BUSINESS FINANCE

LES R. DLABAY

JAMES L. BURROW

THOMSON

SOUTH-WESTERN

Australia • Brazil • Canada • Mexico • Singapore • Spain • United Kingdom • United States

THOMSON

SOUTH-WESTERN

Business Finance

Les R. Dlabay, James L. Burrow

VP/Editorial Director:
Jack W. Calhoun

VP/Editor-in-Chief:
Karen Schmohe

Acquisitions Editor:
Eve Lewis

Sr. Developmental Editor:
Enid Nagel

Editorial Assistant:
Linda Watkins

Sr. Marketing Manager:
Nancy Long

Marketing Coordinator:
Angela Glassmeyer

Sr. Content Project Manager:
Martha Conway

Manager of Technology, Editorial:
Liz Prigge

Technology Project Editor:
Sally Nieman

Manufacturing Coordinator:
Kevin Kluck

Production House:
ICC Macmillan Inc.

Art Director:
Tippy McIntosh

Internal Designer:
Lou Ann Thesing, Thesing Design

Cover Designer:
Lou Ann Thesing, Thesing Design

Cover Images:
© Image Bank

Printer:
Courier—Kendalville
Kendalville, IN

For more information about our
products, contact us at:

Thomson Higher Education
5191 Natorp Boulevard
Mason, Ohio 45040
USA

Uncover the Power of Understanding

Open the pages of **Business Finance** and your classroom suddenly becomes a world of discovery. Whether your course is offered at an Academy of Finance, within a Finance Career Cluster Concentration, or as part of a business curriculum, **Business Finance** provides you with complete coverage.

As a committed instructor responding to ever-changing classroom demands and student needs, you must have tools that are as flexible and as ready to go at a moment's notice as you are. The powerful package accompanying **Business Finance** responds with a wealth of student and teacher resource and support choices with a common thread of built-in flexibility and proven effectiveness.

Student Text Written specifically for high school students, **Business Finance** combines fundamental concepts with a strong lesson-based instructional design, weaving in research opportunities, creative methods of assessment, interesting real-world features, financial calculations, case studies, and academic connections.

Annotated Instructor's Edition Comprehensive teaching notes at point of use in the margins help you create a dynamic learning environment with minimal preparation. Solutions, background information, and projects address different learning styles and abilities.

Instructor's Resource CD Find all the resources you need on one convenient CD. Never be without your teaching materials if there's a computer available.

ExamView® Electronic Testing Software Assessment is a snap with this electronic testing and grading software.

FREE Web Site You and your students can access this free web site for a wealth of online learning tools designed to help students experience economics in your course. Visit thomsonedu.com/school/busfinance today.

Activities Workbook Ideal for students who need additional review.

Adobe eBook Enhance learning with this eBook, complete with photos, graphics, and rich fonts. Additional features allow you to customize the content by highlighting key passages, inserting "sticky notes," and bookmarking pages for reference.

Now You See It

Take a look for yourself at how this dynamic text brings business finance to life for your students day after day with proven learning features and unmatched teaching support. It's everything you need for today's classroom and the understanding that extends well beyond.

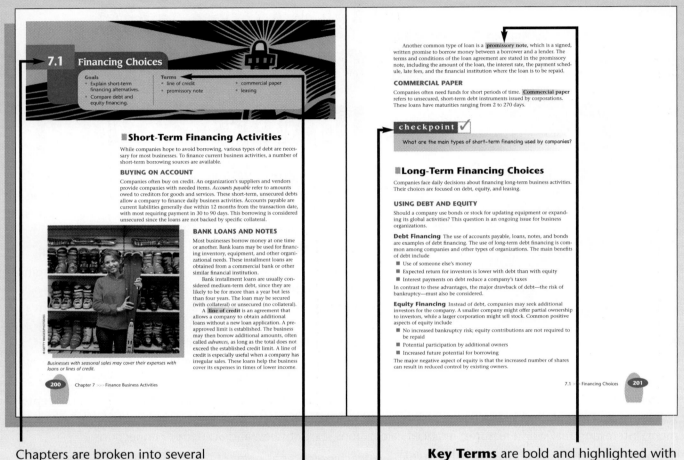

Chapters are broken into several class-length **Lessons.**

Key Terms are bold and highlighted with yellow, emphasizing their importance and allowing students to find them easily.

Prepare students to READ each lesson effectively by previewing **Goals** and **Terms.**

Checkpoints throughout the chapter provide opportunities for informal evaluation of learning.

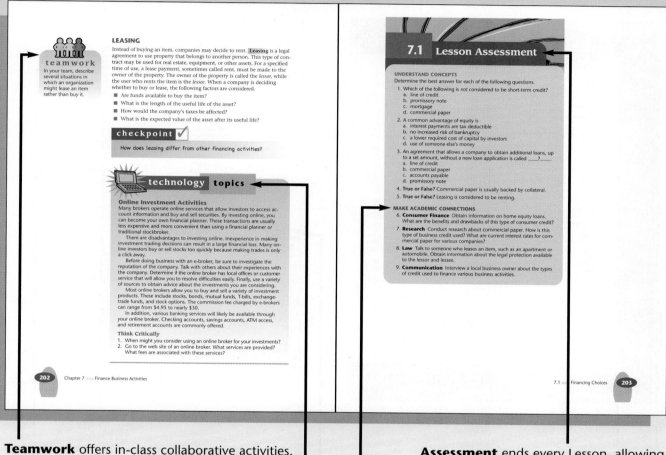

LEASING

Instead of buying an item, companies may decide to rent. **Leasing** is a legal agreement to use property that belongs to another person. This type of contract may be used for real estate, equipment, or other assets. For a specified time of use, a lease payment, sometimes called rent, must be made to the owner of the property. The owner of the property is called the *lessor*, while the user who rents the item is the *lessee*. When a company is deciding whether to buy or lease, the following factors are considered.

- Are funds available to buy the item?
- What is the length of the useful life of the asset?
- How would the company's taxes be affected?
- What is the expected value of the asset after its useful life?

checkpoint ✓

How does leasing differ from other financing activities?

technology topics

Online Investment Activities

Many brokers operate online services that allow investors to access account information and buy and sell securities. By investing online, you can become your own financial planner. These transactions are usually less expensive and more convenient than using a financial planner or traditional stockbroker.

There are disadvantages to investing online. Inexperience in making investment trading decisions can result in a large financial loss. Many online investors buy or sell stocks too quickly because making trades is only a click away.

Before doing business with an e-broker, be sure to investigate the reputation of the company. Talk with others about their experiences with the company. Determine if the online broker has local offices or customer service that will allow you to resolve difficulties easily. Finally, use a variety of sources to obtain advice about the investments you are considering.

Most online brokers allow you to buy and sell a variety of investment products. These include stocks, bonds, mutual funds, T-bills, exchange-trade funds, and stock options. The commission fee charged by e-brokers can range from $4.95 to nearly $30.

In addition, various banking services will likely be available through your online broker. Checking accounts, savings accounts, ATM access, and retirement accounts are commonly offered.

Think Critically

1. When might you consider using an online broker for your investments?
2. Go to the web site of an online broker. What services are provided? What fees are associated with these services?

teamwork

In your team, describe several situations in which an organization might lease an item rather than buy it.

7.1   Lesson Assessment

UNDERSTAND CONCEPTS

Determine the best answer for each of the following questions.

1. Which of the following is *not* considered to be short-term credit?
   a. line of credit
   b. promissory note
   c. mortgage
   d. commercial paper

2. A common advantage of equity is
   a. interest payments are tax deductible
   b. no increased risk of bankruptcy
   c. a lower required cost of capital by investors
   d. use of someone else's money

3. An agreement that allows a company to obtain additional loans, up to a set amount, without a new loan application is called _____?_____.
   a. line of credit
   b. commercial paper
   c. accounts payable
   d. promissory note

4. **True or False?** Commercial paper is usually backed by collateral.

5. **True or False?** Leasing is considered to be renting.

MAKE ACADEMIC CONNECTIONS

6. **Consumer Finance** Obtain information on home equity loans. What are the benefits and drawbacks of this type of consumer credit?

7. **Research** Conduct research about commercial paper. How is this type of business credit used? What are current interest rates for commercial paper for various companies?

8. **Law** Talk to someone who leases an item, such as an apartment or automobile. Obtain information about the legal protection available to the lessor and lessee.

9. **Communication** Interview a local business owner about the types of credit used to finance various business activities.

Teamwork offers in-class collaborative activities. Students work in small groups while developing finance skills and knowledge.

Technology Topics asks students to think critically and in some detail about the impact of technology on companies' financial operations.

Make Academic Connections provides a link between academic subjects and Business Finance.

Assessment ends every Lesson, allowing you to evaluate student comprehension and progress frequently.

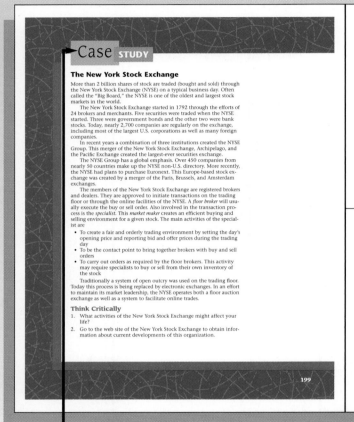

Case STUDY

The New York Stock Exchange

More than 2 billion shares of stock are traded (bought and sold) through the New York Stock Exchange (NYSE) on a typical business day. Often called the "Big Board," the NYSE is one of the oldest and largest stock markets in the world.

The New York Stock Exchange started in 1792 through the efforts of 24 brokers and merchants. Five securities were traded when the NYSE started. Three were government bonds and the other two were bank stocks. Today, nearly 2,700 companies are regularly on the exchange, including most of the largest U.S. corporations as well as many foreign companies.

In recent years a combination of three institutions created the NYSE Group. This merger of the New York Stock Exchange, Archipelago, and the Pacific Exchange created the largest-ever securities exchange.

The NYSE Group has a global emphasis. Over 450 companies from nearly 50 countries make up the NYSE non-U.S. directory. More recently, the NYSE had plans to purchase Euronext. This Europe-based stock exchange was created by a merger of the Paris, Brussels, and Amsterdam exchanges.

The members of the New York Stock Exchange are registered brokers and dealers. They are approved to initiate transactions on the trading floor or through the online facilities of the NYSE. A *floor broker* will usually execute the buy or sell order. Also involved in the transaction process is the *specialist*. This *market maker* creates an efficient buying and selling environment for a given stock. The main activities of the specialist are

- To create a fair and orderly trading environment by setting the day's opening price and reporting bid and offer prices during the trading day
- To be the contact point to bring together brokers with buy and sell orders
- To carry out orders as required by the floor brokers. This activity may require specialists to buy or sell from their own inventory of the stock

Traditionally a system of open outcry was used on the trading floor. Today this process is being replaced by electronic exchanges. In an effort to maintain its market leadership, the NYSE operates both a floor auction exchange as well as a system to facilitate online trades.

Think Critically

1. What activities of the New York Stock Exchange might affect your life?
2. Go to the web site of the New York Stock Exchange to obtain information about current developments of this organization.

199

INTEREST RATES

Interest is paid periodically (usually twice a year) to bondholders based on the bond's face value and its stated interest rate. Then, on the bond's maturity date, the face value is repaid to the investor.

Coupon Rate The coupon rate is the stated annual interest rate for a bond. The annual interest is based on the face value of the bond. For example, an 8 percent, $1,000 bond would have annual interest of $80. This amount is paid to the holder of the bond each year until maturity. The total interest for a year is usually made in two semiannual payments, every six months.

The coupon rate is based on current market interest rates for bonds with comparable risk. This rate is determined during the underwriting process. The monetary policy of the Federal Reserve has a major effect on interest rates. When money is *tight*, interest rates tend to move upward. In contrast, an environment of *loose* money results in lower rates.

Current Yield The actual rate of return for investors will often vary from the coupon rate. As interest rates change, the rate of return required by investors may increase or decrease. The current yield of a bond is the relationship between the amount of interest and the cost of the bond. As interest rates increase, bond values decline, so the current yield is higher.

$$\text{Current Yield (\%)} = \frac{\text{Interest Amount}}{\text{Cost of Bond}}$$

$$\text{Current Yield (\%)} = \frac{\$80}{\$940} = 0.085 = 8.5 \text{ percent}$$

In this situation, the cost (market value) of the bond declined from $1,000 to $940 due to higher interest rates. This lower bond value, in relation to the

FIGURE 7-1			
Bond Ratings			
Quality	**Moody's**	**S&P**	**Description**
High-grade	AAA AA	AAA AA	These ratings are assigned companies judged to be of high quality by all standards; almost no chance of default.
Medium-grade	A BAA	A BBB	Bonds from companies that have many favorable factors with very little chance of default.
Speculative	BA B	BB B	Bonds judged to be somewhat uncertain and a fairly high risk.
Default	CAA CA C	CCC CC C D	Bonds from companies that are of poor standing with extremely poor prospects for making payments to investors; company may have filed for bankruptcy.

Bond ratings are commonly affected by
- The earning power of the company
- Other debts the company currently owes
- The past success and future potential of company management

Bond ratings affect the interest rate a company must offer on its bonds. Lower bond ratings require a high rate to attract investors to the higher risk bond.

Case Study presents an in-depth scenario related to the chapter content and then asks students to analyze the case using critical-thinking skills.

Topics are explained both verbally and mathematically, where appropriate.

Figures provide a summary of important information, graphically organizing information for the student and visually detailing the links and associations between data and associated analysis.

Impact.

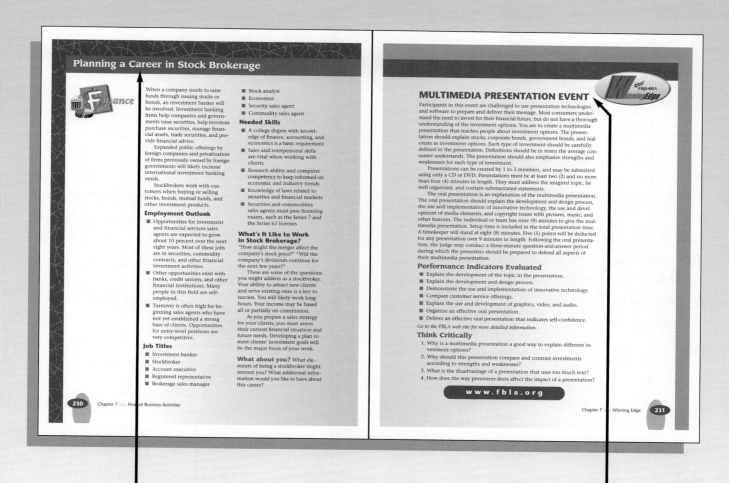

Planning a Career in Stock Brokerage

When a company needs to raise funds through issuing stocks or bonds, an investment banker will be involved. Investment banking firms help companies and governments issue securities, help investors purchase securities, manage financial assets, trade securities, and provide financial advice.

Expanded public offerings by foreign companies and privatization of firms previously owned by foreign governments will likely increase international investment banking needs.

Stockbrokers work with customers when buying or selling stocks, bonds, mutual funds, and other investment products.

Employment Outlook

- Opportunities for investment and financial services sales agents are expected to grow about 10 percent over the next eight years. Most of these jobs are in securities, commodity contracts, and other financial investment activities.
- Other opportunities exist with banks, credit unions, and other financial institutions. Many people in this field are self-employed.
- Turnover is often high for beginning sales agents who have not yet established a strong base of clients. Opportunities for entry-level positions are very competitive.

Job Titles

- Investment banker
- Stockbroker
- Account executive
- Registered representative
- Brokerage sales manager

- Stock analyst
- Economist
- Security sales agent
- Commodity sales agent

Needed Skills

- A college degree with knowledge of finance, accounting, and economics is a basic requirement
- Sales and interpersonal skills are vital when working with clients
- Research ability and computer competency to keep informed on economic and industry trends
- Knowledge of laws related to securities and financial markets
- Securities and commodities sales agents must pass licensing exams, such as the Series 7 and the Series 63 licenses

What's It Like to Work In Stock Brokerage?

"How might the merger affect the company's stock price?" "Will the company's dividends continue for the next few years?"

These are some of the questions you might address as a stockbroker. Your ability to attract new clients and serve existing ones is a key to success. You will likely work long hours. Your income may be based all or partially on commission.

As you prepare a sales strategy for your clients, you must assess their current financial situation and future needs. Developing a plan to meet clients' investment goals will be the major focus of your work.

What about you? What elements of being a stockbroker might interest you? What additional information would you like to have about this career?

MULTIMEDIA PRESENTATION EVENT

Participants in this event are challenged to use presentation technologies and software to prepare and deliver their message. Most consumers understand the need to invest for their financial future, but do not have a thorough understanding of the investment options. You are to create a multimedia presentation that teaches people about investment options. The presentation should explain stocks, corporate bonds, government bonds, and real estate as investment options. Each type of investment should be carefully defined in the presentation. Definitions should be in terms the average consumer understands. The presentation should also emphasize strengths and weaknesses for each type of investment.

Presentations can be created by 1 to 3 members, and may be submitted using only a CD or DVD. Presentations must be at least two (2) and no more than four (4) minutes in length. They must address the assigned topic, be well organized, and contain substantiated statements.

The oral presentation is an explanation of the multimedia presentation. The oral presentation should explain the development and design process, the use and implementation of innovative technology, the use and development of media elements, and copyright issues with pictures, music, and other features. The individual or team has nine (9) minutes to give the multimedia presentation. Setup time is included in the total presentation time. A timekeeper will stand at eight (8) minutes. Five (5) points will be deducted for any presentation over 9 minutes in length. Following the oral presentation, the judge may conduct a three-minute question-and-answer period during which the presenters should be prepared to defend all aspects of their multimedia presentation.

Performance Indicators Evaluated

- Explain the development of the topic in the presentation.
- Explain the development and design process.
- Demonstrate the use and implementation of innovative technology.
- Compare customer service offerings.
- Explain the use and development of graphics, video, and audio.
- Organize an effective oral presentation.
- Deliver an effective oral presentation that indicates self-confidence.

Go to the FBLA web site for more detailed information.

Think Critically

1. Why is a multimedia presentation a good way to explain different investment options?
2. Why should this presentation compare and contrast investments according to strengths and weaknesses?
3. What is the disadvantage of a presentation that uses too much text?
4. How does the way presenters dress affect the impact of a presentation?

www.fbla.org

Planning a Career in... offers a different career profile in every chapter. Career paths, needed skills, and industry opportunities are explored.

Every chapter offers exposure to activities and measures of evaluation for different BPA, DECA, and FBLA competitive events. Give students the **Winning Edge!**

Student-Focused Features for

NET Bookmark encourages students to use the Internet for research. The web site provides a safe portal for students to gather real data for analysis.

NETBookmark

Treasury Direct is a web site run by the U.S. Department of the Treasury that provides information on government securities. Access thomsonedu.com/school/busfinance and click on the link for Chapter 7. Use the Research Center to find out information on Series EE Savings Bonds.

www.thomsonedu.com/school/busfinance

a question of ethics

Investment Fraud

Each year, investors lose more than $1.2 billion to various scams. Especially vulnerable are elderly consumers, who may not completely understand the opportunities they are offered. And, after being scammed, older consumers may be too embarrassed to report their losses to government authorities.

Some of the most common tactics used to attract people to deceptive investment schemes include

- Developing trust, in which con artists create a friendly connection by telling you about their family and asking about yours.
- Offering an impossibly attractive investment opportunity, for example, land that is cheap compared to other real estate or guaranteed returns of over 50 percent.
- Establishing credibility. The scam artist might imply that the investment is safe because it is advertised in *The Wall Street Journal* or mention that the company is "licensed" with the state.
- Creating social pressure by implying that many other people have made this investment. They may even mention names of people the investor knows.
- Generating fear to close the deal, since "you wouldn't want to miss this opportunity."
- Implying limited availability, such as "these are the last two rare coins available."

To avoid becoming a victim of investment fraud, use these guidelines.

1. Investigate before signing and paying any money. Contact federal and state agencies about any complaints against the company. Also, talk with family members and friends about the investment.
2. Avoid "you must sign up today" opportunities. Take your time to determine if the investment is legitimate and appropriate for your situation.
3. Research the company and type of investment. Understand the costs and potential risks.
4. Most important, remember that deals that seem "too good to be true"…usually are!

Think Critically

1. Why do so many people each year get cheated with phony investments?
2. Conduct an Internet search to obtain additional information about various investment frauds. Prepare a summary of your findings.

A Question of Ethics takes a critical look at ethical dilemmas in the workplace and the implications of unethical behavior.

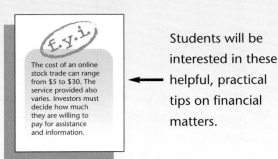

f.y.i.

The cost of an online stock trade can range from $5 to $30. The service provided also varies. Investors must decide how much they are willing to pay for assistance and information.

Students will be interested in these helpful, practical tips on financial matters.

Hands-on Practice

Point Your Browser directs students to activities on the web site.

Finance Around the World investigates the variety of financial decisions that must be made when operating in or with other countries.

Stock Exchanges around the World

Locations of stock exchanges range from Johannesburg to Hong Kong and from Madrid to Lima. More than 150 exist in countries around the world. Each of these organizations serves local companies with trading facilities for buying and selling stocks, bonds, and other securities.

The Prague Stock Exchange started in 1993, the year Czechoslovakia divided into two separate countries—the Czech Republic and Slovakia. As the countries moved from a centrally planned economy under communist rule to a free-market economy, citizens were allowed to invest in stocks.

As the capital of the Czech Republic, Prague is the center of the country's business activities. When it started, the Prague Stock Exchange handled transactions for only seven companies. Today, this exchange has expanded its business to include many more companies. Many of the previously government-controlled businesses are now privately owned. Some of the most popular stocks are companies in the hotel and glass manufacturing industries.

While many local stock exchanges exist, the influence of regional markets is expanding. Euronext was formed in 2000 through a merger of the Paris, Brussels, and Amsterdam stock exchanges. This organization regularly trades stocks of more than 1,250 companies. More recently, Euronext has been acquired by the New York Stock Exchange.

Think Critically

1. How might the activities of stock exchanges in different countries differ from each other?
2. Conduct an Internet search to locate the web site for a stock exchange in another region of the world.

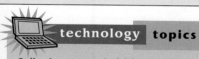

Online Investment Activities

Many brokers operate online services that allow investors to access account information and buy and sell securities. By investing online, you can become your own financial planner. These transactions are usually less expensive and more convenient than using a financial planner or traditional stockbroker.

There are disadvantages to investing online. Inexperience in making investment trading decisions can result in a large financial loss. Many online investors buy or sell stocks too quickly because making trades is only a click away.

Before doing business with an e-broker, be sure to investigate the reputation of the company. Talk with others about their experiences with the company. Determine if the online broker has local offices or customer service that will allow you to resolve difficulties easily. Finally, use a variety of sources to obtain advice about the investments you are considering.

Most online brokers allow you to buy and sell a variety of investment products. These include stocks, bonds, mutual funds, T-bills, exchange-trade funds, and stock options. The commission fee charged by e-brokers can range from $4.95 to nearly $30.

In addition, various banking services will likely be available through your online broker. Checking accounts, savings accounts, ATM access, and retirement accounts are commonly offered.

Think Critically

1. When might you consider using an online broker for your investments?
2. Go to the web site of an online broker. What services are provided? What fees are associated with these services?

Technology Topics asks students to think critically and in some detail about the impact of technology on companies' financial operations.

Integrated Assessment Puts

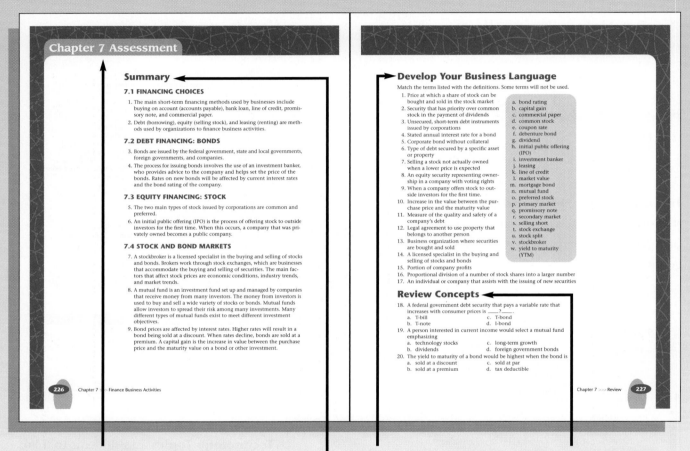

Chapter 7 Assessment

Summary

7.1 FINANCING CHOICES

1. The main short-term financing methods used by businesses include buying on account (accounts payable), bank loan, line of credit, promissory note, and commercial paper.
2. Debt (borrowing), equity (selling stock), and leasing (renting) are methods used by organizations to finance business activities.

7.2 DEBT FINANCING: BONDS

3. Bonds are issued by the federal government, state and local governments, foreign governments, and companies.
4. The process for issuing bonds involves the use of an investment banker, who provides advice to the company and helps set the price of the bonds. Rates on new bonds will be affected by current interest rates and the bond rating of the company.

7.3 EQUITY FINANCING: STOCK

5. The two main types of stock issued by corporations are common and preferred.
6. An initial public offering (IPO) is the process of offering stock to outside investors for the first time. When this occurs, a company that was privately owned becomes a public company.

7.4 STOCK AND BOND MARKETS

7. A stockbroker is a licensed specialist in the buying and selling of stocks and bonds. Brokers work through stock exchanges, which are businesses that accommodate the buying and selling of securities. The main factors that affect stock prices are economic conditions, industry trends, and market trends.
8. A mutual fund is an investment fund set up and managed by companies that receive money from many investors. The money from investors is used to buy and sell a wide variety of stocks or bonds. Mutual funds allow investors to spread their risk among many investments. Many different types of mutual funds exist to meet different investment objectives.
9. Bond prices are affected by interest rates. Higher rates will result in a bond being sold at a discount. When rates decline, bonds are sold at a premium. A capital gain is the increase in value between the purchase price and the maturity value on a bond or other investment.

226   Chapter 7 >>> Finance Business Activities

Develop Your Business Language

Match the terms listed with the definitions. Some terms will not be used.

1. Price at which a share of stock can be bought and sold in the stock market
2. Security that has priority over common stock in the payment of dividends
3. Unsecured, short-term debt instruments issued by corporations
4. Stated annual interest rate for a bond
5. Corporate bond without collateral
6. Type of debt secured by a specific asset or property
7. Selling a stock not actually owned when a lower price is expected
8. An equity security representing ownership in a company with voting rights
9. When a company offers stock to outside investors for the first time.
10. Increase in the value between the purchase price and the maturity value
11. Measure of the quality and safety of a company's debt
12. Legal agreement to use property that belongs to another person
13. Business organization where securities are bought and sold
14. A licensed specialist in the buying and selling of stocks and bonds
15. Portion of company profits
16. Proportional division of a number of stock shares into a larger number
17. An individual or company that assists with the issuing of new securities

a. bond rating
b. capital gain
c. commercial paper
d. common stock
e. coupon rate
f. debenture bond
g. dividend
h. initial public offering (IPO)
i. investment banker
j. leasing
k. line of credit
l. market value
m. mortgage bond
n. mutual fund
o. preferred stock
p. primary market
q. promissory note
r. secondary market
s. selling short
t. stock exchange
u. stock split
v. stockbroker
w. yield to maturity (YTM)

Review Concepts

18. A federal government debt security that pays a variable rate that increases with consumer prices is ____?____ .
   a. T-bill   c. T-bond
   b. T-note   d. I-bond
19. A person interested in current income would select a mutual fund emphasizing
   a. technology stocks   c. long-term growth
   b. dividends   d. foreign government bonds
20. The yield to maturity of a bond would be highest when the bond is
   a. sold at a discount   c. sold at par
   b. sold at a premium   d. tax deductible

Chapter 7 >>> Review   227

Chapter Assessment covers vocabulary building, concept review, financial calculations, case analysis, and the stock market.

Develop Your Business Language assesses student comprehension of the vocabulary of business finance.

Review Concepts uses multiple choice questions to build familiarity with standardized tests, while assessing knowledge of chapter content.

Summary provides a brief review of the key topics from every lesson in the chapter.

Practical Knowledge to the Test

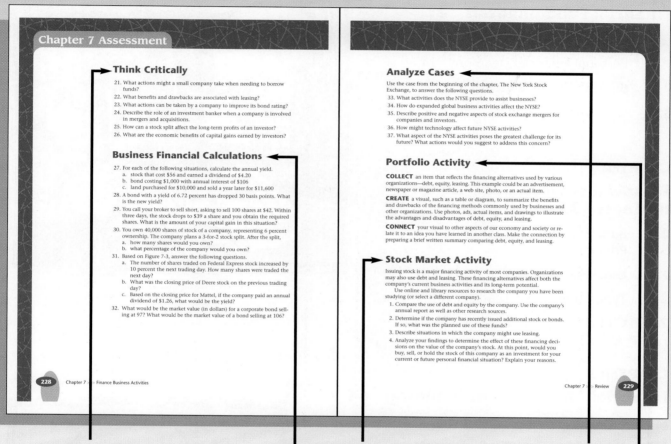

Chapter 7 Assessment

Think Critically

21. What actions might a small company take when needing to borrow funds?
22. What benefits and drawbacks are associated with leasing?
23. What actions can be taken by a company to improve its bond rating?
24. Describe the role of an investment banker when a company is involved in mergers and acquisitions.
25. How can a stock split affect the long-term profits of an investor?
26. What are the economic benefits of capital gains earned by investors?

Business Financial Calculations

27. For each of the following situations, calculate the annual yield.
    a. stock that cost $56 and earned a dividend of $4.20
    b. bond costing $1,000 with annual interest of $106
    c. land purchased for $10,000 and sold a year later for $11,600
28. A bond with a yield of 6.72 percent has dropped 30 basis points. What is the new yield?
29. You call your broker to sell short, asking to sell 100 shares at $42. Within three days, the stock drops to $39 a share and you obtain the required shares. What is the amount of your capital gain in this situation?
30. You own 40,000 shares of stock of a company, representing 6 percent ownership. The company plans a 3-for-2 stock split. After the split,
    a. how many shares would you own?
    b. what percentage of the company would you own?
31. Based on Figure 7-3, answer the following questions.
    a. The number of shares traded on Federal Express stock increased by 10 percent the next trading day. How many shares were traded the next day?
    b. What was the closing price of Deere stock on the previous trading day?
    c. Based on the closing price for Mattel, if the company paid an annual dividend of $1.26, what would be the yield?
32. What would be the market value (in dollars) for a corporate bond selling at 97? What would be the market value of a bond selling at 106?

Analyze Cases

Use the case from the beginning of the chapter, The New York Stock Exchange, to answer the following questions.

33. What activities does the NYSE provide to assist businesses?
34. How do expanded global business activities affect the NYSE?
35. Describe positive and negative aspects of stock exchange mergers for companies and investors.
36. How might technology affect future NYSE activities?
37. What aspect of the NYSE activities poses the greatest challenge for its future? What actions would you suggest to address this concern?

Portfolio Activity

COLLECT an item that reflects the financing alternatives used by various organizations—debt, equity, leasing. This example could be an advertisement, newspaper or magazine article, a web site, photo, or an actual item.

CREATE a visual, such as a table or diagram, to summarize the benefits and drawbacks of the financing methods commonly used by businesses and other organizations. Use photos, ads, actual items, and drawings to illustrate the advantages and disadvantages of debt, equity, and leasing.

CONNECT your visual to other aspects of our economy and society or relate it to an idea you have learned in another class. Make the connection by preparing a brief written summary comparing debt, equity, and leasing.

Stock Market Activity

Issuing stock is a major financing activity of most companies. Organizations may also use debt and leasing. These financing alternatives affect both the company's current business activities and its long-term potential.

Use online and library resources to research the company you have been studying (or select a different company).

1. Compare the use of debt and equity by the company. Use the company's annual report as well as other research sources.
2. Determine if the company has recently issued additional stock or bonds. If so, what was the planned use of these funds?
3. Describe situations in which the company might use leasing.
4. Analyze your findings to determine the effect of these financing decisions on the value of the company's stock. At this point, would you buy, sell, or hold the stock of this company as an investment for your current or future personal financial situation? Explain your reasons.

228 Chapter 7 • Finance Business Activities

Chapter 7 • Review **229**

Think Critically presents questions related to the chapter and asks students to use their critical-thinking skills to provide solutions.

Stock Market Activity provides an opportunity for understanding the relationship between the stock market and financing business enterprises.

Analyze Cases asks students to return to the Chapter-Opening Case and analyze the case using critical-thinking skills.

Business Financial Calculations present the opportunity for students to demonstrate understanding of the math and statistics necessary for proficiency in business finance.

Portfolio Activity outlines projects and activities that students complete to demonstrate proficiency in applying business finance skills.

Contents

Reviewers

Valerie Bentley
Teacher, Business Department
Alcovy High School
Covington, GA

Mable Young Burchfield
Instructional Supervisor
Division of Careers, Technology
Memphis City Schools
Memphis, TN

Susan C. Chambless
Finance Academy Instructor
Hoover High School
Hoover, AL

Karen N. Ceh
Teacher, Business Department
Parkland High School
Allentown, PA

Patricia Deike
Banking and Financial Services Instructor
Regional Occupational Program
Riverside County Office of Education
Riverside, CA

Crystal Force
Director/Teacher
Wolfson Academy of Finance
Jacksonville, FL

Lance Garvin
Business teacher
Pike High School
Indianapolis, IN

Richard T. Gordon
Lead Teacher Business and Applied Technology
Bloomington High School
Bloomington, IL

Meg Hoffman
Teacher, Business Department
Citrus High School
Inverness, FL

Dena Hutcheson Irwin
Teacher, Business Department
Shakamak MSD
Jasonville, IN

Donna A. Jones
Business Instructor and Academy
  of Finance Director
Gloucester High School
Gloucester, VA

Wanda Kline
Business Technology Department Chair
Hamilton Heights High School
Arcadia, IN

Roger C. Lyder
Teacher
Pelham High School
Pelham, NM

Thomas Montoya
Teacher/Coordinator Business
Albuquerque, NM

Kevin Raiford
Business Instructor
Western High School
Las Vegas, NV

Tony R. Renesca
Business Education Instructor
Booker T. Washington Sr. High school
Miami, FL

Authors

Les R. Dlabay is a Professor of Business in the Department of Economics and Business at Lake Forest College in Illinois. Over the years, he has taught more than 30 different courses in high school and college programs. These include Introduction to Finance, Personal Finance, Investments, Financial Accounting, Capital Budgeting, Marketing Research, and Cultural Perspectives of International Business. Dr. Dlabay has presented over 300 workshops and seminars for teachers and other organizations around the country. His "hobbies" include a global food package collection (from over 100 countries) and paper currency from 200 countries, which are used to teach about the economic, financial, cultural, and political aspects of international business.

James L. Burrow has a background in marketing and human resource development. He works regularly with the business community and other organizations as a consultant on marketing and performance improvement strategies including the use of the Internet as an education and training resource. He recently retired from the faculty of North Carolina State University where he served as the Coordinator of the graduate Training and Development Program for over 15 years. Dr. Burrow received degrees from the University of Northern Iowa and the University of Nebraska in Marketing and Marketing Education.

Financial Fundamentals

▶ **Point Your** [Browser]
www.thomsonedu.com/school/busfinance

JPMorgan Chase: Financial Partnerships in Action

For consumers, there are checking accounts, mortgages, and auto loans. Businesses are offered investment banking services and enterprise start-up loans. For governments, there is tax collection and payment processing. JPMorgan Chase, one of the world's largest financial services companies, serves individuals, businesses, and governments.

This global organization, with offices in more than 50 countries, had its beginnings in 1799. In recent years, JPMorgan Chase expanded by buying several other banks and financial institutions. These purchases included Chemical Bank, Manufacturers Hanover, Bank One, First Chicago, and National Bank of Detroit. As the company grew, it offered more services.

For consumers, the company offers a wide variety of banking services. In addition to traditional savings and checking accounts, JPMorgan Chase provides personal investment assistance, credit cards, insurance advice, and various types of loans. Buying a home, purchasing a car, or financing a college education are all available through JPMorgan Chase.

Investment banking is an important service offered to major companies. Serving as an investment banker, JPMorgan Chase assists corporations with issuing stocks and bonds to raise needed capital. This service allows companies to expand their operations, buy new equipment, and market new products. When serving as an investment banker, JPMorgan Chase earns fees and commissions.

While JPMorgan Chase serves the needs of big corporations, small businesses are also important customers. "Chase Online" helps smaller companies to manage accounts, obtain loans, and plan employee benefits. Also available to small business owners are insurance services and assistance with planning retirement for their employees.

The company's international activities include global banking and foreign investments. JPMorgan Chase can obtain foreign currencies for its customers through an international network of banks.

JPMorgan Chase also contributes to charity. Each year, over $140 million is donated to non-profit organizations in the U.S. and around the world. In addition, more than $3 billion of community development lending helps with housing and business start-ups in lower-income areas.

Think Critically

1. What are the main benefits JPMorgan Chase provides individuals, businesses, and government?
2. Conduct a web search for JPMorgan Chase to obtain recent information about the company. What types of financial activities did you learn about?

Goals
- Describe the role of finance in the economy.
- Identify types of financial markets.

Terms
- money
- finance
- inflation
- security
- stock
- bond
- liquidity

■ Financial Activities in Action

Each day, you probably participate in various financial transactions. These financial transactions might include buying items in stores, receiving a paycheck, or borrowing money to purchase a car. These transactions include paying and receiving money as well as using credit.

Money is any item that serves as a method of payment. Most people think of money as coins, bank notes, checks, and debit cards. In the past, items that were used as money included salt, shells, cattle, and gold. Today, several types of online and electronic money are being used.

Your money activities are the basis for financial events in society. **Finance** refers to activities involved with saving, investing, and using money by individuals, businesses, and governments. Every person is involved in finance.

PARTICIPANTS IN FINANCIAL SYSTEMS

When people, businesses, and governments in a country have financial relationships, a *financial system* exists. These financial relationships may include saving, spending, paying taxes, earning interest, receiving a salary, or buying investments. As shown in Figure 1-1, the financial system of a country involves interactions among three main participants.

© GETTY IMAGES/PHOTODISC

Finance touches every person's life.

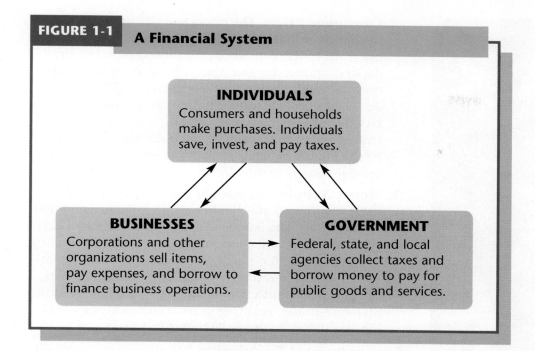

FIGURE 1-1 **A Financial System**

INDIVIDUALS
Consumers and households make purchases. Individuals save, invest, and pay taxes.

BUSINESSES
Corporations and other organizations sell items, pay expenses, and borrow to finance business operations.

GOVERNMENT
Federal, state, and local agencies collect taxes and borrow money to pay for public goods and services.

Individual Consumers and Investors Your first role in the financial system is as a consumer. Every time you buy something, a financial exchange takes place. You are using cash or credit to pay for a purchase. This purchasing is an example of a financial activity.

If you receive a paycheck or a gift of money, you may put this money in a bank account. Or, you may invest the money. These activities are other examples of ways you participate in the financial system.

Businesses Everyone is dependent on the goods and services provided by various companies. These organizations sell items. The money received from these sales pays for operating expenses and hopefully provides a profit for the company.

Companies also borrow money. The use of credit by businesses represents a significant portion of our financial system.

Government You and your neighbors use schools, parks, roads, police protection, and other public services. To pay for these services, government collects taxes and other fees. Federal, state, and local government agencies also borrow money to finance various projects.

FACTORS AFFECTING FINANCIAL ACTIVITIES

The financial systems in society are influenced by many factors. World events as well as consumer saving habits affect the financial environment.

Economic Conditions A country's economic activities are a primary element of finance. Several economic factors have a major effect on financial activities.

1. **Interest Rates** The cost of money affects almost every aspect of finance. Interest rates are determined by the forces of supply and demand. When consumer saving and investing increase the supply of money, interest rates tend to decrease. As borrowing by consumers, businesses, and government increases, interest rates are likely to rise.

Banking is one way individuals participate in the financial system.

Each year, U.S. consumers lose more than $1.2 billion in fraudulent investments. Several federal government agencies are available to assist investors.

2. **Consumer Prices** The prices you pay for items tend to change. **Inflation** is a rise in the general level of prices. In times of inflation, the buying power of the dollar decreases. For example, if prices increased 5 percent during the last year, items that cost $100 a year ago would now cost $105. It now takes more money to buy the same amount of goods and services. In the United States, the *consumer price index (CPI),* published by the Bureau of Labor Statistics, is used to measure the average change in prices.

3. **Money Supply** The amount of money in circulation in an economy is another important influence on financial activities. The money supply, which includes coins, paper currency, and checking accounts, affects spending and borrowing. Too much money in circulation can result in lower interest rates but higher consumer prices. In contrast, too little money in the economy may push up interest rates, resulting in reduced consumer spending and increased unemployment.

Governmental Regulations Without rules, financial systems would be confusing. Imagine if anyone could issue stocks or bonds without being concerned about the value of a company. Many people would be cheated. As a result, governments create regulations for fairness in financial transactions.

In the United States, the Securities and Exchange Commission (SEC), created in 1934, is one of the primary financial regulatory agencies. The main goals of the SEC are (1) to promote clear and full investment information and (2) to protect investors against fraud and deception. Other federal agencies that regulate financial activities include the Federal Reserve System, the Comptroller of the Currency, the Federal Deposit Insurance Corporation (FDIC), and the National Credit Union Administration (NCUA).

Global Business Activities You often buy and use products from around the world. International trade is the basis of many financial activities. When a country exports more than it imports, its *trade surplus* benefits the country's economy. A *trade deficit* (more imports than exports) can hurt a country's economy.

A trade deficit can also affect the value of a nation's money. Since countries use different money systems, the value of currencies vary as a result of global financial transactions. The *foreign exchange rate* is the value of a country's currency in relation to the value of the money of another country. The value of a nation's currency is most influenced by international trade, the nation's political stability, and economic conditions in the country.

checkpoint ✔

Name three economic factors that affect financial activities.

Financial Markets

Whenever you buy or sell something, you participate in a *market*. This market might be a store, an online auction, a garage sale, or a stock exchange in any major city around the world. A *financial market* is a location (physical or online) where buyers and sellers of financial products meet to conduct business.

Financial markets involve the buying and selling of various assets and investments. While some investments are physical (houses, land, gold, rare coins), other investments represent ownership (stocks) or lending (bonds).

A security is an investment instrument issued by a corporation, government, or other organization representing ownership or a debt. Stock is a security representing ownership in a corporation. In contrast, a bond is debt, money that is borrowed by a company or government. In addition to stocks and bonds, other examples of securities include mutual funds, certificates of deposit (CDs), and commodity futures.

TYPES OF FINANCIAL MARKETS

While many types of financial markets exist around the world, as shown in Figure 1-2, they are commonly classified into two major categories: money markets and capital markets.

teamwork

Some people prefer investing in bonds, others prefer stocks. In your team, prepare a list of factors a person might consider when deciding whether to invest in bonds or stocks.

FIGURE 1-2

Types of Financial Markets

Money Markets (short-term debt securities)	Capital Markets (long-term securities)
Treasury Bills	Treasury Notes and Bonds
Certificates of Deposit (CDs)	Corporate and Municipal Bonds
Commercial Paper	Common and Preferred Stock

Money Markets All organizations need money to operate on a daily basis. While sales increase cash flows, often additional funds are needed for short periods of time. *Money markets* are financial markets where short-term debt securities (less than one year) are bought and sold. Some examples of short-term securities are Treasury bills, certificates of deposit, and commercial paper. Investments in these short-term debt securities usually have a lower risk than investments with longer maturities.

Capital Markets When an organization is in need of funds for long-term use, it will become involved in *capital markets*. These markets buy and sell various debt and equity securities that are issued for more than a year.

Debt securities represent borrowing by companies or governments. Examples of debt securities include bonds, issued by corporations, and municipal bonds, issued by state and local governments. In contrast, *equity securities* represent ownership. The most common type of equity security is stock.

VALUE OF SECURITIES

Investors are continually interested in the value of assets they own. Many factors can affect the value of a security. The most common of these are

1. **Supply and Demand** As more people desire a certain investment, the value of it will likely increase. Well-managed, profitable organizations are likely to attract more investors, increasing the value of the company's stock. If demand for a company's stock goes down, the value of it will decrease.

2. **Future Cash Flows** When making an investment, both individuals and companies expect to receive money in the future. Larger amounts of future cash flows will increase the value a person will pay for an investment. The *expected return* is the amount of future cash inflows. The *rate of return* (or *yield*) is the relationship between the amount received and the cost of an investment. For example, if an investor receives $1,000 for a $10,000 investment, the rate of return is 10 percent ($1,000 divided by $10,000).

3. **Risk** Every investor and every business manager must consider risk. These dangers may include changing economic conditions, political uncertainty, and shifting consumer buying preferences.

4. **Liquidity** The value of a security is often influenced by its ability to be converted to cash. **Liquidity** refers to the ease and speed with which an investment can be converted into cash.

5. **Interest Rates** The cost of money, measured by *interest rates*, is another important factor affecting the value of an investment. For example, if interest rates rise, more people will likely put money in savings accounts instead of buying stock. This change will usually result in lower stock values.

DIGITAL VISION

Buyers and sellers meet to conduct business at a stock market.

While investors are likely to consider all of these factors, often the risk-return relationship is of primary importance. Higher-risk investments are connected with higher *potential* returns. A person has the opportunity to make more money, but often will have a loss.

checkpoint ✓

Name five factors that affect the value of securities.

Online Finance Sources

Are interest rates expected to rise? What are the best investments during times of inflation? Should a company use debt or equity to finance a new factory? Search online for the many resources that are available to answer these and other questions. As you study finance, work in finance, and make financial decisions, the following web sites will be of value.

Economic Data and Financial News
Financial Times
The Wall Street Journal
The Economist
Federal Reserve System

Stock and Other Investment Information
Yahoo! Finance
The Motley Fool
Yahoo! Bonds
MarketWatch
BondsOnline
TreasuryDirect

Global Monetary Organizations
World Bank
International Monetary Fund
Inter-American Development Bank
Asian Development Bank
African Development Bank

Foreign Currency Exchange Rates
XE.com
x-rates.com
OANDA

Stock Exchanges around the World
Stock Exchanges Worldwide
BusinessJeeves.com
Site-by-Site International Investment Portal and Research Center
Investormap Global Markets

Think Critically

1. Find one of these web sites and prepare a summary of the features and information that are available.
2. Locate other web sites that would be valuable when studying finance.

UNDERSTAND CONCEPTS

Determine the best answer for each of the following questions.

1. Finance refers to
   a. government actions to collect taxes
   b. business operations in countries around the world
   c. activities involved with saving, investing, and using money
   d. the value of money when inflation is occurring

2. A financial market where short-term debt securities are bought and sold is a _____?_____ market.
   a. foreign exchange
   b. money
   c. capital
   d. liquidity

3. The ease with which an item can be converted to cash is called
   a. exporting
   b. liquidity
   c. risk
   d. rate of return

4. **True or False?** When consumer prices fall, it is commonly called *inflation*.

MAKE ACADEMIC CONNECTIONS

5. **Research** Using Figure 1-1, investigate the three main participants involved in financial systems. Describe what each group receives and sends out (represented by the arrows in the illustration).

6. **Geography** Conduct Internet research about stock markets and other financial markets in various countries around the world. Prepare a short written or oral summary of your findings.

7. **Economics** Select an economic factor (such as interest rates or consumer prices). Using library or online research, obtain current information on this economic factor. Describe how the current situation might affect financial activities.

8. **Culture** Talk to someone who has lived in or visited another country. Ask about the financial activities in that country. What are some similarities and differences compared to financial activities in the United States? Prepare a brief written or oral summary of your discussion with that person.

Goals
- Explain the personal financial planning process.
- Describe common personal financial decisions.

Terms
- personal financial planning
- financial plan
- personal financial goal
- opportunity cost

■ Finance in Your Life

Do you have enough money to buy all you desire? Probably not. The problem of *scarcity* requires that you make financial decisions. Most people want to use their finances to obtain the most satisfaction from the money they have available. Financial and personal satisfaction result from a process called *personal money management* or *personal financial planning*. **Personal financial planning** is the process of managing your money to achieve personal economic satisfaction.

The main benefits of proper personal financial planning include

- Better actions for using your finances
- Effective control of your spending
- Improved personal relationships
- A sense of freedom from financial worries

A comprehensive financial plan can enhance the quality of your life and increase your satisfaction by reducing uncertainty about your future needs and resources. A **financial plan** is a formal report with a summary of your current financial situation along with plans for future financial activities. You can create this document on your own or you can seek assistance from a financial planner or use a money management software package.

Financial advisors can help with personal money management.

INFLUENCES ON PERSONAL FINANCIAL DECISIONS

Your financial situation and the decisions you make are affected by various personal and economic factors. These influences include age and household size as well as interest rates and inflation.

Personal Life Situation Teens spend money differently than people in their 30s or 40s. Personal factors such as age, income, household size, and personal beliefs influence spending and saving patterns. Your life situation is also affected by events such as graduation, dependent children leaving home, changes in health, engagement and marriage, divorce, birth or adoption of a child, retirement, a career change, a move to new area, or the death of a spouse, family member, or other dependent.

Economic Factors As with all financial decisions, economic conditions such as inflation, interest rates, and unemployment will affect your personal financial planning. Higher consumer prices will affect spending habits. Lower interest rates may influence you to borrow money to make a certain purchase.

THE FINANCIAL PLANNING PROCESS

Effective personal financial planning requires a logical system. Personal financial advisors often recommend steps similar to those in Figure 1-3.

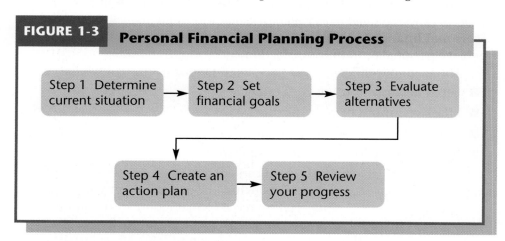

FIGURE 1-3 Personal Financial Planning Process

Step 1 Determine current situation → Step 2 Set financial goals → Step 3 Evaluate alternatives → Step 4 Create an action plan → Step 5 Review your progress

Step 1 Determine Current Situation Personal financial planning activities should start by knowing where you are now. Begin the financial planning process by knowing the amount of your income, savings, living expenses, and debts. Prepare a list of current amounts for items owned (assets) and amounts owed to others (liabilities). In addition, a detailed list of amounts you spend for various items will give you a foundation for your financial decision making.

Step 2 Set Financial Goals Knowing where you are going is important for every aspect of life. As a result, goal setting is central to financial decision making. A **personal financial goal** is a desired outcome for financial planning. Financial goals help you plan, implement, and measure the progress of your spending, saving, and investing activities. As you set personal financial goals, be sure that these desired targets are

- **Realistic** Know that you will not be able to afford certain things.
- **Specific and Measurable** Exact goals help you see your progress. Instead of a goal "to save some money," you should say "to save $200 a month."

teamwork

Create a list of personal financial goals that a person or family might want to achieve. Discuss in your team which ones could be achieved in a year or two, and which ones would take longer.

- **Time-Specific** Your goal should set a specific time limit such as "to pay off credit card debts within 18 months."
- **Action-Based** Explain how you will achieve the goal.

Step 3 Evaluate Alternatives Whenever you make decisions, you should consider various solutions. For example, if you need transportation, alternatives may include buying a car, using public transportation, renting a car, or paying a friend for rides. As you develop alternatives, be sure to consider

1. Continuing the same course of action
2. Expanding your current actions
3. Changing to a new course of action

The more creative you are in developing alternatives, the more likely you will be successful. But, remember that if you decide to be cautious and do nothing, this is also a choice that has consequences.

Opportunity Cost Every course of action you choose to take means you will give up something else. For example, a decision to invest your money in stock may mean you cannot take a vacation. **Opportunity cost** is what you give up by making a choice. These *trade-offs* may not be measured in dollars. The resources you give up (money or time) also have a value that is lost.

One way to measure opportunity cost is with the *time value of money,* which measures the increase in an amount of money as a result of interest earned. Saving instead of spending money today will result in a larger amount in the future. Every time you spend, save, invest, or borrow, consider the time value of money. For example, spending money from a savings account means lost interest earnings. The items you buy may have a higher priority than the amount of interest earned.

Risk Uncertainty is a part of every decision. For example, selecting a college major and choosing a career field involve risk. What if you don't like working in the field you chose or cannot obtain employment in it? Some decisions have a very low risk, such as putting money in an insured savings account. Be sure to gather information about risk before making any financial decision. Good sources of risk information are your experiences and the experiences of others, as well as library and online sources.

© GETTY IMAGES/PHOTODISC

Any purchasing decision has an opportunity cost.

Step 4 Create an Action Plan After you evaluate the alternatives, you should develop an action plan to achieve your goals. For example, you can increase savings by reducing your spending. Or, you might increase your income by working extra time or by getting a second job. To implement your financial action plan, you may need assistance. For example, you may use the services of an insurance agent or an investment broker.

Step 5 Review Your Progress Finally, after you have taken action, regularly review your financial decisions. While an annual review is recommended, changes in your personal situation may require more frequent evaluations. When life events affect your financial needs, the financial planning process will provide a way to adapt to those changes. Regularly reviewing this decision-making process will help you make proper adjustments for your current life situation.

checkpoint ✓

Describe the five steps of the personal financial process.

■Personal Financial Decisions

As you implement the financial planning process, you will make decisions in five areas.

OBTAINING FINANCIAL RESOURCES

People commonly obtain financial resources from employment, investments, or ownership of a business. Your education, talents, and efforts provide a foundation for your future earning potential.

PLANNING THE USE OF FINANCIAL RESOURCES

A wise spending plan, often called a *budget*, is the foundation for achieving personal financial goals. Financial planning is not designed to prevent your enjoyment of life. Wise spending can help you obtain things you want. Quite often, people make unplanned purchases. These impulsive decisions usually result in financial difficulties. Writing down how you spend your money will help you plan today and in the future. Spending less than you receive is the only path for achieving personal financial security.

SAVING AND INVESTING DECISIONS

Your future financial security must start with a regular savings plan. These funds might be needed for emergencies, unexpected bills, replacement of major items, or buying special items. After establishing a basic savings plan, you should consider investments that offer greater financial growth.

Many types of investments are available. People invest for two primary reasons: (1) current income and (2) long-term growth. Financial advisors commonly recommend *diversification*, which is investing in a variety of assets. For example, you may someday own stocks, bonds, mutual funds, real estate, and collectibles such as rare coins.

BORROWING ACTIVITIES

The wise use of credit is necessary to avoid financial difficulties. Many people in our society overuse and misuse credit. These poor financial planning decisions commonly result in household stress, bankruptcy, and other personal and financial troubles.

MANAGING FINANCIAL RISKS

Every financial decision has risks. The use of insurance and other risk management actions benefits both individuals and businesses. When planning your finances, be sure to determine your need for auto, home, health, life, and disability insurance coverage.

Explain five main areas of personal financial decisions.

Dollarization in Ecuador and Elsewhere

As you pay for your purchase in Ecuador with U.S. dollars, you receive some coins in change. While these coins are the size you expect, something is different. You look at the coins and notice these are not U.S. quarters, dimes, and nickels. What's going on?

While the U.S. dollar is the official currency of Ecuador, the country does not have enough U.S. coins to handle the many business transactions. Paper currency is abundant. As a matter of fact, over 60 percent of all U.S. paper money is in circulation outside the United States. But coins are scarce. Due to this shortage, Ecuador had to create its own coins with a similar shape but a different design.

In the late 1990s, Ecuador faced many economic difficulties including high inflation, increased poverty, and a declining value of the *sucre* (its previous currency). Actions to address these problems included adoption of the U.S. dollar as official currency.

Dollarization is the official use of a currency by a country other than its own currency. In addition to Ecuador, other countries that officially use the U.S. dollar include El Salvador, Panama, and East Timor.

The term "dollarization" most often refers to the use of the U.S. dollar by other countries. This word also can indicate when any country uses the currency of another country. For example, Tuvalu, located in the Pacific region, uses the Australian dollar. Monaco uses the euro as its official currency. This small Western European country had previously used the French franc.

Think Critically

1. What are some benefits of dollarization?
2. What are some possible problems with dollarization?
3. Conduct an Internet search to obtain additional information on dollarization. Prepare a summary of your research results.

UNDERSTAND CONCEPTS

Determine the best answer for each of the following questions.

1. The first step of the personal financial planning process is to:
   a. create an action plan
   b. review your progress
   c. determine your current situation
   d. set financial goals

2. Buying insurance is a method of
   a. obtaining financial resources
   b. managing financial risk
   c. borrowing
   d. planning investment decisions

3. Opportunity cost is sometimes called
   a. a trade-off
   b. a personal financial goal
   c. risk management
   d. all of the above

4. **True or False?** A financial plan serves the same purpose as a budget.

5. **True or False?** Diversification refers to owning a variety of investments.

MAKE ACADEMIC CONNECTIONS

6. **Technology** Locate a web site that offers information about making personal financial decisions. Prepare a two-paragraph summary of your findings.

7. **Oral Communication** Conduct an interview with another student. Ask that person about her or his financial goals. Suggest actions to help the person achieve those goals.

8. **Visual Art** Create a flowchart to communicate the five steps of the financial planning process.

9. **Research** Use library or online research to determine common financial planning activities for different stages of life. Prepare a written summary or poster reporting your findings for people in their 20s, 30s, 40s, 50s, and 60s and older.

1.3 Business Financial Activities

Goals
- Describe financial institutions commonly used by businesses and consumers.
- Explain the sources and uses of funds of businesses.

Terms
- deposit institution
- non-deposit institution
- source of funds
- use of funds

■ Types of Financial Institutions

Both individuals and businesses need *financial institutions* to handle money receipts, payments, and lending. These organizations, also called *financial intermediaries,* provide a wide range of financial services. As shown in Figure 1-4, financial institutions are commonly viewed in two main categories—deposit institutions and non-deposit institutions.

FIGURE 1-4

Types of Financial Institutions

Deposit Institutions	Non-Deposit Institutions
Commercial bank	Life insurance company
Savings and loan association	Investment company
Mutual savings bank	Consumer finance company
Credit union	Mortgage company
	Check-cashing outlet
	Pawnshop

DEPOSIT INSTITUTIONS

Deposit institutions, also called *depository institutions,* accept deposits from people and businesses to use in the future. This category of financial institutions includes commercial banks, thrift institutions, and credit unions.

Commercial Banks These financial institutions are often called *full-service banks* and offer a wide range of financial services. Commercial banks offer checking accounts, provide savings accounts, make loans, and offer other services to individuals and businesses. In recent years, many banks have expanded with full-service branch offices in shopping centers and grocery stores.

Thrift Institutions Two types of financial institutions are commonly viewed in this category—savings and loan associations and mutual savings banks. A *savings and loan association* (S&L) specializes in savings accounts and making loans for home mortgages. In recent years, these financial

NETBookmark

Credit unions have provided financial services to their members for many years. Access thomsonedu.com/school/busfinance and click on the link for Chapter 1. Research the history of credit unions in the U.S. and find out about credit unions in your community.

www.thomsonedu.com/school/busfinance

institutions have expanded to offer a greater variety of financial services and have become more like banks. Today, many S&Ls use the words *savings bank* in their names.

While a *mutual savings bank* provides a variety of services, it is organized mainly for savings and home loans. This type of financial institution is owned by the depositors. The profits of the mutual savings bank go to the depositors. Mutual savings banks are located mainly in the northeastern United States.

Credit Unions A *credit union* is a user-owned, not-for-profit, cooperative financial institution. Credit unions are commonly formed by people in the same company, government agency, labor union, profession, church, or community. Serving members only, credit unions accept savings deposits and make loans for a variety of purposes. Today, credit unions also offer a wide range of financial services.

NON-DEPOSIT INSTITUTIONS

The other major category of financial institutions is **non-deposit institutions**. This group includes life insurance companies, investment companies, consumer finance companies, mortgage companies, check-cashing outlets, and pawnshops.

Life Insurance Companies People commonly buy life insurance to provide financial security for their dependents. Besides protection, many life insurance companies also offer financial services such as investments. By investing in companies, life insurance companies help to expand business in an economy.

Investment Companies Investment companies allow people to choose investment opportunities for long-term growth of their money. Many investors in our society own shares of one of the more than 30,000 mutual funds worldwide made available by investment companies.

Consumer Finance Companies These organizations specialize in loans for durable goods, such as cars and refrigerators, and for financial emergencies. While consumer finance companies make loans, they do not accept savings as do banks and other financial institutions.

Mortgage Companies Buying a home is an important activity in the economy. Mortgage companies, along with other financial institutions, provide loans for purchasing a home or other real estate.

© GETTY IMAGES/PHOTODISC

Smart investors keep track of the value of their assets.

Check-Cashing Outlets People without bank accounts often use check-cashing outlets (CCOs) to cash paychecks and for other financial services. CCOs offer a variety of services such as electronic tax filing, money orders, private postal boxes, utility bill payment, and the sale of bus and subway tokens. Most services at a CCO are more expensive than at other financial institutions.

Pawnshops Offering small loans based on the value of some tangible possession (such as jewelry), pawnshops commonly charge higher fees than other lending institutions.

checkpoint ✓

How do deposit institutions differ from non–deposit institutions?

■Sources and Uses of Funds

The availability of money for business operations is a fundamental element of any financial system. The sources (inflows) and uses (outflows) of cash and credit provide necessary funds for current and long-term business activities.

SOURCES OF FUNDS

Businesses and other organizations require money for day-to-day activities. **Source of funds** refers to the inflow of cash that can be used for paying various expenses. Three common sources of funds are available for companies.

1. Revenue refers to the inflow of cash from business operations. These funds result from sales of goods and services. Examples of revenue include store sales for a retailer, premiums for an insurance company, fees for a law office, and tuition for a college or university.

2. Investor funds are the result of money from existing or new owners of a company. Selling the stock of a company is an example of investor funds. Or, if you own a small business, you might ask additional investors to provide funds.

3. Borrowing is common among most businesses and other types of organizations. Loans, notes, bonds, and mortgages are some methods used to borrow funds. This money may be used to expand international trade operations or build a new factory.

USES OF FUNDS

The daily operations of organizations also involve making payments for various business costs and other necessary expenses. The **use of funds** involves outflow of money by a company. Current expenses and capital expenditures are the main uses of funds.

teamwork

In your team, select a business. Prepare a list of current expenses and capital expenditures that this company might use in its operations.

1. *Current expenses* include rent, materials, wages and salaries, utilities, repairs, advertising, supplies, and other necessary business costs. Most business expenses involve items used up in a year or less.

2. *Capital expenditures* are long-term spending for items that will be used over a longer period of time (more than a year). For example, a building or a computer system will probably be paid for and used over several years. These long-term costs, also called *capital projects*, are necessary for companies to produce, store, and deliver goods and services.

checkpoint ✓

What are examples of sources and uses of funds for businesses?

finance **in your life**

Similarities of Personal and Business Financial Planning

Budgeting In a similar way as a company plans its financial activities, a budget is also an important personal financial planning tool. The budgeting process for both households and companies must start with setting goals. Your personal plan for spending will depend on what you want to achieve, such as saving for college or buying a car. A company also sets goals when creating a budget. These goals may include spending more for advertising, building a new factory, or increasing employee salaries. Like your goals, these business goals will affect how a company spends its money.

Financial Statements When you keep track of your income and spending, you are creating an *income statement.* If you create a list of what you own (assets) and what you owe (liabilities), you have started developing a *balance sheet.* These two financial statements, the income statement and balance sheet, are vital financial planning tools for both individuals and companies. A company uses these financial reports to measure its progress. In a similar way, individuals and families can use an income statement and balance sheet to assess spending patterns and calculate the achievement of financial goals.

Banking Services When you open a bank account, you might need to save for the future or make payments using a checking account. In the future, you may need to borrow money to buy a house or a car. These are two examples of loans made to individuals. Banking services used by companies serve a similar purpose. Businesses desire to store money (savings), make payments (checking), and borrow for organizational needs (loans).

Think Critically

1. In what ways are personal and business financial activities similar?
2. Describe possible differences between personal financial planning activities and financial decisions made by businesses.

1.3 Lesson Assessment

UNDERSTAND CONCEPTS

Determine the best answer for each of the following questions.

1. An example of a deposit institution is a
   a. credit union
   b. mortgage company
   c. consumer finance company
   d. life insurance company

2. _____?_____ is an example of a capital expense.
   a. Advertising
   b. Rent
   c. A truck
   d. An electric bill

3. **True or False?** An investment company offers the widest range of financial services.

4. **True or False?** Investments can be a source of funds for a business.

MAKE ACADEMIC CONNECTIONS

5. **History** Investigate the availability of credit unions in your community. Who may join? What services are offered?

6. **Culture** Conduct research about the types of financial institutions in other countries.

7. **Law** Check-cashing outlets and pawnshops frequently charge fees and rates much higher than other financial institutions. Research laws that regulate these financial institutions. Prepare a one-page summary of your findings.

8. **Technology** Research recent developments in electronic banking services. Describe some new services that were not available a few years ago.

Goals
- Identify government financial activities.
- Describe sources of government funds.

Terms
- tax revenue
- income tax
- property tax
- sales tax
- municipal bond

Government Financial Activities

Government plays a significant role in every economic system. Your role as a citizen and voter influences the decisions and actions taken by government. In a private enterprise system, government's role is much less extensive than in other economic systems but is still an important one. The role of government in the economy frequently changes as newly elected officials take office.

Government regulates and oversees business activities.

© GETTY IMAGES/PHOTODISC

FUNCTIONS OF GOVERNMENT

Governments participate in many economic and business activities related to the financial system of a society. Several fundamental roles of government are common, including

- Providing public services for members of the society
- Protecting citizens, consumers, businesses, and workers from dangers
- Regulating financial and other business activities, while promoting competition
- Providing information and assistance to businesses
- Purchasing goods and services for government operations
- Hiring public employees to serve citizens
- Raising revenue to finance various public services and government projects

Each of these roles has either a direct or indirect impact on business activity, economic growth, and the operation of a society's financial system.

LEVELS OF GOVERNMENT

In the United States, three levels of government exist. The public service agencies in each of these levels serve various needs.

Federal Government The main role of the federal government is to oversee the activities that involve two or more states or other countries. In general, the U.S. Constitution gives the federal government the power to regulate foreign trade and interstate commerce.

Business transactions involving companies in more than one state are called *interstate commerce*. For example, a financial institution that conducts business with people in several states would be regulated by the federal government.

State Government State governments regulate business activities within their own boundaries. *Intrastate commerce* refers to business transactions involving companies that do business only in one state. For instance, a lending company that provides loans only within a state's boundaries would be regulated by that state and not the federal government.

Local Government All states have delegated some of their legislative authority to local governments. Local governments include county boards and city or town councils. Local governments commonly provide services needed for an orderly society, such as police and fire protection.

teamwork

Create a list of financial activities, followed by three columns headed individuals, business, and government. In your team, decide which items apply to each group. Place a check mark in one or more columns to indicate if the activity applies to this group.

checkpoint ✓

Describe the activities of the three levels of government.

▮ Sources of Government Funds

Government must have a way to raise money to finance operations and pay wages to its workers. Government income is called **tax revenue.** Governments obtain a large portion of their revenue through the collection of taxes. In addition, governments raise revenue in other ways. Fines for traffic violations and other violations of the law provide revenue for government. Fees and licenses are also a source of income. Certain types of enterprises require a business license. For example, insurance and real estate agents pay a fee for the privilege of conducting business. Governments also charge fees for such things as driver's licenses and fishing privileges.

TAXES

A government establishes tax policies to pay for the services it provides. Taxes are levied on earnings, the value of property, and on the sale of goods and services.

Your earnings as an individual are subject to an income tax. **Income taxes** are levied on the income of individuals. The individual income tax is the largest source of revenue for the federal government. Corporate income taxes also provide government revenue. The corporate income tax is based on business profits.

A major source of revenue for local governments is the real estate **property tax.** This tax is based on the value of land and buildings. Most property tax revenue is used to pay for schools and other local government services, such as police protection and community parks. Businesses also pay a property tax.

The cost of buying things can be increased by a sales tax. A **sales tax** is a state or local tax on goods and services that is collected by the seller. If you buy a can of paint for $15.00 and the state sales tax is 6 percent, the seller collects $15.90 from you. The seller then will pay 90 cents to the state, but you were the one who provided the money for the tax.

Paying taxes is a responsibility of citizens and businesses. You should pay your fair share of tax but not more than your share. Tax laws and policies are established to help make the paying of taxes fair and equitable. Whether a particular tax or tax policy is fair and equitable is always subject to debate. Businesses also pay a lot of taxes to all levels of government.

BORROWING

Government income from taxes and other sources may not always be enough to cover the costs of providing services. Borrowing is another activity of government. When a government wants to build a building, such as a new courthouse or convention center, the funds needed are often raised through borrowing.

Governments often borrow money by selling bonds. When you buy a government bond, you are helping to finance the services provided by government. Banks, insurance companies, and other financial institutions help finance our governments by purchasing bonds in large quantities. By borrowing money, the government becomes a debtor and must pay interest on its debt.

Federal Government Borrowing Bonds issued by the U.S. government are backed by the "full faith and credit" of the federal government. Bonds issued by our federal government are considered the least risky of all debt. The U.S. federal government issues four main types of debt securities.

1. U.S. savings bonds
2. Treasury bills
3. Treasury notes
4. Treasury bonds

State and Local Government Borrowing Many local governments issue bonds to finance various public service projects. A **municipal bond** is a debt security issued by a state or local government. These bonds are commonly issued by states, cities, counties, and school districts. While municipal bonds usually pay lower interest than most other investments, these can still be very attractive for two reasons.

1. They are low in risk.
2. The interest earned is not subject to income tax.

Name the two main sources of funds for governments.

1.4 Lesson Assessment

UNDERSTAND CONCEPTS

Determine the best answer for each of the following questions.

1. ____?____ tax is based on the value of a person's home.
   a. An income
   b. A sales
   c. An import
   d. A property

2. Treasury bills, Treasury notes, and Treasury bonds are issued by the ____?____ government.
   a. state
   b. city
   c. federal
   d. county

3. A(n) ____?____ tax is a common source of revenue for state and local governments.
   a. sales
   b. import
   c. gift
   d. unemployment

4. A(n) ____?____ bond is issued by state and local governments.
   a. savings
   b. municipal
   c. corporate
   d. export

MAKE ACADEMIC CONNECTIONS

5. **Law** Research some of the federal government agencies that exist to regulate financial activities, such as banking and investing. What are the main duties of these agencies? Prepare a brief written summary of your findings.

6. **Culture** Research different systems of government. Explain how history and culture can affect business regulations in various countries.

7. **Careers** Locate information about the process and employment requirements for obtaining a job with the federal or state government.

8. **Visual Communication** Conduct a survey of people to obtain their opinions about which types of taxes are most appropriate to raise government revenue. Prepare a summary data table with your findings.

Summary

1.1 FINANCE IN SOCIETY

1. A financial system involves financial activities among individuals, businesses, and government. Major factors that affect financial activities are changing economic conditions, government regulations, and global business activities.

2. The two major types of financial markets are money markets and capital markets. The value of investment securities is influenced by supply and demand, future cash flows, risk, liquidity, and interest rates.

1.2 PERSONAL FINANCIAL DECISIONS

3. Personal financial planning involves a five-step process: (1) determine current situation, (2) set financial goals, (3) evaluate alternatives, (4) create an action plan, and (5) review progress.

4. The major areas of financial decision-making are obtaining financial resources, planning the use of resources, saving and investing, borrowing, and managing financial risks.

1.3 BUSINESS FINANCIAL ACTIVITIES

5. The major types of deposit institutions are commercial banks, savings and loan associations, mutual savings banks, and credit unions. Non-deposit financial institutions include life insurance companies, investment companies, consumer finance companies, mortgage companies, check-cashing outlets, and pawnshops.

6. Common sources of funds are company revenue, investor funds, and borrowing. The use of funds involves outflow of money for current expenses and capital expenditures.

1.4 GOVERNMENT FINANCES

7. Federal, state, and local governments provide public services, protect citizens and others, regulate financial activities, provide information, purchase goods and services, hire public employees, and raise revenue.

8. The main sources of government funds are taxes and borrowing.

Develop Your Business Language

Match the terms listed with the definitions. Some terms will not be used.

1. Security representing ownership in a corporation
2. Investment instrument issued by a corporation, government, or other organization representing ownership or a debt
3. Money that is borrowed by a company or government
4. Government income
5. What you give up by making a choice
6. Debt security issued by a state or local government
7. Rise in the general level of prices
8. Outflow of money by a company
9. The inflow of cash that can be used for paying various expenses
10. State or local tax on goods and services
11. Any item that serves as a method of payment

a. bond
b. deposit institution
c. finance
d. financial plan
e. income tax
f. inflation
g. liquidity
h. money
i. municipal bond
j. non-deposit institution
k. opportunity cost
l. personal financial goal
m. personal financial planning
n. property tax
o. sales tax
p. security
q. source of funds
r. stock
s. tax revenue
t. use of funds

Review Concepts

12. Taxes are collected by the ____?____ component of a financial system.
    a. agency
    b. business
    c. consumer
    d. government

13. Increased savings will likely cause ____?____ to rise.
    a. interest rates
    b. borrowing
    c. inflation
    d. exports

14. An example of a current operating expense would be
    a. a computer
    b. a building
    c. purchase of land
    d. a truck repair

15. Interstate commerce refers to business
    a. in more than one country
    b. in more than one state
    c. within the same state
    d. in the same city

Think Critically

16. Inflation rates can be deceptive. Many people face *hidden* inflation since the cost of necessities (food, gas, health care), on which they spend most of their money, may rise at a higher rate than non-essential items which could be dropping in price. Explain how the reported inflation rate could be much lower than the actual cost-of-living increases experienced by consumers.

17. Assessing risk in various financial decision situations is important. Describe what is meant by the following types of risk: a. inflation risk, b. liquidity risk, c. business failure risk, d. global risk.

18. What relationship exists between liquidity and the rate of return on an investment?

19. What actions might a person take to avoid using a check-cashing outlet or a pawnshop?

20. Using the list in the section on "Functions of Government" (on page 22), describe a specific action for each of these activities.

21. Consumers pay some taxes directly, such as sales tax and income tax. What are some examples of *indirect* taxes you might pay?

Business Financial Calculations

22. The rate of return on an investment, also called the yield, is the relationship between the yearly (annual) inflow from the investment and the cost of the investment. For example, a $100 savings account that earns $3 would have a 3 percent yield ($3 ÷ $100). Calculate the yield for the following investments.
    a. $8 dividend on a stock that cost $160
    b. $1,000 rent on land that cost $10,000
    c. $74 interest on a bond that cost $960
    d. $5,600 profit from a business that had a startup cost of $78,000

23. Harold Collins made a down payment of $700 on a car and will pay $230 a month for 48 months. What will be the total cost (including both principal and interest) of the vehicle?

24. The Maxwell Construction Company had $184,000 in revenue last year. The company expects its revenue to grow 6 percent a year. What will be the company's revenue two years from now?

25. A city government spends $228,000 a month on public services. Of that amount, 43 percent is used for fire and police protection.
    a. How much is spent each month for fire and police protection?
    b. How much is spent each month for other services?
    c. How much is spent in a year for fire and police protection?

26. In a city in which there are 90,000 employed workers, 18,000 are public employees. Of this number, 6,000 are employed by the federal government, 8,000 by the state, and 4,000 by the city.
    a. What percent of all workers are public employees?
    b. What percent of the public employees are employed by the federal government?
    c. What percent of all employees are employees of the state?

Analyze Cases

Use the case from the beginning of the chapter, JPMorgan Chase: Financial Partnerships in Action, to answer the following questions.

27. What are benefits and concerns associated with a company buying other companies that become part of its organization?
28. Which services of JPMorgan Chase might you consider using to assist you with your personal financial planning activities?
29. Describe various sources and uses of funds for JPMorgan Chase.
30. What are possible government regulations that may affect the business activities of JPMorgan Chase?
31. JPMorgan Chase has asked you to (a) identify an area of concern for the company, and (b) suggest actions that might be taken to address this concern.

Portfolio Activity

To provide tangible evidence of your learning about the financial environment of business, do the following:

COLLECT an item that illustrates financial activity. This example could be an advertisement, newspaper or magazine article, photo, or some other actual item.

CREATE a visual to show various financial activities related to the item you selected. Use photos, other pictures or ads, other actual items, and drawings to illustrate common financial decisions by individuals, businesses, and government, along with factors that might affect these decisions.

CONNECT your visual to other aspects of our economy and society or relate it to an important concept you have learned in another class. Make the connection by preparing a one-minute presentation on financial activities in our society.

Stock Market Activity

The stock market is an important element of the economy and society. Nearly every person owns stock either directly or indirectly, through a mutual fund, retirement account, or other investment. In this project you will learn about many aspects of issuing, buying, selling, and holding stock.

Conduct library and Internet research on the basics of selecting and owning stock investments.

1. Identify how and why people buy stock as an investment.
2. Explain factors a company might consider when planning to issue stock.
3. Describe financial decisions that individuals, businesses, and government might encounter regarding stocks and stock market activities.

"How much should I save for retirement?" "What is the best type of life insurance for my family situation?" "What actions can I take to reduce the amount of debt I owe?"

These and many other questions are answered by people who work in personal financial planning. Employment in this field has a wide range of opportunities. Your work may involve financial planning activities within a company with hundreds of employees. You might work for a social service agency that helps people avoid financial difficulties as a result of a job loss or illness.

Employment Outlook

- Faster than average growth in employment is expected as the personal financial choices faced by people become more complex.
- Employment of financial analysts in large firms will grow as fast as the average for most occupations.
- Community-based and non-profit budget counselors will expand as economic conditions and personal situations result in needed services.

Job Titles

- Credit counselor
- Budget advisor
- Certified financial planner
- Financial data analyst
- Personal financial advisor
- Family money management counselor
- Tax preparer

Needed Skills

- Prospective employees with knowledge in accounting, finance, economics, and other business fields will enjoy the best job possibilities.
- Communication skills are very important when working with individuals and customer groups.
- Continuing education, especially in taxes and estate planning laws, is important.
- Certification of financial planning competencies is available from the Certified Financial Planner Board of Standards and other organizations.

What's It Like to Work in Personal Financial Management?

At 8 a.m., Carla Pohanka leaves for work...in the next room. Carla runs a personal financial planning business out of her home. This morning she is reviewing the files of several clients before advising them about various personal financial decisions. But then, it's time to get on the road.

At 10 a.m., Carla is scheduled to meet with a person who just retired but does not have enough income to cover current living expenses. At noon, she meets with several small business owners who want to create a retirement fund for their employees.

Today, the afternoon is fairly open so Carla can relax or take care of some personal errands. But in the evening, things again get busy. Right after dinner, Carla meets with a family that wants to create a savings and investment program to set aside funds for the children's college educations. Finally, her day ends with a phone call from a client who has a question about recent tax law changes.

What about you? What personal financial situations faced by people might result in a need for hiring someone trained as a financial planner or budget counselor?

PUBLIC SPEAKING I

The Public Speaking I event focuses attention on effective speaking skills. Personal finance is an important issue for individuals and families. Financial goals become reality when budgets include savings and investments. Many people lack the financial discipline necessary to reach future goals. "Personal Financial Decisions for Future Happiness" is the topic for your speech. Your speech must emphasize the importance of financial planning for young people. The speech should emphasize the importance of disciplined savings and investments for future financial success.

The speech should be four (4) minutes in length and must reflect one or more of the nine (9) FBLA-PBL goals. The speech should include facts and working data from credible sources. The speech should be well organized, contain substantiated statements, and be written in an acceptable business style. Participants may use notes or note cards when delivering the speech. Participants are not allowed to use visual aids and a microphone for their speeches.

During the speech, a timekeeper will stand at three (3) minutes. When the speaker is finished, the time used by the participant will be recorded, noting a deduction of five (5) points for any time under 3:31 or over 4:29 minutes. Students will present their speeches to judges and other students.

Performance Indicators Evaluated

- Define clearly the importance of financial planning for individuals and families.
- State clearly the purpose of the speech.
- State clearly the objectives of the speech.
- Accomplish the purpose of the speech.
- Use solid examples to reinforce the objectives of the speech.
- Demonstrate self-confidence, poise, and good voice projection.
- Incorporate appropriate gestures and eye contact.
- Project confidence when presenting the speech.
- Deliver a sincere, interesting, clear, creative, convincing, and concise speech.

Go to the FBLA web site for more detailed information.

Think Critically

1. Why must personal financial planning begin at an early age?
2. What is a major financial downfall for many individuals and families?
3. How can future goals motivate people to prepare financial plans?
4. Why should a speech about "Personal Finance" include examples that are relevant for the audience?

www.fbla.org

Financial Environment of Business

Point Your [Browser]
www.thomsonedu.com/school/busfinance

Case STUDY

Caught Up in the Economy

Cam had always wanted to own his own business. He wanted the challenge of making the decisions that determined whether he would succeed or fail. He sorted through many ideas before settling on a delivery service for local retailers. Many of the local businesses were losing sales to online businesses. Customers liked the convenience of shopping from home and having products delivered to their doors by UPS or FedEx.

He developed a win-win idea for local businesses and their customers. He would deliver any order of $25 or more to a local customer. He would charge the retailer 10 percent less than the shipping cost that would be charged by the major parcel shipping companies. And he guaranteed same-day delivery for orders placed before noon, overnight delivery for afternoon orders during the week, and Monday morning delivery for any weekend order.

Cam's business grew quickly as customers had positive experiences with his rapid delivery service. Businesses that had not used his service before began to call him for local delivery. Customers got to know Cam and his reliable service. He had never had a complaint of a late or damaged delivery. He added a part-time assistant so he did not have to work long hours every day and felt he would soon be able to add another delivery vehicle and a full-time employee.

As Cam celebrated the first anniversary of his business, he was beginning to feel some pressure due to two unplanned and uncontrollable circumstances. Due to a world-wide energy crisis, gas prices had jumped 20 cents a gallon during the year and experts predicted they would continue to rise over the next six months. At the same time, a new national parcel delivery service had entered the competition with FedEx and UPS. To fight the new business, the established companies had temporarily reduced the shipping rates they charged by an average of 10 percent. While Cam believed the price cut was temporary, he was receiving less for each delivery based on the way he calculated his fees. He knew the larger companies could maintain lower prices longer than he could as the owner of a new small business. Based on those two events, Cam's plans to expand his business were on hold. In fact, they had him teetering on the edge of an unprofitable business.

Think Critically

1. What are the similarities and differences between the two events Cam is facing and their effect on his business?
2. What alternatives are available to Cam for dealing with rising gas prices and reduced delivery charges?

2.1 Basic Economic Systems and Principles

Goals
- Identify and describe basic economic principles.
- Discuss how economic decisions are made.

Terms
- economics
- scarcity
- choice
- resources
- demand
- supply
- market price
- market economy

■ Understanding Economics

The economy and the factors that drive the economy have a major effect on both businesses and consumers. Financial decisions are influenced as much by the state of the economy as by any other factors. Effective financial planning and decision making requires an understanding of the economy and economic principles.

You can't watch a news program on television or read the headlines of a newspaper without encountering the term economics. Yet ask almost anyone the meaning of economics or how economics affects their daily lives and you may have a hard time getting a meaningful answer. What is it that makes economics so important yet so difficult to understand?

DEFINING ECONOMICS

Economics is defined as a science, meaning that it is based on facts and principles. The principles can be used to explain events and predict what is likely to happen in the future if certain things occur. Since economics is a science, it can be used to make decisions.

Economics is the science of decision making about the allocation of scarce resources. If people had everything they needed, there would not be a need for economics. In reality people have a large number of needs and limited resources to fill those needs. Economists are scientists who study how decisions can be made that result in the best match of needs and resources. The science of economics can help an individual decide how to plan a personal budget in order to satisfy both immediate needs and long-term needs. Economics can help politicians and bureaucrats decide on the best monetary policies to increase a country's standard of living.

There are great differences in needs and the availability of resources. In your own neighborhood, some people need very little to be satisfied while others are not satisfied even as they spend large sums of money on a variety of products and services. Some people have large sums of money and other resources, while others have almost none. The same differences in needs and resources occur in your community and state as well as in various countries and regions of the world. In some areas people have high levels of consumption and a wealth of resources, while in other places people have difficulty surviving and almost no useful resources. Because of the great differences in needs and the availability of resources, economic decision making can be difficult and complex.

ECONOMIC PRINCIPLES

Several important principles define the science of economics.

Scarcity and Choice   Scarcity means that people have wants and needs that are greater than can be satisfied with the available products and services. Because of scarcity, individuals have to make choices. Choice means deciding which wants and needs will be satisfied and which will go unsatisfied.

Limited Resources   Resources are the means available to develop solutions for unsatisfied wants and needs. An individual's resources are time, money, and skills. People can use their personal resources to create solutions for their needs. They can use their time and skills to earn money so they can purchase the products and services they want.

Companies and countries also have resources. There are three categories of those resources. *Natural resources* are the materials in the world around us. They include land, water, minerals, forests, and even animals. Some natural resources such as timber and water are renewable if managed wisely. They can be replaced or renewed for a continuing supply. Other resources are non-renewable with a limited supply. Examples of important non-renewable resources are oil and coal. There is no exact replacement for non-renewable resources when their supply is gone.

© GETTY IMAGES/PHOTODISC

Natural resources such as land and forests must be managed wisely.

The second category of resources available to countries and businesses is capital resources. *Capital resources* are the human-made goods used in the production of other products and services. Examples of capital resources include factories, machines, tools, and vehicles and the many products used by businesses in their operations. Money used by businesses to purchase the things they need is also considered a capital resource.

The final category of economic resources is human resources. *Human resources* are people and their skills, including both physical and mental abilities. In economics, human resources are sometimes referred to as labor. Entrepreneurs, managers, and employees use their abilities to plan, produce, and sell the products and services needed by consumers.

technology topics

Technology and Economics

Technology plays a very important role in economics. New technology can affect the availability of products and services. Technology may allow a greater number of products to be produced faster and at a lower cost. It may also result in superior products that make older products obsolete. Technology can also change the demand for products and services. Individuals with technology skills can work for higher salaries and wages, giving them more money to spend. Technology such as the Internet can make people aware of products and services that weren't available in the past and can make it easier and often cheaper to purchase them.

Think Critically

1. Identify specific technologies that have resulted in major changes in the following industries: agriculture, transportation, entertainment.
2. What are some negative economic effects that technologies have had on individuals, businesses, and countries?

Supply and Demand **Demand** is the amount of a product or service that individuals want to buy to satisfy their wants and needs. **Supply** is the quantity of a product or service that has been produced by businesses with the hope of making a profit from sales to customers. Several things can affect the demand and the supply of products and services. If products or services do not meet the needs of individuals or if there are better alternatives, the demand for those products or services will be low. If businesses cannot obtain the resources needed to produce a product or service or if those resources are very expensive, the supply will be low.

The supply and demand of goods and services are not usually in balance. People have unlimited wants and needs. The availability of resources limits the supply of products and services. Individuals use their available money to buy goods and services, and they want to get the greatest amount of needs satisfaction for the money they spend. Businesses use their financial and nonfinancial resources to produce and sell goods and services. They obtain money from their customers when products are sold. They want to sell products that will provide the greatest return on the money they invested to produce and sell the products.

The price of a product or service provides the balance between supply and demand. If the price of a product is low, more people will be able to purchase it and will see it as a greater value. Demand for the product will increase. The lower price results in a greater demand. If the price of a product is high, businesses will make a higher profit and will be willing to provide more products for sale. The higher price results in a higher supply. The price at which an equal number of products will be produced and purchased is known as the **market price**. Prices of goods and services rise and fall based on supply and demand.

teamwork

The prices of some products tend to rise over time while others decline. Make a list of products where the market price is rising and another list of those with declining prices. Compare the lists and discuss what might influence whether prices rise or fall.

checkpoint ✓

Describe three important principles of economics.

■Making Economic Decisions

There are two levels of economic decisions. Businesses and individuals make decisions about what to produce and what to consume. Businesses must decide how to use the resources they have available to produce and sell products and services. Their goal is to make the most profitable decisions. Individual consumers must decide how to use the resources they have available to purchase products and services. Their goal is to get the greatest satisfaction from their decisions. The level of economic decisions related to the choices of individuals and businesses is known as *microeconomics*.

The second level of economic decisions is known as macroeconomics. *Macroeconomics* relates to economic decisions made at a national level. Countries have limited resources and must be able to use those resources to meet the goals of the country and provide a reasonable standard of living and quality of life for their citizens. To do that, the people responsible for economic planning for the country must make three important decisions.

1. What products and services will be produced?
2. How will the needed products and services be produced?
3. For whom will the products and services be produced?

TYPES OF ECONOMIC SYSTEMS

The way a country makes the three economic decisions determines the type of economy it has. In a *traditional economy,* economic decisions are made in much the same way they always have been. There is very little government influence or control in a traditional economy. The basic needs of individuals and families are unchanged for generations. They do the same work using many of the same tools and procedures that their ancestors did. People use their time, skills, and tools to meet their basic needs and sustain their lives in the best way they know how.

In a traditional economy, the same methods of production have been used for generations.

In a *command economy*, the government has the primary influence on economic decisions. Government decision-makers determine what goods and services are needed and how and when they will be produced. They influence the work people do since the work will be devoted to producing the needed products and services. The government also determines what is available for consumers to purchase as well as the prices that will be charged.

A **market economy** is based on the combination of the decisions made by individual consumers and businesses. All businesses can decide what they will produce and how. They also have the freedom to set the price they think is appropriate for their products and services. Individual consumers can also decide how they will spend their money. They are free to buy the products and services they want and determine how much they are willing to pay for each choice.

THE U.S. FREE ENTERPRISE ECONOMY

Most countries do not have a pure form of any of the three economic systems. Developing countries in Africa and Eastern Asia that had traditional economies are now using more central government planning as well as experimenting with a market economy. Strong central economies in countries such as China are allowing some individual land ownership for farmers as well as the development of small businesses while still maintaining many government controls. European countries that have market economies also have government ownership or control of many social and human service activities.

The United States has always had a commitment to a market economy, maintaining principles of individual ownership of property and freedom for consumers and businesses to control their own economic decisions. However, laws developed and enforced by federal and state governments regulate the economy and maintain balance and fairness in the marketplace. Government restricts some economic activities that are considered harmful to citizens and regulates others to make sure consumers have access to essential products and services such as water and electricity. The government even owns and operates some business activities such as schools, police and fire protection, and the postal service when it is determined that government ownership is for the public good.

The mixed economy of the United States is often referred to as a *free enterprise economy*. It is based on several important principles designed to protect and promote the economic freedoms of individual consumers and businesses. Those principles include:

1. **Right of Private Ownership** People have the right to own property. They can buy and sell property including homes, cars, businesses, and other material goods. The ownership and use of individual property is protected by law as long as it doesn't interfere with the rights of others. Businesses own the resources needed to produce products and services so they can control the basic economic decisions of what will be produced and how it will be produced.

Consumers can decide what to buy and how much to spend.

2. **Freedom of Choice** Each consumer and each businessperson has freedom of choice. Consumers can decide what and when to buy and how much money to spend. Businesses are free to enter into or end any business activity. They can decide what to produce, the quantity to produce, and the prices they want to charge.

3. **Competition among Businesses** Anyone can start and operate a business if they have the resources and ability. If there is a strong consumer demand for a product or service, it is likely that several businesses will offer it. If a business is profitable, it can expect that other businesses will compete for those profits. Competition increases the number of product choices and helps to control the prices at which products and services are sold.

4. **Consumer Influence on Economic Activity** There are few restrictions on how consumers spend their money. Because of competition, consumers usually have choices among several businesses for the products and services they want. There will be differences in the variety, quality, and price of products. Consumer decisions determine which products and services are sold as well as which businesses are successful.

5. **A Limited Government Role in the Economy** Due to the individual freedoms in a free enterprise economy, the government plays a very limited role. The primary purpose of government is to help ensure the long-term health and stability of the economy. The government exerts some economic influence through laws regulating business practices and competition. A federal monetary policy influences business decisions and consumer spending by raising and lowering taxes, regulating the amount of money in circulation in the economy, and influencing interest rates charged to businesses and consumers.

checkpoint ✓

What is the difference between microeconomics and macroeconomics?

2.1 Lesson Assessment

UNDERSTAND CONCEPTS

Determine the best answer for each of the following questions.

1. The science of economics is needed because
   a. today people have everything they need
   b. governments must make all economic decisions
   c. people have unlimited wants and needs and limited resources
   d. people can't be trusted to make good decisions

2. The economic principle that people have more wants and needs than can be satisfied with the available products and services is
   a. choice
   b. scarcity
   c. limited resources
   d. supply and demand

3. The ____?____ of a product or service provides the balance between supply and demand.
   a. available money
   b. resources
   c. market price
   d. unlimited wants

4. **True or False?** The level of economic decisions related to the choices of individuals and businesses is known as microeconomics.

5. In a ____?____ economy, the government holds the primary influence on economic decisions.
   a. traditional
   b. market
   c. command
   d. free enterprise

MAKE ACADEMIC CONNECTIONS

6. **Economics** List three examples of each type of economic resources.

7. **Visual Art** The relationship of supply and demand is often pictured as a graph by economists. Use an economics textbook or the Internet to locate a graph illustrating a supply and demand relationship. Show the graph to the other students in your class and orally describe the meaning of the information in the graph.

8. **Research** Identify three countries each of which provides an example of one of the three types of economic systems. Use the Internet or resources from your school library to gather economic information about the countries. Prepare a table that compares the three countries to illustrate the differences in their economies.

9. **Critical Thinking** Briefly describe what each of the principles of free enterprise means to you as an individual.

10. **Communication** Review recent newspapers and business magazines. Identify and study three articles describing actions taken by federal or state government related to the economy. Prepare a one-paragraph summary of each article, describing the action of the government and the reason the action was taken.

2.2 Legal Forms of Business

Goals
- Recognize differences in the legal forms of business ownership and organization.
- Explain financial implications of the business ownership decision.

Terms
- sole proprietorship
- partnership
- corporation
- limited liability company (LLC)

■ Organizing a Business

A business is easy to form in a free enterprise economy. If a person wants to start a business, it is a matter of deciding what will be bought and sold and how to attract customers. Thousands of people operate small enterprises from their own homes with little thought about how the business is organized and whether it is following proper business procedures. The *form of business ownership* determines the financial, managerial, and legal responsibilities of business owners.

IMPORTANCE OF THE ORGANIZING DECISION

There are several factors that should encourage any business owner to be thoughtful about how their business is organized and operated. All business owners, even those with small businesses requiring little time and money to operate, want their businesses to be successful. That means they want to make a profit and have the business grow. Most new businesses fail due to poor financial planning and lack of adequate financial resources.

The way a business is organized plays a major role in its financial condition. It will determine how much money is available to start the business, how additional funds can be obtained when needed, how income and expenses are allocated and accounted for, and even the amount of taxes paid by the business and business owner. The way a business is organized also determines how investors are compensated for their risk.

ROLE OF GOVERNMENT

Government plays a limited role in a free enterprise economy. The two primary ways governments are involved in the organization of businesses are in legal requirements and taxation.

Government has a responsibility to protect the health and safety of citizens, prevent a major imbalance of competition among businesses and between businesses and consumers, and encourage economic growth. Governments pass laws and regulations related to those responsibilities. Many business activities must be licensed and must conform to specific conditions and procedures. The government may inspect business operations or require businesses to report information about their organization and its operations.

Taxes are a fact of life for almost everyone, and businesses are no exception. Governments collect various types of taxes to fund their operations and services. Depending on the type of business organization and business activities, businesses and business owners may be subject to

- Taxes on business and personal income
- Sales tax on products and services sold
- Employment taxes for Social Security, Medicare, and Medicaid
- Property taxes on real estate and other assets
- Special taxes imposed on particular types of businesses, products and services, or operations

LEGAL FORMS OF BUSINESS OWNERSHIP

Determining the legal form of organization for a business should be done carefully to obtain the best circumstances for financing the business, maintaining profitability, and meeting government operating and taxation requirements. The four most common forms for U.S. businesses are sole proprietorship, partnership, corporation, and limited liability company.

Sole Proprietorship A sole proprietorship is a business owned and managed by one person. All financial and operating decisions are made by the owner of the business. The single owner is totally responsible for the success or failure of the business. A sole proprietorship can be formed with almost no legal requirements.

Partnership A partnership is a business owned and managed by two or more people under the conditions of a legal written agreement. The agreement identifies each partner's financial obligations, managerial and operational responsibilities, and how the partnership can be expanded or dissolved.

Corporation A corporation is a distinct legal entity formed by completing required legal documents in a specific state. It is owned by one or more shareholders who have invested in the business and is managed by a board of directors. A corporation is treated legally as if it were an individual, meaning it can enter into contracts and is subject to taxes and business laws.

Limited Liability Company A newer legal form of business ownership is the limited liability company (LLC). Limited liability companies combine features of the partnership and corporation, offering some of the advantages of each. They are formed with a written agreement that is simpler than the documents required of a corporation and more like a partnership agreement. LLCs offer more financial protection for investors than a partnership and similar to that given to stockholders of a corporation.

checkpoint ✓

Why should business owners carefully consider the legal form of ownership for their business?

■Analyzing Forms of Business Ownership

Why would a business owner want to operate a business as a corporation rather than a sole proprietorship? What advantages are offered by forming a limited liability company rather than a partnership? Many factors enter into the decision, including the amount of individual responsibility and control, the simplicity or complexity of forming and managing the business, and differences in legal requirements and liability. One of the major considerations is the financial implications of owning and operating each type of business.

SOLE PROPRIETORSHIP

In a sole proprietorship, the owner has total responsibility for and control over the business. The proprietor must provide financing to start the business from his or her own savings or obtain additional financing from investors in the form of loans, credit, or other financial arrangements. The owner is also responsible for all business debts. If the business fails, the owner is personally liable for the full amount of losses. That amount may be greater than the amount originally invested by the owner.

In return for those financial risks, the sole proprietor receives all profits made by the business but must pay any required income and employment taxes on those profits. Those taxes will be assessed at the individual income tax rates of the federal, state, and local governments. Depending on the level of personal income of the owner, those tax rates may be higher than tax rates for other ownership forms.

Because there is only one owner, it may be difficult to obtain financing for the sole proprietorship. Banks and other investment sources may be concerned about the capabilities of the sole owner as a manager, especially for a new business. They may consider it too much of a risk to loan money since there is nothing more than the assets of the business and the personal resources of the owner to pay back the loan. The life of the business is dependent on one person. If the owner dies or is unable to continue business operations, the business must close or be sold, creating immediate financial pressure. The capital resources of a sole proprietorship may be limited based on the financial standing of the owner.

A sole proprietor takes on all the risks and all the benefits of ownership.

Business partners share the risks and rewards of ownership.

teamwork

Develop a simple partnership agreement for a business. Prepare four statements that describe your agreements about financing, management and operations responsibilities, and the sharing of profits and losses. How do the interests and skills of each partner influence your decisions?

PARTNERSHIP

Partnerships are similar to sole proprietorships from a financing viewpoint. The individual partners are responsible for providing and obtaining the financing. Each partner has responsibility and liability for the debts of the business. If one partner is unable to pay his or her share of those debts, another partner can be required to pay from personal resources.

The advantage of a partnership is that there are more financial resources from two or more people than from one owner. Because the combination of partners adds expertise and skill as well as greater coverage for any business liabilities, it may be easier to obtain financing from banks, suppliers, and other investors. A disadvantage is that management decision making is shared, sometimes complicating business matters.

The life of a partnership is generally limited to the life of any partner or the decision by one partner to end the business relationship. In that way, partnerships are similar to sole proprietorships. The business could come to a sudden end, making it more risky for those providing financing. Most partnership agreements include procedures for ending the partnership, adding partners, or selling the ownership of one partner. In that way, while the specific partnership may end, the business may continue under a new partnership agreement.

Partnership income is passed through to each partner under the terms of the partnership agreement. Taxes are assessed at the individual tax rates of each owner.

A special form of partnership is the limited partnership. A *limited partnership* includes one or more general partners and other limited partners. General partners have operating responsibilities and are liable for all of the business's debts. Limited partners are investors. They cannot participate in day-to-day operations and management decisions. In return, their liability is limited to the amount of their investment. Limited partnerships add financial strength, but may raise questions for other investors due to the limited financial liability of many of the partners.

CORPORATION

Most large businesses and an increasing number of small businesses organize as corporations. Because of the legal status of corporations, they offer many financial advantages to owners as well as to those who have financial relationships with the business.

The ownership of a corporation is controlled by the sale of stock. A *private corporation* can limit the number of owners and who is allowed to purchase stock. A *public corporation* issues stock that is sold on the open market, so anyone with the money to pay for a share of stock can be an owner. Because stock can be bought and sold, the life of the corporation is unlimited. It can continue as long as the company is financially successful.

The ownership and management of a corporation is separated. Overall direction of the corporation is in the hands of a board of directors. Day-today leadership and operations is handled by people with management expertise hired by the directors. Due to the breadth of involvement and specialized expertise, the success rate of corporations is much greater than sole proprietorships or partnerships. They have a much lower financial risk for investors and other companies offering financing to the business.

Initial financing is easier to obtain for public corporations since it is accomplished through the sale of shares of stock. One investor does not need a great deal of money to become an owner. Hundreds of individuals as well as other businesses and organizations can purchase stock with different levels of investment. A major benefit of investing in a corporation is that the liability of a stockholder is limited to the amount invested. Even if the corporation has losses well beyond the value of its assets, investors will have no greater liability than the cost of their stock.

The major financial disadvantage of corporations is that profits can be taxed twice. First, corporations must pay taxes on their profits. The corporate tax rate may be lower than many individual tax rates. Stockholders also expect corporations to pay dividends. *Dividends* are a percentage of corporate earnings allocated to each share of stock. Stockholders must pay individual income tax on the value of dividends received. Also, when stock is sold, the owner may have to pay taxes on any increase in value of the stock from the time it was purchased.

Most corporations are legally known as *Subchapter C corporations*. That name comes from Subchapter C of the Internal Revenue Service code, which regulates how the income and expenses of most corporations are treated for purposes of taxation. A special circumstance that avoids the double taxation is a Subchapter S corporation. *Subchapter S corporations* are smaller corporations that have special tax rules from the Internal Revenue Service and many states. Paperwork is simplified and profits are not taxed at the corporate rate. Instead, earnings flow through to the stockholders. The stockholders then pay individual taxes on their earnings. Stockholder liability is still limited to the amount of the original investment. Because of the special rules and limitations on size, access to large amounts of financing is reduced.

LIMITED LIABILITY COMPANY (LLC)

The limited liability company is a unique form of business ownership that combines advantages and disadvantages of partnerships and private corporations. Ownership is restricted to the partners. Similar to a corporation, the partners have limited liability for the debts of the firm. Like a partnership, income is taxed at the individual rate of each owner based on the profits distributed. The LLC is relatively new and has not been fully legally tested in many states. Many investors are reluctant to provide financing until those legal concerns are clarified. The financial health of the business is very dependent on the resources of the owners and their management capabilities.

In a recent year, 25 million U.S. businesses filed tax returns. Of the total, 72 percent were sole proprietorships, 20 percent were corporations, 5 percent were partnerships and 3 percent were LLCs. The combined annual revenue of all businesses was over $20 trillion.

checkpoint ✓

Why does the corporate form of ownership offer more likelihood of greater initial financing than either the sole proprietorship or partnership?

Financial Activities of a Business Start-Up

Many people think about starting their own business but most do not. The most common reason given is "I didn't have enough money to get the business started." It is true that many businesses require thousands of dollars just to open the doors and many thousands more to continue operations long enough to make a profit. And it is also true that most people who want to start a business do not have the personal savings, cannot find investors, and are unable to get a start-up loan from a bank.

Some creative entrepreneurs have found innovative ways to obtain the money they needed to start their businesses. Here are some examples.

Jon was able to start a lawn care business by bartering. He traded services with other businesses when he didn't have enough money on hand to buy them. He provided an equal value of lawn care services in exchange for printing of brochures and business cards, legal expenses, and repair and maintenance of his equipment. He didn't receive any cash for that work but also didn't have to directly pay for those expenses.

Ervin had restored an antique car that had increased in value over the years. He sold the car for over $40,000, which he used to start a web design business. Ervin knew he would miss the car but felt the sale was worth it to be able to open his business.

Sheila and her husband owned a home on which they had paid over 40 percent of the mortgage. They obtained a home equity loan equal to 50 percent of their home's current value. Sheila used the money to open a day care center. She knew they were risking the loss of their home if the business didn't succeed, so she planned carefully for the business.

Eunice used much the same strategy when she borrowed against a paid-up life insurance policy. The insurance policy remained in effect and the amount of the loan would be deducted from the payout to her beneficiaries in the event of her death.

Nadji was particularly creative when locating funding to start a business to build custom outdoor furniture. He had a very good credit rating with high credit limits on his two credit cards. He used the credit cards to purchase needed tools and materials. He already had three orders from customers and asked them for a 10 percent deposit which he used for his other immediate expenses. While the interest rate on the amount financed with his credit cards was high, he was able to complete the orders in three months. He earned enough money from those sales to pay off his credit card balances and purchase materials and supplies for the new orders he had received.

Think Critically

1. Each of the creative financing methods is risky. How would you determine if the risk was worth taking to start a new business?
2. Identify several other innovative ways that a prospective business owner might obtain several thousand dollars to help finance a new business.

2.2 Lesson Assessment

UNDERSTAND CONCEPTS

Determine the best answer for each of the following questions.

1. The form of business ownership determines which type of responsibility of the owner?
   a. financial
   b. legal
   c. managerial
   d. all of the above

2. Most new businesses fail due to poor _____?_____ planning.
   a. financial
   b. production
   c. managerial
   d. none of the above

3. A _____?_____ is a business owned and managed by two or more people under the conditions of a legal written agreement.
   a. sole proprietorship
   b. partnership
   c. corporation
   d. none of the above

4. **True or False?** Ownership in a limited liability company (LLC) is controlled through the sale of stock.

5. The major financial disadvantage to the ownership of a corporation is
   a. each owner is individually liable of all losses
   b. corporate tax rates are usually higher than individual rates
   c. corporate profits are subject to double taxation
   d. stock prices can decrease in value as well as increase

MAKE ACADEMIC CONNECTIONS

6. **Technology** Prepare a computer presentation of at least three slides describing reasons that business owners should carefully consider the legal form of business ownership and organization.

7. **Debate** Form two teams and prepare for a debate on the topic "The U.S. federal government should take a more active role in protecting consumers and increasing business competition." Your teacher will explain the debate rules and assign the position each team will take.

8. **Communication** Write a one-page persuasive paper discussing the form of business ownership that you would use to start a business.

9. **Math** Use the Internet to determine the federal tax rates for individual income and corporate income for the most recent year. Calculate the amount of taxes that would be paid by a sole proprietor and by a corporation (no stockholder dividend) for the following taxable incomes.
   a. $50,000   b. $295,000   c. $916,000

10. **Math** If each of the above incomes is divided between two partners rather than a sole proprietor, how much tax would each partner pay based on the individual tax rates? What is the difference between the total taxes paid by both partners and the taxes paid by the sole proprietor for each of the taxable incomes?

Goals
- Discuss the purpose and general structure of financial markets.
- Describe the major types of financial markets.

Terms
- financial market
- financial return
- financial risk
- term
- commodity markets
- capital markets
- stock market
- money markets

■ The Need for Financial Markets

"Money makes the world go around" is more than the lyrics of a song. Money really does make the financial world go around. Money allows companies to obtain the resources they need to operate their businesses. Companies use money to build factories and assembly lines; purchase equipment, raw materials and supplies; and pay the salaries of the personnel needed to produce goods that can be sold to customers.

Consumers need money for large and small items, one-time and every-day purchases. Homes, automobiles, food, clothing, entertainment, and vacations all require money. From inexpensive daily purchases to the very costly items that require both savings and loans, money is the resource that allows consumers to meet their wants and needs.

EXCHANGING FINANCIAL RESOURCES

Some people need money while others have money. For people who have a short- or long-term financial need, the options are to earn the money or to borrow from those who have money in order to meet those needs. People who have money can use their financial assets to earn even more. They can invest or loan the money to those with financial needs in order to get a financial return.

For most people, buying a home involves a long-term loan.

© GETTY IMAGES/PHOTODISC

While it is possible for individuals who need money and those who have money to make individual agreements on the terms of their exchange, that procedure would be difficult and certainly time-consuming. Financial markets and financial institutions have developed to make those exchanges easier and more convenient. A **financial market** is an organized process for the exchange of capital and credit. Common financial markets are stock markets, bond markets, commodity markets, and currency markets. Some basic principles of financial exchange guide the activities of those markets and institutions.

PRINCIPLES OF FINANCIAL EXCHANGE

People who need to borrow money from others must pay to do so. People who loan or invest money with others do so to obtain a financial return. A **financial return** is a profit earned from an investment. Most investments are made to gain the greatest financial return. However, investments come with financial risks. A **financial risk** is the possibility that an expected profit will not be achieved. Investments are evaluated to determine the level of risk. Investments with higher financial risks offer the opportunity for a greater financial return, while low-risk investments offer a lower return. With greater risk, there is a higher probability that the expected return will not be realized. The low-risk investments pay less but have a greater likelihood of achieving the expected return.

The **term** of an investment is the length of time the invested money is controlled by others. Long-term investments may be made for many years or even without an ending date identified. Short-term investments may only have a term of a few days or a few months.

Businesses use money to pay for the resources needed to run the business. Money can be obtained by offering ownership in the business or by obtaining long- and short-term financing from non-owners. Ownership financing in sole proprietorships, partnerships, and limited liability companies comes directly from the resources of the owners. Those ownership investments typically are made for the life of the business. Ownership financing in corporations comes from the sale of stock. Stock in public corporations is bought and sold regularly. Some stock owners hold their stock in companies for many years, while others hold the stock for only a short time.

Non-owners provide both short-term and long-term financing for businesses. A typical way for businesses to obtain financing without offering ownership is to borrow money from financial institutions. Short-term and long-term *loans* to purchase raw materials, inventory, supplies, and equipment or to pay ongoing operating costs are often obtained from banks or from the suppliers of the goods purchased. Expensive purchases of property such as land or buildings are financed with *mortgages*. Companies and other organizations such as state and local governments, schools, and universities may issue *bonds* that promise to pay investors an identified interest rate for a specified time period.

teamwork

With your team, consider the following questions: Under what circumstances might an investor choose to assume a greater financial risk for a higher possible return? When is it better to choose a lower risk but a lower return?

checkpoint ✓

How is financial risk related to financial return?

■Common Financial Markets

Financial markets assist in the exchange between buyers and sellers. When a large group of people have interests in the same products and financial resources, a market serves as a common location where those resources can be bought and sold. Sellers want to obtain the highest possible price for the resources they own. Buyers want to purchase those resources at the lowest possible price. Financial markets help to identify the supply and demand for a specific resource in order to determine its current market price. The financial market also manages the exchange between buyers and sellers with policies and procedures for placing orders, making payments, and transferring ownership.

COMMODITY MARKETS

Commodity markets trade raw materials and other basic production resources. Oil, electricity, grain, livestock, chemicals, metals, and gold are examples of commodities. Major commodity markets include the Chicago Board of Trade, the New York Mercantile Exchange, the London Metal Exchange, and the International Petroleum Exchange of London. There are even very specialized commodities exchanges such as the New Orleans Cotton Exchange and the Coffee, Sugar, and Cocoa Exchange in New York.

Two types of markets exist for the sale of commodities. *Spot markets* buy and sell products for immediate (on-the-spot) delivery. *Futures markets* are contracts negotiated for the sale of products at some future date. For example, an airline may negotiate a futures contract for a large amount of aviation fuel to be delivered in six months so they will have an adequate supply at a guaranteed price. A farmer may negotiate a futures contract to sell cattle at a specific price to be delivered in four months. By negotiating a certain future price for each of the commodities, the airline knows what its fuel costs will be and the farmer knows what price he will receive for the cattle when they are ready for market. Negotiated prices reduce some of the risk in the purchase and sale of commodities.

DIGITAL VISION

Sugar is traded at a specialized commodity exchange.

STOCK MARKETS

A stock market is the organized exchange of the ownership shares of public corporations. The buying and selling of stock occurs in *stock exchanges*. Stock exchanges used to be physical locations where representatives of buyers and sellers actually met to negotiate for the purchase and sale of stocks. Today with the development of computer technologies and the Internet, sales are often completed electronically. The New York Stock Exchange still places buy and sell orders on the trading floor of the exchange located on Wall Street in New York City. Another major U.S. stock exchange, NASDAQ, is a virtual exchange. There is no physical trading floor at its New York office. All offers and bids between sellers and buyers are matched electronically.

OTHER FINANCIAL MARKETS

Companies use other methods to obtain financing. Capital markets are used to finance intermediate or long-term debt of one year or longer. Stock markets are one type of capital market. Another is the bond market. A *bond* is a financial instrument that obligates the issuer to pay the bondholder the principal plus agreed-upon interest at the end of a designated period. Bonds are often issued for terms of 5, 10, and 20 years or even longer. *Bond markets* offer newly issued bonds of companies and government agencies for sale as well as buying and selling existing bonds.

Money markets specialize in buying and selling financial instruments for short time periods of a year or less. The federal government offers short-term securities known as *treasury bills*. Some cities offer municipal notes to obtain cash for city operations. The government securities are repaid from taxes or other revenues.

A common form of money market financing familiar to many individuals are *certificates of deposit* (CDs) offered by banks and other financial institutions. Businesses raise money needed for short-term operating expenses by selling *commercial paper*. The various types of short-term securities are sold and traded through banks, government offices, and securities dealers.

PRIMARY AND SECONDARY OFFERINGS

When an organization makes stock available for the first time or issues new bonds, it is known as a *primary offering*. The primary offering is also referred to as the *initial public offering* (IPO). Primary offerings are used to raise new capital for an organization. That organization receives the proceeds from the sale of the IPO.

Buyers may choose to hold the stock and bonds or they may decide to resell them. When an investor offers stocks and bonds for resale, they are known as a *secondary offering*. The original organization is not involved in the secondary sale, so it does not receive any money. The value of securities increase and decrease based on supply, demand, economic conditions, and other market factors. Investors buy and sell securities on the secondary market with the hope of making a profit on their eventual sale.

checkpoint ✓

What is the difference between a primary and a secondary offering?

UNDERSTAND CONCEPTS

Determine the best answer for each of the following questions.

1. The uncertainty that an expected profit will not be achieved is a financial ____?____.

   a. market   c. risk
   b. return   d. investment

2. **True or False?** The term of an investment is the interest rate to be paid.

3. A typical way for businesses to obtain financing without offering ownership is to ____?____ money from financial institutions.

4. A ____?____ exists to facilitate the exchange of things of value between buyers and sellers.

   a. stock   c. bank
   b. financial market d. none of the above

5. **True or False?** Stock exchanges need to have physical locations where representatives of buyers and sellers actually meet to negotiate for the purchase and sale of stocks.

MAKE ACADEMIC CONNECTIONS

6. **Research** Review a daily newspaper and identify five different opportunities for investing money identified in articles, advertisements, or special features. Describe each of the types of investments, the organization or company offering the investment, and the level of risk and return of the investment.

7. **Math** Recently the U.S. government offered Series EE Savings Bonds at an interest rate of 3.70 percent. Interest is compounded semiannually, meaning the interest is added to the principal every six months. If you purchase $2,500 of the bonds, calculate the interest earned and the total value of your investment at the end of each year for a five-year period.

8. **Critical Thinking** Write a two-page report discussing and comparing the use of ownership and non-ownership financing to expand a small business that is currently organized as a sole proprietorship.

9. **Visual Art** Prepare a table that identifies 10 different commodities that are publicly traded. Develop a separate column for the type of commodity, the name of the commodity exchange, the city and country where the exchange is located, and the current price of the commodity.

10. **Communication** Prepare a two-minute speech on the risks and rewards of the stock market as a way for individuals to invest some of their money.

■ Going Global

It is difficult today for most businesses to operate without being affected by the global business environment. Changing technology in communications makes information exchange around the world almost instantaneous. Improvements in production processes and distribution methods make it possible to move raw materials, supplies, and finished goods quickly from place to place. This allows lower-cost production and access to customers in many countries. Trade agreements negotiated between countries and regions of the world reduce trade restrictions and encourage free trade.

Corporate ownership is often multinational. Business investments are made with little regard for country boundaries. Whether by choice or not, businesses are facing global competition and are adjusting their decisions and operations to reflect the global marketplace. A **global business**, or *multinational business*, is a company that transcends national boundaries and is not committed to a single home country.

IMPORTANCE OF INTERNATIONAL BUSINESS

Over the past 20 years, U.S. business investments in other countries have grown from under $500 billion to nearly $2.5 trillion. At the same time, foreign companies have made business investments in the United States. Those foreign investments have grown from about $200 billion to over $1.5 trillion over the 20-year period. Multinational investments have been made in almost all industries.

© GETTY IMAGES/PHOTODISC

Many businesses today operate internationally.

Those investments are not limited to ownership of companies in other countries. Businesses may form formal partnerships or less formal working agreements. One company may share a technology or process with another, offer management help, or provide a business activity that is needed by the foreign company for effective competition in a new market. One of the major forms of international investment is providing long-term and short-term loans and other types of financing to foreign businesses.

Reasons for companies to make international business investments include

1. To expand their markets
2. To increase operating efficiency and reduce costs
3. To reduce political, legal, and regulatory hurdles they might otherwise face in other countries
4. To diversify their operations
5. To gain a greater return on their investments

a question of ethics

Guidelines for Ethical Decision Making

You are offered a free trip to visit factories in several other countries if your company uses the services of a particular bank. Do you do it? Each day, people make many financial decisions. These choices of actions may be viewed differently in different countries. In some societies, people expect you to do business with family members. In other places, payments or gifts are expected before you are able to do business. Many financial situations can create ethical concerns. Ethics are principles of right and wrong used to guide personal and business decisions. When considering the ethics of financial situations, three guidelines are commonly used.

1. **Is the action legal?** Laws vary among states and around the world. Most financial organizations base company decisions on the laws in their home countries. When a conflict occurs, managers will also consider factors such as professional standards and the potential effects of an action on society.

2. **Does the action violate professional or company standards?** Professional and company standards frequently exceed the law. These standards can help to ensure that financial decisions will be in the best interest of both the company and society.

3. **Who is affected by the action and how?** An action may be legal and within professional or company standards. But decision makers should also consider possible effects on employees, consumers, competitors, and the environment.

Think Critically

1. What are some examples of situations faced by financial managers and individual investors that may require using these ethical guidelines?
2. Describe how business activities might be affected if no ethical guidelines existed.
3. Research an ethical situation that has been in the news. How did this situation affect companies, workers, investors, and others?

PROBLEMS FACED IN INTERNATIONAL BUSINESS

It is not easy to shift business activities from one country to another. Each country has different political, economic, and legal environments. The culture of business in the new country may mean a different approach to business relationships, different management practices, and even different beliefs about ethical issues. Specifically, businesses have to consider

1. Language and cultural differences affecting company employees and customers

2. Differences in the stability of the government that might result in political risks

3. Different economic philosophies leading to more or less government influence on the economy and on businesses

4. Different money systems and fluctuating monetary values between currencies

checkpoint ✓

List several reasons businesses may want to make multinational business investments.

■ International Finance

International business requires international finance. Money flows from one business to another across country borders. Individual and organizational investors look to foreign markets for investment opportunities. Special considerations affect international finance.

FOREIGN CURRENCIES AND RATES OF EXCHANGE

When products and services are bought and sold globally, payments move from one country to another. Usually each country has its own currency. The currency of another country is a **foreign currency.** If a U.S. business wants to purchase goods from a member of the European Union it will need to convert U.S. dollars to euros. In the same way, if a Japanese automobile manufacturer ships pickup trucks to Mexico, pesos will need to be converted to yen. To make the conversion from one currency to another, an exchange rate must be established. An **exchange rate** is the value of one currency in terms of another. Exchange rates in the U.S. are often expressed in terms of how much of a foreign currency is required to purchase one dollar. For example 1.23 CAD/USD means that it takes 1.23 Canadian Dollars to purchase one U.S. Dollar.

© GETTY IMAGES/PHOTODISC

International currency is exchanged at a foreign exchange market.

teamwork

Use the Internet to follow stock indexes of the stock markets of three countries for several days. Discuss your observations and what they might say about the business and economic environment of the countries.

Exchange rates are established in the foreign exchange market. The **foreign exchange market** is where one currency is exchanged for another. The foreign exchange market is not one organization or one location. It is a series of interconnected entities including large banks, governments, multinational businesses, and smaller retail businesses that exchange small amounts of currencies for individuals.

There is not just one exchange rate at a given time between two countries' currencies. The exchange rates cannot vary a great deal or it would make exchanging currencies too difficult and risky. Today's technology allows participants involved in currency exchanges to compare rates worldwide and make exchanges where they can get the best rates.

The foreign exchange market is the largest trading market in the world, handling over \$$1^1/_2$ trillion each day. The largest volume of currency exchange occurs in the United Kingdom, which accounts for nearly 1/3 of all exchanges. The other countries with large exchange volumes are the United States and Japan.

The exchange rate for a country's currency is based on the supply and demand for that currency. If few U.S. dollars are available for exchange yet a large amount are demanded, the exchange rate will increase. The difference in the value of a country's imports and exports affects supply and demand and therefore the exchange rates. If the U.S. is importing more goods than it is exporting, it will need to convert more U.S. dollars to other currencies. Converting to other currencies increases the demand for those currencies and decreases the exchange rate for U.S. dollars.

INTERNATIONAL CAPITAL INVESTMENTS

One way for businesses and individual investors to participate in the global economy is to invest in businesses from other countries. Those investments can be in the form of direct investment through short-term and long-term loans to foreign or multinational businesses. Investors will want to consider the rate of return on the investment compared to other possible uses of their money. They will want to study the possible risk of the investment. Risks may be higher or lower than similar investments in U.S. firms.

A second method of international investment is by participating in foreign stock markets. While the U.S. stock markets offer trading in many international businesses, many countries have their own stock exchanges that offer stock trading for the corporations headquartered in their countries. Trading rules and procedures may be different from one exchange to another, so investors need to have expert advice and assistance before participating in a new stock market.

The major U.S. exchanges have well-known market indexes that provide information on the overall performance of the stock market. Those include the Dow Jones Industrial Average, the NASDAQ Composite, and the Standard and Poor's (S&P) 500. The stock markets of other countries have their own market indexes.

Germany: XETRA DAX	Great Britain: FT-SE 100
Japan: Nikkei 225	Hong Kong: Hang Seng

checkpoint ✓

What determines a country's foreign exchange rate?

UNDERSTAND CONCEPTS

Determine the best answer for each of the following questions.

1. **True or False?** A global business is not committed to a single home country.

2. Over the past 20 years, U.S. business investments in other countries have grown to nearly
   a. $500 billion
   b. $1 trillion
   c. $2.5 trillion
   d. $5 trillion

3. Which of the following is NOT a reason for companies to make international business investments?
   a. to increase operating efficiency and reduce costs
   b. to reduce political, legal, and regulatory hurdles they might otherwise face in other countries
   c. to diversify their operations
   d. all of the above are appropriate reasons

4. **True or False?** The value of a country's imports and exports has no effect on the exchange rate for its currency.

MAKE ACADEMIC CONNECTIONS

5. **Research** Develop a table that compares the currency exchange rates of four different countries.

6. **Economics** Use the Internet to identify four multinational companies that produce products you have purchased and used. List each company name, the country in which it began, and its primary product.

7. **Law** Use the Internet, magazines, or newspapers to locate information on a company that faces a legal, ethical, or political problem resulting from business activities in another country. Prepare a written summary of the issues and how the company is attempting to resolve the problem it faces.

8. **Critical Thinking** Some people are concerned that international business competition hurts U.S. businesses and consumers. Gather information that provides evidence of the benefits of international business competition. Write a one-page persuasive essay based on the information you collect.

9. **Careers** Identify a multinational company for which you would like to work. Gather information on the company, the countries in which it has operations, and an international job offered by the company that interests you. Prepare a letter that could be sent to the company expressing your interest in the company and the reasons the international job appeals to you.

Summary

2.1 BASIC ECONOMIC SYSTEMS AND PRINCIPLES

1. Financial decisions are influenced as much by the economy as by any other factors. Effective financial planning and decision making requires an understanding of the economy and economic principles.

2. Businesses and individuals make decisions about what to produce and what to consume. Microeconomics is about economic decisions related to the choices of individuals and businesses. Macroeconomics is about economic decisions made at a national level.

2.2 LEGAL FORMS OF BUSINESS

3. The way a business is organized plays a major role in its financial condition. It will determine how much money is available to start the business, how additional funds can be obtained when needed, how income and expenses are allocated and accounted for, and even the amount of taxes paid by the business and business owner.

4. Many factors enter into the decision about the form of business ownership. These include the amount of individual responsibility and control, the simplicity or complexity of forming and managing the business, and differences in legal requirements and liability. A major consideration is the financial implications for owning and operating each type of business.

2.3 TYPES OF FINANCIAL MARKETS

5. Financial markets and financial institutions have developed to facilitate exchanges between those who need money and those who have money. A financial market is an organized process for the exchange of capital and credit. Some basic principles of financial exchange guide the activities of those markets and institutions.

6. Sellers want to obtain the highest price possible for their resources while buyers want to purchase those resources at the lowest price. Financial markets help identify the available supply and demand for a specific resource in order to determine the market price at a particular time. The market manages the exchange between buyers and sellers.

2.4 GLOBAL FINANCIAL ACTIVITIES

7. Corporate ownership is often multinational and business investments are made with little regard for country boundaries. A global or multinational business is a company that transcends national boundaries and is not committed to a single home country.

8. International business requires international finance. Money must be exchanged from one country's currency to that of the other country. Businesses and individual investors participate in the global business economy by investing in businesses of other countries.

Develop Your Business Language

Match the terms listed with the definitions. Some terms will not be used.

1. Uncertainty that an expected profit will not be achieved
2. Organized exchange of the ownership shares of public corporations
3. Company that transcends national boundaries and is not committed to a single home country
4. Science of decision making about the allocation of scarce resources
5. Organized process for the exchange of capital and credit
6. Business owned and managed by two or more people under the conditions of a legal written agreement
7. Where one currency is exchanged for another
8. Currency of another country
9. Length of time invested money is controlled by others
10. Trade raw materials and other basic production resources

a. capital markets
b. choice
c. commodity markets
d. corporation
e. demand
f. economics
g. exchange rate
h. financial market
i. financial return
j. financial risk
k. foreign currency
l. foreign exchange market
m. global business
n. limited liability company (LLC)
o. market economy
p. market price
q. money markets
r. partnership
s. resources
t. scarcity
u. sole proprietorship
v. stock market
w. supply
x. term

Review Concepts

11. Which of the following is NOT one of the important decisions that must be made about a country's economy?
    a. How much money is needed?
    b. What products and services will be produced?
    c. How will the needed products and services be produced?
    d. For whom will the products and services be produced?

12. Which type of business does not end when the current owner dies or sells his or her ownership in the business?
    a. sole proprietorship
    b. partnership
    c. corporation
    d. none of the above

13. What two things must be balanced when selecting an investment?
    a. cost and benefit
    b. risk and return
    c. income and expenses
    d. supply and demand

14. The largest trading market in the world is
    a. the New York Stock Exchange
    b. NASDAQ
    c. the Chicago Board of Trade
    d. the foreign exchange market

Think Critically

15. Identify five ways that the U.S. economy affects the lives of you, your family, and your community. They can be both positive and negative.

16. Many people start their day with a bowl of breakfast cereal. Consider all of the resources needed to produce a box of cereal. Make a list of the resources you think would be needed and classify them as natural resources, capital resources, or human resources.

17. Why do most people start new businesses as a sole proprietorship when a corporation offers greater protection for the assets invested?

18. Why is there a need for secondary offerings for stock and bonds as well as a primary offering? Even though the company issuing the stocks and bonds does not benefit directly from secondary offering sales, how can those sales have a positive effect on that company?

19. The exchange rates for foreign currencies are of great concern to businesses involved in foreign trade. In what ways do those exchange rates affect individual consumers?

Business Financial Calculations

20. An electronics company can use its resources to produce either digital cameras or cellular phones. It costs $87 to produce each camera and $58 to produce each phone. In the current market it will be able to sell 8,500 cameras at $127 each or 12,750 phones at $92 each. What will be the difference in the company's profit for each of the choices?

21. In a recent year the federal corporate tax rate was 15 percent on income up to $50,000 and 25 percent for income from $50,000–$75,000. In the same year, the individual income tax rate was 0 percent for income up to $7,500, 15 percent for income from $7,500–$30,500 and 25 percent for income from $30,500–$74,000. What would be the difference in income tax paid by a person who organized a small business as a corporation versus a sole proprietorship with a business income of $69,800?

22. Allan has a grain farm in Iowa. His cost for raising corn is $2.28 per bushel. He sold his corn crop at three different times on the commodity market. In June after his corn was planted he sold half of his anticipated 300,000 bushel crop on the futures market for $2.32 per bushel. In November he sold 90,000 bushel at $2.30 per bushel on the spot market. The next April, he sold the remaining 60,000 bushel for $2.25. What were Allan's income, costs, and profit or loss from each sale? What were his income, costs, and profit realized from the entire crop?

23. A U.S. manufacturer placed an order with a German company for some specialized production equipment. The final cost of the order was $78,500 EUR. From the time negotiations began until the order was completed and payment needed to be made, the currency exchange rate between the U.S. dollar and the Euro has gone from $1.252 USD/EUR to $1.273. How much more did the U.S. company have to pay based on the rate change? What was the percentage of price increase in U.S. dollars?

Analyze Cases

Use the case from the beginning of the chapter, Caught Up in the Economy, to answer the following questions.

24. How do the economic principles of scarcity, choice, and supply and demand apply to the situation Cam faced when the established parcel delivery companies reduced their prices?

25. Describe how each of the principles of the U.S. free enterprise economy is illustrated in the case. How have those principles benefited Cam? How are they related to the problems he currently faces?

26. Cam started his business as a sole proprietorship. How might he be able to respond differently to the competitive situation he is facing if the business was organized as a partnership or a corporation?

27. What are the reasons Cam's new business has been so successful when other parcel delivery services are available? How might Cam use the positive experiences of his customers and the local demand for his delivery service to respond to the price cuts of the large competitors?

Portfolio Activity

To provide tangible evidence of your learning about the financial environment of business, do the following:

COLLECT an example of a product, service, or business activity that illustrates global business competition. The example could be an advertisement, newspaper or magazine article, product, or another type of example.

CREATE a visual to show how several economic principles apply to the example you have collected. Use photos, other pictures, or drawings to illustrate the economic impact on businesses and consumers.

CONNECT your visual to other items already in your class portfolio or relate it to an important concept you have learned in another class. Make the connection by preparing a one-minute presentation on the economic role of global business competition.

Stock Market Activity

The value of stock is affected by many factors. Economic, social, and political conditions can influence the market price of stocks in different industries. As consumer spending patterns change, some companies benefit while others suffer. Demographic trends such as population shifts can affect the profits and stock prices of various companies.

Conduct library and Internet research on an industry of your choice. (An industry is a group of companies involved in similar business activities.)

1. Identify the main companies in the industry. Describe the competitive situation among these companies.

2. Explain how economic conditions might affect the stock value of the companies in this industry.

3. Describe recent social trends or government actions that might have a positive or negative influence on the stock value of the companies in this industry.

Planning a Career in Economics

Government & Public Administration

Economics may not seem like a career area, but economists can be found in all types of industries and businesses. The need for people with an understanding of the intricate workings of the national and world economies is vital to the success of companies and the economic health of our country. People with the capability to gather and analyze economic data, predict economic changes and the effects of those changes on business decisions, and communicate complex mathematical information to business and government leaders will be in high demand in the future.

Employment Outlook

■ Employment of economists is expected to grow more slowly than average for all occupations over the next 10 years. Demand is rising for economic analysis in virtually every industry. More than half of all economists are employed by the federal and state governments.

■ Academic positions for economists will grow as those currently employed near retirement. Demand for high school economics teachers is also expected to grow.

■ Employment growth should be the fastest in private industry, especially in management, scientific, and technical consulting services.

Job Titles

■ Economist
■ Financial analyst
■ Market analyst
■ Public policy consultant
■ Researcher or research assistant
■ Econometrician

Needed Skills

■ Well-developed quantitative skills and preparation in mathematics, statistics, survey design, and computers.

■ Minimum of a bachelor's degree with increasing demand for an MBA. Top economists hold a PhD.

■ Excellent communication skills to present quantitative data and make understandable recommendations to decision-makers.

What's It Like to Work in Economics?

The real estate market has been very good. The economy is strong and mortgage rates are at low levels. Many young couples are buying their first homes and current homeowners are upgrading to bigger and more expensive houses.

Yet Jackson is worried. As the lead economist for a national homebuilder, he provides recommendations to company executives to help them decide whether to continue to purchase land for new housing developments and to increase the number of construction crews to keep up with current demand.

The stock market is increasingly volatile with a few predictions of a major downward adjustment. The Federal Reserve chairman has recently hinted at increasing the federal funds rate, which could result in higher mortgage rates. Jackson is spending more and more time poring over a variety of economic data. His advice will affect company plans and more importantly, company profits.

What about you? What appeals to you about economics careers? What will you have to do to achieve success in this career field?

GLOBAL MARKETING TEAM EVENT

The Global Marketing Team Event is a team event that consists of 2–4 members. All members of the team must be dressed in business attire when giving the presentation. Each member must contribute. The event requires participants to demonstrate knowledge and understanding of management and international business concepts. The team will develop a written international marketing plan that identifies the customer base and consumer behavior in different cultures. The plan must include title page, table of contents, synopsis or mini-plan, and company goals. The marketing plan must include descriptions of customers and their needs, pricing strategy, and the competition. The marketing plan must demonstrate a strong understanding of global financial activities, including global currencies, legal paperwork, contracts, and insurance. The Global Marketing Team will have ten (10) minutes to present their plan to the judges. Flash cards will be used to give participants two (2) minute and one (1) minute warnings. Judges have an additional five (5) minutes to ask questions.

Topic Your business (Heartland Foods) wants to market beef and other agricultural products to Japan. Japan is a huge potential market for the products that your company produces efficiently. Japanese have a high demand for the top quality beef produced in the United States. Trade depends upon a strong dollar, continued strong diplomatic relations between the U.S. and Japan, a high-quality product, and no disturbing publicity like "Mad Cow Disease."

Performance Indicators Evaluated

- Demonstrate knowledge and understanding of management and international business concepts.
- Communicate research in a clear and concise manner both orally and in writing.
- Demonstrate teamwork skills needed to function in a global marketing environment.
- Demonstrate an understanding of price and international exchange rates.
- Demonstrate effective persuasive and informative communication and presentation skills.
- Recognize economic, social, legal, and technological trends that affect global marketing.
- Develop a written international marketing plan.

Go to the BPA web site for more detailed information.

Think Critically

1. Why is it important to understand the culture when developing a marketing plan?
2. Why is insurance important when conducting international business?
3. Why is it important to understand the economic system of the country where you want to conduct business?
4. Who are two professional experts that a business should contact for advice when considering expansion into international markets?

www.bpa.org

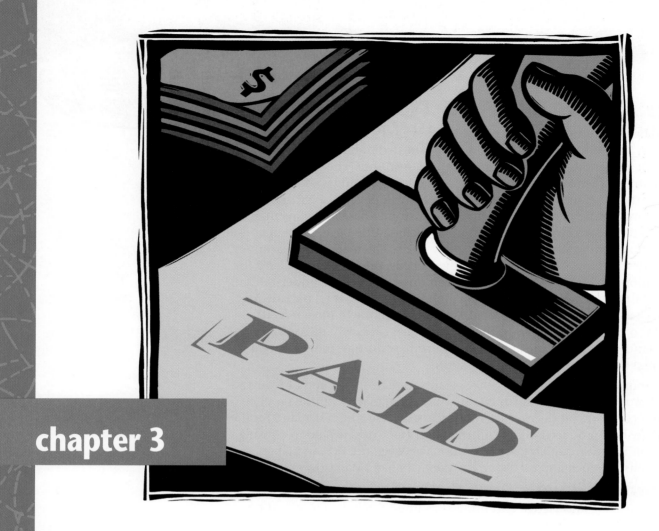

chapter 3

Financial Management Planning

3.1 BUSINESS FINANCIAL GOALS

3.2 UNDERSTAND FINANCIAL STATEMENTS

3.3 DEVELOP A FINANCIAL BUDGET

3.4 INTEREST AND TIME VALUE OF MONEY

Point Your [Browser]
www.thomsonedu.com/school/busfinance

Case STUDY

Apple Computer: A New Life

Few companies get a second chance. Apple Computer has fought back from the brink of financial failure several times.

Apple Computer was the creation of Steve Jobs and Steve Wosniak. When they introduced the Apple II in 1977, the personal computer moved from being primarily a desktop tool for businesspeople to a computer that individuals could afford and use. It was a one-box computer and monitor that was easy to assemble and simple to use. They developed their own easy-to-use and reliable operating system rather than relying on the established Microsoft software used on most computers. Since Apple was reluctant to license the operating system to other companies, it never achieved the widespread use of Microsoft Windows.

Apple received recognition for continuing innovation with a series of unique products including the Lisa computer, the Newton handheld computer, and the PowerMac G4 Cube. They also refined their operating software resulting in OS X, a faster, more flexible, easy-to-update operating system. However, the company struggled with operations and management issues. Steve Jobs was replaced as the head of Apple in 1985 and left the company. A series of CEOs worked on marketing, new product development, partnerships with other companies, and other strategies, but failed to return the company to its original success. Many business and financial experts predicted that the company would not survive.

Jobs was rehired by Apple in 1996 and soon was reinstated as CEO. He recommitted the company to a narrowly focused set of innovative products and concentrated on exploiting the growing popularity of the Internet. In fact, he often used the title iCEO to demonstrate his belief in the importance of the Internet focus. The first new company success was iTunes, a software system that made it easy to download, manage, and listen to music on the computer. That was quickly followed by the iPod, which has become the world's most popular portable media player. Apple opened the online iTunes Music Store, selling individual songs as downloadable music files inexpensively.

The company's financial condition has rebounded with a rising stock price, excellent cash flow, and a return to profitability. Additional new product plans including partnerships with companies such as Nike and Disney suggest Apple has been able to reinvent and reestablish itself.

Think Critically

1. How could Apple Computer be a leader in innovation yet financially unsuccessful?

2. Use a Web search to identify new product ideas Apple is developing on its own and in partnership with other companies. Do you believe they continue to focus on innovative ideas?

Goals
- Describe the three primary financial goals of businesses.
- Identify the characteristics of effective financial goals.

Terms
- business financial goals
- creditor
- principal
- interest
- collateral

■Financial Needs of Business

Financial health is a critical factor in the success of any business. A business that has good financial resources is in a position to take advantage of opportunities, combat competition from other businesses, and respond to problems it encounters. Without those resources, the business will be in a constant struggle to survive.

Business owners and managers pay constant attention to the financial position and financial health of the overall business and of its major operating units. Financial management determines the current financial health of the company. It also determines the amount of money needed for all business activities and operations, where the financing will be obtained, and how planned activities and operations will contribute to the overall financial health of the business.

SET FINANCIAL GOALS

The first step in financial management for a business is to establish financial goals. **Business financial goals** establish direction for the financial plans of a business. Business financial goals are developed to respond to three main financial needs.

1. A business must meet its financial obligations and pay its debts.
2. A business must provide a competitive rate of return for its investors.
3. A business must finance future growth and improvement to remain competitive.

MEET CURRENT FINANCIAL OBLIGATIONS

All businesses need money to operate. Typically the owners of the business are not able to provide all of the money a business requires. Creditors provide additional money to pay for business operations. A **creditor** is an individual or an organization that provides funds to a business, with repayment of the funds and agreed-upon interest due at a future date. Regular payments of **principal**—the amount of money borrowed—and **interest**—the amount paid for the privilege of borrowing money—must be made to all creditors. A bank may provide a loan to purchase equipment or to finance construction of a building. A supplier may offer credit for thirty or sixty days or longer to help finance the purchase of raw materials, supplies, or equipment. Financial management recognizes the amounts owed to creditors and determines how those obligations will be repaid as they become due. It also determines whether the company is in a good position to borrow additional funds from creditors when financial resources are needed.

The sale of products and services by the business also provides money to finance operations. All sales have related costs to the business, so income from sales does not automatically translate into profits for the business. The sale of goods and services usually results in cash coming in to the business. Cash is important to pay for ongoing expenses. If the amount of income received from sales does not exceed the costs of producing the sales, the financial position of the business will decline. That means the business will have a more difficult time meeting financial obligations because sales were not profitable. Another part of financial management is determining the profitability of a company's products and services and how to improve the financial position resulting from ongoing business operations.

Businesses may borrow money to finance new construction or expansion.

PROVIDE COMPETITIVE FINANCIAL RETURN TO INVESTORS

People invest money with the expectation of making a good financial return, or profit, on their investment. They will generally invest their money where they can receive the highest rate of return within the level of risk they are willing to take. If a business is not able to make adequate profits to pay its investors a competitive financial return, it will be unable to attract additional money from investors when needed. It will also run the risk that investors will take their money from the business and reinvest it where a higher return is available.

Owners of sole proprietorships, partnerships, and even small corporations may be willing to accept a comparatively low rate of return on the money they have invested for a time. The operation and success of the business is an important part of their lives and they are usually seeking more from the business than the highest possible rate of financial return. People who invest in a larger corporation as stockholders, on the other hand, have little personal interest in the ongoing business operations. They are primarily concerned about the money they have invested and the return they are receiving on that investment. If they see that the return is not comparable to what they can receive from other investment choices, they will quickly sell their stock. There is pressure on corporate management to maintain a competitive rate of return and provide evidence that the financial position of the company is healthy and improving. That pressure has led to some notable legal problems for executives as well as company failures as a result of fraudulent financial and accounting transactions. Recent examples include Enron and WorldCom.

teamwork

"A business needs to grow and improve in order to be successful." Do you agree or disagree with that statement? Discuss it with your teammates and provide reasons to support each of the positions.

Financial management determines how funds will be returned to owners in the form of salaries and dividends at a level that satisfies their expectations and that is competitive with alternative investments. Financial managers are sensitive to the needs and perceptions of investors. They make financial decisions designed to maintain an appropriate rate of return and positive relations with important investors.

FINANCE BUSINESS GROWTH AND IMPROVEMENT

If you study the history of today's largest businesses, each of them started as a small business. There is no guarantee that growth will assure the success of a business. Large businesses run into financial difficulties that may lead to bankruptcy. Not every business needs to grow into a giant company with billions of dollars of sales and thousands of employees. But even small businesses look for new customers, higher sales, and greater profits.

© GETTY IMAGES/PHOTODISC

Not every small business must become large, but most try to attract new customers and attain greater profits.

Businesses can finance growth through attracting additional investments, borrowing more money from creditors, or reinvesting profits. Each of those alternatives requires the business to be financially healthy. Only investors who are in a position to accept a very high risk of losing their money will place money in a business experiencing financial difficulties. Investors expect to receive compensation for assuming high risk. For example, they may demand a greater percentage of ownership of the business than the amount they invested would typically warrant. They may negotiate an agreement that if the business fails they are the first to receive money after creditors have been paid.

A creditor is not likely to loan money or to finance a purchase for a company experiencing financial difficulties. Credit terms extended in those situations will usually command a higher interest rate, a shorter term of the loan, or a part of the business as collateral. **Collateral** is an asset promised by a business to a creditor if repayment of a loan isn't completed. Any creditor providing a large amount of financing will want to have assurance that the financial health of the business is strong. That way, creditors reduce the risk that they will not be repaid for the money loaned.

Financial management carefully prepares for growth and expansion and determines the best ways to finance the growth through additional investments, seeking credit, using company profits, or a combination of these choices. Financial managers prepare the necessary financial documents and information needed by prospective investors and creditors in order to successfully obtain the financing.

checkpoint ✓

What are the three main financial needs of a business?

■Establish Financial Goals

Business financial goals, just like personal financial goals, must be clear and specific. It is not enough for managers to state that the business will provide an adequate investor return or to devote some of the profits earned to future expansion.

CHARACTERISTICS OF EFFECTIVE GOALS

Business financial goals must have several elements to be effective. Business financial goals must be

- Specific
- Realistic
- Measurable
- Established for an identified period of time

Specific A *specific* financial goal is directed at a particular business action. For example "to increase the profitability of all new product introductions after six months of sales by 1.5 percent" directs efforts at a specific business activity—new product introductions. Everyone knows what part of business operations must receive attention in order to achieve the goal.

Realistic A *realistic* financial goal must be possible. It can stretch the organization to perform better than it has in the past, but it cannot be so high as to be unrealistic. In the example above, the goal was to increase profitability of new sales by 1.5 percent within six months. If in the past, profitability from new sales had never increased more than 0.3 percent, the new goal is probably not realistic.

Measurable A *measurable* goal identifies the financial performance that is expected to change. It must be a goal for which the business is able to gather information and evaluate the results. In the example, the goal is to increase profits from new product sales. If some costs cannot be matched to specific products or if information is not collected on a monthly basis, the goal cannot be measured.

Identified Time Finally, an *identified time* allows adequate time for the business to improve the identified performance as well as a time frame in which the business usually measures performance. In this case, the goal establishes a standard for improving the profitability of new products within six months. That amount of time is realistic for a new product to become established in a market and accepted by customers.

Example If a company regularly introduces new products and wants to improve the profitability of those products, the established goal "to increase the profitability of all new product introductions after six months of sales by 1.5 percent" establishes an important financial performance target for the company. Achieving the goal will demonstrate that the financial performance of an important business activity is improving. Company managers and employees will use the goal to determine how they can increase sales and control costs of the new products in order to meet the standard established at the end of six months. Financial managers can gather and analyze the data and provide updated information to company employees on the progress that is being made toward achieving the goal.

technology topics

A Bank in a Kiosk

Estimates are that 15 percent of U.S. households do not use banks. That means they don't have savings or checking accounts and seldom have credit cards since most require a bank account for approval. The "un-banked" still need financial services. Self-service kiosks placed in convenience stores, malls, and other public locations are meeting that need. Financial services kiosks allow consumers to withdraw cash, purchase money orders, cash paychecks, transfer money, pay utility and telephone bills, and purchase prepaid credit, debit, and gift cards. Some kiosks are even set up to allow customers to receive their wages in cash from employers or their pensions or other payments from the government. In addition to the value the kiosks provide to people who do not have bank accounts, they also provide convenient access to financial services for people who do have bank accounts. You can quickly pay a bill while filling up your gas tank or purchasing a cup of coffee.

Think Critically

1. Why would a convenience store want to have a self-service kiosk offering financial products?
2. Do you believe that banks should view the kiosks as competition? Why or why not?

When asked by *Fortune* magazine in 2006 to select companies they most admire other than their own, businesspeople worldwide identified four U.S. companies in the top five. They are General Electric, Procter & Gamble, FedEx, and Johnson & Johnson. One non-U.S. company, Toyota Motors, also appeared in the top five.

DETERMINE FINANCIAL PRIORITIES

Over a period of years, companies must be able to accomplish each of the three financial goals. They must have adequate levels of investment, be able to meet short- and long-term credit obligations, and finance growth plans. One of these goals may be more important than the others at a certain time or based on circumstances facing the business. An important financial management responsibility is determining the immediate and long-term financial needs of the business and establishing appropriate goals.

Companies facing increasing competition or rising costs may want to concentrate on meeting current financial obligations. They may set goals to improve productivity or increase profitability. Other goals may be to reduce the amount of credit owed and increase their cash position.

A company that is focused on growth needs to determine how that growth will be financed. Will the company choose to increase the amount of investment by offering additional stock for sale or will it choose to finance the growth through increased borrowing from creditors? In either case, the financial position of the company will need to be strong.

Increasing the attractiveness of the company to investors may mean working to increase stock value or dividend rates. To appeal to creditors, the company must have adequate assets to cover the increased expenses of the credit payments. The financial priorities of the company will help to determine the types of specific financial goals that will be needed.

Identify the four characteristics of effective business financial goals.

UNDERSTAND CONCEPTS

Determine the best answer for each of the following questions.

1. Which of the following is NOT one of the main financial needs of a business?
   a. A business must provide a competitive rate of return for its investors.
   b. A business must meet its financial obligations and pay its debts.
   c. A business must finance future growth and improvement to remain competitive.
   d. A business must make a profit on all of its activities.

2. A ____?____ financial goal is directed at a particular business action.
   a. measurable
   b. specific
   c. realistic
   d. clear

3. **True or False?** A business that wants to finance growth needs to be financially healthy.

4. A ____?____ is an individual or an organization that provides funds to a business with a repayment of the funds and agreed-upon interest due at a future date.

5. **True or False?** A company should address all three of the main financial goals at the same time rather than selecting one as a priority.

MAKE ACADEMIC CONNECTIONS

6. **Technology** Various investments provide different rates of return to investors but also have different levels of risk. Use the Internet to identify the annual rate of return an investor could receive for placing $10,000 in each of the following investment choices one year ago: a checking account, a 12-month certificate of deposit, purchasing gold on the commodity market, buying stock in Wal-Mart. How do the investment choices differ in the level of risk for the investor?

7. **Speech** Prepare a two-minute persuasive speech saying why having an adequate supply of cash may be more important to a new business than showing a profit at the end of the first year of operations.

8. **Research** Identify three different types of creditors a business could use to finance a new computer purchase. Prepare a table that compares the advantages and disadvantages of the three alternatives.

9. **Math** A company established a goal to increase the ratio of assets to liabilities by 5 percent within one year. At the beginning of the year, the assets were $1,565,898 and liabilities were $1,326,527. At the end of the year, the assets were $1,964,025 and liabilities were $1,598,296. Calculate the change in assets and liabilities from the beginning to the end of the year. Calculate the increase or decrease in the percentage (ratio) of assets to liabilities from the beginning to the end of the year. Did the company meet its goal?

Understand Financial Statements

Goals

- Explain the purpose and elements of a balance sheet.
- Explain the purpose and elements of an income statement.
- Explain the purpose and elements of a cash flow statement

Terms

- financial statements
- balance sheet
- assets
- depreciation
- liabilities
- owner's equity
- income statement
- cash flow statement

■ The Balance Sheet

Businesses prepare financial statements to report financial information. **Financial statements** are specific reports prepared according to accepted accounting standards that provide financial information about an enterprise. The three primary financial statements—the *balance sheet*, the *income statement*, and the *cash flow statement*—are used to understand the financial health of a business and to make financial decisions. The three types of statements are used not only in businesses but by government agencies, nonprofit organizations, and even individuals who prepare personal financial statements to apply for a loan, purchase a home, or make a substantial investment.

In order to be useful for decision-making, financial statements must be understandable, reliable, and comparable. *Understandable* means that the forms are organized in the same way so they can be read and interpreted by both financial experts and people who have a general understanding of financial concepts and principles. *Reliable* means the statements contain objective and unbiased information so it can be trusted by those who must use the information. *Comparable* means that information from financial statements prepared for different time periods or even for different companies can be compared.

To meet those requirements, financial statements are created following guidelines established by the Financial Accounting Standards Board and endorsed by the American Institute of Certified Public Accountants. Public corporations are required by the Securities and Exchange Commission (SEC) to prepare financial statements and have them audited by an independent certified public accountant. The statements and audit reports must be available for public review.

An accountant provides financial information that is useful for business decision-making.

BALANCE SHEET COMPONENTS

The **balance sheet**, also known as the statement of financial position, identifies the assets, liabilities, and equity of a business as of a specific date. The balance sheet describes what the company owns, what it owes, and its value to the owners. The balance sheet is organized around the basic accounting equation.

> Assets = Liabilities + Owner's Equity

A balance sheet provides a "snapshot" of the financial status of a business at a specific date. Balance sheets are always prepared at the end of the fiscal year for a company. They are also often prepared quarterly or monthly so changes in the financial position of a company can be readily identified. The values can change quickly based on management decisions and company performance, so it is important to examine several consecutive balance sheets to determine if changes are occurring and the values of those changes. A sample balance sheet is shown in Figure 3-1.

FIGURE 3-1

Sample Balance Sheet

BALANCE SHEET

December 31, 20xx

Assets		Liabilities and Owners' Equity	
Current Assets		**Current Liabilities**	
Cash	$ 24,500	Note Payable	$86,090
Accounts Receivable	85,445	Loans Payable	25,540
Inventory	128,900	Accounts Payable	38,800
Prepaid Expenses	20,050	Taxes Payable	27,600
Operating Supplies	12,300	**Long-Term Liabilities**	
Long-Term Assets		Mortgage	498,200
Investments in Subsidiaries	825,000	Pensions Payable	560,000
Vehicles	93,200	**Total Liabilities**	1,236,230
Land	86,235		
Buildings	657,000	**Owner's Equity**	
Capital Equipment	394,500	Stock	$707,825
Less: Accumulated Depreciation	(29,450)	Capital Surplus	225,000
		Retained Earnings	128,625
Total Assets	$2,297,680	**Total Liabilities and Owner's equity**	$2,297,680

Assets All of the things a business owns and uses as a part of business operations are **assets**. Everything from the buildings, land, and equipment to office supplies and inventory are assets of a business. Assets are categorized on the balance sheet according to the length of time they will be available for use by the business. *Current assets* have a short life of less than a year. If necessary, current assets can be quickly converted to cash. Common types of current assets for many businesses are cash, inventory, materials and supplies, and accounts receivable. *Long-term assets* have a longer life of a year or more and often define the nature of the business. Common types of long-term assets are buildings, land, equipment, patents, investments made by the company for a period longer than a year, and other owned resources used by the business.

The value of most long-term assets decreases over time. A decline in the value of an asset as it ages is known as **depreciation.** The balance sheet reflects both the original value of the asset and its depreciated value. The method used to calculate depreciation is established by federal tax laws.

Liabilities Those things that the business owes to others are **liabilities.** Anything the business has purchased, leased, or used but not yet paid for results in a liability. The amount of the loan or lease must be included in the liabilities section of the balance sheet.

Just as with assets, there are two categories of liabilities. *Current liabilities* are those that will be paid for within a year. *Long-term liabilities* are any for which payment will not be made in full for more than a year. Common types of current liabilities are accounts payable, which are purchases for which suppliers have provided short-term credit, loans that must be repaid quickly, and wages and taxes owed. Long-term liabilities include mortgages on land and buildings, long-term purchase agreements, and multi-year leases on equipment.

Owner's Equity The total value that all owners and investors have in the firm is **owner's equity.** In a corporation, owner's equity is the value of all stock and any profits being held by the business. In proprietorships and partnerships, owner's equity is the total amount the owners have invested in the business and the increase (or decrease) in value of the business resulting from its operations.

ANALYZING A BALANCE SHEET

The balance sheet lists the values of everything owned and owed by a business. As its name implies, a balance sheet must be in balance. The difference between the value of all current and long-term assets and all current and long-term liabilities is the owner's equity. Therefore, to balance the financial position of a business

> Assets − Liabilities = Owner's Equity

If liabilities increase in relation to the value of assets, owner's equity declines. If assets increase more than the value of liabilities, owner's equity increases.

The changes in values of assets, liabilities, and owner's equity can be compared over time. How has the value of specific types of assets or total assets changed during a one-year period? Has owner's equity increased or decreased during that time? What specific assets or liabilities changed in value to affect owner's equity? Another important type of analysis is to compare specific values on a balance sheet with each other. A common comparison is to determine the relationship of current assets and current liabilities to the value of total assets. If the percentage of current liabilities to total assets is increasing faster than the percentage of current assets to total assets, the business may run into a problem in paying its short-term debts. More detailed discussion of the analysis of balance sheets and other financial statements will occur in later chapters.

checkpoint ✓

What is the basic accounting equation around which a balance sheet is organized?

Income Statement

The balance sheet presents a company's financial position on a specific date. The second financial statement, the income statement, provides a view of the financial changes in a business that have occurred during a specified period of time. It documents all income and expenses during that period and the resulting profit or loss earned. A sample income statement is shown in Figure 3-2. Just like the balance sheet, an income statement needs to be prepared at least once a year but is usually prepared very frequently, often once a month. Recognizing changes in income, expenses, and profits is very important for effective financial management.

FIGURE 3-2

Sample Income Statement

INCOME STATEMENT

January 1 – June 30, 20xx

Revenue from Sales	
Product 1	$454,125
Product 2	283,143
Sale of Services	181,443
Less: Product Returns	(18,200)
Total Sales Revenue	**$900,511**
Cost of Sales	
Product 1	202,204
Product 2	123,118
Services	61,240
Total Cost of Sales	**$386,562**
Gross Profit (Loss)	**$513,949**
Operating Expenses	
General & Administrative	$43,292
Sales & Marketing	201,389
Non-Management Salaries	92,100
Research & Development	21,214
Operations Expenses	78,225
Total Operating Expenses	**$436,220**
Interest Paid	8,200
Income before Taxes	**$69,529**
Taxes Paid	11,127
Net Income	**$58,402**

teamwork

Discuss with your team members what you can learn from an income statement about a company's strengths and weaknesses that you cannot learn from a balance sheet. What does a balance sheet offer that cannot be learned from an income statement?

All sources of revenue or income received by the business are listed on the income statement. Those sources are commonly income from the sale of products and services and interest earned from savings and investments. To make sure that income is reported accurately, any reductions in the income received such as the value of products returned by customers must be deducted. Subtracting the cost of goods sold results in the gross profit for the business.

Following the calculation of gross profit, all expenses are itemized and subtracted. Items such as salaries, rents, leases, interest payments on loans and mortgages, supplies, utilities, insurance, maintenance, and repairs are common business expenses listed on an income statement. Usually income before taxes is calculated followed by subtracting the amount of taxes paid. The result is the business' net income or loss for the period.

ANALYZING AN INCOME STATEMENT

Just as with the balance sheet, a full understanding of the profit or loss earned by a business requires a detailed analysis of the income statement. Each category of revenues and expenses should be compared from month to month and year to year to note changes that show improvement or decline in factors contributing to profits or losses. Comparing individual items within one income statement also offers important information. For example, comparing the value of sales to the cost of goods sold or net sales to salaries can show whether those expenses are consuming an appropriate percentage of the specific revenue item. Finally, comparing specific elements of a company's financial performance with the performance of similar companies or same-industry averages is an important type of analysis.

checkpoint ✓

How is profit or loss calculated on an income statement?

Cash Flow Statement

Neither the balance sheets nor the income statements disclose all of the important financial information needed to understand a company's financial strengths or weaknesses. Financial data reported on both statements does not necessarily reflect the actual cash received and spent by the business during the time period represented. If a customer purchases a product on credit, the money may not be received for some time after the actual sale. In

© GETTY IMAGES/PHOTODISC

A business keeps track of its financial health using financial statements.

the same way, if the business obtains a loan or buys equipment or supplies on credit, money will not be spent until payments are made to the creditors.

Having access to an adequate supply of cash is important to every business. A lack of cash may mean that too much credit is being extended to customers or the company has too many current liabilities. A **cash flow statement** is prepared to show how cash is used by a business during a specified time period. A sample statement is shown in Figure 3-3.

FIGURE 3-3

Sample Cash Flow Statement

STATEMENT OF CASH FLOW

For the six months ending June 30, 20xx

Beginning Cash Balance	$10,867
Cash Receipts	
Cash Sales	$2,574,828
Asset Sales	526,800
Receipts on Accounts Receivable	198,560
Receipts on Loans Receivable	33,210
Contributed Capital	325,000
Total Cash In	$3,658,398
Available Cash	$3,669,265
Cash Payments	
Salaries	$1,023,530
Other Operating Expenses	1,729,633
Loan Payments	324,910
Capital Expenditures	88,620
Tax Payments	46,173
Total Cash Out	$3,212,866
Net Cash Flow	$445,532
Ending Cash Balance	$456,399

The statement separates cash flows into categories of cash receipts and cash payments. Receipts are reported by specific types of revenues such as cash sales, payments received from customers, interest received, and owner's investments. Common categories of cash payments are payments to creditors, payments of salaries, utilities, and taxes, and cash purchases of equipment and supplies. The result of the analysis of cash flow is a net increase or decrease in the company's cash balance for the period.

Analysis of the cash flow statement compares the company's cash position from one time period to the next, whether the amount of available cash is increasing or decreasing, and how cash is being generated and used. The analysis will help decision-makers decide if the company's ability to pay for current expenses is improving or declining. It will also help to explain whether the company has adequate resources to finance ongoing operations and growth or whether it will have to seek other sources of financing.

checkpoint ✓

What important financial information is not reflected in either the balance sheet or the income statement?

Using a Personal Budget

Are you one of those people who is always wondering where your money went? Have you intended to save for college, a car, or your own apartment, but don't seem to have enough money to pay your current expenses? Businesses rely on budgets to make sure they have adequate resources to meet current expenses and to anticipate future financial needs. You can do the same thing.

Budgeting provides information to help you understand your financial resources and current spending patterns. With a budget you have a clear picture of what income you receive and how you use that income to meet current needs and future goals.

First, establish your real income. To be able to budget you have to know how much money you earn each week or month. Be honest. Don't expect that your parents or grandparents may give you money or that you can earn a quick extra amount by mowing a lawn or taking a babysitting job. What do you regularly receive from your part-time job, allowance, or earnings on a savings account? That is the amount you must use to budget expenses.

Second, identify what you really spend. It's just like counting calories. You often forget many of the things you eat each day and you surely don't remember everything you purchase. You need a specific list of the categories of your regular expenses and an accurate amount you spend each week or month. You may need to record all expenditures for several weeks and months to get an accurate understanding of where your money goes.

Third, balance real income with real expenses. Are you spending everything you earn each week? Do your expenditures really reflect how you want to spend your money considering both immediate and future wants and needs? Most people need to find ways to reduce their current expenditures to be able to save more for important future needs. Planning and following a budget helps you make those difficult decisions.

Finally, apply the 60/40 rule. A good rule to balance immediate and long-term needs is to budget 60 percent of your income on your regular expenses—those things you know you have to purchase each week or month. Then reserve 40 percent for other expenses that are not regular purchases. Those expenses can include savings for education, a car, or future expenses when you are on your own. You might establish a special savings for personal rewards—a vacation or a special purchase. You may want to save 10 percent just for fun money. But be careful you don't tap into your other savings.

Think Critically

1. What can you do with a personal budget if you find your current expenses just meet or even exceed your income?
2. Based on your current personal financial circumstances, do you believe you could apply the 60/40 rule in your budget? Why or why not?

3.2 Lesson Assessment

UNDERSTAND CONCEPTS

Determine the best answer for each of the following questions.

1. Which of these terms is NOT a part of the basic accounting equation?
   a. income
   b. liabilities
   c. assets
   d. owner's equity

2. **True or False?** The balance sheet reflects the original value of an asset but not its depreciated value.

3. **True or False?** The income statement presents a company's financial position on a specific date.

4. After all expenses and taxes are subtracted from a company's gross profit, the result is the company's
   a. net worth
   b. profit or loss
   c. cash flow
   d. revenue

5. Specific types of revenues such as cash sales, payments received from customers, interest received, and owner's investments are all cash ____?____.

MAKE ACADEMIC CONNECTIONS

6. **Technology** Templates are available through various Internet web sites that provide a relatively easy way to construct and complete the calculations for financial statements. Search the Internet to locate a simple template for a balance sheet and an income statement. Transfer the information from Figures 3-1 and 3-2 into the appropriate template. Make sure the final calculations are correct and then print the two financial statements.

7. **Ethics** When the managers of a large company intentionally misrepresent the financial condition of the company to make it appear better than it actually is, negative consequences can result for stockholders, creditors, employees, and others. Use the Internet or library to gather information on a company that failed due to fraudulent financial practices. Prepare a one-page report on the case, identifying the ethical issues involved and the negative consequences of the fraud.

8. **Math** Use the information in Figure 3-1 to calculate the following ratios: (1) current assets to long-term assets, (2) each category of assets to total assets, (3) current liabilities to long-term liabilities, (4) each category of liabilities to total liabilities, (5) total assets to owner's equity, and (6) total liabilities to owner's equity. How do the ratios help you to understand the financial health of the company? What additional information would be useful in analyzing the company's financial condition?

Goals
- Recognize the purpose of budgeting and types of financial budgets.
- Understand the process for developing a financial budget.

Terms
- financial budget
- budget discrepancies
- operating budget
- capital budget
- trend analysis

■ Plan the Financial Future

An important tool for financial planning is the financial budget. A **financial budget** is a projected financial statement for a specific future time period. Financial budgets should be carefully prepared based on considerations of future events that could affect the business' financial performance and condition.

THE PURPOSE OF BUDGETING

Will the company's sales be higher or lower in six months? Will production costs increase? If so, by how much? Are there enough employees to meet sales expectations? What will happen to operating expenses if sales increase or decline? Can the profitability of the company be improved? Each of these questions relies on an understanding of future financial conditions of the business. The answers provide important information for managers and employees to develop realistic production, marketing, and operating plans that can be supported by the company's financial resources and contribute to strengthening its financial position.

Budgeting requires that planners project into the future and understand factors that can affect specific elements of the business' finances. Budgets that are not accurate will mislead managers, investors, creditors, and others who use the budgets to make decisions. Without an accurate budget, the business may not be able to meet short- and long-term financial obligations. It may miss out on opportunities that lead to growth and profitability.

Budgets serve as a road map for monitoring business activities and performance. If a budget is established for a period of six months or a year, the specific items in the budget can be monitored during that time to see if the financial results of company operations are matching the budgeted amounts. If not, managers can determine what has occurred that is not consistent with the planning used to develop the budget. Changes can be made to

Financial budgets help a business plan for the future.

© GETTY IMAGES/PHOTODISC

attempt to bring financial performance in line with the budget or to modify the budget to reflect the changing conditions and performance.

When the time period for which the budget was developed has ended, financial statements are prepared to reflect actual financial performance. Those statements are then compared to the budget to determine the accuracy of the budget. An analysis of budget discrepancies, differences between budgeted amounts and actual financial performance, will help to improve understanding of factors affecting financial performance and improve the accuracy of future budgets.

TYPES OF FINANCIAL BUDGETS

The primary types of financial budgets are the operating budget, cash budget, and capital budget.

Operating Budget An operating budget projects all income and expenses for the operations of a business for a specific future time period. It estimates all types of income, operating costs, expenses, and the projected profit or loss from operations. A large company will usually develop operating budgets for smaller operating units such as a division, a specific factory or business location, or a product group. Those operating budgets are then combined into a full budget for the entire company.

An operating budget projects whether operations for the budgeting period will be profitable. That allows for adjustments to be made in income and expenses to achieve profitability goals.

Cash Budget A *cash budget* is the estimate of the flow of cash into and out of a company for a specified time period. Whether a company is making or losing money at a particular time, it must have adequate cash on hand to meet immediate financial obligations. Because the availability of cash is so very important to the short-term financial health of a company, the cash budget is one of the most critical financial planning tools. Cash budgets are often prepared for a six-month or even year-long period of time but are divided into month-by-month projections of cash flow. An example monthly cash budget is shown in Figure 3-4.

FIGURE 3-4

Sample Monthly Cash Budget

CASH BUDGET	
January 1 – 31, 20xx	
Beginning cash balance	**$545,300**
Cash Inflow	
Collections on accounts receivable	$752,000
Cash sales	483,000
Total Inflow	**$1,235,000**
Cash Outflow	
Payments on accounts payable	$520,000
Cash expenses	110,500
Payments on long-term debt	750,000
Quarterly dividend payable	50,000
Total Outflow	**$1,430,500**
Estimated ending cash balance	**$ 349,800**

Capital Budget A capital budget is a plan to acquire and finance long-term assets of a business. It projects the need for, cost, and value of capital assets. Capital budgets include assets such as land, buildings, and equipment that have a lifespan of more than a year. A capital budget includes costs of acquiring, expanding, upgrading, improving, and renovating the major assets of a company. It can even include purchasing another company or selling existing assets. Because capital items are usually very expensive, decisions about what capital expenditures are needed, when to purchase, and how much can be spent are critical to the financial health of a company.

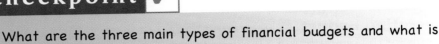

What are the three main types of financial budgets and what is the purpose of each?

teamwork

An example of a personal budgeting decision similar to a business' capital budget is deciding whether to purchase an expensive automobile or save for the upcoming costs of college. Discuss with your team how individuals can make difficult choices among expensive alternatives that will require payments for several years.

■ Prepare a Financial Budget

Budgets will not be useful if they are not accurate. Having an incomplete or inaccurate budget may be a greater problem than having no budget at all. People may be misled by inaccurate budget information and make poor decisions. A budget should be prepared carefully following a systematic process, drawing on information from inside and outside the company.

STEPS IN BUDGET PREPARATION

Each type of budget is different. Each is a part of the overall financial plan of the business and contributes to its financial condition. Each of the business budgets should be prepared using the same sources of information and the same systematic process.

1. **Identify the type of budget and the categories of financial information included in the budget.** An operating budget estimates all income and expenses of a company. A cash budget looks at cash inflows and outflows during the budgeted time period. A capital budget analyzes the long-term costs and contributions of capital assets. The categories of financial information should be the same as those used in the company's financial statements.

2. **Organize the information categories to reflect the financial calculations that must be completed in the budget.** For example, the operating statement is organized according to the profitability equation

   Income − Expenses = Profit or Loss

   All categories of income and expenses needed to calculate gross and net profit are included in the operating budget.

   The cash budget uses the formula

   Cash Receipts − Cash Payments = Net Cash Flow

   As with the operating budget, all categories of cash receipts must be listed followed by each type of cash payment. Subtracting payments from receipts provides net cash flow. That amount is used to predict what the company's cash balance will be at the end of the budgeting period.

Adding new employees will affect a business' budget.

3. **Gather and analyze internal and external information that will affect the budget.** Internal financial information is gathered from current and past financial statements and the financial records of the company. Budgets must reflect planned changes in the organization. If products are being discontinued or added, if the company is undertaking a new marketing strategy, or if new employees are being added or payrolls increased, those changes need to be reflected in the projected financial data in the budgets. The strategies and plans of the business that will be implemented during the budget period provide important information for budget planning.

Analysis of the accuracy of prior budgets will help improve budget planning. If any of the categories of financial information are regularly under- or overestimated, adjustments should be made in the current budget.

Factors outside the company are also important budget considerations. Economic conditions can affect future financial performance. Inflation, a slow economy, rising interest rates, or changes in taxes or regulations might influence overall financial performance or specific elements of a business' costs. Increasing competition, changes in technology, or international business conditions might pose challenges or open opportunities that must be reflected in budgets.

4. **Select the method of calculating budgeted amounts.** By how much will each of the amounts in a budget change from the prior budget? It is not likely that each amount can be adjusted just by increasing or decreasing it a specific percentage. Certain budget items are related to other items, so a change in one will have a particular effect on the other. If sales are projected to increase by a certain amount, payroll costs will need to increase to pay for the additional production and sales efforts. Payroll often is calculated as a specific percentage of production or sales.

Trend analysis is a valuable method of developing budgets. **Trend analysis** examines financial performance over several periods of time to determine patterns. The patterns can then be used to improve forecasting.

5. Complete the budget by making the necessary financial calculations. The gathered information is used to calculate all of the required budget items. The completed budget then becomes a planning, decision-making, and communications tool for the business.

checkpoint ✓

Why is analysis of internal and external information an important part of budget development?

¥£€$ finance around the world

Origins of World Currencies

You have probably heard of the dollar, the peso, and the euro. But how about the baht, the kwacha, and the rand? With over 200 countries in the world, many currency names exist.

Some monetary units, like the peso, are used in more than one country. The word *franc* is used as the currency name by over 25 countries in Africa and other places. These nations were influenced by France through colonization and other global activities. Similarly, the *shilling* is used in Kenya, Somalia, Tanzania, and Uganda, which were previously British colonies.

Some monetary unit names have unusual origins. The *quetzal* in Guatemala is the name for a bird with a long tail. In Malawi and Zambia, the *kwacha* is based on the slogan "New dawn of freedom."

The word *peso* means "weight." The first pesos, coined in Spain in 1497, were also known as *pieces of eight.* The pieces were made of eight *reals,* a Spanish word for royal, which was also a common coin at the time. Each real weighed slightly less than 424 troy grains and consisted of silver 0.93 fine. Today, the peso is the monetary unit of Mexico, the Philippines, and several Latin American countries.

In the United Kingdom, the *pound sterling* has been the currency for over 900 years. Introduced in 1158, It was originally an old English silver coin made of 92.5 percent sterling silver and weighed 1/20 a troy ounce (about 1.555 grams). *Pound* comes from "pund," which is from the Latin word "pondus," meaning "weight." *Sterling* is most likely from an old English word "steorra," meaning "star"—a small star appeared on early pennies. However, another explanation also exists. At one point, the English referred to their coins as Easterlings, a region with skilled metal refiners. "Easterling silver" may have become "sterling silver."

What about the *dollar*? Where does that name come from? *Dollar* comes from the 16th century German word "thaler." This was short for "Joahimsthaler," which was a coin made from metal mined in Joahimsthal, a town in what is now the Czech Republic. Over time, the name became associated with the money of the United States and over 30 other countries.

Think Critically

1. What factors influence the names of the currency used in different countries?
2. Conduct an Internet search to locate additional information about the name origins and current values of various world currencies.

3.3 Lesson Assessment

UNDERSTAND CONCEPTS

Determine the best answer for each of the following questions.

1. The difference between a financial budget and a financial statement is that the budget
   a. is projected
   b. has less information
   c. is not accurate
   d. none of the above

2. **True or False?** A budget discrepancy is the difference between a budgeted amount and actual financial performance.

3. A(n) _____?_____ budget projects all income and expenses for the operations of a business for a specific future time period.

4. Which financial budget is typically prepared for the shortest period of time?
   a. operating
   b. cash
   c. capital
   d. all are prepared for one year

5. **True or False?** The most accurate method to calculate the amounts in a budget is to apply a specific percentage of increase or decrease.

MAKE ACADEMIC CONNECTIONS

6. **Oral Communication** Prepare a short oral presentation that discusses the similarities and differences of financial statements and financial budgets.

7. **Math** The budgeted amount of sales for an operating budget is $1,938,592. The actual amount of sales at the end of the period was $2,285,492. Calculate the budget discrepancy in actual dollars and as a percentage of the budgeted amount.

8. **Research** Use the Internet to complete research on the use of trend analysis by businesses. Prepare a chart, graph, or other visual that illustrates how trend analysis can be used to aid business decision-making.

9. **Economics** Read the business section of a newspaper or review articles in a current business magazine. Identify one projected change in the U.S. economy and another one in the international economy. Develop a one-page written report describing each of the changes and discussing how each change could affect the operating budget of a business.

3.4 Interest and Time Value of Money

Goals
- Discuss how interest rates affect investment decisions.
- Understand how to calculate the time value of money on investments and loans.

Terms
- interest rate
- future value
- time value of money
- present value

■ The Meaning of Interest

You deposit $1,000 in a savings account paying 5 percent annual interest. At the end of the year you have $1,050. You might think it hardly seems worth it when you consider what you could have purchased with the $1,000. If you simply left the $1,000 in the account, its value would double in 14 years. If you were able to add $100 each month to that savings, at the end of the same 14 years your savings account would be valued at over $26,000. Would that amount make it worth saving the money rather than spending it immediately?

Compound interest makes saving worthwhile.

UNDERSTAND INTEREST RATES

Interest is the amount charged to a borrower for the use of the lender's money. If you are the borrower, you must repay more than you borrowed to compensate the lender for the time you used the money and the risk to the lender than you might not repay it. In the same way if you place some of your money in a bank or in another investment, you expect that the value you receive for allowing others to use your money will be greater than the amount you invested.

The amount of interest a lender receives is based on the interest rate. An **interest rate** is the cost of borrowing money, expressed as a percentage of the amount borrowed, usually over a period of one year. Interest is either paid as simple interest or compound interest. With *simple interest,* the amount of interest is calculated at the end of each year based on the total amount loaned. *Compound interest* pays interest not only on the total amount borrowed but also on the interest that has been earned.

CALCULATE SIMPLE INTEREST

Determining the amount of interest owed or earned can be easy or it may be complicated. The formula for determining simple interest is

$i = Prt$ i = interest
P = principal
r = interest rate
t = time (the length of the loan or investment in years)

Adding the interest, i, to the principal, P, will yield the total amount that is earned from the investment or that needs to be repaid for a loan.

Example If $1,000 is loaned at 5 percent simple interest, at the end of two years $100 in interest has been earned.

$1,000 × 0.05 × 2 = $100   simple interest at the end of 2 years

CALCULATE COMPOUND INTEREST

If the interest is compounded annually, the interest at the end of the first year is added to the amount loaned and that amount is used to calculate the interest earned at the end of the second year.

Example Rather than $100 earned from simple interest, the lender now has earned $102.50 of interest.

$1,000 × 0.05 = $50
$1,050 × 0.05 = $52.50
$50 + $52.50 = $102.50   compound interest at the end of 2 years

Interest can be compounded at various times. In the example, interest was compounded once a year, but it could be compounded quarterly, monthly, or even daily. The frequency of the compounding affects the total amount of interest paid. The more frequent the compounding, the higher will be the total interest and therefore the return on the investment. The same $1,000 invested for two years at 5 percent compounded daily would earn $1,105.16.

teamwork

Under the Truth in Lending Act, information on credit and finance terms must be made "clearly and conspicuously" to consumers by a business. This means that disclosures must be legible and reasonably understandable. Locate examples of credit information in newspaper and magazine ads. Discuss with your team members whether you believe the examples meet the legal requirement or not.

CALCULATE FUTURE VALUE

Calculating the effects of compounding interest is a bit more complex. The formula has to account for the rate and amount of compounding during the time of the loan or investment. **Future value**, *FV*, is the amount to which an amount of money will grow in a defined period of time at a specified investment rate. The formula for calculating the future value of a loan or investment with compound interest is

$$FV = P(1 + i)^n$$

FV = future value of the investment or loan
P = principal
i = interest rate per period of compounding
n = number of compounding periods in the length of the loan

It is important to recognize that i is not the annual interest rate unless interest is compounded only once a year. If interest is compounded quarterly, the annual interest rate would be divided by 4 to determine the interest rate per compounding period. Therefore, 5 percent interest compounded quarterly would be an interest rate of 1.25 percent, or 0.0125. If that same interest is compounded monthly, the interest rate per compounding period is 5/12 percent, 0.4167 percent, or 0.004167.

In the same way n is only the number of years of the investment or loan if interest is compounded annually. For quarterly compounding of a three-year loan, $n = 12$, 3 years $\times$ 4 periods per year. Monthly compounding would yield an n of 36, 3 years $\times$ 12 periods per year.

Future Value, *FV*, is the total amount of principal and interest. To determine the amount of interest earned or due, subtract the principal of the loan or investment from the future value.

$$I = FV - P$$

ACTUAL RATE OF INTEREST

Knowing the actual rate of interest is very important in evaluating an investment or deciding to borrow money. Usually the stated rate is the annual rate disregarding compounding. So, the cost of a loan may be stated as a 10 percent annual rate or the rate on a certificate of deposit may be listed as a 4.25 percent APR (annual percentage rate). The effective interest rate is the actual rate paid by the borrower or earned by the investor and includes compounding. If the interest charged for the loan with a 10 percent APR is compounded quarterly, the effective interest rate is 10.38 percent. The certificate of deposit with a stated interest rate of 4.25 percent if compounded daily pays an effective interest rate of 4.44 percent.

checkpoint ✔

What is the difference between simple interest and compound interest?

Time Value of Money

How do businesses decide whether they should borrow or invest money? An investment decision involves more than just seeing if a company has cash available that is not currently being used for anything. A borrowing decision must consider factors other than that the company has a need for additional cash or assets. Investment and borrowing decisions are influenced by the time value of money. The **time value of money** is the difference in purchasing power of an amount of money at a future date. The time value of an amount of money is affected by inflation. *Inflation* is the general increase in the price of all goods and services over time. Because of inflation, you will be able to purchase less at a future date than you can today with the same amount of money. The value is also affected by interest rates that must be paid for loans or that can be earned on investments.

The time value of money compares the future value with the present value of an amount of money. *Future value* is the amount to which an amount of money will grow in a defined period of time at a specified investment rate. **Present value** is the current value of an amount of money to be received at a future date based on a specified investment rate.

Time value of money is used to determine the value of investments. Investments are affected by both inflation and interest rates. Investment decisions are based on what can be purchased now versus what can be purchased with the same amount of money in the future considering the effects of inflation and interest rates. To make an investment worthwhile, the amount earned by the end of the investment period should be greater than the rate of inflation over the same time period. Obtaining a loan to have money to use today makes financial sense if the present value of the money is higher than the value of the money including interest when the loan is repaid.

© GETTY IMAGES/PHOTODISC

The time value of money is the change in purchasing power of an amount of money over time.

PRESENT VALUE EXAMPLES

Businesses encounter several situations where they need to determine the present value of money. If a company wants to borrow money, the lender will charge interest for the time the company uses the money. A typical procedure is for the lender to discount the loan. A *discount* is the amount of money subtracted from a loan at the time of lending equal to the interest charged by the lender.

For example, if a business borrows $10,000 for one year from a bank at an interest (discount) rate of 8 percent, the bank will subtract $800 ($10,000 × 0.08). The actual amount of money received by the business is $9,200. At the end of the year, the business must repay the bank $10,000. Using this example, the present value of the $10,000 that must be repaid in one year is $9,200. If the business needed the full $10,000 it would have to borrow $10,870, as shown in the following equation

$$\$10,870 - (\$10,870 \times 0.08) = \$10,000.40$$

Another example of the use of present value is when a company has a large amount of accounts receivable from customers but needs cash immediately. It can sell those accounts to another business for a discounted value. That business will then attempt to collect the full value of the accounts from customers in the future when payments are scheduled.

If a company has $30,000 of accounts receivable that are due in 90 days, another company may offer to discount them at an annual rate of 20 percent. Since 90 days = 1/4 of a year, the effective interest rate is 0.20 ÷ 4 = 0.05 or 5 percent. The discount amount is $30,000 × 0.05 = $1,500. The present value of the $30,000 accounts receivable is $30,000 − $1,500 = $28,500.

© GETTY IMAGES/PHOTODISC

Interest rates and inflation affect the decisions made by a business owner.

FUTURE VALUE EXAMPLES

A business may face questions such as

- **Question 1** If we borrow $380,000 today to replace outdated equipment and the terms are 8 percent for 5 years compounded quarterly, what is the total cost of the purchase?

- **Question 2** If we invest $20,000 per month in an employee retirement account at an annual interest rate of 6 percent compounded monthly, what will be the value of the fund in 10 years?

Businesses may borrow money to replace outdated equipment.

Each of these questions requires the calculation of future value of money. The formula for calculating future value that appeared earlier in this lesson assumed one principal amount invested at a specific interest rate for an identified time period. That formula will work to answer the first question.

Question 1 To determine the total cost of the equipment purchase, the calculation is

$$FV = PV (1 + i)^n$$
$$FV = \$380{,}000 (1 + 0.02)^{20}$$
$$FV = \$380{,}000 \times 1.4859$$
$$FV = \$564{,}642$$

Question 2 The second question requires a more complex calculation. Not only is interest being compounded each month, the principal is being increased every month as well. The formula to determine the future value of the retirement fund is

$$FV = PMT\,[((1 + i)^n - 1) \div i]$$

PMT = payment
i = interest rate per period of compounding
n = number of compounding periods in the length of the loan

The annual interest rate is 6 percent so the monthly interest rate is 6/12 percent or 0.5 percent or 0.005. The investment is for 10 years and compounded monthly so there are $10 \times 12 = 120$ compounding periods.

$$FV = \$20{,}000\,[((1 + 0.005)^{120} - 1) \div 0.005]$$
$$FV = \$20{,}000\,(1.8194 - 1) \div 0.005$$
$$FV = \$20{,}000 \times 163.88$$
$$FV = \$3{,}277{,}600$$

METHODS OF CALCULATING TIME VALUE OF MONEY

Calculation of the time value of money can be accomplished using a variety of techniques. Several methods are described in Figure 3-5. The examples illustrate calculations of a $10,000 investment at an interest rate of 5 percent compounded annually. The future value of the investment after 10 years is approximately $16,200. Slight differences in the figures in the examples are the result of rounding.

checkpoint ✓

What two factors affect the time value of money?

FIGURE 3-5

Alternatives for Calculating Time Value of Money

Method	Process and Results
MATHEMATICAL FORMULAS The most basic method of time value of money calculations involves the use of a formula. Formulas for calculating PV and FV are given in this lesson.	The future value after 10 years of a $10,000 investment at an interest rate of 5 percent compounded annually is $FV = PV(1 + i)^n$ $\$16{,}288.95 = \$10{,}000\,(1 + 0.05)^{10}$
TIME VALUE OF MONEY TABLES Instead of calculating with a formula, you can use time value of money tables. The numeric factors presented ease the computational process. Sample tables are included in Appendices A–D.	Using the tables in Appendices A–D $10,000 × Future Value of $1, 5 percent, 10 periods $10,000 × $1 × 1.629 = $16,290
FINANCIAL CALCULATOR Handheld financial calculators are programmed with various financial functions. Both future value and present value calculations may be performed using the appropriate keystrokes.	With a financial calculator, use the following keystrokes. Amount 10,000 PMT Time periods 10 N Interest rate 5 I Result FV $16,288.95
SPREADSHEET SOFTWARE Excel and other software programs have built-in formulas for various financial computations, including time value of money.	When using a spreadsheet program, use the following formula = FV(rate, periods, amount per period, single amount) = FV(0.05, 10, 0, 10000) = $16,288.95
WEB SITES Many time value of money calculators are available online. Some only address simple questions while others compute complex problems.	Some easy-to-use calculators for computing the time value of money and other financial computations are located at www.kiplinger.com/tools cgi.money.cnn.com/tools www.finance.cch.com/tools/calcs.asp

3.4 Lesson Assessment

UNDERSTAND CONCEPTS

Determine the best answer for each of the following questions.

1. **True or False?** An investment grows faster with compound interest than with simple interest at the same interest rate.

2. Which of the following is NOT one of the factors used to calculate interest?
   a. principal
   b. rate
   c. time
   d. value

3. The amount to which an amount of money will grow in a defined period of time at a specified investment rate is the
   a. present value
   b. current value
   c. future value
   d. time value

4. **True or False?** The time value of money can be computed using a specialized handheld financial calculator.

MAKE ACADEMIC CONNECTIONS

5. **Economics** Use the Internet and locate the five highest interest rates currently being paid for a minimum $10,000 investment. Create a table that compares the investments. Include the name of the organization offering the investment, the type of organization, the minimum term of the investment, the annual percentage rate, and the effective interest rate. Compare your table with those of other students.

6. **Math** Calculate the amount of interest that would be earned on an investment of $5,500 for two years at a simple interest rate of 8.5 percent. How much more interest would be earned if the interest was compounded quarterly for the two years?

7. **History** List five common household products used in your home that would have been used by a family in the mid-1900s. Research the current cost to purchase each of the products in your community. Then using the Internet or other information sources, identify what each product would have cost approximately 50 years ago. Create a poster or other visual that compares the prices from the two time periods. Prepare a short oral presentation that discusses reasons for the price differences.

8. **Technology** Use three of the methods shown in Figure 3-5 to calculate the future value of an investment of $8,000 for 5 years at 6 percent interest compounded quarterly. For each method write a brief description of the process you used to complete the calculation. Show the numeric values used and the result of each calculation.

Summary

3.1 BUSINESS FINANCIAL GOALS

1. Business financial goals are developed to respond to three main financial needs. A business must provide a competitive rate of return for its investors. It must meet its financial obligations and pay its debts. And it must finance future growth and improvement to remain competitive.

2. Business financial goals must have several elements to be effective. The goals must be specific, realistic, measurable, and established for an identified period of time.

3.2 UNDERSTAND FINANCIAL STATEMENTS

3. Financial statements are used to understand the financial health of a business and make financial decisions. The balance sheet identifies the assets, liabilities, and owner's equity of a business as of a specific date.

4. The income statement provides a view of the financial changes in a business that have occurred during a specific period of time. It documents income and expenses and the resulting profit or loss.

5. A cash flow statement is prepared to show how cash is used by a business during a specified time period. A lack of cash may mean that too much credit is being extended to customers or the company has too many current liabilities.

3.3 DEVELOP A FINANCIAL BUDGET

6. Financial budgets are prepared based on considerations of future events that could affect the business' financial performance and condition. The primary types of financial budgets are the operating budget, cash budget, and capital budget.

7. Budgets are not useful if they are not accurate. A budget should be prepared carefully following a systematic process and drawing on information from inside and outside the company.

3.4 INTEREST AND TIME VALUE OF MONEY

8. An interest rate is the cost of borrowing money, expressed as a percentage of the amount borrowed, usually over a period of one year. The amount of simple interest is calculated at the end of each year based on the total amount loaned. Compound interest is paid not only on the total amount borrowed but also on the interest earned.

9. Time value of money is used to determine the value of investments. Investments decisions are based on what can be purchased now versus what can be purchased with the same amount of money in the future considering the effects of inflation and interest rates.

Develop Your Business Language

Match the terms listed with the definitions. Some terms will not be used.

1. Total value that all owners and investors have in the firm
2. All of the things a business owns and uses as a part of business operations
3. The difference in purchasing power of an amount of money at a future date
4. Identifies the assets, liabilities, and equity of a business as of a specific date
5. Differences between budgeted amounts and actual financial performance
6. Projected financial statement for a specific future time period
7. Decline in the value of an asset as it ages
8. Amount of money borrowed
9. Plan to acquire and finance long-term assets of a business
10. Asset promised by a business to a creditor if repayment of a loan isn't completed
11. Amount paid for the privilege of borrowing money
12. Examines financial performance over several periods of time to determine patterns
13. Establish direction for the financial plans of a business

a. assets
b. balance sheet
c. budget discrepancies
d. business financial goals
e. capital budget
f. cash flow statement
g. collateral
h. creditor
i. depreciation
j. financial budget
k. financial statements
l. future value
m. income statement
n. interest
o. interest rate
p. liabilities
q. operating budget
r. owner's equity
s. present value
t. principal
u. time value of money
v. trend analysis

Review Concepts

14. Which of the following is one of the main financial needs of a business?
    a. A business must provide low prices for competitors to remain competitive.
    b. A business must meet its financial obligations and pay its debts.
    c. A business must avoid growing to a large size in order to maintain effectiveness and efficiency.
    d. All are correct.

15. Effective business financial goals must have each of the following elements except
    a. They must be specific.
    b. They must be realistic.
    c. They must be open-ended.
    d. They must be established for an identified period of time.

Think Critically

16. Describe why the financial health of a company affects the way it can respond to competition, problems, and opportunities. Should a company try to maintain a large amount of unused capital and cash to be able to respond to unanticipated circumstances? Why or why not?

17. How can a company be profitable but not have enough cash to meet immediate financial obligations? Is it possible for a company to have a large amount of cash on hand but not be profitable? Explain.

18. If you were the owner of a business and could choose the method of financing growth, would you prefer to invest more of your own personal money, attract additional investors, borrow money from creditors to be repaid, or wait to make additional profits to reinvest in the business? Analyze the advantages and disadvantages of each choice.

19. Prepare two written financial goals for a business and show how the goals meet all of the characteristics of effective goals.

20. If you had to choose one of the three main financial statements to learn about the overall financial health of a business, which would you choose and why? If you wanted to learn about the current financial performance, which statement would be the most helpful? Why?

21. Describe why both inflation and interest rates should be considered by a business when choosing among investments and when deciding whether to borrow money to finance a major purchase.

Business Financial Calculations

22. Calculate the simple interest and compound interest earned for each of the investments using the information from the table.

Amount invested	Interest rate	Compounding period	Length of investment	Simple interest	Compound interest
$10,000	5.0	annual	2 years		
$150,000	6.5	quarterly	1 year		
$1,490,500	8.0	monthly	18 months		

23. Use the information from Figure 3-1 to calculate
    a. The percentage of current liabilities to current assets
    b. The percentage of total liabilities to total assets
    c. The percentage of current assets to total assets
    d. The percentage of total owner's equity to total assets

24. A business needs to borrow $75,000 from the bank to replace a damaged delivery vehicle. It will be able to repay the loan in six months. The bank will discount the loan and charge an annual interest rate of 7.5 percent. What amount must the company borrow in order to receive the needed money?

25. If your grandparents deposit $500 in an investment account for your college education each year from the time you are born and the account pays 5 percent compounded quarterly, what will be the total amount in the account when you turn 18 years old?

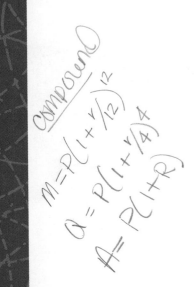

Compound

$$M = P(1 + \frac{r}{12})^{12}$$

$$Q = P(1 + \frac{r}{4})^4$$

$$A = P(1 + R)$$

Analyze Cases

Use the case from the beginning of the chapter, Apple Computer: A New Life, to answer the following questions.

26. If you were an investment business looking for new companies that held a great deal of promise for growth and financial return, what would you have thought about the strengths and weaknesses of Apple Computer in the late 1970s? Do you think Apple Computer provides a more or less risky investment opportunity today than it did in the first few years of its existence? Justify your opinion.

27. If you analyzed current balance sheets of Apple Computer and compared them to the balance sheets of the first few years of its operations, what differences would you expect to see other than a much larger business?

28. One of Apple's unique competitive strengths has been that it has concentrated on being innovative rather than providing products that are similar to its competitors. Why do you believe that strategy resulted in some of the past financial problems for the company? Why have products like iPod and iTunes improved the company's financial health?

Portfolio Activity

COLLECT an example of a balance sheet and an income statement from a public corporation. Recent financial statements are often available on a company's web site.

CREATE a visual to demonstrate how the two financial statements provide important information about the company's financial health.

CONNECT your visual to other items already in your class portfolio or relate it to an important concept you have learned in another class. Make the connection by preparing a one-minute presentation on the importance of being able to understand financial statements.

Stock Market Activity

As companies plan their strategy for success, various factors must be considered. Setting organizational goals, preparing a budget, and analyzing financial statements are activities involved in business financial planning. Appropriate planning along with successful implementation of these plans will likely have a positive affect on a company's stock price.

Select a company that you will research and analyze. Conduct library and web research, and obtain a copy of the company's annual report to

1. Identify recent and current goals of the company.
2. Determine the extent to which these goals have been achieved.
3. Assess how financial performance has affected the company's stock price.
4. Describe potential actions that might be appropriate for future company success.
5. Maintain a record of the company's stock value with the date and closing price. Note any major company, economic, or news developments that may affect stock prices.

Planning a Career in Government Financial Planning

The federal government is a major employer, with over 3 million employees. State and local governments add another 7 million jobs. Financial career opportunities in government are interesting, varied, and offered at all levels of government and in most agencies. A growing demand for finance expertise exists in the FBI, IRS, military, and Homeland Security.

Every government agency and office is involved in budget planning and budget management. Financial planners, accountants, auditors, investment analysts, and financial managers make important decisions about government services, budget management, tax planning, collections, and auditing. Financial expertise is required to support lawmakers. Government agency managers consider financial policies, develop a broad range of laws, and maintain effective and balanced budgets.

Employment Outlook

- Good employment prospects in government finance careers are projected for the near future, with major employment growth in the IRS focusing on tax collections and enforcement and in the Defense Department working with procurement and contract management. State and local government positions are expected to grow at an even faster pace than federal.
- Pay scales for government employment are lower than equivalent jobs in the private sector. Job security is often better with excellent benefits at the federal level.

Job Titles

- Auditor
- Contract specialist
- Budget analyst
- Cash management specialist
- Financial institution examiner
- Intelligence specialist
- Internal revenue agent
- Finance policy specialist

Needed Skills

- Well-developed quantitative skills and preparation in mathematics, statistics, and computer finance and business applications.
- Varied education levels with opportunities for graduates of two- and four-year colleges. Specialized and managerial positions require a B.A. and often an M.B.A. or Master's in Accounting.
- Accuracy, objectivity, and attention to detail with an understanding of financial policies and procedures.

What's It Like to Work in Government Budget Planning?

The federal budget of the United States outlines annual expenditures of over $2.5 trillion. The complete budget and its supporting materials consume over 1000 printed pages. Personnel in the Federal Office of Management and Budget complete the federal budget under the direction of the President of the United States. The OMB coordinates the planning efforts and compiles the individual budgets of every government office and agency. Budget planning and preparation is a continuing job involving thousands of employees from technicians to managers and administrators. When completed, the budget is presented to Congress, where it is analyzed, modified, and passed into law.

What about you? What do you see as the advantages and disadvantages of a finance career in government? What type of agency or career area would appeal to you most?

ENTREPRENEURSHIP EVENT

The BPA Entrepreneurship Event challenges participants to develop an operating plan and operational structure for a small business. Each participant selects a legal form of business that is appropriate for their small business. The business plan developed in this event includes financial goals, a budget, and other necessary financial statements.

Each contestant will develop a business plan that cannot exceed ten (10) single-spaced pages. The business plan is for a start-up business in the student's community or local area. The business plan must market a new product. Students should conduct extensive research to determine what type of new business would be successful in their community or region. The business plan must convince bankers and venture capitalists that the idea has great profit potential. Most businesses take up to three years to earn a profit. The proposed business plan must show enough financial depth to weather the early years of operation.

The business plan must include title page, table of contents, executive summary, description of proposed business, objectives of the business, proposed business strategies, products and/or services, form of ownership, management, market analysis, customer profile, competition, short-range operational goals, financial analysis, and supporting documentation.

PERFORMANCE INDICATORS EVALUATED

■ Demonstrate knowledge and understanding of entrepreneurship.
■ Communicate research clearly and concisely, both orally and in writing.
■ Demonstrate effective persuasive and informative communication and presentation skills.
■ Develop a written business plan for a start-up business.
■ Identify the target market for the business.
■ Understand the demographics of the target market.
■ Identify the competition and strategies to attract business.
■ Identify strengths, weaknesses, opportunities, and threats (SWOT) for your business idea.
■ Demonstrate oral presentation skills when presenting the business plan.
■ Develop a business plan to market a new product for a start-up business.

Go to the BPA web site for more detailed information.

Think Critically

1. What is the value of research when proposing a new business idea?
2. How should the target market be involved before presenting a start-up business proposal?
3. Why do most entrepreneurs need substantial savings before proposing a start-up business?
4. Why is the executive summary so important?

w w w . b p a . o r g

chapter 4

Maintain and Analyze Financial Records

4.1 ACCOUNTING PRINCIPLES AND PRACTICES

4.2 MAINTAIN AND USE FINANCIAL RECORDS

4.3 FINANCIAL MANAGEMENT ANALYSIS TOOLS

4.4 FINANCIAL ANALYSIS AND DECISION MAKING

Point Your [Browser]
www.thomsonedu.com/school/busfinance

Case STUDY

Accenture: Making the Right Move

Accenture is the world's largest management and technology consulting firm. In 2005 it had revenues of more than $17 billion and net income of $940.5 million. Its clients include 87 of the Fortune Global 100, more than two-thirds of the Fortune Global 500, and government agencies in 24 countries. Accenture focuses on helping its clients identify and enter new markets, increase revenues in existing markets, improve operational performance, and deliver products and services more efficiently. The firm is organized around 18 industry specialties ranging from utilities, insurance, and technology to e-government, human resources, and learning.

The success of Accenture is remarkable considering its short history as an independent company and the problems it faced in its development. Accenture started as a consulting division of Arthur Andersen, the international accounting firm that failed as a result of its work with Enron. Arthur Andersen was one of the first accounting firms to recognize the need to offer financial consulting services to its clients. Its first major consulting client was General Electric in 1953. It worked with GE to determine the feasibility of an automated manufacturing and financial management system at a time when computers were first being used in business.

Due to concerns about administrative and financial relationships and ethical issues about the relationships between consulting and auditing responsibilities for clients, Andersen Consulting separated from Arthur Andersen in the early 1990s. Financial ties remained and led to infighting and negative relations between the two companies. The problems were resolved in 2000 with a total split and a new name for the consulting firm. Accenture was suggested by an employee in a naming contest and was a word developed from the phrase "accent on the future." It was selected both to reflect the company's commitment to be a global leader in business innovation and also as a word that would not be offensive anywhere in its worldwide market.

Accenture became a publicly traded company in 2001 when its stock IPO (Initial Public Offering) raised $1.7 billion in its first day. Accenture's world headquarters is in New York City but it is officially incorporated in Bermuda. Accenture has been criticized for that decision since Bermuda is known as a "tax haven country" where businesses incorporate to avoid U.S. taxes.

Think Critically

1. How might Accenture have fared if it had remained a consulting division of Arthur Andersen during the Enron scandal?

2. Why do you believe Accenture broadened its consulting focus from financial issues to a broad range of business processes? What positive and negative effects could that have on a business?

Goals
- Identify important accounting activities and procedures.
- Recognize assumptions, principles, and professional practices that guide accountants' work.

Terms
- accounting
- equities
- fundamental accounting equation
- accounts
- accounting transaction
- accounting cycle
- accrual accounting
- due care

■ Finance and Accounting

The study of finance provides information to individuals, businesses, and organizations on how to raise, allocate, and use monetary resources. Financial planning takes into account the current financial position of the organization, its immediate and long-term financial needs, and the risks in any alternatives being considered.

Both accounting and finance are involved in helping individuals and organizations make effective financial decisions. Some people think accounting and finance are essentially the same. There are major differences, even though both are important in effective financial management. **Accounting** is responsible for organizing a system of financial records, recording financial data, and preparing, analyzing, and interpreting financial statements. The financial records and financial statements must be timely, and they must be free of errors and bias. Generally Accepted Accounting Principles (GAAP) guide the work of the accounting profession. In the U.S., Generally Accepted Accounting Principles are developed and enforced by the Financial Accounting Standards Board (FASB). Accountants must also follow the accounting rules and regulations of each country in which a business operates, as well as the International Accounting Standards (IAS), when applicable.

Finance refers to saving, investing, and using money by individuals, businesses, and governments. Finance is broader than accounting and consists of three interrelated areas.

- *Money and capital markets,* which deals with determining monetary needs and obtaining adequate capital and cash
- *Investments,* which focuses on analyzing and choosing among investment alternatives while considering returns and risks
- *Financial management,* which applies management principles to financial decision-making for organizations

One way to look at the difference between accounting and finance is that accounting focuses on history and finance focuses on the future. Accountants analyze the financial performance of individuals, businesses, and organizations to determine what happened. Finance, on the other hand, uses historic and current financial information to predict and plan for the future. Both are essential to effective financial management. Decision-makers must understand the financial past to plan for the financial future.

PRINCIPLES OF ACCOUNTING

For hundreds of years, businesses have tracked their financial progress as an important measure of success. The primary goal of accounting is to determine the value of the resources of a business and

STOCKBYTE

Equipment is a tangible asset of a business.

the financial claims on those resources. The financial claims on a company's resources are known as **equities.** Those claims come from both creditors and owners. Accounting organizes the classification and analysis of resources using the fundamental accounting equation.

The Accounting Equation The **fundamental accounting equation** is

Assets = Liabilities + Owner's Equity

Assets are the resources used by a business in its operations. They include tangible resources such as land, buildings, equipment, inventory, employees, and cash and intangibles such as patents, copyrights, trademarks, and even the image and goodwill of the business. *Liabilities* are claims against the business resources by those to whom the business has financial obligations. Those claims includes loans, accounts payable, taxes payable, and other obligations. *Owner's equity* is the financial interest in the business held by all owners. Ownership is determined by the legal form of the organization— sole proprietorship, partnership, corporation, cooperative, or other legal form. Owner's equity is made up of both the investments of all owners and any undistributed earnings of the business. The financial records for each of the specific assets, liabilities, and categories of owner's equity are known as the business' **accounts.**

Accounting Transactions The resources of the organization and the claims on those resources must remain balanced. Any changes in the resources of an organization must be reflected on both sides of the accounting equation by additions to or reductions from the company's assets and

The value of all inventory held by U.S. retailers at the end of 2004 was $461.2 billion. Nearly two-thirds of that inventory was held by automobile dealers and auto parts suppliers.

corresponding additions to or reductions from liabilities or owner's equity. Any time revenue moves into or out of the business or any time the value of an account changes, it must be reflected in the accounts of the business so that the accounting equation remains balanced.

An accounting transaction is the act of recording a financial activity that results in a change in value of an organization's resource. The transaction will result in financial *entries* in the accounts of the business in a way that maintains their balance with each other. For example, if a company pays a bill to a creditor, the amount of that liability account (accounts payable) is reduced. At the same time, the amount of the company's cash (an asset account) is also reduced since cash was used to pay the creditor. The two reductions maintain the balance among the accounts. In the same way, if the company makes a sale to a customer for cash, the value of inventory is reduced and the value of the cash account is increased. Other accounts may be affected depending on whether the sale resulted in a profit or loss but the overall accounting equation remains in balance after the transaction is recorded.

Recording Transactions The basic requirement for maintaining complete financial records for a business is that all financial transactions must be recorded. Recording financial transactions and maintaining records of those transactions is the primary responsibility of accountants. Each transaction should be identified through a source document. In accounting, a *source document* is the original record of a transaction. Common examples of source documents are sales receipts, invoices, checks, and computer records such as printouts of cash register transactions. Using source documents, transactions are recorded in business records called *journals*. The *journal entry* identifies the key information for the transaction, including date, amount, purpose, and the accounts affected. The financial effect on each account is noted so that the accounting equation stays in balance after the transaction is recorded.

Financial Statements A business uses financial statements to understand and analyze the financial performance and health of the business. *Financial statements* are specific reports prepared according to accepted accounting standards that provide financial information about an enterprise. The three primary financial statements—the *balance sheet,* the *income statement*, and the *cash flow statement*—are summary reports prepared at regular times using the company's financial records.

THE ACCOUNTING CYCLE

Financial information must be available for decision-makers in an understandable form and a timely manner. It would be impossible for everyone needing financial information to review all of the financial transactions of the business every time a decision needs to be made. Accountants regularly summarize financial data and prepare financial reports following the accounting cycle. The accounting cycle is a series of steps performed to ensure the completeness and accuracy of accounting records and to prepare summary financial statements. Completing those steps is called "closing the books" for the company and provides a summary of the business' finances as of a particular date. Normally the accounting cycle is completed monthly, quarterly (every three months), and at the end of the company's fiscal (financial) year. The steps in the accounting cycle are summarized in Figure 4-1.

Steps 3, 4, and 6 are unique accounting activities designed to ensure the accuracy and integrity of the company's financial records. In Step 3, a trial balance of accounts is prepared. The trial balance is a worksheet constructed in the format of the accounting equation. It lists the values of all accounts and determines whether the total of accounts is balanced. If the totals do not balance, accounts and journal entries must be reviewed to identify and correct errors.

In Step 4, adjustments to account balances are made. It is important that all financial statements reflect the accurate financial

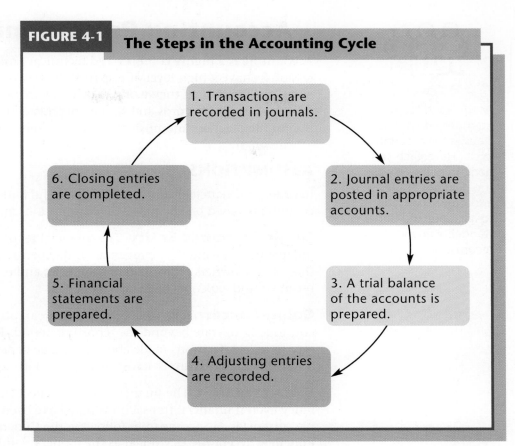

FIGURE 4-1   **The Steps in the Accounting Cycle**

1. Transactions are recorded in journals.

2. Journal entries are posted in appropriate accounts.

3. A trial balance of the accounts is prepared.

4. Adjusting entries are recorded.

5. Financial statements are prepared.

6. Closing entries are completed.

position of a business as of a specific date. Some accounts reflect earnings or payments for multiple accounting periods. For example, employees may have earned wages for the ending days of the accounting period but paychecks have not yet been issued. The account recording employee wages must be adjusted to reflect the actual wage expenses of the company for the actual period the work was performed. In the same way, the company may have made a six-month insurance payment but some of the cost of that insurance applies to months following the date financial statements are prepared. In this case an adjustment to the insurance expense account will reflect the actual cost of insurance for the time covered by the statements.

Finally, in Step 6 closing entries are made after financial statements are completed. Closing entries prepare all accounts for the next accounting cycle. In completing the financial analysis and financial statements, accountants create temporary accounts to identify income, expenses, and earnings related to the specific accounting period. The balances of the temporary accounts are returned to their original locations and the temporary accounts are closed through a series of closing entries.

checkpoint ✓

What is the purpose of the accounting cycle?

teamwork

Assign each team member one of the steps in the accounting cycle. Have each student, in order, explain the purpose of the step and how it contributes to accurate and understandable financial records.

■ Accounting Professional Practices

Accounting is a highly complex and technical profession. Accounting professionals have a high level of responsibility for the financial success of the companies for which they work. Inaccurate, incomplete, or improperly prepared accounting records and statements misrepresent the financial condition of the business and mislead those who rely on the accountants' work.

ASSUMPTIONS

In order for financial information to be useful and reliable, accounting procedures are based on the following assumptions and principles.

Single Economic Entity The financial reporting is for an identifiable, independent business. The revenues and expenses are kept separate from those of the owners or from other businesses and reflect the total and unique revenues and expenses of the business.

Going Concern The financial data is for an ongoing business that will continue to operate beyond the reporting period. This assumption is necessary to reflect decisions made about the value of assets and the allocations of revenues and expenses across financial reporting time periods.

Monetary Unit The financial records reflect the use of one stable currency even if financial transactions may have been completed using multiple currencies. U.S. companies following the Generally Accepted Accounting Principles accept the U.S. dollar as the monetary unit. There is no adjustment for inflation in reporting monetary values.

Periodic Reporting The financial basis of business operations can be recorded and analyzed in specific and regular time periods, usually monthly, quarterly, and annually. The use of common and consistent reporting periods is necessary to compare past, current, and future financial performance.

ACCOUNTING PRINCIPLES

Certain accepted accounting principles are used to value and record financial data.

Historic Costs Companies record and report the value of resources based on their acquisition costs rather than their current market value. The values are more stable and comparable and there is less opportunity to misstate values of resources by applying a subjective, current value assessment.

Revenue Recognition Companies are expected to record revenues when they are actually earned, not when payment is received. In the same way, expenses are recorded when they are actually applied to the operation of the business, not when payment is made. The accounting procedure that recognizes revenues and expenses when they are incurred rather than when cash is received or spent is known as **accrual accounting.**

Expense and Revenue Matching Financial reports are expected to match expenses with related revenue. Expenses are costs of products and services needed for business operations and for increasing the revenue of the business. The matching principle is used to show how much it costs to earn specific revenue. Only when there is no reasonable connection between an expense and any revenue generation can an expense be charged at the time it is incurred.

Full Disclosure A company's financial statements and supporting information should contain all relevant facts and explanations needed to accurately reflect the company's financial position and make it understandable. Information that does not contribute to understanding and that is costly to obtain and prepare should not be included.

Accounting financial data must be for an ongoing, operating business.

Standard Practice and Conservatism Accounting procedures used to record, analyze, and report financial information should follow industry practices. When choosing between two interpretations or solutions, the one that will be least likely to overstate assets and income should be chosen.

PROFESSIONAL PRACTICES

As with most professions, accounting is defined by a number of professional practices. Those practices specify requirements and expectations for people who are employed in the profession and provide assurances to the businesses employing professional accountants of the quality and standards they can expect.

Professional Competence Accountants are expected to have sufficient competence to perform required tasks. Accounting competence includes knowledge of accounting rules and standards and the judgment to apply the rules and standards appropriately. The primary rules of accounting are the Statements of Accounting Standards, Generally Accepted Accounting Principles, and applicable laws and regulations of government agencies.

Many accounting responsibilities require a great deal of technical knowledge to understand the business and its operations or to complete complex data analysis and financial calculations. If a person does not have adequate technical knowledge to complete the financial analysis, he or she is required to complete the necessary research, consult with experts, or recommend that another person who has the needed technical expertise be assigned to the task.

Accountants must exercise due care in completing their tasks.

Due Care and Sufficient Data

Accountants are expected to exercise due care in performing their duties. **Due care** is a commitment to completing all tasks thoroughly and with the highest level of quality. Often the details of financial transactions are not easy to obtain or understand. By exercising due care, accountants use their knowledge and abilities to obtain complete and accurate information when preparing financial records. They need to serve the best interests of the company, its employees, and others who rely on the financial information by being ethical and objective. They must make sure that everyone they work with and supervise completes assigned tasks correctly and completely.

Independence and Integrity Accountants must remain objective and not knowingly misrepresent information or allow others, either subordinates or superiors, to do so. There may be pressure in an organization to present the most positive financial picture. That is particularly true if the company is trying to obtain financing or attract investors. There are several recent examples of top-level corporate executives who attempted to misrepresent the financial condition of their organizations in order to hide management and operating problems. The accountants and accounting firms working for those companies faced immense pressure to comply with the executives' demands and several failed to meet their professional obligations to maintain their independence and follow accepted accounting practices.

Every accountant has the responsibility to report all relevant information, report it honestly, and correct any inaccurate or misleading information in financial records and reports. If there are concerns about the quality or accuracy of the work, it is the obligation of the accountant to make those concerns known to management, provide relevant documents and applicable rules and regulations, and, if necessary, ask other experts to review the information.

checkpoint ✔

Provide an example of each of the professional practices expected of accountants.

4.1 Lesson Assessment

UNDERSTAND CONCEPTS

Determine the best answer for each of the following questions.

1. Recording an activity that results in a change in value of an organization's resource is done through
   a. financial statements
   b. financial transactions
   c. the accounting cycle
   d. the accounting equation

2. **True or False?** Accounting deals with the financial future of a business while finance deals with its past.

3. Which of the following is *not* a purpose of completing the accounting cycle?
   a. to ensure the completeness and accuracy of accounting records
   b. to prepare summary financial statements
   c. to close the books of a company in order to report on its financial condition as of a specific date
   d. all of the above are purposes

4. **True or False?** A business should use common and consistent financial reporting periods in order to compare past, current, and future financial performance.

5. The accounting principle of _____?_____ states that a company's financial statements and supporting information should contain all relevant facts and explanations.
   a. revenue recognition
   b. historic costs
   c. full disclosure
   d. conservatism

MAKE ACADEMIC CONNECTIONS

6. **Government** Identify one federal department or agency that regulates accounting practice or financial reporting. Prepare a short written explanation of the type of regulation and how it affects the work of accountants.

7. **Visual Art** Use an accounting textbook or the Internet to gather information on the accounting cycle. Identify one type of accounting form that is used for each step in the cycle. Create a poster modeled after Figure 4-1 that includes an illustration of the accounting form for each of the steps.

8. **International Studies** Identify three countries that are major trading partners with U.S. businesses. Gather information on each country's accounting standards. Compare similarities and differences with the U.S. approach.

Goals
- Describe the importance of accurate, complete, and secure financial records for a business.
- Discuss important uses and users of a business' financial records.

Terms
- information system
- information integrity
- annual report

■Develop and Maintain a Business Records System

All business information is important. Companies devote significant financial and human resources to plan, build, maintain, and secure a complex and comprehensive information system. An **information system** is a structured set of processes, people, and equipment for converting data into information. An effective business information system is under direct management control and is designed to be usable throughout the organization. The system is designed to integrate hardware, software, information, data, applications, communications, and the people who generate, record, and use the information. The components of an effective information system are users, data collection devices, data sharing devices, analysis/interpretation of information, organizational structures, and processes.

TYPES OF FINANCIAL INFORMATION

Among the types of information maintained in an information system, financial information is one of the most important. The information system of an organization must collect, record, store, and securely maintain all financial data, records, and reports. Financial information occurs in many forms. The common types of business financial information include

- ■ **Data** raw facts related to financial transactions of the company
- ■ **Records** a collection of related data organized in a form that can be retrieved and viewed
- ■ **Reports** the organized presentation of financial data, often with notes, providing specific information on the financial condition or position of the organization

INFORMATION INTEGRITY

The people in charge of an information system as well as each person with access to the system have a responsibility to maintain the integrity of the information. **Information integrity** means that information remains unchanged from its source and has not been accidentally or maliciously modified, altered, or destroyed. Problems with the integrity of information systems are commonly seen.

An example of a problem with information integrity is that a store scanner may not record the accurate price of a product.

- A supermarket scanner is not programmed to record the accurate price of a product.
- Personal credit reports are incorrect due to lack of care by employees responsible for reporting and recording information.
- People working with personal data in an organization's database download it to a laptop where it is essentially unsecured.
- Companies hit by natural disasters such as hurricanes and floods lose essential records.

Each time a situation occurs where data is lost, destroyed, recorded inaccurately, or misused, people's confidence in the organization as well as its information systems and the information itself is shaken. It is particularly important that people maintain their belief in the quality and integrity of a company's financial information. They must feel that they can rely on that information when making decisions about investments and other financial dealings with the company. A lack of confidence and trust will cause people to be reluctant to engage in financial dealings with the business.

MAINTAINING FINANCIAL RECORDS

Developing and maintaining a financial records system that has integrity and the confidence of those who use and rely on the information requires decisions in several areas. Those areas and specific procedures are described in Figure 4-2 on the next page.

checkpoint ✓

Provide examples that show the differences among financial data, records, and reports.

teamwork

Discuss with team members why each of the components of an information system is necessary in a business. Develop a list of criteria a business might use to determine if their information system is effective and secure.

FIGURE 4-2

Effective and Secure Information Systems

Record Selection

What types of records are needed to

- conduct your type of business and make effective management decisions
- meet stockholder information expectations
- determine your financial progress and health
- meet government reporting and tax requirements
- protect ownership, contractual, and intellectual property rights

Information Maintenance

What hardware, software, and other system components are needed to

- maintain the amount and types of information used in your business
- allow access to critical information
- accurately track the financial progress and health of the company
- make information easily accessible, usable, and understandable by all with legitimate information needs

Information and System Security

What special measures have been taken to

- secure information and important documents away from the business site in case of disaster
- meet the storage requirements of original and legal documents
- provide ready access to critical documents and information in times of crisis or disaster
- provide necessary security for access, reasonable use, and modification of information

Legal Integrity

What are the legal considerations regarding the need to

- authenticate original records and documents
- meet legal requirements for electronic versus hard copy records
- meet government requirements for documentation, review, and retention

System Maintenance and Improvement

What procedures and authority are in place to

- regularly review the quality of the information system and procedures
- meet industry standards and government record-keeping requirements
- remove nonessential records when they are no longer needed
- securely destroy records that are no longer being maintained
- remove roadblocks to efficient information access, use, and exchange
- provide funds to maintain and update information system components

▉Using Financial Records

Financial information is important to the business and to everyone interested in or affected by the company's financial performance. Information must be organized to be meaningful and usable. Accounting is responsible for collecting, recording, and organizing financial data into records and reports. Those financial reports and other information are then used by others to draw conclusions and make decisions that affect the financial future of the company.

USERS AND USES

The primary users of financial reports and information are company managers and decision-makers, investors, creditors, and government regulators. Each has a particular need and use for the information.

The primary responsibility of managers and company decision-makers is to operate a profitable business and maximize shareholder value. They make decisions about capital expenditures to make sure business assets are as productive as possible. They review the operations and results of each part of the business to increase productivity and profitability and control expenses. Managers must maintain sufficient working capital to continue operations and invest funds not currently being used.

Investors are concerned about the financial performance of a company to achieve their investment objectives. The major objective of investing is to maximize the value of the investment. That can be achieved through the

technology topics

Using New Technology Wisely

Many companies adopt new technologies thinking they will receive a good return on their investment through reduced personnel costs and productivity gains. However, experience in many companies shows that getting a good return depends on the type of technology purchased and its use. If a company just purchases equipment and provides training to employees without changing how work is done, the result is usually a loss on the investment. If the company analyzes specific jobs to see how each job can become more efficient and then purchases the needed technology, the return is modest—10 to 20 percent. However, if an entire business process is reorganized and supported with technology, companies see returns of up to 300 percent. Just providing data entry workers with new computers and software gets little return. Automating the entire data entry and recordkeeping system will give the company a small return. A comprehensive process integrating financial management with planning, operations, and customer service using technology will be expensive initially, but will give the greatest return on investment in the long run.

Think Critically

1. Why does providing individual employees with the latest technology and training often cost more than it returns to the company?
2. Why might a business spend money on technology when it is not likely the investment will save the company any money?

Business financial information is important to owners, investors, creditors, and the government.

increasing value of the investment itself and the regular earnings from the investment. For example, with stock ownership, value increases as stock prices increase and earnings are achieved through the payment of dividends.

Creditors are concerned that the company has adequate assets to secure the amount of money they loan to the business. More important from the creditor's viewpoint is whether the business is generating adequate cash to meet the payment schedule. Creditors want to make sure that the financial condition of the business is strong enough to make it a good credit risk for the length of the loan.

The interest of the government in a business' financial records is twofold. Businesses are required to pay taxes and other fees based on their legal and financial status. In addition, a variety of government regulations require financial disclosures from businesses. Those disclosures include specific financial data as well as information on financial recordkeeping and financial decision-making procedures.

PRIVATE AND PUBLIC RECORDS AND REPORTS

Requirements differ on the types of financial information companies must disclose. Much of the financial data and records of businesses are private, including records of all financial transactions. The records can be controlled and information shared based upon the decisions of management as long as all legal requirements are met. In general, privately owned companies are not required to publicly disclose financial information.

Corporations whose stock is publicly traded do have a public reporting requirement. Those companies must provide an annual report to all stockholders. An **annual report** is a statement of a company's operating and financial performance issued at the end of its fiscal year. Annual statements often include a letter from the chief executive, a narrative discussion of the year's operations, and plans for the future. In addition, the Securities and Exchange Commission requires public corporations to file a *Form 10-K* each year. It is similar to an annual report but may be even more detailed. The 10-K includes information about the company history, organizational structure, equity, holdings, earnings per share, subsidiaries, and audited financial statements.

checkpoint ✓

What requirements for public reporting of financial information must publicly owned corporations meet?

a question of ethics

What Led to the Sarbanes-Oxley Act?

As the country started into the new century, public confidence in big business and accounting practices was shattered with several major back-to-back scandals. The most famous was Enron, a Houston-based energy company that had been the darling of investment bankers and the business press. *Fortune* magazine named Enron "America's Most Innovative Company" for six consecutive years. In late 2001, it all came crashing down when Enron filed for bankruptcy, becoming the largest bankruptcy in U.S. history. It cost thousands of employees their jobs and, even worse, the retirement savings they had invested in the company as the stock price plummeted from over $90 to under $1 per share. The blame for the company's failure was placed on several company executives for illegal financial transactions in moving assets and expenses among company entities as well as approving fraudulent accounting to hide the transactions. The company's auditing firm, Arthur Andersen, was convicted of obstruction of justice and disbanded.

The Enron bankruptcy was followed quickly by several other scandals that exposed serious problems with accounting practices and the oversight provided by auditing firms. WorldCom's founder, Bernard Ebbers, and several other executives manipulated stock prices, misused the Board of Directors to approve illegal compensation plans, and illegally inflated the value of the company's assets by over $11 billion. Tyco experienced a similar problem with overvalued stocks, illegal executive pay, and misleading financial statements. Two top executives were accused of the theft of $600 million from the company. Based on the scandals, several leading public accounting firms—Deloitte & Touche, Ernst & Young, KPMG, and PricewaterhouseCoopers—were charged with negligence as auditors of their clients' financial information and reports.

The federal government responded quickly to restore the public's confidence in corporate finance and accounting practices. The Sarbanes-Oxley Act was passed in July, 2002 by overwhelming majorities in Congress. It established new or more stringent standards for all U.S. public company boards, management, and public accounting firms. It has been called the most important piece of legislation affecting corporate governance, financial disclosure, and public accounting since the securities laws of the 1930s. Executives and corporate directors are held responsible for understanding and approving financial statements, auditing committees and firms must have independence from conflicts of interest or executive pressure, and new enforcement provisions and stiff criminal penalties are established. Rules regulating executive compensation are also imposed.

Think Critically

1. What circumstances likely led to large public auditing companies getting caught up in the major corporate scandals?
2. Use the Internet to review business and public reactions to Sarbanes-Oxley. What are the views in support of and opposition to the law?

UNDERSTAND CONCEPTS

Determine the best answer for each of the following questions.

1. All of the following are components of an information system except
   a. users
   b. data collection devices
   c. data sharing devices
   d. all of the above are components

2. **True or False?** Three common types of business financial information are data, records, and reports.

3. Information ____?____ means that information remains unchanged from its source and has not been accidentally or maliciously modified, altered, or destroyed.
   a. control
   b. management
   c. integrity
   d. integration

4. **True or False?** The primary responsibility of managers and company decision-makers is to increase sales and satisfy customers.

5. The Securities and Exchange Commission requires publicly traded corporations to
   a. pay a dividend
   b. restrict compensation for top executives
   c. pay a minimum tax each year
   d. provide an annual report to all shareholders

MAKE ACADEMIC CONNECTIONS

6. **Visual Art** Use textbooks or the Internet to locate and study examples of a computerized information system. Use a computer graphics program or poster board and colored markers to prepare a visual depiction of the components of the system. Label each component and be prepared to describe how the system operates.

7. **Research** Use newspapers, magazines, and the Internet to research the problems business face with information integrity. Prepare a three-column table that identifies (1) the problem, (2) the damage resulting from the problem, (3) what the business did to correct the problem.

8. **Debate** Form two teams and prepare for a debate on this topic: "The legal requirement that public corporations must publish detailed financial information interferes with competition and a business' right to privacy." Your teacher will explain the debate rules and assign the position each team will take.

Goals
- Identify the primary purpose and activities of financial management.
- Describe important tools used in financial management.

Terms
- chief executive officer (CEO)
- chief operating officer (COO)
- chief financial officer (CFO)
- equity financing
- debt financing
- retained earnings
- solvency

■Financial Management Activities

The overall objective of financial management is to maximize the wealth of the owners. Considering the nature of the business and the risk assumed by investors, owner's equity should increase at a rate equal to or better than other investments. Financial managers determine the best mix of assets for a business, how to acquire them, and how to use them to get the best possible financial return from their use.

THE STRUCTURE OF FINANCIAL MANAGEMENT

A corporation is guided by a board of directors. The board of directors represents the shareholders in oversight of the business. It is their responsibility to set direction for the business and establish corporate policy, hire and determine the compensation of the key executives, and review major business decisions.

The employed management of a corporation is headed by the chief executive officer. The **chief executive officer (CEO)** is charged with carrying out the strategy and policy of the board of directors. The CEO provides leadership for management and employees, sets long-term operational direction, and is accountable to the board for all company activities and results.

Typically, the two positions reporting to the CEO and having primary responsibility for managing the business are the chief operating officer and the chief financial officer. The **chief operating officer (COO)** directs the actual operations of the business while the **chief financial officer (CFO)** is responsible for planning and managing its financial resources.

Under the CFO are a number of managers. The top-level financial managers in many companies are the *treasurer* and *controller*. Both of these positions are supported by a number of financial specialists. The treasurer has responsibility for the management of a company's cash, investments, and other financial resources as well as relationships with investors and creditors. The controller is in charge of accounting and the financial records of the organization and provides support for executives and other managers in understanding and using financial data and reports. The efforts of the entire

Businesses plan for investment in assets like equipment and materials.

financial management team are directed at accomplishing the overall goal of the business—to maximize ownership wealth.

FINANCIAL MANAGEMENT DECISIONS

Financial management is focused on investment decisions. Three major types of investment decisions define the work of financial management in businesses. Those decisions are (1) what investments need to be made, (2) how the investments should be financed, and (3) how the business' investments can be efficiently managed.

Asset Planning Investments are made to acquire the assets needed for business operations. The assets needed are determined by the activities of the business and its size. Financial managers work with operations management as well as other managers in the organization to determine what investments in land, buildings, equipment, materials, and other major assets are needed at the current time and in the future. In some cases assets must be added, and in other instances assets can be reduced. One of the most interesting and challenging investment decisions is the area of mergers and acquisitions. Deciding to purchase an existing company or merge the resources of two or more companies is a major financial decision of a company, as is the decision to sell a major part of the business to reduce the company's size and focus its efforts.

Asset Financing Once decisions are made on the best mix of assets for a business, financial managers determine how to finance the acquisition of those assets. The two major ways to finance asset acquisition are equity financing and debt financing. **Equity financing** offers an ownership interest in the company to investors. Corporate equity financing is done through the sale of stock. **Debt financing** is the use of borrowed money to obtain needed assets. Individuals or institutions providing the debt financing become creditors who receive payment in the form of principal and interest. Creditors also have a claim on company assets if repayment is not made. Long-term debt financing is usually done by issuing bonds or signing promissory notes and mortgages. Common methods of short-term financing are obtaining *trade credit* (buying on credit from vendors and suppliers), *operating loans* from financial institutions, and *commercial paper* (short-term

teamwork

Discuss the advantages and disadvantages of equity and debt financing from the viewpoint of the company and from the viewpoint of the investor.

money market securities). Investment decisions are made by comparing alternatives based on both financial and nonfinancial advantages, disadvantages, payoffs, and risks to the business.

Asset Management The third role of financial management in business is to ensure that assets are managed as efficiently as possible. Once again, the primary goal of this activity is to maximize the return on the company's assets. Fixed assets such as buildings and equipment are maintained by operations management. Financial management is concerned with maximizing the financial life of those assets, depreciation costs, and replacement.

Managing the liquid assets of a business is an important focus of financial managers. Liquid assets are cash, accounts receivable, inventory, owned stock, and a variety of short-term investments (such as money market funds, certificates of deposit, and securities). As with the management of fixed assets, financial managers are concerned with obtaining the maximum use and value of the company's liquid assets.

checkpoint ✓

What are the three major types of investment decisions that define the work of financial managers in business?

■Financial Analysis Tools

Corporate finance is responsible for recommending the financial decisions a business should make and for the data and analyses used to make the decisions. Long-term financing decisions determine the types of capital assets needed by the company, how the assets contribute to the company's financial position, and how they will be financed. Short-term financial planning involves decisions about working capital and maintaining an appropriate balance between current assets and current liabilities. Both long- and short-term financial planning is done using the financial data, records, and reports of the business.

USING FINANCIAL RECORDS AND REPORTS

To make effective financial decisions, managers study the value of assets, liabilities, and owner's equity, the revenues and expenses generated by the business, the company's stock position, and its use of earnings. They are concerned about the changes in the financial condition and position of the business over time, its current status, and projections for the future. The primary sources of information for those decisions are

- Financial statements—balance sheet, income statement, statement of cash flow, and other supporting statements
- Records of the business for specific assets, liabilities, and owner's equity, as well as revenue and expense records
- Budgets prepared to plan capital acquisition, working capital, cash flow, and earnings

Each of the records and reports is studied for three purposes.

1. Determine current values of each of the business' important financial elements, changes that have occurred compared to prior periods, and values projected for future periods

2. Identify the relationships among the current values, the amount and nature of changes from prior periods, and how relationships will be affected based on future plans

3. Compare, when possible, these values, their relationships, and proposed changes with those of comparable businesses

BALANCE SHEET

The balance sheet is a picture of the financial condition of the business as of a specific date. The important information contained in the balance sheet is the firm's total assets and their division between long-term and current assets, the total liabilities and their division between long-term debt and current liabilities, and the owner's equity and how it is divided among types of equity as well as the value of retained earnings. **Retained earnings** are profits earned by a company that are not paid to shareholders as dividends.

The balance sheet can provide a view of the current financial position of the company. Is it financially strong or not? The strength of a company can be seen by its overall financial value. Essentially that means how much money the owners would have if the assets and liabilities were converted to cash. This question is only theoretical, because if a business attempted to convert its assets immediately, the assets would not be able to be sold at their actual value. The question also cannot be directly answered from the balance sheet because long-term assets are not carried at their actual value. Age, condition, depreciation methods, and other factors can affect their actual value. In general, the balance sheet shows whether the value of assets is much greater than the value of liabilities or not. If the value of assets is significantly higher it can be assumed that there is greater stockholder value than if liabilities are close to assets in value.

A more important measure of the current financial position is its working capital. Working capital is determined by subtracting current liabilities from current assets. A healthy working capital balance gives companies flexibility in operations. They can invest for growth, add needed assets, and respond to competitive pressures. Excess working capital can be invested for additional earnings. A company with positive working capital is attractive to investors and lenders.

A final component of the balance sheet is the owner's or shareholders' equity. It is normally made up of the value of all classes of stock and retained earnings. Retained earnings are available for financing growth, reducing debt, or investment to generate additional earnings. Of course, stockholders are interested in the earnings they receive on their investment. Earnings that have been retained have not been paid out to stockholders as dividends. A high value in retained earnings may be positive for company executives, but not for stockholders or prospective investors.

In addition to studying and comparing the current values on the balance sheet, changes in value from prior time periods is also important. Categories of assets, liabilities, and owner's equity can be compared with the same categories in previous time periods. Changes in relationships

Until recently, there were no easy ways for financial information to be moved automatically between different software applications. XBRL (Extensible Business Reporting Language) is an electronic format designed to solve the problem. It is being cooperatively developed by over 200 corporations, accounting firms, and regulators. It will allow the automatic exchange of financial information among software applications anywhere in the world via the Internet.

between assets and liabilities should be analyzed as well. Are assets, liabilities, and owner's equity changing? If so, is the change positive or negative for the financial health of the business? Is working capital improving or not? Have profits been distributed to shareholders, held in retained earnings, or used to finance needed assets or reduce debt?

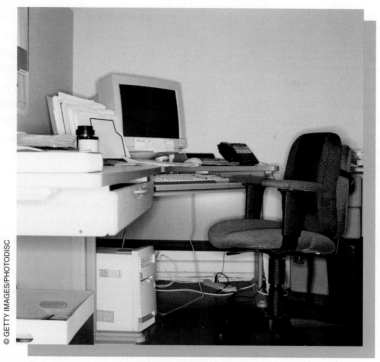

© GETTY IMAGES/PHOTODISC

The age and condition of office equipment affects its value.

INCOME STATEMENT

The income statement provides a summary and detail about the financial performance or profitability of business operations over an identified period of time. Sales and the costs to generate those sales, other sources of revenue, and all operating, administrative, and other business expenses are detailed in the income statement culminating in net earnings for the period.

Focusing on the income statement for one time period provides a limited amount of information. It shows the values and relationships among the major activities of the business that generate revenue and earnings. The cost of sales compared to net sales, the types and values of various expenses, net income before and after taxes, and the relationship of net income to revenues are important information from the income statement. This information describes the efficiency of various parts of the business' operations as well as the effectiveness of the company in converting resources into revenues and profits.

Greater understanding of the business' financial performance comes from comparisons of income statements over several time periods—monthly, quarterly, and annually. How are revenues and the sources of revenues changing? Are various costs increasing as a direct measure and as a proportion of other values? Is the business improving in profitability and in efficiency and effectiveness of generating revenues and profits? Comparing the actual amounts from the income statement with budgeted amounts helps to improve financial planning for future periods.

Comparisons with the income statements of other companies should be approached cautiously since many factors unique to the business influence the actual values of income and expense items. Comparison of the relationships of cost of sales and net income to revenue may be helpful in analyzing the competitive performance of the business.

CASH FLOW STATEMENT

Cash flow is the movement of cash into and out of a business. It demonstrates the solvency of a business. **Solvency** is the ability of an organization to meet its financial obligations as they become due. Cash flow is a very important short-term measure of a business' financial health. A business may generate a large amount of cash in a full year of operations and end with a healthy cash position. If that company has several months in which cash inflows do not meet cash payment requirements it will need to obtain short-term financing. Statements of cash flow are prepared and analyzed frequently, at least monthly.

The analysis of cash flow should be approached carefully. Cash is certainly not the equivalent of profit. A company can have a large cash balance yet be struggling with profitability. In the same way, a profitable company may have difficulty generating cash for immediate needs. As a general conclusion, a company with an increasing positive cash flow is a healthy company.

Cash is generated in one of three ways and each provides important information about company operations. *Cash from operating activities* describes the revenues from the primary work of the business such as the sale of products and services. A company needs to be able to generate a positive cash flow consistently from its operations. Some operations will not generate a positive cash balance. The cash flow can vary significantly from month to month and quarter to quarter in some businesses such as those with seasonal sales. *Cash from investing activities* describes revenues earned from purchasing or selling assets. Examples include stock ownership in other companies, securities, real estate, and the purchase and sale of long-term assets. The third category of cash is *cash from financing activities*. Those activities include cash from the sale of stock and from taking on long- or short-term debt (loans and notes). Each of the categories reports cash reductions as well as cash revenues. For example, when a retailer uses cash to purchase inventory, it reduces the cash balance for operating activities.

There is not a particular cash balance that is an indication of financial health. It is more important to look for major changes in cash flow, areas where cash balances are small or negative, and the types of activities that are generating or consuming cash. Comparing a company's cash position to the cash flow of its major competitors is meaningful since a company that is not maintaining an equivalent amount of cash may find itself in a difficult position.

checkpoint ✓

What are the primary sources of information for making financial decisions in a business?

4.3 Lesson Assessment

UNDERSTAND CONCEPTS

Determine the best answer for each of the following questions.

1. **True or False?** To maximize ownership wealth, owner's equity should increase at a rate equivalent to or better than other investments considering the nature of the business and the risk assumed by investors.

2. The ____?____ is the executive who is accountable to the board of directors for all company activities and results.
   a. CEO
   b. COO
   c. CFO
   d. CDE

3. ____?____ financing offers an ownership interest in the company, while ____?____ financing uses borrowed money to obtain capital.

4. Which of the following is *not* one of the primary sources of information for financial decisions in a business?
   a. financial statements
   b. specific financial records
   c. financial transaction data
   d. financial budgets

5. **True or False?** Retained earnings refers to the amount of cash that the business has reserved to pay accounts receivable and loans.

MAKE ACADEMIC CONNECTIONS

6. **Critical Thinking** Some people believe that corporations should have other priorities than maximizing ownership wealth. Write a two-page critical analysis paper in which you discuss the positive and negative effects that priority can have on a company.

7. **Math** In the first half of the year, a company's balance sheet showed current assets of $845,281 and current liabilities of $582,936. At the end of the year, current assets were valued at $728,910 and current liabilities totaled $523,992. Calculate the amount of working capital at the end of each accounting period and the percentage change in current assets, current liabilities, and working capital.

8. **Careers** Gather information on the differences in the job responsibilities of a corporate treasurer and controller. Create an illustration of the main differences in the daily work of the two financial managers.

9. **Technology** Use the Internet to locate a copy of a business' balance sheet, income statement, and statement of cash flow. Using each of the financial statements, identify information that provides evidence of the company's financial condition and performance. Prepare a software presentation of the financial information you selected and a description of its meaning.

4.4   Financial Analysis and Decision Making

Goals
- Recognize important financial ratios used to analyze the financial condition of a business.
- Discuss how ratios aid in financial decision making.

Terms
- financial ratios
- ratio analysis
- financial leverage
- operating income
- benchmark company

Understanding Financial Ratios

Analysis of a business' financial information over time is very important in understanding management's approach to financial planning, the company's competitive position, and its attractiveness to investors. Financial managers pay a great deal of attention to financial records and financial statements of their own company and of competing companies. One important tool for analyzing financial statements is financial ratios. **Financial ratios** are comparisons of important financial data used to evaluate business performance. The financial data used to calculate ratios comes from the company's financial statements.

Ratio analysis is the study of relationships in a company's finances in order to understand and improve financial performance. Ratio analysis includes comparing relationships in current performance, making comparisons between current and past performance, and comparing the financial

Financial managers analyze company performance using financial ratios.

© GETTY IMAGES/PHOTODISC

performance of the business with competitors' performance. Ratio analysis is used to determine areas of financial strength and weakness in order to make decisions that will strengthen the company's financial position.

There are many financial ratios that can be calculated. Financial managers and investors decide which ratios provide the information for the decisions they need to make. Ratios can be categorized in terms of the important types of financial performance and decisions in a business.

LIQUIDITY RATIOS

No matter how profitable a company is, an important measure of its financial health is its ability to pay debts on time. To be able to finance short-term debt, a company should be in a favorable liquid position. That means it either has a good cash balance or other current assets than can be converted quickly to cash without substantial loss of their value. Commonly used liquidity ratios are the current ratio and the quick ratio.

Current Ratio A measure of the ability to meet current debt.

$$\text{Current Ratio} = \frac{\text{Current Assets}}{\text{Current Liabilities}}$$

The current ratio shows how well the company is prepared to pay current liabilities, those debts that will come due within a year. Of course it is expected that a business have more current assets than current liabilities. A strong position in most industries is a ratio of 2:1. Financial managers and investors will look at the current assets to determine how quickly they can be converted to cash and the value of the assets listed on the company's balance sheet to make sure it is an accurate reflection of an asset's real cash value.

Quick Ratio (acid test) A more precise liquidity measure that reduces the value of current assets by the value of the inventory.

$$\text{Quick Ratio} = \frac{\text{Current Assets} - \text{Inventory}}{\text{Current Liabilities}}$$

Current assets cannot all be disposed of quickly in order to obtain cash to pay a company's short-term debts. Inventory is a particular problem in some industries. An inventory level is developed and maintained to meet customer needs over a period of time. If it must be liquidated quickly, prices may have to be reduced dramatically. By reducing the value of current assets by the value of the inventory, the quick ratio provides a more specific value of available current assets to cover the liabilities. The quick ratio does not have to be as high as the current ratio since the current assets used are highly liquid. A ratio of 1:1 may be acceptable in many industries.

© GETTY IMAGES/PHOTODISC

Prices may have to be reduced dramatically to liquidate inventory.

ASSET MANAGEMENT RATIOS

Businesses use their assets to make money. Assets produce sales and sales generate profits. A company that can use assets efficiently by keeping their values low in relation to sales and profits is financially stronger than companies that require a higher value of assets for the same results. Asset management ratios compare the value of key assets to sales performance.

Inventory Turnover Ratio Measures the efficiency of a company in maintaining inventory to generate sales.

$$\text{Inventory Turnover Ratio} = \frac{\text{Net Sales}}{\text{Average Inventory}}$$

A company doesn't earn money on its inventory until it is sold. The more rapidly inventory is sold, the lower the amount of financing required. If a company can maintain low inventory levels and still have high sales volume, it is using inventory very efficiently. Some industries require a lower volume of inventory or have lower total inventory costs to generate sales. Other industries require a high inventory level or the cost of inventory is quite high. A business with a low ratio should be evaluated to see if the inventory is dated or obsolete or if there is another reason that it is not being converted to sales more quickly.

Total Assets Turnover Ratio Measures how efficiently all assets generate sales.

$$\text{Total Assets Turnover Ratio} = \frac{\text{Sales}}{\text{Total Assets}}$$

The total assets turnover ratio is similar to the inventory turnover ratio except that it focuses on the efficient use of all company assets. By comparing the value of all current and fixed assets to sales, the company can determine if it has a reasonable amount of assets for the sales being produced. A low value suggests assets are not being used efficiently. Some businesses also calculate a *fixed assets turnover ratio* to examine the efficiency of land, buildings, and major equipment.

Businesses such as auto dealerships have a high cost of inventory.

Accounts Receivable Turnover Ratio Measures how quickly credit sales are converted to cash.

$$\text{Accounts Receivable Turnover Ratio} = \frac{\text{Total Credit Sales}}{\text{Accounts Receivable}}$$

The accounts receivable turnover ratio identifies how quickly customer accounts are paid. Higher ratios mean that accounts receivable are collected quickly. Long collection periods usually result in losses when older accounts are not paid. Some companies use total sales rather than total credit sales to determine the accounts receivable turnover. Another related ratio is the *average collection period ratio,* determined by dividing accounts receivable by the average daily sales. This ratio identifies how many days on average it takes to collect accounts receivable. A smaller number of days demonstrates effective credit procedures.

DEBT MANAGEMENT RATIOS

Using debt to finance some parts of a business' operations allows owners to maintain control of the business with a lower level of investment. If debt is used effectively it is possible to get a higher rate of return on the use of the money than the actual cost of the debt. Using debt financing to increase the rate of return on assets is known as **financial leverage.** As long as a company can pay its debts when they come due, a high level of debt financing is not necessarily a problem. Stockholders like to see higher debt ratios as long as the firm is profitable because they provide higher potential earnings. Creditors on the other hand get concerned when debt ratios are high because they have fewer claims on assets if the business should fail.

Debt Ratio Measures how much of a company's assets are owned by creditors.

$$\text{Debt Ratio} = \frac{\text{Total Debt (current and long-term liabilities)}}{\text{Total Assets (current and long-term)}}$$

The appropriate ratio is guided by the industry in which the company operates and the financial stability of the company. A stable company with a long operating history can carry a ratio where debt is greater than 50 percent of total assets. A new company, risky industry, or volatile economy may require a ratio where debt is one-third or one-fourth of the asset value. Related debt management ratios are total debt divided by net worth, which provides a direct comparison of equity and debt financing levels; and long-term debt divided by total assets, which shows the extent to which the company's assets are financed by long-term debt.

Times-Interest-Earned Ratio Shows how well-positioned the company is to pay interest on its debt.

$$\text{Times-Interest-Earned Ratio} = \frac{\text{Operating Income}}{\text{Total Interest Charges}}$$

A high times-interest-earned ratio means the company has a high margin of safety in being able to pay creditors. Operating income would have to decline significantly before the company would be at risk from its creditors. To be particularly cautious, the ratio could be calculated by using the total of interest and principal charges rather than just the interest. Most creditors are satisfied if interest payments are kept up to date, but to remove debt obligations a business needs adequate income to make full payments.

teamwork

Have each team member select three financial ratios he or she believes would be the most important in determining whether to purchase a company's stock. As a team compare the choices and discuss the reasons for each person's choices.

PROFITABILITY RATIOS

All of the financial decisions and operations of a company ultimately result in bottom-line performance. Both financial managers and investors are interested in tracking improvement in profitability and comparing it to the profitability of competitors as well as the results that could be obtained from other possible investments.

Profit Margin on Sales Ratio Measures the profit generated by each dollar of sales.

$$\text{Profit Margin on Sales Ratio} = \frac{\text{Net Profit}}{\text{Net Sales}}$$

The main revenues of a business come from sales. The greater the return on sales, the more efficient is the business. A lower ratio may indicate there is pressure on prices so little margin is available for profit after expenses have been paid. To assist with that analysis, companies calculate the *gross profit margin ratio* which divides gross profit by net sales. Carrying a high level of debt with accompanying interest payments could also reduce the profit margin on sales. The effect of interest and taxes on profit margins can be determined by calculating the *operating profit margin ratio*. It is determined by dividing operating income by net sales. **Operating income** is the company's earnings before interest and taxes.

Return on Total Assets Ratio Measures the company's earnings on each dollar of assets.

$$\text{Return on Total Assets Ratio} = \frac{\text{Net Income}}{\text{Total Assets}}$$

This ratio is particularly meaningful to managers, creditors, and investors because it evaluates the efficiency of the assets of the company. Does the company have too much money invested in assets based on the profit or are the assets particularly effective in generating income? When managers make plans for capital investments, consideration of the contribution to this ratio will be very important. A similar important profitability ratio is the return on equity ratio.

Most revenues of a business come from sales.

Return on Equity Ratio Measures how each dollar of investment by stockholders contributes to net income.

$$\text{Return on Equity Ratio} = \frac{\text{Net Profit}}{\text{Stockholders' Equity}}$$

MARKET PERFORMANCE RATIOS

The final set of ratios examines the overall financial performance of the business in contributing to shareholder value. The results are usually examined over several years to see changes in the company's performance. These ratios are considered by both stockholders and the board of directors as important evidence of the effectiveness of executive leadership. Market performance ratios are most useful as a way to compare the financial performance of similar companies or of several companies being considered for investment purposes.

Earnings per Share Ratio Measures the amount of profit earned by each share of stock.

$$\text{Earnings per Share Ratio} = \frac{\text{Net Income}}{\text{Number of Shares Issued}}$$

If the company issues preferred stock, the dividends paid to preferred stockholders are subtracted from net income before dividing by the number of shares of common stock issued. Preferred stockholders receive a specified dividend which affects the overall earnings for other stockholders.

Price Earnings Ratio A measure of the strength of a company's earnings in affecting the price of its stock.

$$\text{Price Earnings Ratio} = \frac{\text{Market Stock Price}}{\text{Earnings per Share}}$$

When investors decide on the price to pay for a company's stock, an important consideration is the earnings they expect to receive on their investments. A company with a strong record of earnings is likely to command a higher price than one with poor earnings.

Market to Book Ratio The relationship between the value of stock as recorded on the company's balance sheet and its value determined by the stock price.

$$\text{Market to Book Ratio} = \frac{\text{Market Price per Share}}{\text{Book Value per Share}}$$

The book value of stock is calculated by dividing the stockholder equity by the number of shares issued. Market to book ratios are often greater than 1, meaning that investors are willing to pay more for stock than it is valued by the company. One of the reasons is that accounting valuations are conservative so the value of assets listed on the balance sheet is lower than their actual value. Also, a company has intangible assets such as goodwill that affect its market value.

checkpoint ✓

What are the five categories of financial ratios?

Use Financial Ratios

Comparative financial analysis should be done using companies in the same industry with similar characteristics.

Financial ratios should be used carefully because they are only general measures of a company's financial condition. Ratios calculated from only one set of a company's financial statements can be used to examine current relationships among key financial elements. For example, ratios can illustrate the proportion of assets and liabilities that are liquid versus long-term or the proportion of assets that are owned versus financed. That one-time analysis may point out strengths of the company's current financial position and performance and, more importantly, identify areas of concern if ratios indicate potential problems with some of the proportions.

Those relationships are likely to change over time, so comparing ratios over several time periods provides a better picture of the company's financial condition. Another use of ratios is to compare specific aspects of the company's financial condition and performance with that of similar businesses. Examining industry trends in financial performance using financial ratios is an important part of financial analysis.

DEVELOP A FINANCIAL ANALYSIS PLAN

Companies follow these steps to use financial ratios in financial planning.

1. Organize financial records and statements in order to access the information needed to calculate ratios.

2. Determine the key financial ratios needed to evaluate financial performance and develop financial goals. Consider the major areas of financial decisions (asset planning, asset financing, and asset management) as well as the categories of financial information needed (liquidity, asset management, debt management, profitability, and market performance).

3. Develop baseline data by calculating the first set of ratios. Because companies maintain historic financial records and financial statements, financial ratios for prior years can be calculated to serve as baseline information. Financial ratios can be calculated for several years to study the history of the company's financial performance.

4. Identify sources of comparative information in order to compare the company's financial performance with other companies. Comparison should be made with companies in the same industry and with a select group of companies that have similar characteristics affecting financial performance, such as the corporate ownership structure, age of the company, company size defined by sales and assets, and geographic location of major operations and markets.

5. Identify benchmark companies to serve as financial performance targets. A **benchmark company** is a competitor that has historically demonstrated outstanding financial performance.

f.y.i.

Each year, Dun and Bradstreet publishes *Industry Norms and Key Business Ratios*. It analyzes financial data for hundreds of types of businesses organized by industry. The publication provides examples of typical statements as well as 14 key financial ratios for each industry.

6. Run analyses and calculate ratios regularly. Once-a-year analysis might be misleading because the financial data such as cash flow, sales, inventory level, and accounts receivable and payable may change dramatically from quarter to quarter. Complete trend analysis where ratios are monitored over an extended period of time looking for trends that indicate improving or declining financial conditions.

7. Use the results of ratio analysis as one factor in establishing financial goals and implementing changes in business activities designed to improve financial performance.

SOURCES OF COMPARATIVE INFORMATION

One of the uses of financial ratios is to compare specific aspects of a company's financial performance with other companies. Since most public corporations are required to publish financial statements at least annually, it is relatively easy to obtain comparative financial information. Investors also use financial statement information and financial ratios to evaluate companies in order to make sound investment decisions. Many companies serving investors collect and publish that information. Figure 4-3 lists several useful sources of comparative financial information for public corporations.

Industry and trade associations frequently collect information from their members and provide comparative financial performance data. Often that information is provided only to members or to others for a fee. Some organizations make information available to the public for free.

checkpoint ✓

What is a benchmark company and how is it used when analyzing financial ratios?

FIGURE 4-3

Sources of Comparative Financial Performance Information

Securities and Exchange Commission (SEC) The Securities and Exchange Commission's EDGAR (Electronic Data Gathering and Retrieval) database of all filings of public companies (www.sec.gov/edgar.shtml)

Hoover's Online A searchable database that contains detailed company and industry information including financial information, company history, competitors, and product information (www.hoovers.com/free/)

Yahoo! Finance A comprehensive online research service including corporate reports, company information, earnings, analyst reports, and several research tools (biz.yahoo.com/r/)

MSN Money A comprehensive business and investing web site providing industry and individual company information (moneycentral.msn.com/detail/stock_quote)

InvestorGuide.com Offers a wide range of current and historic information on thousands of publicly traded companies with comparisons to major competitors (www.investorguide.com/)

Analyzing Personal Financial Progress

"Why do I never seem to have enough money at the end of the month?"

"How will I ever have the money to purchase a house?"

"How can I be sure I will have enough savings to retire?"

Each of these questions reflects the importance of personal financial planning. They demonstrate on a personal level the same types of financial issues facing businesses. Being able to pay bills at the end of the month is a matter of cash flow. Financing a major purchase such as a home requires taking on long-term debt. Planning for retirement requires increasing your personal net worth. Just as executives carefully study reports to plan for growth and profitability, individuals need to maintain financial records and develop expertise in financial analysis.

Financial ratios can be an important personal financial planning tool. In order to use financial ratios you will need to prepare a balance sheet and an income statement. The following ratios provide useful information on your current status and guidance on what you can do to improve your personal financial health.

- Do you have enough cash and liquid assets to pay immediate expenses?

  Current Ratio = Current Assets ÷ Current Liabilities

- What proportion of your assets is really owned by your creditors?

  Debt to Total Assets Ratio = Total Liabilities ÷ Total Assets

- How much debt do you own compared to your net worth?

  Debt to Equity Ratio = Total Liabilities ÷ Owner's Equity

- How does your income compare to the value of your assets and your personal net worth?

  Net Return on Assets Ratio = Net Profit (income) ÷ Assets

  Net Return on Equity Ratio = Net Profit (income) ÷ Owner's Equity

Think Critically

1. What changes in the relationship of assets, liabilities, and owner's equity would indicate improving personal financial health?
2. How could an individual begin to make those financial changes?

4.4 Lesson Assessment

UNDERSTAND CONCEPTS

Determine the best answer for each of the following questions.

1. **True or False?** The financial data used to calculate ratios comes from the company's financial statements.

2. ____?____ ratios measure a company's ability to meet its short-term financial obligations and its use of working capital.
   a. liquidity
   b. asset management
   c. profitability
   d. market performance

3. A company's debt ratio measures how much of a company's assets are owned by
   a. stockholders
   b. the federal government
   c. creditors
   d. all of the above

4. **True or False?** Financial ratios should not be compared with those of competitors since each business is unique and has different financial goals.

5. Publicly held companies are required to publish their financial statements annually by
   a. the Internal Revenue Service
   b. the Securities and Exchange Commission
   c. Hoover's
   d. their industry association

MAKE ACADEMIC CONNECTIONS

6. **Math** Use one of the web sites referenced in the lesson to locate the financial statements of a corporation that is headquartered in your state. Find the information needed to calculate three financial ratios. Complete the calculations to show the company's performance for each ratio. Show all of your work.

7. **Research** Use the Internet to gather information on the use of benchmarking. Prepare a one-page report that discusses how a company can use benchmarking to improve its financial performance and the value of benchmarking as a business tool.

8. **Law** Research the Sarbanes-Oxley Act of 2002. What problems was it supposed to correct, and how has it affected businesses in a positive and negative way? Prepare a three-minute oral report on your findings.

9. **Critical Thinking** Prepare a chart in which you identify one financial ratio that you believe would provide important information for each of the following groups: company executives, shareholders, and creditors. Include a short description of each ratio and why you selected the ratio for the group.

Summary

4.1 ACCOUNTING PRINCIPLES AND PRACTICES

1. Accounting is responsible for organizing a system of financial records, recording financial data, and preparing, analyzing, and interpreting financial statements.

2. Inaccurate, incomplete, or improperly prepared accounting records and statements misrepresent the financial condition of the business and mislead those who rely on the accountants' work.

4.2 MAINTAIN AND USE FINANCIAL RECORDS

3. The components of an effective information system are users, data collection devices, data sharing devices, analysis/interpretation of information, and organizational structures and processes.

4. Financial reports and other financial information are prepared by accountants and used to draw conclusions and make decisions that affect the financial future of the company.

4.3 FINANCIAL MANAGEMENT ANALYSIS TOOLS

5. Financial management is responsible for asset management in a business. It determines the best mix of assets for a business, how to acquire them, and how to use them to get the best possible financial return from their use.

6. To make effective financial decisions, managers study the value of assets, liabilities, and owner's equity, the revenues and expenses generated by the business, the company's stock position, and its use of earnings. They are concerned about the changes in the financial condition and position of the business over time, its current status, and projections for the future.

4.4 FINANCIAL ANALYSIS AND DECISION MAKING

7. An important tool for analyzing financial statements is financial ratios. Ratio analysis includes comparing relationships in current performance, making comparisons between current and past performance, and comparing the financial performance of the business with competitors' performance.

8. Ratios calculated from a company's financial statements can be used to examine current relationships among key financial elements. Comparing ratios over several time periods provides a better picture of the company's financial condition. Another use of ratios is to compare specific aspects of the company's financial condition and performance with that of similar businesses.

Develop Your Business Language

Match the terms listed with the definitions. Some terms will not be used.

1. The ability of an organization to meet its financial obligations as they become due
2. A statement of financial performance issued at the end of a fiscal year
3. Study relationships in a company's financial resources in order to understand and improve financial performance
4. Commitment to completing all tasks thoroughly and with the highest level of quality
5. Offers an ownership interest to investors
6. Steps completed to ensure the accuracy of accounting records
7. A set of processes, people, and equipment for converting data into information
8. Profits earned by a company that are not paid to shareholders as dividends
9. Financial records for assets, liabilities, and categories of owner's equity
10. Using debt financing to increase the rate of return on assets
11. Responsible for carrying out the strategy and policy of the board of directors

a. accounting
b. accounting cycle
c. accounting transaction
d. accounts
e. accrual accounting
f. annual report
g. benchmark company
h. chief executive officer
i. chief financial officer
j. chief operating officer
k. debt financing
l. due care
m. equities
n. equity financing
o. financial leverage
p. financial ratios
q. fundamental accounting equation
r. information integrity
s. information system
t. operating income
u. ratio analysis
v. retained earnings
w. solvency

Review Concepts

12. Which of the following is a responsibility of finance rather than accounting?
    a. organizing a system of financial records
    b. recording financial data
    c. analyzing and choosing among investment alternatives
    d. preparing financial statements

13. Which of the following is the first step in the accounting cycle?
    a. financial statements are prepared
    b. a trial balance of accounts is prepared
    c. journal entries are posted in the appropriate accounts
    d. transactions are recorded in journals

14. The accounting procedure that recognizes revenues and expenses when they are incurred rather than when cash is received or spent is known as
    a. expense and revenue matching
    b. accrual accounting
    c. the accounting cycle
    d. full disclosure

Chapter 4 >>> Review   **135**

Chapter 4 Assessment

Think Critically

15. Why does a company need both accounting and finance personnel? What types of problems might occur if accounting and finance personnel do not cooperate and work effectively together?

16. Many types of activities occur in a business that result in the need for an accounting transaction. Make a list of at least ten activities that would occur in a large retail store that would result in an accounting entry. Classify each as revenue moving in, revenue moving out, or another type of activity that results in a change in an account.

17. Assume that students in your school are expected to exercise *due care* in performing their duties just as accountants are. Provide several examples of how that might affect the daily activities of students.

18. What does it mean that the board of directors represents the shareholders of a corporation? Do you believe that a focus on shareholders and profit may lead to the types of ethical problems that have been seen in some large corporations recently? Why or why not?

19. What is the difference between liquidity and profitability? How can a company that is liquid have problems with profitability? How can a profitable company have liquidity problems?

Business Financial Calculations

20. Complete the following accounting equations by calculating the missing values.

Assets	Liabilities	Owner's Equity
$1,046,326	$583,221	
	862,210	$923,010
$542,119		$210,990

21. An accountant needs to convert financial transactions completed in a foreign currency to U.S. dollars. Calculate the values of each of the following transactions using the conversion rate provided.

Foreign Currency	Transaction Amount	Conversion Rate	U.S. Dollar Value
Brazilian Real	96,054 BRL	1/0.46 USD	
EU Euro	182,250 EUR	1/1.27 USD	
Mexican Peso	23,295 MXN	1/0.092 USD	
Chinese Yuan	965,880 CNY	1/0.125 USD	

22. Calculate each financial ratio using the information provided.
   a. current ratio: current assets $865,921, current liabilities $441,020
   b. quick ratio: current assets $428,200, current liabilities $301,905, inventory $25,025
   c. accounts receivable turnover: total credit sales $986,550, accounts receivable $96,010

Analyze Cases

Use the case from the beginning of the chapter, Making the Right Move, to answer the following questions.

23. In your opinion, what changes in business and the economy led to the rapid growth and success of Accenture?

24. Why do you believe the executives and employees of Accenture wanted to separate themselves from the large accounting firm, Arthur Andersen, even before that company was hit with scandal?

25. Do you think that personnel employed as consultants by Accenture should have expertise in finance and accounting? Why or why not?

26. What is your view of the image Accenture tried to create by the choice of a new company name? Make several creative recommendations that Accenture could consider to strengthen its image.

27. Use the Internet to review Accenture's most recent financial statements. What evidence do you see that suggests Accenture is maintaining a strong financial position? What problems, if any, do you see? Provide information from the statements to support your analysis.

Portfolio Activity

COLLECT examples that illustrate the work of financial personnel in business and government. Examples can be products, forms, ads, or other materials.

CREATE a visual to show how business activities are affected by the examples you have collected. Use photos, drawings, or other types of images to show the role of financial personnel in organizations.

CONNECT your visual to other items already in your class portfolio or relate it to an important concept you have learned in another class. Make the connection by preparing a one-minute presentation on the role of financial analysis for businesses, investors, and the economy.

Stock Market Activity

Before buying stock in a business, it is useful to review its financial records. In this project you will learn about analyzing the information that can be found in the reports of a company.

Use Internet and library resources and the annual report for the company you have been studying (or select a different company).

1. Review the balance sheet and income statement of the company. How do the company's assets, liabilities, equity, revenue, expenses, and net income compare to recent years?

2. Prepare a ratio analysis using the ratios presented in this chapter. Compare these ratios to other companies in the same industry.

3. Continue to record of the company's stock value. Note any company, economic, or news developments that may affect stock prices.

Planning a Career in Accounting

The economy runs on money, and accountants maintain the financial records required by individuals, companies, and government agencies. There are four categories of accounting professionals. Public accountants work independently and perform a broad range of accounting activities for their clients. Management accountants are employed by large companies and maintain the financial records they require. Government accountants work in the public sector maintaining the records of government agencies and auditing private businesses and individuals whose activities are subject to government regulations or taxation. Internal auditors review the records of their companies to insure the accuracy and honesty of records and reports.

Employment Outlook

- Employment opportunities for accountants are excellent. Increasing financial regulations and greater government scrutiny of business financial practices require more accounting professionals.

- As economies expand worldwide, increased business activity requires more people to manage financial transactions.

- New opportunities are emerging in the area of forensic accounting, where specialized accountants scrutinize financial transactions looking for white-collar crime.

Job Titles

- Accountant
- Junior accountant
- Auditor
- Budget analyst
- Cost accountant

Needed Skills

- A B.A. in accounting, with a M.A. in accounting or an MBA either required or preferred for many jobs.
- To advance in the profession, accountants must pass the four-part Uniform CPA Examination.
- An aptitude for mathematics to be able to analyze, compare, and interpret facts and figures.
- Proficiency in accounting and auditing computer software.

What's It Like to Work in Accounting?

Maggie is getting ready again for one of the peak times for accounting employees in her company. At the end of every quarter and especially at the end of the year, no one is allowed to schedule a vacation and everyone can expect that workdays may be 10–12 hours or longer.

Maggie knew when she became an accountant that a major responsibility was to close the books at the end of each accounting period. She remembered over 20 years ago when she got her first corporate accounting job that all records were completed manually. Rather than the two weeks it currently takes to complete the process, she and her colleagues scheduled almost a month. "Thank goodness for computerized records and accounting systems," Maggie thought. But even two weeks is now thought to be too slow, and the company is working to find ways to speed the process. "Our managers can't wait that long to have the important financial information they need," Maggie's boss said at their last planning meeting.

What about you? What appeals to you about the work of accountants? What would you have to do to prepare for a career in this field?

MARKETING MANAGEMENT SERIES EVENT ROLE PLAY

The DECA Marketing Management Series Event consists of a 100-question test and a related role-play. The role-play consists of a written scenario for the student to review. The Marketing Management Series Event involves decisions related to a product or service to sell; a situation involving communications, human relations, economics or professional development; or a business management consideration. The role-play participant must translate what they have learned into effective, efficient, and spontaneous action. A list of five performance indicators specific to the scenario is included in the instructions, indicating what the participant must accomplish during the role-play.

Participants have 10 minutes to prepare notes for their response to the role-play. During the first 10 minutes of the role-play, participants will explain their solution to the role-play problem. The judge has up to five (5) additional minutes to ask questions about the role-play solution.

Role Play Situation You are the manager for Bank On Us (a national bank) in Fall Creek (a growing community with 60,000 people). The average family income in Fall Creek is $82,000 per year and 78% of the population has a college degree or some college education. Since the grand opening of your bank, eight competitors have located within a five-block radius of your bank. The Regional Bank On Us president has asked for your management strategy to train employees to sell additional customer services to current customers. The president has also asked you for a promotional plan to capture business from the large number of people moving into your community. All management strategies that you suggest must be cost effective and reap the desired results. You must demonstrate an understanding of the demographics for your community, characteristics of the target market, and top customer expectations for a bank.

Performance Indicators Evaluated

- Demonstrate a clear understanding of the bank's mission.
- Understand the demographics and banking needs of the community.
- Explain cost-effective strategies to increase business for the bank.
- Present a clear plan of action to meet the goals of the bank.
- Demonstrate a clear understanding of banking services and the competitive nature of the banking industry.

Go to the DECA web site for more detailed information.

Think Critically

1. Why is customer service such a high priority for banks?
2. Why is it important for a manager to understand the competition in the banking industry?
3. How are bank employees related to the bank's overall goals?
4. How have bank teller positions changed due to the amount of competition in the banking industry?

www.deca.org

Short-Term Financial Activities

► **Point Your [Browser]**
www.thomsonedu.com/school/busfinance

Nestlé's Liquidity and Brand Activities

With cash and other current assets of more than $30 billion, the Nestlé Company serves over two billion customers in more than 180 countries. Selling chocolate, instant coffee, baby formula, and bottled water, Nestlé is the world's largest food and beverage company with over 120 brands.

The company started in 1866 when Henri Nestlé, a pharmacist, created formula for babies. Chocolate was added in the 1920s as the company started to expand its product line. Today, with headquarters in Vevey, Switzerland, Nestlé employs about 250,000 people and has factories or operations in almost every country in the world.

More recently, Nestlé has also expanded into other product lines. The company has significant investments in Alcon Inc. (ophthalmic drugs, contact lens solutions, and equipment for ocular surgery) and in cosmetics through the L'Oréal brand.

Nestlé is the world's number one food company in terms of sales. They are the world leader in coffee, with the Nescafé brand, and one of the world's largest bottled water and baby-food producers. In 2001, Nestlé purchased Ralston Purina to become a major competitor in the pet food market. The company uses a strategy of growing existing products through innovation and renovation.

In producing its hundreds of different products, Nestlé must make extensive use of raw materials from around the world. Maintaining inventories is a significant part of the company's activities. Relationships with farmers and other suppliers require coordination among hundreds of organizations.

Production facilities must have the proper items in the proper quantities at the proper time. Payments to suppliers (cash outflows) and receipts from Nestlé's customers (cash inflows) provide the foundation for day-to-day financial activities. While a major seller of bottled water and hot chocolate, Nestlé must also be concerned with another type of *liquidity!*

Think Critically

1. What types of short-term financial activities are necessary for the Nestlé Company to be successful?
2. Conduct an Internet search for Nestlé to obtain recent information about the company's business and financial activities. What are some of the major actions the company has taken?

Goals
- Explain the steps involved in developing a cash budget.
- Identify the elements of working capital.

Terms
- cash budget
- account receivable
- working capital
- current assets
- current liabilities
- account payable
- current ratio

■ Cash Budgeting Process

"It's time to pay the rent for our office space." What if you don't have the money for this payment?

Planning cash inflows and outflows is one of the most important financial activities of an organization. A tool used for this purpose is a **cash budget**, which is an estimate of future cash receipts and cash payments for a specified period of time.

A cash budget allows a company to prepare adequately for its short- and long-term financial activities. The main benefits of a cash budget are to

- ■ Plan for cash inflows to pay operating expenses
- ■ Decide if short-term borrowing needs exist
- ■ Create an ability to pay debts on schedule
- ■ Determine potential cash shortages
- ■ Plan for long-term spending, also known as *capital expenses*

As shown in Figure 5-1, a cash budget has three main sections: cash receipts, cash payments, and cash excess or shortage.

© GETTY IMAGES/PHOTODISC

Cash sales are a major portion of some companies' cash receipts.

FIGURE 5-1

Cash Budget

Cash Receipts	January	February	March	1st Quarter Total
Cash sales	$7,200	$6,400	$6,800	$20,400
Collection on account	14,800	11,100	13,400	39,300
Other cash receipts	2,300	1,700	2,200	6,200
Total Cash Received	$24,300	$19,200	$22,400	$65,900

Cash Payments	January	February	March	1st Quarter Total
Variable expenses	$9,200	$13,600	$8,300	$31,100
Fixed expenses	8,600	8,600	8,600	25,800
Other cash expenses	1,400	2,600	900	4,900
Total Cash Payments	$19,200	$24,800	$17,800	$61,800
Cash Excess (Shortage)	$5,100	($5,600)	$4,600	$4,100

CASH RECEIPTS

Money coming into an organization is vital for business operations. These funds are necessary to pay workers and for other company expenses. Most organizations have three main sources of cash receipts.

Cash Sales Stores and other businesses sell various products and services for cash. Often these transactions are a major portion of the company's cash receipts. Cash sales for various types of organizations may include service fees, repair revenue, commission income, tuition, and donations.

Collections on Account When companies sell on credit, cash will not be received immediately. Instead, a customer pays later, maybe a month or longer. When customers buy on credit, the money owed for these purchases creates an **account receivable.** Collections on account are an important source of cash receipts for organizations that sell on credit.

The time required to collect from credit customers has to be estimated. This projection is usually based on past collection trends. For example, 80 percent of a company's customers may pay within 30 days. When preparing a cash budget, this cash receipt amount would appear in the month after the sale is made. If the company estimated sales on account of $100,000 in a month, the business would expect $80,000 to be collected on account during the next month from those sales. Of course, additional cash would be received from on account sales in prior months.

Other Cash Receipts Finally, a business may receive cash from other sources. These cash receipts can be the result of selling unneeded supplies or old equipment. A company may rent excess space to another business. At other times, money from dividends or interest earned may be received. Most often, these types of cash inflows will vary and may not be easily budgeted.

One other source of cash receipts is borrowing or issuing additional stock. When a company expects to have a shortage, a loan may be obtained or the business may seek money from additional investors.

Research studies report that poor management of cash flows is a common cause of business failure.

CASH PAYMENTS

Estimating the amount of money going out is the second major element of the cash budgeting process. Most companies and other organizations have three main types of cash payments.

teamwork

In your team, select a business in your community. Create a list of possible cash receipts and cash payments for this organization.

Variable Cash Expenses Many types of payments are different each month. For example, utilities such as electricity and water will usually change from month to month depending on usage. Utility expenses are examples of *variable* cash expenses. Other variable expenses may include wages, supplies, materials, repairs, and advertising.

Fixed Cash Expenses Some business payments are constant from month to month. Expenses such as rent, insurance premiums, or loan payments are examples of *fixed* cash expenses.

Other Cash Payments A company may encounter additional cash expenses that are not related to day-to-day operations. Some examples of these other cash payments can include interest on loans, dividends to investors, and income taxes. Payments for capital expenses, such as equipment or buildings, may be included in the cash budget. Often, companies make use of a capital budget to plan for these expensive assets.

CASH EXCESS OR SHORTAGE

When comparing expected cash receipts and cash payments, the result will be a cash *excess* or *shortage*. An excess, when receipts exceed payments, may be deposited in a bank account or invested. A cash shortage must be covered by borrowing.

Financial planning for a business usually requires that a minimum cash amount will be available at all times. This amount will depend on various factors, such as expected future cash flows and company needs. The minimum cash amount should allow a company to pay workers and other operating expenses for a month. Having an adequate cash balance allows an organization to be prepared for unexpected situations without needing to borrow. Too small a cash reserve has obvious consequences. A large cash balance

Rental of office space is a fixed cash expense.

also has costs. Maintaining a large cash reserve means these funds cannot be used for other purposes, such as inventory or new equipment.

CASH CONTROL METHODS

Cash can be a major target for theft. To assure safekeeping of an organization's money, various guidelines are suggested. These include

- Clear procedures for handling cash that are communicated to all staff members
- A system that divides responsibilities among those who receive and those who deposit cash
- A process that separates the preparation and approval of cash payments

Traditionally, companies used the principle of "deposit all cash received, and make all payments by check." This rule helped to avoid the possibility of inappropriate use of currency (bank notes and coins). Today, since many payments are made electronically, additional procedures must be developed. Various computer programs are available to manage and control cash activities. This software helps companies track receipts and payments while building in procedures that reduce opportunities for theft and fraud.

checkpoint ✓

How is a cash excess (or shortage) calculated?

■ Working Capital

In addition to cash, every organization makes use of other items in its daily financial activities. **Working capital** is the difference between current assets and current liabilities.

ELEMENTS OF WORKING CAPITAL

As shown in Figure 5-2, the working capital of a company consists of two major elements: current assets and current liabilities.

FIGURE 5-2

Working Capital

Current Assets	−	Current Liabilities	=	Working Capital
items of value that will be converted to cash within a year		amounts due to be paid within a year		
Examples		**Examples**		
cash, accounts receivable, inventory		accounts payable, taxes, short-term loans		

Current Assets Items of value in an organization that will likely be converted into cash within a year are called **current assets**. These assets commonly include cash, accounts receivable, inventory, and other liquid

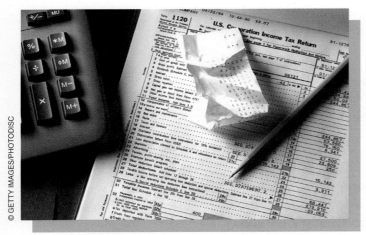

Taxes are considered a current liability.

assets. Current assets are the basis of day-to-day financial activities such as paying expenses, collecting money from customers, and selling items to generate a profit.

Current Liabilities Organizations also have debts that will be paid shortly. Current liabilities are amounts owed that need to be paid within the next year. One of the most common current liabilities is accounts payable. These are amounts owed to suppliers and others for items bought on credit by the company. Other current liabilities would include any short-term debts of the organization, such as loans coming due or taxes owed.

MANAGING WORKING CAPITAL

Working capital is an indication of the amount of net liquid assets a company has available to build its business. This number can be positive or negative. Companies with negative working capital (current liabilities exceeding current assets) may lack the funds necessary for growth. The organization may have too much short-term debt or may not be carrying enough items in inventory. In general, businesses with more working capital have a greater potential for success. These companies can expand and improve their business activities.

Too many current assets may indicate that a company is not using available funds wisely. Excess levels of inventory or not collecting accounts receivable on time suggests a weak financial situation.

To determine an appropriate level of working capital, a company might calculate its current ratio. This number, sometimes also referred to as the *liquidity ratio,* is calculated by dividing current assets by current liabilities. When this ratio is 1.0 or greater, the company has adequate current assets to cover debts coming due shortly. If the current ratio is below 1.0, the company may not be able to pay upcoming bills on time.

If a company has total current assets of $1,000,000 and its total current liabilities are $800,000, its current ratio would be 1.25 ($1,000,000 divided by $800,000). Is this an appropriate current ratio? A simple answer is "it depends!" When assessing the current ratio (or other financial ratios) of a company, consider three factors.

■ The current ratio of the company in the past few years

■ The current ratios of other companies in the same industry

■ Current economic conditions

An analysis of these items will help a company decide if it needs to increase or decrease the amount of current assets and liabilities.

checkpoint ✓

How is working capital calculated?

business in action

Cash Flows for Nonprofit Organizations

Millions of low-income, unemployed, and self-employed people are without adequate health insurance. To assist these persons, community health care facilities are formed to provide medical services.

These health care clinics are often organized on a nonprofit basis. The organizations usually have three main sources of cash inflows.

1. Grants
2. Donations
3. Fees from clients

Staff members are continually seeking funding sources and applying for grants. State and federal government agencies provide opportunities to finance health care programs for lower-income populations. Foundations also exist to serve various social needs. These charitable organizations, often funded by major corporations, provide grants to serve people in difficult economic situations.

Donations to these health clinics are tax deductible since they are tax-exempt, nonprofit organizations. Donors report amounts given to charitable organizations on federal income tax returns to reduce their taxable income. To attract additional donations, clinics often plan marketing and promotional activities. A community health fair can expand awareness of preventive health practices while also increasing potential donations.

The fees received from clients are often a minor portion of cash inflows. While patients are often charged a small amount, it still may be more than they can afford. Service is rarely denied to those not able to pay.

As health care costs rise, clinics encounter increasing operating expenses and need additional sources of cash. They also try to improve efficiency and reduce operating costs. For example, reducing inventory levels until supplies are needed can lower costs. Having supplies donated may also be a strategy.

Many nonprofit organizations do not use the most modern financial recordkeeping procedures. Efforts to use improved cash budgeting systems can help health clinics and other nonprofit organizations better plan their cash receipts and spending activities.

Think Critically

1. What additional cash flow sources might be considered by nonprofit health clinics?
2. Name other types of nonprofit organizations. Describe their cash flow sources.
3. Talk to a person who works for a nonprofit organization. Obtain information about their cash flow sources and other financial activities.

UNDERSTAND CONCEPTS

Determine the best answer for each of the following questions.

1. The major source of cash receipts for most companies is
   a. borrowing
   b. sales
   c. money from the government
   d. earnings from interest and dividends

2. The difference between current assets and current liabilities is
   a. a cash excess
   b. a cash shortage
   c. the current ratio
   d. working capital

3. **True or False?** A loan due in five years is an example of a current liability.

4. **True or False?** A current ratio of 0.94 indicates that a company has current assets that exceed its current liabilities.

MAKE ACADEMIC CONNECTIONS

5. **Communication** Interview a business owner or worker to obtain information about the common sources of cash receipts and typical cash payments in the organization.

6. **Visual Art** Prepare a flowchart (on a poster or using computer software) to present the steps for preparing a cash budget. Use a variety of visuals to present this process.

7. **Technology** Develop a spreadsheet template that could be used to create a cash budget for a business or other organization.

8. **Research** Select a company and locate its most recent annual report online.
   a. Identify the organization's current assets and current liabilities for the past two years.
   b. Calculate the company's current ratio.
   c. What conclusions can you make about the company's financial situation?

Goals
- Describe the types of inventory for a company.
- Identify costs associated with inventory and manufacturing.

Terms
- inventory
- direct materials
- work in process
- finished goods
- inventory turnover
- breakeven point
- variable costs
- fixed costs

▪ Inventory Activities

Companies that make or sell goods must have products available for shipping and selling. **Inventory** is the merchandise an organization plans to sell to customers. Sometimes called *merchandise inventory,* these items are part of a company's current assets. Like other current assets, inventory is considered to be fairly liquid.

TYPES OF INVENTORY

The inventory of a retailing company consists of products in its stores that will be sold to customers. These items may include shirts, MP3 players, packaged food, or hammers. Retailers have finished (ready-to-use) products in inventory. In contrast, as shown in Figure 5-3, a manufacturing company will have likely three types of inventory items—direct materials, work in process, and finished goods.

Direct Materials

Every manufacturing company uses parts and supplies to create the items that they sell. **Direct materials**, also called *raw materials,* are unfinished goods used by a manufacturer to create a finished product.

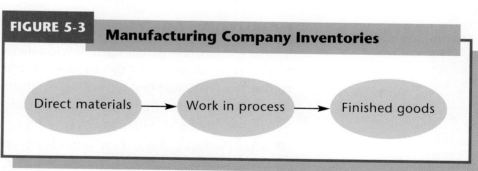

FIGURE 5-3 Manufacturing Company Inventories

Direct materials → Work in process → Finished goods

The direct materials for different types of manufacturing companies will vary. For example, a food processing company will make use of raw fruits and vegetables, packaging materials, and labels. An automobile assembly plant is likely to have over 8,000 different parts.

Work in Process During the production process, items in various stages of completion are called **work in process**. These items, also called *unfinished goods,* have value added to them. Some raw materials, labor activities, and other expenses have been used to create the work-in-process items.

Inventory turnover is an important measure of a company's success.

Finished Goods Products that have completed the manufacturing process and are ready to sell are **finished goods.** These inventory items are ready to be shipped to various wholesalers and retailers.

The sale of the final product is vital to the success of an organization. A measure commonly used to determine how many times inventory is sold and replaced is **inventory turnover.** This measure is calculated by dividing sales by inventory. The resulting ratio provides an indication of how many times the average inventory has been sold. Low turnover is an unhealthy sign, indicating excess stock and/or poor sales. The higher the turnover, the better the inventory is being managed.

INVENTORY CONTROL METHODS

Similar to cash, companies must develop methods to prevent loss of inventory. The loss of inventory can be expensive for an organization. Actions commonly recommended to control inventory loss include

- Create a system of documentation to check product type and amounts of incoming and outgoing items
- Separate responsibilities for authorizing, order preparation, and shipping of inventory
- Conduct a regular physical inventory (at least once a year) to count the actual items in stock
- Use technology such as bar codes, scanners, and radio frequency identification (RFID) to update records and monitor product locations

What are the three types of inventory that a company may have?

Cost Management

The efficient use of materials and labor to create products to sell is the main focus of many companies. In a retailing business, the desired items must be available when requested by customers. In a manufacturing business, the costs of production must be analyzed in order to operate a profitable enterprise.

INVENTORY COSTS

Holding inventory has a cost. First, an *opportunity cost* exists, since the money and space consumed by inventory cannot be used for other business needs. Next, actual financial costs of inventory also are present. These include

1. Storage and tracking costs
2. Insurance, taxes, and interest
3. Losses due to spoilage, damage, and theft

Companies face a difficult situation when deciding how many products to keep on hand. Having too large an inventory can result in higher storage costs and losses due to outdated products. In contrast, too small an inventory can result in lost sales. For example, if a restaurant runs out of a popular menu item, customers may hesitate to visit the restaurant in the future. The company must take appropriate action, which may include the need to find additional suppliers to meet customer demand.

BREAKEVEN ANALYSIS

In the production process, companies must calculate the costs of goods being manufactured. Determining the breakeven point gives the approximate sales volume required to just cover costs, below which production would be unprofitable and above which it would be profitable. Breakeven analysis focuses on the relationship between fixed cost, variable cost, and profit.

Variable Costs Labor costs, production materials, and utilities are considered variable costs. These business expenses change in proportion to the level of production. Although the variable cost per item stays the same, total variable cost increases as production levels rise.

Fixed Costs Business expenses that do not change as the level of production changes are called fixed costs. These expenses include rent, property tax, managers' salaries, and insurance. If a company pays $4,000 a month to rent a factory, that amount will be the same whether 20 radios are produced or 20,000 radios are produced.

Breakeven Point The process to calculate the breakeven point involves two steps.

Step 1 Determine the *gross profit,* which is the difference between the variable costs and the selling price. For example, a shirt costs $6 (variable costs) to make and sells for $10. The gross profit per item is $4.

Selling Price − Variable Costs = Gross Profit per Unit

$$\$10 - \$6 = \$4$$

teamwork

In your team, select a manufacturing company. Identify the variable and fixed costs for this organization.

Step 2 To obtain the breakeven point, divide the total fixed costs by the gross profit per unit. If the company has $24,000 in fixed costs, it must sell 6,000 units to cover all of its fixed costs.

$$\text{Total Fixed Costs} \div \text{Gross Profit per Unit} = \text{Breakeven Units}$$

$$\$24,000 \div \$4 = 6,000 \text{ units}$$

At the breakeven point, a company has no profit. Selling fewer items than the breakeven point will result in a loss. Sales higher than the breakeven point will result in a profit for the business.

checkpoint ✓

What common costs are associated with holding inventory?

technology topics

Radio Frequency Identification (RFID) Devices for Inventory Control

A warehouse manager must keep track of inventory. In the past, the warehouse manager would hope the items were in the warehouse or on a truck. Today, inventory can be tracked with accuracy using radio frequency identification devices (RFIDs). Through electronic tracking, RFIDs tell the exact location of inventory. This system reduces theft and misplaced inventory. Two components make up an RFID system. First, the data-loaded tag (the *transponder*) is attached to the item to be tracked. These computer chips have small antennas that transmit a unique code to an inventory control system. Second, a reader (the *transreceiver*) captures the tag's data using radio waves. This data is then sent to a computer for processing.

Manufacturers are implementing RFID tags on cases and pallets of their products for improved inventory control. Eventually, individual products will also be tagged. Retail stores will use RFID tagging. RFID systems increase efficiency within the supply chain. The ability to replenish shelves faster results in fewer out-of-stock items. It is expected that the tags will ultimately replace the current bar code technology.

What are the implications of RFID for consumers? Here is one possibility: while walking in a mall, you receive a text message on your cell phone. You are informed that a certain item is on sale at a store as you walk by that exact store. This message could be both convenient and frightening.

RFID tags in clothing labels and other products will allow tracking of both products and people. These devices are already being used for highway toll lanes, pets, library books, and baggage tracking by airlines. In the future, RFIDs may be used in homes to turn on appliances and monitor heating and security.

Think Critically

1. Discuss the benefits and concerns of RFID for companies and consumers.
2. Conduct online research to obtain additional information about RFID use in various business and home settings.

5.2 Lesson Assessment

UNDERSTAND CONCEPTS

Determine the best answer for each of the following questions.

1. Partially completed products are commonly referred to as
   a. direct materials
   b. work in process
   c. finished goods
   d. labor costs

2. **True or False?** An inventory turnover calculation will tell a company the profit on each item sold.

3. The ____?____ is the level of sales at which a product has neither a profit nor a loss.

4. ____?____ is an example of a fixed cost.
   a. electricity
   b. supplies
   c. wages
   d. rent

MAKE ACADEMIC CONNECTIONS

5. **Visual Art** Select a product. Obtain photos of the materials and labor involved in creating this item. Present your visuals in a poster or computer presentation.

6. **Geography** Use a map to identify natural resources that exist in various regions of the world. Describe what types of products could be created from these materials.

7. **Research** Conduct library or online research to determine the costs of shoplifting. What actions are commonly taken to prevent this crime?

8. **Math** Based on the following situation, calculate (a) the breakeven point and (b) the profit or loss at 2,000 units of sales:

   selling price $40, variable cost/unit $32, total fixed costs $12,600

Goals
- Describe compensation methods used by companies.
- Explain activities associated with preparing the payroll.

Terms
- compensation
- wages
- salary
- payroll record
- direct deposit

■ Employee Pay Systems

Another short-term financial activity of interest to companies and their employees is payroll. Every organization hopes to pay its workers at a level that will encourage loyalty and excellent performance. **Compensation** refers to the wages or salary along with other financial benefits paid to employees.

TYPES OF COMPENSATION

The compensation payments received by workers are commonly viewed in two major categories: direct and indirect.

Direct Compensation Money received for work efforts is referred to as *direct compensation*. These payments can include wages, salary, commissions, overtime, and bonuses. In some work settings, direct compensation can be affected by a *shift differential*. For example, in some types of work a person may be paid a higher rate for working nights or weekends.

Indirect Compensation Payments made by an employer on behalf of an employee are *indirect compensation*. These items commonly include various employee benefits such as insurance, pension funds, and educational expenses.

COMPENSATION METHODS

The methods used to determine the amount a person is paid can vary. In some companies workers are paid on the basis of an hourly rate. In other organizations, employees may earn a percentage of the sales they make.

Wages and Salary Many employees are paid on an hourly basis. **Wages** refer to the earnings of workers calculated on an hourly basis. A person's total earnings are determined by the hourly rate of pay multiplied by the number of hours worked. **Salary** refers to earnings calculated on the basis of a time period, usually weekly, bi-weekly, or monthly.

Piece Rate In some manufacturing situations, workers may be paid on a *piece rate*. Earnings are determined on the basis of each unit of output. For example, in an electronics assembly plant, workers may be paid 45 cents for each item assembled, and they can produce between 40 and 45 items per hour. These workers would earn between $18 and $20.25 an hour.

IMAGE SOURCE

Some businesses offer fitness programs as an employee benefit.

teamwork

In your team, prepare a list of the benefits and limitations of hourly wages compared to a weekly or monthly salary. Consider this issue from the perspective of both the worker and the company.

Commission In various professions, compensation may be based on sales volume. *Commission* is compensation earned by salespeople or others as a percentage of sales. Some retail store sales staffs and many field sales personnel earn a living based on commission.

A person who only works on commission may receive a *draw*. This amount is an advance in earnings to provide the worker with an income to meet necessary living expenses. The amount of the draw is eventually subtracted from future commission earnings.

EMPLOYEE BENEFITS

As part of a compensation package, most businesses provide employees with various additional benefits. The most common benefits are insurance (health, life, and disability), paid or unpaid vacation time, sick leave, continuing education expenses, and retirement plan deposits.

In an effort to recruit and retain quality employees, companies may offer other types of benefits. Such benefits might include fitness and wellness programs, discounts for company products and services, mileage, transportation and parking fees, and participation in community service during company time.

checkpoint ✓

How do wages differ from salary?

■Payroll Activities

Maintaining payroll records and preparing payments is an ongoing financial activity. While time cards were often used in the past to determine pay, today most payroll procedures are processed electronically.

PAYROLL PREPARATION AND TAXES

A **payroll record** is the form that documents each employee's pay history. This form also includes each employee's name, Social Security number, address, other personal information, tax information, and eligibility for benefits.

The payroll record provides complete information of an employee's *gross pay,* which is the person's total earnings. In addition, a record of the *net pay* is also maintained. Net pay is the amount, after various deductions, which is paid to each employee. The payroll record is also used to keep track of current and year-to-date taxes and other deductions.

Income Taxes
The federal government of the United States requires that federal income tax be withheld from workers' pay. This money is then sent to the U.S. Treasury. Each year, in April, taxpayers file their federal tax return to determine if they owe additional money or if they will receive a refund.

All but seven states have a state income tax. Deductions for this tax are also taken from the current earnings of workers. Many cities, such as Cincinnati, Detroit, Grand Rapids, and New York City, have a city income tax.

Social Security and Medicare
In 1934, Congress created the Social Security system to provide retirement benefits to eligible workers. This deduction may be listed as FICA (Federal Insurance Contributions Act). FICA also funds disability insurance and survivor benefits through Social Security.

In 1965, Medicare was created to provide health insurance for people aged 65 and older. Payroll deductions for this program also fund health coverage for eligible disabled people under age 65.

Payroll taxes cover Social Security and Medicare benefits.

Other Voluntary Deductions In addition to the required government payroll deductions, employees often opt for other deductions that provide various benefits. These voluntary deductions might include

- Health or life insurance
- Savings for future personal use
- Deposits to retirement funds
- Charitable donations
- Union dues or dues for other employee organizations

Employer Taxes In addition to the taxes deducted from an employee's earnings, other taxes are the responsibility of the business. Unemployment insurance is a cooperative program between the federal and state governments. This coverage is financed through federal and state employer payroll taxes.

The Federal Unemployment Tax Act (FUTA) requires companies to pay money to fund state workforce agencies. In addition, FUTA covers the costs of unemployment benefits and job service programs in all states. State unemployment taxes are paid to state agencies and are used to pay benefits to eligible unemployed workers.

Employers also match the amount deducted from employee earnings for FICA and Medicare. For every dollar subtracted from workers' pay for these taxes, the company pays a dollar. That amount is then sent to the federal government for these retirement and insurance programs.

PAYROLL PAYMENT METHODS

The methods used by companies to distribute payroll funds can vary from traditional systems to electronic programs.

Check Payments Traditionally, workers have been paid by check. These documents most often included a *payroll stub,* which provided employees with a summary of their total pay and deductions for the current pay period as well as for the year to date.

Direct Deposit Today, people are writing fewer checks and using more online payment services. With the expansion of electronic banking, most employers offer **direct deposit.** Direct deposit is a system that electronically transfers net pay into an employee's bank account. The employee still receives a payroll stub, but it also can be provided electronically.

Prepaid Bank Cards In the United States, over 20 million people do not have access to bank accounts. These are mostly lower-income workers and recent arrivals to the country. To assist these employees, some companies issue a *prepaid bank card* with the amount of the person's pay. Also called *stored value cards,* these electronic devices may be used to obtain cash and make purchases at stores.

checkpoint ✓

Name common payroll taxes encountered by workers and employers.

5.3 Lesson Assessment

UNDERSTAND CONCEPTS

Determine the best answer for each of the following questions.

1. Which compensation method is used in a factory that pays workers an hourly rate?
   a. wages
   b. salary
   c. piece rate
   d. commission

2. **True or False?** Employee benefits are considered to be indirect compensation.

3. An example of a voluntary payroll deduction is
   a. federal income tax
   b. Medicare
   c. savings account deposit
   d. Social Security

4. **True or False?** In most states, taxes for unemployment insurance are deducted from a worker's pay.

MAKE ACADEMIC CONNECTIONS

5. **Economics** Research changes in average earnings and the cost of living for workers during the past five years. Prepare a graph comparing the data you obtained.

6. **Research** Survey 10 people about the types of taxes they pay. Ask them which type of tax they think is most fair for people in our society.

7. **History** In the past, many workers were paid with cash. Explain some of the problems associated with this type of payroll payment method.

8. **Technology** Conduct research about new developments with stored value cards and prepaid bank cards. What types of electronic payroll systems may be used in the future?

Goals
- Explain the elements of a credit policy.
- Describe accounts receivable management activities.

Terms
- credit policy
- capacity
- unsecured loan
- credit terms
- aging of accounts receivable

▪ Credit Policy

Sales on account are very common in most businesses. Extending credit to customers is an activity offered by nearly every company. When deciding who can buy on account, organizations create a **credit policy**, which details the guidelines used for approval of credit customers.

WHO WILL BE GRANTED CREDIT?

Most organizations that provide credit consider three main factors when deciding who will be allowed to buy on credit.

1. The ability of the borrower to repay money owed is known as **capacity**. This potential is based on income and other cash sources of the credit applicant. Also considered is the amount of additional debt the borrower currently owes.

© GETTY IMAGES/PHOTODISC

Items of value such as land, a house, or a car can be used as collateral.

2. In some credit situations, a specific asset, known as *collateral,* is used to secure a loan. Common items of value such as stocks, bonds, real estate, or vehicles are used for this purpose. They can be sold, if necessary, in order to satisfy the debt. Many credit situations are **unsecured loans**, which have no specific collateral. Unsecured credit relationships involve a higher risk than those with collateral.

3. The past credit history of the borrower is also considered when deciding whether to grant credit. Information on the credit rating of a person or company may be obtained from a credit reporting agency.

WHAT ARE THE CREDIT CONDITIONS?

Once a person is accepted to buy on account, a company must decide how soon the funds must be repaid. **Credit terms** are the conditions under which credit is extended by a lender to a borrower. These conditions address various elements of the agreement, such as

- Whether the buyer or the seller will pay delivery changes
- The number of days in which payment is expected
- Penalty or interest for late payments
- Discounts for early payments

CREDIT TERMS

Credit terms are often expressed as

2/10, n/30

The 2 is the percentage of discount (2 percent) offered to the customer if the invoice is paid within 10 days. The n/30 indicates that the full (or net) amount is due within 30 days.

For example, a $100 sale on May 1 would allow a customer to pay only $98 ($100 minus $2 discount) if the invoice is paid by May 11 (within the 10-day discount period). If payment is not made by May 11, the full amount ($100) is due by May 31.

When the credit terms do not involve a discount, the terms could be expressed as n/30 or n/60. In these situations, the full amount would be due in 30 or 60 days.

A customer who has not been approved for credit in advance is expected to pay cash upon delivery of the good or service. Sometimes the terms of a sale may require payment prior to delivery.

teamwork

With your team, describe a situation in which a person would likely be granted credit and a situation in which a person might be denied credit.

checkpoint ✓

What three factors are commonly considered when deciding whether to grant credit?

■Receivable Management

After a customer makes a purchase and is sent an invoice, an account receivable is created. At this point, the customer must follow the terms of the sale. If payment is due within 30 days and is not received, some actions may be necessary.

CREDIT MANAGEMENT ACTIVITIES

A credit manager continually monitors a company's receivables to avoid uncollectible accounts. This process actually starts as soon as credit is granted.

When reviewing past due accounts, a credit manager may use a process called **aging of accounts receivable.** This activity involves categorizing accounts receivable based on how long they have been due. The first category would be "Current" or "Not Past Due," which are the accounts that are still within the original credit period, such as 30 days. Other categories commonly used are "30 Days Overdue," "31–60 Days Overdue," and "Over 61 Days Overdue." This process can help a credit manager make wiser decisions when granting credit. Having many past due accounts usually indicates a need to reassess the process being used to sell on account.

The longer an account is overdue, the less likely it will be collected. At some point, an account may be considered *uncollectible*. These bad debts then become expenses of the company.

DEBT COLLECTION PROCEDURES

Once an account is past due, credit managers may take one or more of these actions.

1. Contact the debtor to remind the person of the amount that is due.

2. Provide a stronger reminder; encourage the customer to contact the company to make payment arrangements. Most companies will negotiate a settlement since some amount received is better than none.

3. Consider legal action (such as small claims court) or use of a debt collection agency.

© GETTY IMAGES/PHOTODISC

Companies evaluate customers according to an established credit policy.

To protect customers from unreasonable debt collection actions, the Fair Debt Collection Practices Act was enacted in 1978. This legislation protects a person from inappropriate actions by debt collectors; for example

- A person may not be contacted by a debt collector at unreasonable times or places, such as before 8 a.m. or after 9 p.m.

- A person may not be called at a place of employment, if contact at work is prohibited by an employer.

- The debt collector may not tell anyone other than the debtor and the debtor's attorney that money is owed.

checkpoint ✓

What information is provided by the aging of accounts receivable?

¥£€$ finance around the world

A Muslim Perspective on Borrowing

Riba is the Arabic term for interest. In the holy book of Islam, the Qur'an, charging Riba is forbidden. Riba is viewed as having three components.

1. The amount that exceeds the sum borrowed—the finance charge
2. This excess amount in relation to the time of the loan
3. The credit transaction requiring repayment of this predetermined surplus (finance charge)

These elements jointly make up a situation in which Riba exists. Any credit transaction or borrowing which has these elements is considered a transaction of Riba.

The Qur'an and Ahadith (teachings of the Prophet Mohammed) are very clear about interest. "Allah will deprive usury of all blessing, but will give increase for deeds of charity" (Qur'an 2: 276). To keep from paying Riba, Muslims are encouraged to follow these money management guidelines.

- Use debit cards instead of credit cards to avoid paying more than the actual price of the product
- Cancel one or more credit cards currently in use
- Create and carefully follow a specific shopping list
- Develop a careful plan for spending and for paying off credit accounts
- Work with a friend for support with these activities

Obedience in carefully following these actions will allow a person to avoid the future trap of Riba.

Think Critically

1. What are wise actions related to the use of credit?
2. Conduct an Internet search to obtain information on the use of credit and attitudes toward borrowing in different cultures.

5.4 Lesson Assessment

UNDERSTAND CONCEPTS

Determine the best answer for each of the following questions.

1. An unsecured loan is
   a. a loan paid within 30 days
   b. a loan that has no collateral
   c. a loan to a customer who has no credit history
   d. a loan for which a government agency is the lender

2. **True or False?** Credit terms refer to the price of a product when buying on account.

3. An invoice with the credit terms 1/15, n/45 would mean a customer may qualify for a ____?____ discount within a certain time period.
   a. 1 percent
   b. 15 percent
   c. 45 percent
   d. no discount is available

4. **True or False?** Many past due accounts usually indicates that a company is very selective in granting credit.

MAKE ACADEMIC CONNECTIONS

5. **Culture** Talk to a person who has lived in another country. Ask that person about common procedures used when selling to customers. To what extent is credit used? What are common payment methods?

6. **Research** Locate a sample credit card application or a document used to apply for a loan. How are various information items on the form used to decide if a person will be granted credit?

7. **Communication** Talk with a person who works in extending credit or is involved with collection of accounts about the hardest part of the job. Report to the class the main findings of your conversation.

8. **Law** Conduct online research to obtain additional information about the Fair Debt Collection Practices Act. Prepare a short summary of your findings.

Summary

5.1 CASH BUDGET AND WORKING CAPITAL

1. A cash budget is prepared by (1) estimating cash receipts, (2) estimating cash payments, and (3) calculating the cash excess or shortage.

2. Working capital is the difference between current assets and current liabilities. Current assets include cash, accounts receivable, and other liquid assets. Current liabilities are amounts to be paid in the next year.

5.2 INVENTORY MANAGEMENT

3. A manufacturing company will usually have three types of inventory items: direct materials, work in process, and finished goods. Inventory control methods can include a system of documentation, separate responsibilities, a regular physical inventory, and use of technology.

4. Common inventory costs include storage and tracking costs, insurance and taxes, and losses due to spoilage, damage, and theft. Production companies use a breakeven analysis to find the profit of products.

5.3 PAYROLL MANAGEMENT

5. Direct compensation includes wages, salary, commission, overtime, and bonuses. Indirect compensation includes payments made by an employer on behalf of an employee for items such as insurance, pension funds, and educational expenses.

6. Common payroll deductions include federal, state, and city income tax; Social Security and Medicare taxes; and voluntary deductions for items such as health or life insurance, savings, deposits to retirement funds, charitable donations, and union dues.

5.4 CREDIT SALES AND RECEIVABLES

7. Credit is granted to customers on the basis of (1) capacity, the ability of the borrower to repay money owed; (2) collateral, a specific asset used to secure a loan; and (3) the past credit history of the borrower. Credit terms are the conditions under which credit is extended by a lender to a borrower. These terms clearly communicate if the buyer or the seller will pay delivery changes, penalties or interest for late payments, and discounts for early payments.

8. Credit managers use aging of accounts receivable to manage past due accounts. Debt collection procedures are used to reduce the uncollectible accounts of a company.

Develop Your Business Language

Match the terms listed with the definitions. Some terms will not be used.

1. Wages or salary along with other financial benefits paid to employees
2. Conditions under which credit is extended by a lender to a borrower
3. Products that have completed the manufacturing process and are ready to sell
4. Amounts owed that need to be paid within the next year
5. Number calculated by dividing current assets by current liabilities
6. Loans that have no specific collateral
7. Business expenses that do not change as the level of production changes
8. Money owed for the purchases customers buy on credit
9. The difference between current assets and current liabilities
10. Unfinished goods used by a manufacturer to create a finished product
11. Manufactured items in various stages of completion
12. Amounts owed for items bought on credit

a. account receivable
b. accounts payable
c. aging of accounts receivable
d. breakeven point
e. capacity
f. cash budget
g. compensation
h. credit policy
i. credit terms
j. current assets
k. current liabilities
l. current ratio
m. direct deposit
n. direct materials
o. finished goods
p. fixed costs
q. inventory
r. inventory turnover
s. payroll record
t. salary
u. unsecured loan
v. variable costs
w. wages
x. work in process
y. working capital

Review Concepts

13. In a cash budget, a shortage would occur when
    a. cash receipts exceed cash payments
    b. working capital is declining
    c. current assets are less than current liabilities
    d. cash payments exceed cash receipts
14. An example of a current asset is
    a. a building
    b. equipment
    c. inventory
    d. land
15. In a breakeven analysis, ____?____ would be considered a variable cost.
    a. a manager's salary
    b. insurance
    c. rent
    d. utilities
16. indirect compensation includes
    a. commission
    b. employee discounts
    c. overtime pay
    d. wages and salary
17. Credit terms commonly include the
    a. price of the product
    b. time of the credit period
    c. name of lending company
    d. amount of taxes on the sale

Think Critically

18. A cash budget and an income statement have many similarities. What are the main differences between these two documents?

19. When an organization is preparing a cash budget and expects to encounter a shortage, what actions might it take to avoid the shortage?

20. Create a list of procedures you would recommend to a company to prevent the theft of cash and inventory.

21. In the breakeven analysis, fixed costs are constant. Over time, these expenses can change. Give some examples of fixed costs that change over time.

22. Describe the pay system that you believe would be the best for both the workers and the company.

23. What do you believe is the most important factor to be considered when deciding to grant credit to a customer? Explain your answer.

Business Financial Calculations

24. In preparing its cash budget, Ying Electronics projected cash receipts of $47,890 and cash payments of $41,674. Do these amounts represent a cash excess or shortage? For what amount?

25. Hamilton Auto Parts has current assets of $789,500 and current liabilities of $688,560. What is the amount of working capital? What is the company's current ratio?

26. Marge Rodriguez earns $14 per hour plus time and a half for any hours she works over 40 in a pay period. In a recent pay period, she worked 46 hours.
    a. How much is her regular pay?
    b. How much is her overtime pay?
    c. If Marge had $172 deducted for income taxes and $54 for Social Security and Medicare, what is the amount of her net pay?

27. Manor Industries issued an invoice to a customer on March 17 for $560 with credit terms of 3/10, n/45.
    a. If the customer wishes to take the discount, by what date must the invoice be paid?
    b. If the customer takes the discount, what amount will be paid?
    c. if the discount is not taken, by what date must this invoice be paid?

28. In preparing an aging of accounts receivable report, the credit manager determined that 0.04 percent of amounts due were more than 90 days overdue. If the company had accounts receivable of $456,773, what amount was more than 90 days overdue?

Analyze Cases

Use the case from the beginning of the chapter, Nestlé's Liquidity and Brand Activities, to answer the following questions.

29. Describe various economic, social, and political factors that might affect the cash flows of Nestlé.

30. What actions might be necessary for Nestlé to maintain needed levels of inventory?

31. Locate Nestlé's most recent annual report. Calculate its working capital and current ratio for the two most recent years. Be sure to convert the amounts from Swiss francs (CHF) to U.S. dollars. What conclusions can you make about the results?

32. Nestlé often buys smaller food companies and sells off weaker product lines. Identify a company that Nestlé might purchase or select an existing brand of Nestlé that might be sold to another company. Based on your analysis of current assets and liabilities, explain why the new company should be purchased or the existing brand should be sold.

Portfolio Activity

COLLECT information about the current assets of a company (cash, receivables, inventory). This information could be in the form of an article, advertisements, Web resources, photos, or some other actual items.

CREATE a summary table or other visual to report on the assets selected. Use photos, other pictures or ads, other actual items, and drawings to illustrate various types of current assets commonly used by businesses and other types of organizations.

CONNECT your visual to other aspects of finance, the economy, and society, or relate it to an important concept you have learned in another class. Make the connection by preparing a short essay or oral presentation about the relationship of current assets to other topic areas.

Stock Market Project

Stock prices are affected by a variety of financial activities. An analysis of a company's inventory, receivables, and other aspects of short-term finances can provide information about the current performance and future potential of the organization.

Use Internet and library resources to research the company you have been studying (or select a different company).

1. List the amounts of the company's cash, inventory, receivables, and other current assets for the two most recent years available.

2. Obtain the amount of current liabilities for the two most recent years.

3. Calculate the company's working capital and current ratio.

4. Discuss how these findings may affect the stock value of the company.

Planning a Career in Inventory

Transportation, Distribution & Logistics

They are needed everywhere...in stores, factories, hospitals, and government offices. Inventory workers make sure the correct items are in the right place at the right time.

Inventory employment offers a range of work opportunities. You may be involved in ordering parts or supplies. Or, you might be responsible for creating and implementing a system to prevent theft.

Most inventory workers have interactions with supply chain members, including suppliers, shipping companies, distributors, and retailers. Knowledge of every aspect of business is very useful.

Employment Outlook

- The fastest growth in employment will be in technology-based inventory positions.
- About one-third of procurement clerks work for federal, state, and local governments.
- Over 40 percent of purchasing agents are employed in wholesaling and manufacturing.

Job Titles

- Procurement clerk
- Purchasing agent
- Buyer
- Inventory control manager
- Warehouse manager
- Loading dock supervisor
- Director of purchasing
- Materials manager
- Distribution manager
- Overseas shipping manager

Needed Skills

- Prospective employees with knowledge in marketing, retailing, logistics, international trade, and other business fields will have the best job possibilities.
- Communication skills are important when working with individuals both within and outside your organization.
- Skill with computer application software and other technology is vital.
- Strong ability to organize and schedule people and resources is important.
- Education beyond high school is required for most managerial and advanced positions.

What's It Like to Work in Inventory?

Just as you arrive at work, a customer calls to ask if the new products have been shipped. A few minutes later, the southern region sales manager stops by for information about expected prices for incoming goods. Still later, one of your staff reports that the wrong part was received—all 7,000 of them.

Work in inventory provides a great variety of activities. Your ability for creative problem solving along with a calm approach will help to reduce the stress that will almost always be present.

What about you? What aspect of inventory careers might be of interest to you? How might you best prepare for a career in this field?

FINANCIAL ANALYSIS TEAM DECISION MAKING EVENT

The Management Team Decision Making Events provide opportunities for participants to analyze a combination of elements essential to the effective operation of a business in the financial industry. Each management team is composed of two members. Team members will be given a decision-making case study situation involving a management problem in the financial industry. A list of seven performance indicators specific to the scenario is included. Participants must accomplish these tasks during the role-play.

Each team will have 30 minutes to study the situation and organize their analysis using a management decision-making format. Participants may use notes taken during the preparation time. Participant teams will meet with the judge for a 15-minute interview. The team will spend not more than 10 minutes to describe their analysis of the situation. Both members of the team must participate. The judge will spend the remaining 5 minutes questioning the participants about their plan. Each participant must respond to at least one question. Participants are allowed to use a personal laptop computer and/or a handheld digital organizer.

You have been hired by a new upscale department store as a financial consultant to make suggestions for increasing sales. Currently the store pays all employees an hourly wage. The store has asked you to develop a commission plan that will result in employees selling more merchandise. The store is also considering offering their own credit card in order to increase sales. You must cover the strengths, weaknesses, opportunities, and threats of both strategies that the store is considering. Then you must make a solid recommendation for increasing sales. Your strategy should be based upon the store's budget, payroll management system, and inventory management. You are also in charge of presenting the new commission plan to employees. Many of the employees are resistant to this change.

Performance Indicators Evaluated

- Understand the importance of accurate payroll records.
- Explain the value of paying employees commission.
- Determine strategies to increase sales.
- Analyze current sales records to make recommendations for the future.
- Explain the advantages and risks associated with credit sales.
- Understand strategies to increase sales.
- Communicate a new payroll plan that involves commission to employees.

Go to the DECA web site for more detailed information.

Think Critically

1. Why must a company look at current financial records before making changes to reach new financial goals?
2. Why would employees resist earning commission?
3. Why does offering a store credit card increase possible sales?
4. What new threats are associated with offering the store credit card?

www.deca.org

Long-Term Financial Activities

▶ **Point Your** [Browser]
www.thomsonedu.com/school/busfinance

Case STUDY

Capital Spending in New York City

Bridges and road repairs. School buildings and libraries. Buses and fire trucks. This is just a partial list of New York City's capital spending. Each year, the city spends more than $4.5 billion for new and replacement items. In New York City, a capital project is defined as the construction, reconstruction, acquisition, or installation of a physical public improvement. The value must exceed $35,000 and the project should have a useful life of at least five years. Some of the city's capital spending is shown below.

What $10 Million in Capital Spending Buys	
Housing	100 units of housing for the homeless mentally ill
Transit	6 high technology subway cars/25 hybrid diesel-electric buses
Sanitation	54 dual-bin recycling trucks
Fire	11 ladder trucks
Education	7 classrooms
Transportation	Resurfacing 100 lane-miles of city streets
Environment	8,000 feet of water mains (new construction)

The day-to-day operating expenses of the city are funded by taxes, *general obligation* municipal bonds, and other government revenue sources. Many capital projects are financed by another type of municipal bond, the *revenue bond*. Repayment of these bonds occurs using the revenue from the specific project, such as a toll bridge or a sports stadium. In addition, a city may receive a state, federal, or private grant to help finance capital projects that provide public benefits.

A city as large as New York will always have more needs than funding. To best serve the people, a capital budget priority process is used. The procedure starts with public hearings held by the city's 59 Community Boards. Then, various city agencies submit estimates of their capital needs. After the mayor presents the preliminary capital budget, additional public hearings are held. Next, the city council holds hearings to develop recommendations on the mayor's proposal. After revisions, the capital budget is adopted by the city council.

Think Critically

1. Describe examples of business and government capital projects in your community.
2. Conduct an Internet search to obtain information on: (a) the capital budgeting activities of governments, and (b) the current value of municipal bonds issued by New York City.

Goals
- Describe types of capital projects used in business.
- Explain factors that affect capital spending decisions.

Terms
- capital project
- intellectual property
- mutually exclusive projects
- complementary projects

■Capital Spending Activities

Each day, capital assets serve an important role in your life. The food you eat is processed with equipment. Your classes are in a school building. You may drive or ride in a motor vehicle. A **capital project** involves the construction or purchase of a long-term asset, such as buildings and equipment. These items are also called *capital expenditures,* and the process may be referred to as *capital spending.* Every organization needs and uses five main types of capital projects.

REPLACEMENT PROJECT

Buildings get old. Aging machinery can no longer be repaired. When capital projects wear out, companies must replace them. Failure to replace items in a timely manner can result in higher costs, lost sales, and reduced profits.

© GETTY IMAGES/PHOTODISC

Buses are an example of a capital expenditure.

COST-SAVING PROJECT

New technology makes it possible for companies to obtain equipment that reduces operating costs. Computerized temperature controls can reduce energy bills in offices and factories. Robotics may increase production efficiency.

NEW PRODUCT OR NEW MARKET

Companies are continually attempting to expand profits through new products or new customers. When a new product is manufactured, revised or additional equipment is usually needed. This type of capital spending occurs in hopes that company sales and profits will increase.

New technology can increase production efficiency.

Many of today's new products involve **intellectual property**, which are *intangible assets* used by companies. These assets commonly include trademarks, brand names, copyrights, patents, and software licensing agreements. For many businesses, intellectual properties are some of their most valuable assets. Companies such as Coca-Cola, Disney, and McDonald's depend on their famous names and characters to attract customers and sell products.

When a company decides to sell in a new market, capital spending will likely be required. New stores, office space, or factories are needed in the new geographic region.

GOVERNMENT-REQUIRED PROJECT

Every organization faces government regulations that require compliance. For example, to reduce pollutants in the air or water supply, a production company may be required to use certain equipment. To provide for employees or customers with special needs, an organization may be required to adapt doorways, stairs, or work areas.

SOCIAL BENEFIT PROJECT

Finally, a company may undertake a project not directly related to its business operations. In an effort to improve employee satisfaction, a decision might be made to build health club facilities or improve parking. Community involvement may include developing a recreational area for young people.

teamwork

Select a company. In your team, identify an example of each type of capital project for this company.

checkpoint ✓

Describe the five main types of capital projects.

■Project Selection Factors

As a company considers certain capital projects, different circumstances may affect these choices. For example, the high cost of one project may result in rejecting several others. Selecting a certain project might create a need for other actions by the company.

The decision to buy new trucks may result in the need to build a new loading dock to accommodate them.

INDEPENDENT PROJECTS

Quite often, the capital projects being considered are *independent,* meaning that the projects are not affected by each other. However, other limitations may be present. Capital limitations are present in almost every decision-making situation. Organizations do not have unlimited funds for their capital spending activities, so choices among several projects must be made.

MUTUALLY EXCLUSIVE PROJECTS

The selection of a project can sometimes affect other choices. **Mutually exclusive projects** involve situations in which the acceptance of one project does not allow acceptance of others. For example, land used for a warehouse will not be available to build additional office space. A capital decision to use factory space for manufacturing clothing will not allow this same space to be used for a food processing facility.

COMPLEMENTARY PROJECTS

The selection of one capital project can result in a need to accept another one. **Complementary projects** exist when two or more projects are dependent on one another. For example, a decision by a delivery company to buy new energy-efficient trucks may result in the need to build a new loading dock to handle the different design of the new vehicles.

How do mutually exclusive projects differ from complementary projects?

6.1 Lesson Assessment

UNDERSTAND CONCEPTS

Determine the best answer for each of the following questions.

1. **True or False?** Capital spending refers to payment by companies for current operating expenses.

2. Purchase of new machinery to substitute for outdated equipment is an example of a ____?____ project.
   a. cost-saving
   b. replacement
   c. government-required
   d. social benefit

3. **True or False?** Mutually exclusive projects allow a company to accept more than one project.

4. Which of the following would be complementary projects?
   a. a delivery truck and a customer service office
   b. a day care center and a new factory
   c. a reconstructed bridge and highway resurfacing
   d. updated computers and community assistance vehicles

MAKE ACADEMIC CONNECTIONS

5. **Visual Art** Create a poster or computer presentation with photos and other visuals representing the five main types of capital projects.

6. **Economics** Research capital spending to determine how this economic activity creates jobs and other economic benefits. Prepare a short written or oral summary.

7. **Law** Research government regulations that can result in a need for capital spending by companies.

8. **Environment** Observe government-required and social-benefit capital projects in your community that help the environment. What other types of capital projects could be beneficial for reducing air and water pollution?

6.2 Capital Budgeting Process

Goals
- Discuss the steps in the capital budgeting process.
- Explain factors that affect the cost of capital.

Terms
- cost of capital
- cost of debt
- cost of equity
- optimal capital structure
- weighted average cost of capital (WACC)

■ Making Capital Decisions

Capital spending, the purchase of long-term assets, is vital for the current and future success of every organization. Buildings, production equipment, computers, trucks, and machine tools are just a few of the capital items commonly used by companies.

The method for choosing capital projects is a significant task for managers. *Capital budgeting* is the process of selecting long-term assets, such as equipment and buildings. As shown in Figure 6-1, this process may be viewed in five steps.

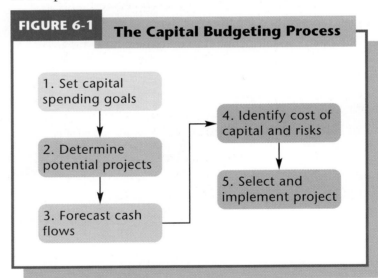

FIGURE 6-1 The Capital Budgeting Process

1. Set capital spending goals
2. Determine potential projects
3. Forecast cash flows
4. Identify cost of capital and risks
5. Select and implement project

1. SET CAPITAL SPENDING GOALS

The capital projects selected by a company should be influenced by organizational goals. The goals of a business may include expanding sales, reducing costs, and increasing profits. Financial theory emphasizes that the goal of a business should be to *maximize the value of the firm*. This objective is commonly measured by the market value of the company's stock. Increasing a company's market value involves both short-term profits and long-term growth. Every capital decision should increase the company's attractiveness among current owners and potential future investors.

For nonprofit organizations, capital spending goals are slightly different. For these groups, capital projects will be chosen to meet goals such as improved community services, reduced operating costs, and expanded visibility to attract additional donations.

2. DETERMINE POTENTIAL PROJECTS

After an organization's capital spending goals are clearly identified, different projects will be considered. For example, if providing customer service is a priority, spending for new computers to answer customer questions may be appropriate. If improving distribution is a necessity, a new warehouse or additional delivery trucks might be considered.

3. FORECAST CASH FLOWS

Next, managers must identify sources and estimate amounts of cash flows for the project. These income and expense items will be the basis for a quantitative project analysis. The two main sources of cash inflows are (1) additional net sales and revenues, and (2) reduced operating expenses. Lower operating expenses create a positive cash flow since money not going out is like money coming in.

When estimating cash flows, managers must be sure to consider only the *additional* amounts—those that are the direct result of the project. A company's sales may increase or expenses decrease as a result of other factors. A valid analysis must specifically identify the cash inflows and outflows that are a direct result of the capital project being considered.

Another issue to consider when forecasting cash flows is inflation. Often, future cash flows for a project will increase each year. The real value of these amounts may actually be lower due to inflation. A manager's ability to consider inflation when estimating future cash flows is important for a valid analysis.

When forecasting cash flows, *depreciation* is not considered. Depreciation refers to the decrease in the value of an item as a result of time and use. Even though depreciation is a business expense, it is not a cash outflow for capital budgeting purposes. Depreciation is handled this way since it is a *non-cash* item, that is, money is not paid out when depreciation is recorded. This amount is taken into consideration as a start-up cost for a project.

DIGITAL VISION

Communication equipment or computers might be a necessary investment to improve customer service.

4. IDENTIFY COST OF CAPITAL AND RISKS

Financing the capital project is the next step a manager must consider. **Cost of capital** is the interest rate used to evaluate a capital project. This percentage is often called the *discount rate,* as it is used to do present value calculations.

At this point, managers will also identify and assess potential risks. These uncertainties can range from inflation and lower consumer spending to new government regulations and natural disasters. Risk is often considered in the analysis by using a higher cost of capital. For example, the usual cost of capital for a company may be 7 percent. When evaluating a project of higher risk, using a cost of capital of 8 percent or higher may be appropriate.

5. SELECT AND IMPLEMENT PROJECT

Managers next decide which of the capital projects will be selected. This analysis will involve both quantitative elements such as cash flows and qualitative factors such as company strengths and weaknesses.

Finally, at the completion of this process, the management team puts the project into operation. The project will now require participation by a variety of people in the organization.

checkpoint ✓

What are the steps of the capital budgeting process?

■ Cost of Capital

A significant component of capital budgeting is financing. Companies have two main sources of capital when financing their activities: debt and equity. The cost of using other people's money is an important consideration. *Cost of capital,* also called *required rate of return,* is the rate required by lenders and investors who are letting the company use their money.

COST OF DEBT

Borrowing is a common practice among organizations. Bonds, loans, and other types of debt are major funding sources. **Cost of debt** is the rate of return required by creditors. This percentage is the rate that lenders expect to receive when allowing someone to use their money. For example, an 8 percent bond issued by a company means the cost of debt is 8 percent.

Several common benefits are associated with using debt.

- The company is using the money of others, allowing the business to keep its funds available for other uses.
- The risk for creditors is lower since debts are legal obligations.
- The cost of capital is lower than other funding sources as a result of the lower risk for lenders.
- Interest payments on debt are tax deductible as a business expense.

COST OF EQUITY

The required rate of return for stockholders is not as obvious as for creditors. **Cost of equity** is the required return of the owners in a company. This amount is the percentage company owners expect to earn based on the money they have invested in the company.

For example, you might have $100,000 invested in a company and expect the profits to be 10 percent. Any profit of less than $10,000 would be disappointing. You might encourage the company to take a different direction. Or, you might sell your ownership in the company to another investor. Company owners (stockholders), like creditors, expect a certain rate of return. This return might be in the form of a share of the profits (dividends) or in the form of increased market value of the company.

OPTIMAL CAPITAL STRUCTURE

Some debt (with a lower cost of capital than equity) is beneficial to a company, but too much debt can result in difficulties. While the cost of debt is lower than the cost of equity, as an organization takes on more debt, its risk increases. More debt increases the likelihood of the company missing debt payments and going bankrupt. In an attempt to have an appropriate balance between the amount of debt and equity, an **optimal capital structure** is the goal. This structure is the financing combination of a low cost of capital and maximum market value.

One of the most important managerial decisions is how much debt and how much equity to use. Factors to consider include

- The current amount of the company's current debt obligations
- The company's ability to borrow additional funds or issue additional bonds
- The sensitivity of stockholders regarding the current risk of the company due to existing debt
- The past and expected future profitability of the company

WEIGHTED AVERAGE COST OF CAPITAL (WACC)

When creating the capital budget, companies develop a **weighted average cost of capital (WACC)**. The WACC is calculated by multiplying the proportions of debt and equity times the capital cost for each. For example, if a company has 30 percent debt at a cost of 8 percent and 70 percent equity at a cost of 10 percent, the WACC would be

$$\text{WACC} = \left(\begin{array}{c}\text{Percent}\\\text{Debt}\end{array} \times \begin{array}{c}\text{Cost of}\\\text{Debt}\end{array}\right) + \left(\begin{array}{c}\text{Percent}\\\text{Equity}\end{array} \times \begin{array}{c}\text{Cost of}\\\text{Equity}\end{array}\right)$$

$$\text{WACC} = (0.30 \times 0.08) + (0.70 \times 0.10)$$

$$\text{WACC} = 0.024 + 0.07 = 0.094 = 9.4\%$$

You might think that the WACC declines as a company takes on more debt. This is true, but only up to a certain portion of debt. As more debt is used, risk increases to create a higher cost of both debt and equity, resulting in a higher WACC.

Every organization attempts to minimize its WACC. This will occur when a certain combination of debt and equity is used. The exact combination will vary for every company and changes as risk (from increased use of debt) and interest rates change. Managers continually analyze various economic and company factors to arrive at the optimal capital structure.

checkpoint ✓

Why is the cost of debt lower than the cost of equity?

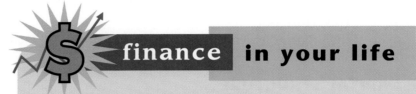

finance in your life

Using Time Value of Money to Plan Personal Financial Goals

"My child is going to college in ten years. If I save $4,000 a year at a 5 percent interest rate, how much will be available for his education?" This example is just one way people use time value of money calculations to reach their financial goals. For each financial planning situation, regular deposits to a savings or investment account are required. Using time value of money, you can determine the future value or the amount you should save or invest to achieve a specific goal for the future. The calculations for this situation would be as follows.

$4,000 × future value of a series, 10 years, 5 percent

$4,000 × 12.578 (see Appendix D) = $50,312

Saving $4,000 a year for 10 years, earning 5 percent, results in having $50,312.

Ben Wallace wants to have $50,000 available over the next 10 years to help with his parents' retirement expenses. If he earns an average of 8 percent on his investments, what amount must he invest each year to achieve this goal? The calculations for this situation are as follows.

$50,000 ÷ the future value of a series of deposits, 10 years, 8 percent

$50,000 ÷ 14.487 (see Appendix D) = $3,452.80

Ben needs to invest approximately $3,450 a year for 10 years at 8 percent to achieve his desired financial goal.

Think Critically

1. Describe other situations in which time value of money calculations could assist people with achieving their personal financial goals.
2. Identify a personal financial goal for your future. Prepare a calculation for this goal.

UNDERSTAND CONCEPTS

Determine the best answer for each of the following questions.

1. According to financial theory, the major goal of a business organization should be
   a. higher sales
   b. lower customer complaints
   c. a high market value
   d. a low level of debt

2. **True or False?** Projects with a higher risk will usually be evaluated with a lower cost of capital.

3. A common benefit of debt is
   a. lower risk than equity
   b. interest payments reduce the amount of taxes
   c. stockholders may not receive their dividends
   d. reduced chance of company bankruptcy

4. **True or False?** If a company has no debt, its WACC would be the same as its cost of equity.

MAKE ACADEMIC CONNECTIONS

5. **Visual Art** Using photos and other visuals, create a flowchart to communicate the steps of the capital budgeting process.

6. **Communication** Interview a person who works for a nonprofit organization. Obtain information about their capital spending and the process used to analyze capital projects.

7. **Research** The cost of debt is related to bond yields. Using online or library resources, obtain current data for the rate investors are earning on corporate bonds for some companies of your choice.

8. **Communication** Talk to five people to ask them about the risks they consider when investing in stock. What were the major considerations mentioned? Were the answers from some of the people similar?

Goals
- Describe tools used to analyze capital projects.
- Explain factors that influence capital project decisions.

Terms
- payback method
- net present value (NPV)
- internal rate of return (IRR)
- sunk cost

■ Capital Decision Tools

How might a company decide which capital project to accept? Several decision-making approaches are available to guide this process.

PAYBACK METHOD

If a project that costs $10,000 brings in $2,500 a year, the payback is four years. The **payback method** is used to determine the how long it will take for the cash flows of a capital project to equal the original cost. In the following situation, new machinery that will reduce operating expenses costs $42,000. With the annual amount of savings for each year shown, the payback would be five years.

Year	Cash flows
1	$10,000
2	9,000
3	9,000
4	8,000
5	8,000

In this example, it takes until the fifth year for the total cash flows to exceed the original cost of $42,000.

The payback method has been commonly used for many years. Managers find this method easy to use. The payback method has two drawbacks. First, payback favors short-term projects which may not be in the best interest of the company. Second, this method does not consider the *time value of money*, which is a significant financial analysis tool.

NET PRESENT VALUE

To address the major problem with the payback method, that it does not consider the time value of money, another tool was created. **Net present value (NPV)** calculates the present value of cash flows for a project minus the initial investment. Three elements are necessary to use the NPV method.

1. *Initial investment* is the cost of the project, such as new equipment or a building. The initial investment is also called the *start-up cost* or the *initial outlay*.

2. *Cash flows* are the yearly amounts of increased sales or decreased costs. These funds are the financial benefits of the capital project.

3. *Cost of capital* is the interest rate the company will use to calculate the present value of the cash flows. This percentage is also called the *discount rate*.

CALCULATE NET PRESENT VALUE

Calculating net present value involves three steps.

Step 1 Calculate the present value of the cash flows using a 10 percent cost of capital.

Year 1	$4,500
Year 2	$4,500
Year 3	$4,500

$4,500 × present value of a series (see Appendix C)

$4,500 × 2.487 = $11,192

Step 2 Subtract the initial cost of $10,000 from the total in Step 1 to obtain the NPV.

NPV = $11,192 − $10,000 = $1,192

Step 3 Evaluate the result. In this situation, the projected cash flows have a present value of $11,192, which is greater than the initial cost of $10,000. The result is a positive NPV of $1,192.

In general, if the NPV is positive, accept the project. If the NPV is negative, reject the project. When considering several projects, accept the one with the highest NPV.

Managers should be aware of the limitations of NPV analysis. First, while the initial outlay is based on reliable costs, the projected cash flows are estimates. Accuracy of these projected figures will depend on the skill and experience of managers. Also, the cost of capital used in the analysis may change. Additional risk or increased interest rates can result in a higher cost of capital with a lower NPV.

A survey of companies indicates that the net present value method is used most often by companies to evaluate capital projects. After NPV, the internal rate of return (IRR) and the payback method are the next most popular analysis techniques.

© GETTY IMAGES/PHOTODISC

The start-up cost of a capital project is only one element of NPV.

INTERNAL RATE OF RETURN

Managers are often interested in the rate of return of a project. The internal rate of return (IRR) is the discount rate at which the net present value is zero. IRR provides decision-makers with the rate of return for a capital project. Several methods can be used to calculate IRR. First, financial calculators will likely have an IRR function key. In addition, software or on-line calculators are available to determine the internal rate of return. Least desirable, but sometimes necessary, is using the trial-and-error method.

A major drawback of IRR is that it reports a percentage rather than a dollar amount. One project may have an IRR of 17 percent while another is only 8 percent. The first project may only involve $100,000 while the second is for $1.2 million. The IRR looks more attractive for the smaller project, but the company will likely maximize its value by accepting the larger project.

checkpoint ✓

What three decision-making tools are commonly used to evaluate capital projects?

■ Additional Analysis Factors

In the process of using the various methods to evaluate capital projects, some additional issues should be considered.

OPPORTUNITY COST

Whenever a decision is made to take one course of action, something else is given up. *Opportunity cost* is the value of the alternative that is given up when a decision is made. Sometimes these opportunity costs may involve items that cannot be measured in monetary value.

When a capital projects decision is being made, working capital is an example of an opportunity cost. Cash, accounts receivable, and inventory are usually required for the operation of a project. While these items are still in the company, they are not available to be used for other purposes. Since these current assets are not available for use in other ways, their value is an opportunity cost of the project.

SUNK COST

Companies may have situations in which an expense must be paid whether a project is accepted or not. For example, the cost to research a new project will occur whether or not the company decides to produce the item. A sunk cost is an expense that has been paid that will not affect capital decisions. These expenses may include equipment that has been purchased but that may or may not be used. Sunk costs are not considered in a capital spending analysis since the decision to accept or reject the project will not affect whether the expense will occur.

RISK ANALYSIS

Uncertainty is present in all financial decisions. These risks may be viewed from geographic, economic, social, and political perspectives.

Geography Changing weather conditions can ruin agricultural crops. A rough terrain can result in difficulties with transportation. Various geographic factors can be the basis of increased capital project risk.

Economic Conditions Higher prices, changing currency values, and low consumer spending create uncertainty. Economic risks such as inflation and changing interest rates must be considered in the capital budgeting process.

Social and Cultural Factors In one country, a certain action may be considered a bribe. In another culture, the same action may be viewed as an accepted way of doing business. Cultural differences as a result of traditions, religion, and family relations can create uncertainty when doing business in different regions. While these situations are not directly influenced by government actions, these circumstances may be viewed as *informal* trade barriers.

Political and Legal Restrictions In contrast, specific government regulations restricting certain business activities are *formal* trade barriers. Packaging laws, import taxes, and labor safety standards can affect the cost and success of a capital project. Political risk is also affected by changes in governments as a result of elections or military action.

teamwork

Describe a business situation in which a company is creating a new product. In your team, identify geographic, economic, social-cultural, and political-legal factors that could create risk for the company.

checkpoint ✓

How do opportunity costs and sunk costs differ?

technology topics

Handheld and Online Financial Calculators for Capital Project Analysis

Financial handheld calculators (such as TI BA II and HP 12C) provide users with built-in business finance functions. The prices of these devices range from under $30 to over $600, depending on the complexity of calculations offered. Many managers and students use these calculators for easy computations when doing net present value (NPV) and internal rate of return (IRR) analyses.

Online calculators are also available. These web-based tools can be accessed for fast and easy analysis of capital projects. Several web sites are set up so a user can enter the data, click the calculate button, and receive the results. These online calculators may also provide a basic interpretation of the results.

Think Critically

1. Locate an online calculator for net present value (NPV) and internal rate of return (IRR).
2. Compare the benefits of handheld and web-based financial calculators.

UNDERSTAND CONCEPTS

Determine the best answer for each of the following questions.

1. **True or False?** The payback method is common in companies due to the ease of its use.

2. The most accepted method for evaluating capital projects is
   a. payback
   b. net present value
   c. internal rate of return
   d. the risk analysis process

3. Which of the following NPV elements is most accurate because it requires the least estimating?
   a. cash flows
   b. start-up costs
   c. risk
   d. cost of capital

4. In some countries, being expected to hire family members before others would be an example of _____?_____ risk.
   a. geographic
   b. economic
   c. cultural
   d. political

MAKE ACADEMIC CONNECTIONS

5. **Communication** Select a possible capital project. Create a presentation (using photos, ads, online articles, and other visuals) to communicate the (a) initial costs, (b) cash flows, and (c) cost of capital.

6. **Culture** Talk with a person who has lived or worked in another country. Find information about capital projects in that culture. How do businesses and governments determine which projects to implement?

7. **Research** Conduct Internet or library research to obtain additional information about types of risks and how risks are analyzed for capital budgeting decisions.

8. **Geography** Locate a map for a region of the world. Describe geographic factors that could create a risk for companies doing business in that area.

Goals
- Explain business growth and expansion actions.
- Identify actions for reducing global business risks.

Terms
- centralized organization
- decentralized organization
- horizontal integration
- vertical integration
- diversification
- joint venture

Business Growth Actions

Organizations continually seek out and evaluate capital decisions that will provide current profits and long-term growth. Managers make decisions that they hope will improve the company's future success.

ORGANIZATIONAL STRATEGIES

When planning for successful growth and expansion, a company must consider the structure of its organization. In a **centralized organization**, decisions are made at company headquarters. This type of structure allows for better control but may not be as flexible when adapting to local market needs around the world.

An example of a vertical integration merger is a food processing company that buys its own farmland.

© GETTY IMAGES/PHOTODISC

teamwork

In your team, describe situations in which centralized business activities might be preferred to a decentralized organization.

In contrast, a **decentralized organization** allows company decisions to be made at lower levels of the organization. In these companies, managers of local stores and factory supervisors in different countries have greater authority. They can make decisions about advertising and branding without consulting corporate headquarters.

EXPANSION METHODS

Often, growth of a company can be the result of a merger, for example, if a supermarket chain buys other grocery stores. **Horizontal integration** is a merger between two or more companies in the same type of business. The benefits of this situation include higher income levels as well as an ability to buy materials and supplies more efficiently, in larger quantities.

Another type of merger is **vertical integration.** In this situation, a company expands through increased involvement in different stages of production and distribution. A food processing company may buy its own farmland and obtain a shipping company. Vertical integration is especially used in developing economies where outsourcing of various business functions may not be possible.

PRODUCT VARIATIONS

Companies often grow by offering more and different products. New flavors, different package sizes, and varied brands can create business expansion. For example, in recent years new cereal products have included freeze-dried fruit and additional types of grains.

DIVERSITY OF MARKETS

Expanded business activities can also be a result of new markets. A *market* is defined as where and to whom a business sells. Business locations can grow in different regions of the country or into other countries. Geographic expansion may also occur when a company sells in a variety of areas—urban, suburban, small town, and rural. The audience of a business also may expand. Instead of just selling to younger consumers, a company may adapt its products to attract older customers.

Some companies sell only to households and individual consumers. These are referred to as B2C (business to consumer). For example, a home lawn-care service or housecleaning business would be B2C. In contrast, B2B (business to business) organizations sell to other businesses. A company that repairs buses or a business that supplies parts to an electronics manufacturer would be considered B2B. Many companies expand to cover both B2C and B2B activities. An auto repair firm may service cars for individuals (B2C) while also providing oil changes for business vehicles (B2B).

checkpoint ✓

How does a centralized organization differ from a decentralized one?

■Reducing Global Risks

Financial, economic, and other business risks are an ongoing concern for managers in every setting. These uncertainties are intensified when doing business in another country. To reduce international business risk, four actions are suggested.

CONDUCT BUSINESS IN SEVERAL REGIONS

If a company's global business activities are focused on one or two countries, the organization faces a risky situation. If political unrest or poor economic conditions occur, lower profits are likely. If a company manufactures and sells products in several regions of the world, the risk is reduced.

DIVERSIFY PRODUCT LINES

Dependency on one or two products can be risky. If demand for a company's main product declines, profits may disappear. Producing and selling a variety of items can reduce risk. **Diversification** is the offering of a variety of products or services. While this term most often refers to investing in different types of securities and industries, it is also valid for capital projects.

A diversified product portfolio may include cookies and crackers, ice cream, bottled water, cosmetics, and oral hygiene products in the same company. This portfolio of products will allow a company to balance lower sales in one division with higher sales in its other product lines.

Conducting business in several regions reduces global risk.

© GETTY IMAGES/PHOTODISC

INVOLVE LOCAL OWNERSHIP

Working with a local owner can be viewed favorably by a country's government. A company that is completely owned by people from another country is viewed with more suspicion, creating greater risk.

The use of local partnerships can reduce this uncertainty. A **joint venture** is an agreement between two or more companies to share a business project. These types of arrangements between companies in different countries can contribute to business success for all parties involved.

EMPLOY LOCAL MANAGEMENT

Hiring local managers can create favorable relationships in a foreign business environment. These supervisors have knowledge of local customs and cultural business practices. A working environment involving local managers will usually reduce risk.

checkpoint ✓

What actions can be taken to reduce global business risk?

Toshiba's Production Facility in Thailand

In 2006, Toshiba, a Japanese company, announced construction of a new semiconductor production facility in the Bangkadi Industrial Park, about 35 kilometers north of Bangkok. This new facility expands the company's manufacturing capacity for semiconductors and other electronic components. With increased demand for small-signal devices in Asian markets, the company hopes to strengthen its overall profitability.

Using capital project analysis techniques, Toshiba has decided to increase production in the Bangkok factory. The initial construction of the new building was expected to take about eight months. This first phase of the multi-year building plan had an estimated cost of 2 billion yen (approximately 700 million Baht—the currency of Thailand). When completed, the new building will have a total production area of over 8,000 square meters and will employ 9,000 workers. This plant will use high-efficiency production lines to reduce manufacturing costs.

One of Toshiba's main corporate strategies involves selection of capital projects with the newest technology. This investment in Bangkok uses state-of-the-art manufacturing equipment. This capital project decision allows the company continued leadership potential in the high-growth semiconductor business around the world.

Think Critically

1. What are some of the benefits of this capital project?
2. What analysis process did the company likely use when considering this project?
3. Conduct an Internet search about Toshiba. Obtain updated information about this production facility and other company activities.

6.4   Lesson Assessment

UNDERSTAND CONCEPTS

Determine the best answer for each of the following questions.

1. A company in which decisions are made by top-level managers is a
   _____?_____ organization.
   a. centralized
   b. decentralized
   c. horizontal
   d. vertical

2. **True or False?** Decentralized organizations usually have managers making decisions in different geographic regions.

3. Horizontal integration allows a company to
   a. reduce risk by selling a wide variety of products
   b. combine with other companies in a similar business
   c. provide local managers with decision-making authority
   d. be involved with different stages of production and distribution

4. **True or False?** A diversified company usually has higher risk than a non-diversified organization.

MAKE ACADEMIC CONNECTIONS

5. **Visual Art** Using photos, ads, packages, labels, or other visuals, create a presentation to communicate the characteristics of (a) centralized and decentralized organizations, and (b) horizontal and vertical business activities.

6. **Law** Horizontal mergers can result in a monopoly with reduced competition and few consumer choices. Obtain information about monopolies and antitrust laws, which are designed to prevent monopolies. Prepare a short written or oral summary of your findings.

7. **Technology** Find examples of online B2C and B2B business activities. Describe the elements of these two types of business activities.

8. **Research** Using Internet or library sources, locate an example of a joint venture. Describe the partnership and explain the benefits for the companies involved.

Summary

6.1 CAPITAL PROJECTS

1. Capital spending refers to construction or purchase of a long-term asset, such as buildings and equipment. The main types of capital projects are replacement projects, cost-saving projects, new products or markets, government-required projects, and social benefit projects.

2. Independent projects are not affected by other projects. Mutually-exclusive projects involve situations in which the acceptance of one project does not allow acceptance of others. Complementary projects exist when two or more projects are dependent on one another.

6.2 CAPITAL BUDGETING PROCESS

3. The five steps of the capital budgeting process are (1) set capital spending goals, (2) determine potential projects, (3) forecast cash flows, (4) identify the cost of capital, and (5) select and implement the project.

4. Cost of capital has two elements. The cost of debt is the rate of return required by creditors. The cost of equity is the required return of the owners in a company. The optimal capital structure is the financing combination with a low cost of capital and maximum market value.

6.3 CAPITAL PROJECT ANALYSIS

5. Three main capital budgeting decision methods are commonly used: (1) the payback method, (2) net present value (NPV), and (3) internal rate of return (IRR).

6. Sunk costs are expenses that have been incurred and cannot be recovered. The risks of a capital project are commonly created by geography, economic conditions, social and cultural factors, and political and legal restrictions.

6.4 BUSINESS EXPANSION STRATEGIES

7. In centralized organizations, decisions are made at company headquarters. A decentralized organization allows business decisions to be made at lower levels of the organization. Horizontal integration is a merger between two or more companies in the same type of business. With vertical integration, a company expands through increased involvement in different stages of production and distribution.

8. Reducing global business risk may be achieved by conducting business in several regions, having a diverse product line, involving local owners, and employing local management.

Develop Your Business Language

Match the terms listed with the definitions. Some terms will not be used.

1. Discount rate at which the net present value is zero
2. Business decisions are made at lower levels of the organization
3. Acceptance of one project does not allow acceptance of others
4. Two or more projects that are dependent on one another
5. Expenses that have been incurred and cannot be recovered
6. Agreement between two or more companies to share a business project
7. Business decisions are made at company headquarters
8. Construction or purchase of a long-term asset, such as buildings and equipment
9. Intangible assets used by companies
10. Rate of return required by creditors
11. Present value of cash flows for a project minus the initial investment
12. Offering of a variety of products or services

a. capital project
b. centralized organization
c. complementary projects
d. cost of capital
e. cost of debt
f. cost of equity
g. decentralized organization
h. diversification
i. horizontal integration
j. intellectual property
k. internal rate of return (IRR)
l. joint venture
m. mutually exclusive projects
n. net present value (NPV)
o. optimal capital structure
p. payback method
q. sunk cost
r. vertical integration
s. weighted average cost of capital (WACC)

Review Concepts

13. A government-required capital project would be
    a. new machinery to lower operating costs
    b. pollution control equipment to reduce water waste
    c. development of a new product to sell in South America
    d. a day care facility for the children of employees

14. The cost of capital is most influenced by
    a. the required return of lenders and owners
    b. the corporate tax rate
    c. government actions to reduce pollution
    d. competition from foreign companies

15. Which will be the lowest for a company?
    a. cost of debt
    b. cost of equity
    c. WACC
    d. cost of invested funds

16. Which of these would be considered a sunk cost?
    a. depreciation for a currently owned building
    b. materials for production of vehicles
    c. electricity for the company's office
    d. taxes owed for current profits

Think Critically

17. Piracy and counterfeiting of software, videos, and other products is a concern of many companies. How are businesses and consumers affected by this illegal activity?

18. Efforts to maximize the value of a company are considered by many to be the major financial goal of business organizations. Describe other business goals, and explain how these other goals are likely to contribute to increased company value.

19. Cash flows can result from reduced operating expenses, in which "money not going out is like money coming in." Explain this idea and give an example of how a capital project could reduce a company's expenses.

20. How might the capital budgeting activities of a nonprofit organization be different from the capital spending decisions of a company?

21. What guidelines would you suggest to managers when they are deciding whether to use debt or equity to finance a capital project?

22. Other than those mentioned in the chapter, what actions might a company take to reduce risk?

Business Financial Calculations

23. For the following situation, what is the payback (in years)?

    Initial cost: $1.5 million

    Cash flows: Year 1 $300,000, Year 2 $400,000, Year 3 $500,000, Year 4 $400,000, Year 5 $300,000

24. What is the net present value (NPV) for the following situation? Should this capital project be accepted? Explain your answer.

    Initial cost: $78,000

    Cost of capital: 8 percent

    Cash flows: Year 1 $28,000, Year 2 $37,000, Year 3 $34,000

25. A company is considering a one-year investment that costs $100,000. The investment would earn $15,000 during that year. What is the internal rate of return on this investment?

26. In the following situation, calculate the weighted average cost of capital (WACC).

    Proportion of debt: 40 percent

    Cost of debt: 6 percent

    Proportion of equity: 60 percent

    Cost of equity: 9 percent

Analyze Cases

Use the case from the beginning of the chapter, Capital Spending in New York City, to answer the following questions.

27. What are potential difficulties faced by organizations that do not spend adequate amounts on capital projects?

28. Create a list of items that would be in the city's (a) operating budget and (b) capital budget.

29. In the 1970s, New York City was in a difficult financial situation and was unable to make debt payments on time. How would this problem affect the city's ability to sell municipal bonds? What effect would this problem have on the rate paid on the bonds?

30. Contact a local government agency to obtain information about the capital spending activities planned for the next few years.

31. If you were asked to set priorities for the capital budget of New York City, (a) describe actions you might take to decide which capital projects would be most important, and (b) suggest some capital projects that might be most important for New York City in the next few years.

Portfolio Activity

COLLECT an item that illustrates a capital project for a company or government agency. This example could be an advertisement, newspaper or magazine article, photo, or some other actual item.

CREATE a video or an in-class presentation with visuals to communicate the planning, decision-making, financing, and implementing of the capital project.

CONNECT your presentation to other aspects of our economy and society or relate the capital project to a concept you have learned in another class. Make the connection by preparing a short essay to discuss the capital project in relation to other topics.

Stock Market Activity

The stock value of a company reflects the beliefs of investors about the organization's financial decisions. The capital projects selected by managers will be the basis for current profits and long-term growth.

Use Internet and library resources to research the company you have been studying (or select a different company).

1. Describe recent capital projects of the company.

2. Explain the methods used by the company to finance its long-term operations.

3. Discuss how these capital projects may affect the stock value of the company.

Planning a Career in Capital Project Analysis

Every organization is dependent on capital assets for current operations and long-term success. Purchasing new equipment, constructing additional buildings, and buying updated computers are just some of the capital spending activities of businesses. These decisions are based on an analysis process that takes into account financial and economic factors.

In addition to businesses, the need for capital decision-making experts in government positions and with nonprofit organizations will continue to be vital.

Employment Outlook

- Overall employment for financial managers is expected to grow about as fast as the average for all occupations through 2014.

- Potential exists for expanded career opportunities in businesses with growth expectations. As companies increase their domestic and international operations, new capital projects will be considered.

- Government and nonprofit agencies will have a strong demand for capital budget experts. To serve various public needs, these agencies are likely to place a stronger emphasis on capital spending activities.

Job Titles

- Capital analyst
- Capital budget analyst
- Capital budgeting manager
- Credit risk capital analyst
- Venture capital analyst

Needed Skills

- Knowledge in the areas of finance, accounting, economics, real estate, and risk management are fundamental for success.

- Analytical skills, computer competency, and financial forecasting modeling are necessary to plan capital spending in terms of business and economic conditions.

- Ability to work collaboratively with people in several departments within an organization, taking a team leadership role when necessary.

- Strong consideration is given to candidates with an MBA (Masters in Business Administration) and CPA (Certified Public Accountant).

- Global business activities require knowledge of cross-cultural situations and foreign economic environments.

What's It Like to Work in Capital Project Analysis?

"Today's agenda will include finalizing the capital budget, analysis of the proposed new computer system, and a decision on funding the new factory in Asia."

You might think, "That's a lot for just one meeting!" But remember, capital project work has many elements.

In addition to these work duties, you will likely be involved preparing follow-up reports about the implementation and actual costs of capital projects.

What about you? What elements of a career in capital project analysis could be of interest to you? How might you best prepare for a career in this field?

MARKETING RESEARCH EVENT

The Marketing Research Event provides an opportunity for 1–3 participants to demonstrate marketing research skills. The event consists of two major parts: the written document and the oral presentation by participants. The written document, a marketing research study, accounts for 70 points. The oral presentation accounts for the remaining 30 points of the 100 points.

Participants may use visual aids for their presentation. The oral presentation consists of 10 minutes for participants to explain the project followed by 5 minutes for the judge's questions. Participants are to assume the role of management trainee. They have been asked by the business manager of a major stock brokerage firm (the judge) to develop a promotional campaign. Participants will conduct the necessary market research and develop a promotional campaign for the firm's customer service offerings. The judge will evaluate the presentation, focusing on the effectiveness of public speaking and presentation skills and how well the participants respond to questions that the judge may ask following the presentation.

Participants will choose a stock brokerage/investment company and describe the business's current customer service offerings. The business's customer service offerings must then be compared to services offered by the competition. Participants will design and conduct a marketing research study to determine preferred customer service offerings. Based on the comparison and research, the participants will identify new customer service offerings for the business. Then the participants will develop a promotional campaign to promote the business's proposed customer service offerings.

Performance Indicators Evaluated

- Identify the business's customer service offerings.
- Design a marketing research study to determine the clientele's customer service preferences.
- Conduct the market research.
- Compare customer service offerings.
- Recommend improvements for customer service offerings.
- Prepare a promotional campaign to promote the business's proposed customer service offerings based on the market research.
- Present the research findings and proposed promotional campaign to the business's manager in a role-play situation.

Go to the DECA web site for more detailed information.

Think Critically

1. Why is it important for a company to know what the competition offers for customer service?
2. Why is accurate marketing research so important?
3. What is the advantage of a company using a third party to conduct research and make recommendations?
4. What incentives can be used to encourage customers to participate in a marketing research survey?

www.deca.org

chapter 7

Finance Business Activities

7.1 FINANCING CHOICES

7.2 DEBT FINANCING: BONDS

7.3 EQUITY FINANCING: STOCK

7.4 STOCK AND BOND MARKETS

▶ **Point Your** [Browser]
www.thomsonedu.com/school/busfinance

Case STUDY

The New York Stock Exchange

More than 2 billion shares of stock are traded (bought and sold) through the New York Stock Exchange (NYSE) on a typical business day. Often called the "Big Board," the NYSE is one of the oldest and largest stock markets in the world.

The New York Stock Exchange started in 1792 through the efforts of 24 brokers and merchants. Five securities were traded when the NYSE started. Three were government bonds and the other two were bank stocks. Today, nearly 2,700 companies are regularly on the exchange, including most of the largest U.S. corporations as well as many foreign companies.

In recent years a combination of three institutions created the NYSE Group. This merger of the New York Stock Exchange, Archipelago, and the Pacific Exchange created the largest-ever securities exchange.

The NYSE Group has a global emphasis. Over 450 companies from nearly 50 countries make up the NYSE non-U.S. directory. More recently, the NYSE had plans to purchase Euronext. This Europe-based stock exchange was created by a merger of the Paris, Brussels, and Amsterdam exchanges.

The members of the New York Stock Exchange are registered brokers and dealers. They are approved to initiate transactions on the trading floor or through the online facilities of the NYSE. A *floor broker* will usually execute the buy or sell order. Also involved in the transaction process is the *specialist*. This *market maker* creates an efficient buying and selling environment for a given stock. The main activities of the specialist are

- To create a fair and orderly trading environment by setting the day's opening price and reporting bid and offer prices during the trading day
- To be the contact point to bring together brokers with buy and sell orders
- To carry out orders as required by the floor brokers. This activity may require specialists to buy or sell from their own inventory of the stock

Traditionally a system of open outcry was used on the trading floor. Today this process is being replaced by electronic exchanges. In an effort to maintain its market leadership, the NYSE operates both a floor auction exchange as well as a system to facilitate online trades.

Think Critically

1. What activities of the New York Stock Exchange might affect your life?
2. Go to the web site of the New York Stock Exchange to obtain information about current developments of this organization.

Goals
- Explain short-term financing alternatives.
- Compare debt and equity financing.

Terms
- line of credit
- promissory note
- commercial paper
- leasing

■ Short-Term Financing Activities

While companies hope to avoid borrowing, various types of debt are necessary for most businesses. To finance current business activities, a number of short-term borrowing sources are available.

BUYING ON ACCOUNT

Companies often buy on credit. An organization's suppliers and vendors provide companies with needed items. *Accounts payable* refer to amounts owed to creditors for goods and services. These short-term, unsecured debts allow a company to finance daily business activities. Accounts payable are current liabilities generally due within 12 months from the transaction date, with most requiring payment in 30 to 90 days. This borrowing is considered unsecured since the loans are not backed by specific collateral.

© GETTY IMAGES/PHOTODISC

Businesses with seasonal sales may cover their expenses with loans or lines of credit.

BANK LOANS AND NOTES

Most businesses borrow money at one time or another. Bank loans may be used for financing inventory, equipment, and other organizational needs. These installment loans are obtained from a commercial bank or other similar financial institution.

Bank installment loans are usually considered medium-term debt, since they are likely to be for more than a year but less than four years. The loan may be secured (with collateral) or unsecured (no collateral).

A **line of credit** is an agreement that allows a company to obtain additional loans without a new loan application. A pre-approved limit is established. The business may then borrow additional amounts, often called *advances*, as long as the total does not exceed the established credit limit. A line of credit is especially useful when a company has irregular sales. These loans help the business cover its expenses in times of lower income.

Another common type of loan is a **promissory note**, which is a signed, written promise to borrow money between a borrower and a lender. The terms and conditions of the loan agreement are stated in the promissory note, including the amount of the loan, the interest rate, the payment schedule, late fees, and the financial institution where the loan is to be repaid.

COMMERCIAL PAPER

Companies often need funds for short periods of time. **Commercial paper** refers to unsecured, short-term debt instruments issued by corporations. These loans have maturities ranging from 2 to 270 days.

checkpoint ✓

What are the main types of short-term financing used by companies?

▮Long-Term Financing Choices

Companies face daily decisions about financing long-term business activities. Their choices are focused on debt, equity, and leasing.

USING DEBT AND EQUITY

Should a company use bonds or stock for updating equipment or expanding its global activities? This question is an ongoing issue for business organizations.

Debt Financing The use of accounts payable, loans, notes, and bonds are examples of debt financing. The use of long-term debt financing is common among companies and other types of organizations. The main benefits of debt include

- Use of someone else's money
- Expected return for investors is lower with debt than with equity
- Interest payments on debt reduce a company's taxes

In contrast to these advantages, the major drawback of debt—the risk of bankruptcy—must also be considered.

Equity Financing Instead of debt, companies may seek additional investors for the company. A smaller company might offer partial ownership to investors, while a larger corporation might sell stock. Common positive aspects of equity include

- No increased bankruptcy risk; equity contributions are not required to be repaid
- Potential participation by additional owners
- Increased future potential for borrowing

The major negative aspect of equity is that the increased number of shares can result in reduced control by existing owners.

teamwork

In your team, describe several situations in which an organization might lease an item rather than buy it.

LEASING

Instead of buying an item, companies may decide to rent. **Leasing** is a legal agreement to use property that belongs to another person. This type of contract may be used for real estate, equipment, or other assets. For a specified time of use, a lease payment, sometimes called rent, must be made to the owner of the property. The owner of the property is called the *lessor,* while the user who rents the item is the *lessee.* When a company is deciding whether to buy or lease, the following factors are considered.

- Are funds available to buy the item?
- What is the length of the useful life of the asset?
- How would the company's taxes be affected?
- What is the expected value of the asset after its useful life?

checkpoint ✓

How does leasing differ from other financing activities?

Online Investment Activities

Many brokers operate online services that allow investors to access account information and buy and sell securities. By investing online, you can become your own financial planner. These transactions are usually less expensive and more convenient than using a financial planner or traditional stockbroker.

There are disadvantages to investing online. Inexperience in making investment trading decisions can result in a large financial loss. Many online investors buy or sell stocks too quickly because making trades is only a click away.

Before doing business with an e-broker, be sure to investigate the reputation of the company. Talk with others about their experiences with the company. Determine if the online broker has local offices or customer service that will allow you to resolve difficulties easily. Finally, use a variety of sources to obtain advice about the investments you are considering.

Most online brokers allow you to buy and sell a variety of investment products. These include stocks, bonds, mutual funds, T-bills, exchange-trade funds, and stock options. The commission fee charged by e-brokers can range from $4.95 to nearly $30.

In addition, various banking services will likely be available through your online broker. Checking accounts, savings accounts, ATM access, and retirement accounts are commonly offered.

Think Critically

1. When might you consider using an online broker for your investments?
2. Go to the web site of an online broker. What services are provided? What fees are associated with these services?

UNDERSTAND CONCEPTS

Determine the best answer for each of the following questions.

1. Which of the following is *not* considered to be short-term credit?
   a. line of credit
   b. promissory note
   c. mortgage
   d. commercial paper

2. A common advantage of equity is
   a. interest payments are tax deductible
   b. no increased risk of bankruptcy
   c. a lower required cost of capital by investors
   d. use of someone else's money

3. An agreement that allows a company to obtain additional loans, up to a set amount, without a new loan application is called ____?____.
   a. line of credit
   b. commercial paper
   c. accounts payable
   d. promissory note

4. **True or False?** Commercial paper is usually backed by collateral.

5. **True or False?** Leasing is considered to be renting.

MAKE ACADEMIC CONNECTIONS

6. **Consumer Finance** Obtain information on home equity loans. What are the benefits and drawbacks of this type of consumer credit?

7. **Research** Conduct research about commercial paper. How is this type of business credit used? What are current interest rates for commercial paper for various companies?

8. **Law** Talk to someone who leases an item, such as an apartment or automobile. Obtain information about the legal protection available to the lessor and lessee.

9. **Communication** Interview a local business owner about the types of credit used to finance various business activities.

Goals
- Describe the main types of government and corporate bonds.
- Explain activities associated with issuing bonds.

Terms
- mortgage bond
- debenture bond
- investment banker
- coupon rate
- bond rating

■ Types of Bonds

To raise money for current operations or future expansion, most governments and corporations sell bonds. A *bond* is a certificate representing a promise to pay a definite amount of money at a stated interest rate on a specified *maturity date* (due date). Bonds are similar to promissory notes issued by individual borrowers.

When you buy a bond, you are lending money to the organization issuing the bond. You become a *creditor* of the organization.

GOVERNMENT BONDS

Borrowing is a major source of funds for most government agencies. Federal, state, and local governments issue a variety of bonds.

U.S. Savings Bonds One of the safest investments for people with small amounts to invest is U.S. government savings bonds. Series EE savings bonds, which come in denominations from $50 to $10,000, pay interest through a process called discounting.

STOCKBYTE

States may issue municipal bonds for such projects as toll roads.

A Series EE bond is bought at half its face value. A $50 bond costs $25 and, at the end of its full term, pays at least $50. The difference between the purchase price and the redemption (payoff) value is the interest earned. The interest earned is determined by the length of time the bond is held. The time it takes for a savings bond to mature will vary depending on the current interest rate being paid.

One other type of savings bond is the I bond. These investments pay an interest rate that is lower than the rate of other savings bonds, but they pay a variable rate that increases with inflation.

NET Bookmark

Treasury Direct is a web site run by the U.S. Department of the Treasury that provides information on government securities. Access thomsonedu.com/school/busfinance and click on the link for Chapter 7. Use the Research Center to find out information on Series EE Savings Bonds.

www.thomsonedu.com/school/busfinance

Federal Government Bonds The federal government also borrows. The U.S. Treasury issues three major types of debt securities. The difference among them is the length of time to maturity.

1. **Treasury Bills** T-bills are short-term borrowing, with maturities from 91 days to one year.

2. **Treasury Notes** T-notes have maturities from one to ten years.

3. **Treasury Bonds** T-bonds are long-term borrowing, with maturities ranging from 10 to 30 years.

Debt securities are also issued by other federal agencies. These include the Federal National Mortgage Association (often called Fannie Mae), the Federal Housing Administration (FHA), the Government National Mortgage Association (Ginnie Mae), and the Federal Loan Mortgage Corporation (Freddie Mac). Bonds issued by these agencies pay a slightly higher interest rate than Treasury Department securities.

State and Local Government Bonds States, cities, counties, school districts, and other taxing entities borrow to fund various projects. Bonds issued by local and state governments are called *municipal bonds,* or munis.

Two types of municipal bonds exist. A *general obligation bond* is backed by the full faith, credit, and taxing power of the government issuing the bond. A *revenue bond* is repaid with the income from the project that the bond was issued to finance, such as a toll bridge or stadium.

Municipal bonds have an advantage over bonds issued by companies. Often, interest earned on municipal bonds is exempt from federal and most state income taxes. A tax-exempt investment results in a higher return. Consider these two situations.

■ Investment A, a corporate bond paying $100 in interest that is taxable, results in the investor keeping less than $100, since taxes must be paid on the interest earned.

■ Investment B, a municipal bond paying $100 in interest that is not taxed, resulting in a higher return since the investor keeps the entire $100.

This higher rate of return, often referred to as the *taxable equivalent yield,* would be the comparable rate of return had the interest been subject to income taxes.

Foreign Government Bonds

To finance roads, schools, and military equipment for their nations, foreign governments also issue bonds. These debts are a direct obligation of a foreign government. Foreign governments may issue two types of bonds.

1. **External bonds** These bonds are intended for investors in another country. Interest and principal are paid in the currency of the country in which investors live. External bonds of countries intended for purchase by investors in the U.S. are called *dollar bonds*.

2. **Internal bonds** These bonds are aimed at investors in the country issuing the bond and are payable in the native currency. Foreign government bonds that are payable in several currencies are known as *multiple currency bonds*.

The value of foreign government bonds is based on the same factors as other bonds, including the economic and political stability of the government issuing the bonds. Investors in these bonds commonly face additional risk, such as varied exchange rates, currency instability, and changes in administrations.

Foreign governments issue bonds to finance infrastructure improvements such as roads.

CORPORATE BONDS

Investing in bonds is quite different from investing in stock. When you invest in stock, you are an owner of the company. When you buy a bond, you are lending money to the company. Bonds issued by corporations are called *corporate bonds*.

Mortgage Bonds One type of corporate bond is a mortgage bond. This type of debt is secured by a specific asset or property. The collateral for a mortgage bond may be equipment, a building, or land. For lenders, a mortgage bond is safer than other types of bonds since a pledge of an asset in the event of default reduces the risk.

Debenture Bonds A corporate bond without collateral is a debenture bond. This is an unsecured debt bond whose holder has the claim of a general creditor on all assets of the issuer not pledged specifically to secure other debt.

Other Features of Corporate Bonds A *callable bond* allows the company to pay off the debt before the maturity date at a specified price. A

teamwork

In your team, prepare a list of business situations for which a company may decide to issue bonds.

convertible bond can be exchanged for common stock in the same company. This conversion of a bond to stock will occur according to terms set forth in advance. The agreement will list the set number of shares that will be issued for each bond.

GLOBAL COMPANY BONDS

Companies based in other countries also issue bonds. A corporation may issue debt securities in more than one region at a time. For example, a European company may issue bonds for sale in both its home region and in Japan. These bonds will most likely be issued both in the currency of the home country (euro) and the other country (yen). Global bonds are usually issued by businesses with an international reputation and high credit rating.

checkpoint ✓

How do mortgage bonds differ from debenture bonds?

▮Issuing Bonds

Every bond has a *face value,* also called the *maturity value* or *par value,* that indicates the amount being borrowed. Most corporate bonds issued in the United States have a face value of $1,000. Around the world, bonds may be issued with different face values. In the United Kingdom, bonds traditionally are issued for 100 pounds sterling. In Brazil, the standard amount is 1,000 reals, while in South Africa it is 100 rand.

The *maturity date* is the date when the bond, which is a loan, must be repaid. Corporate bonds in the U.S. may be issued for any time period, but they are most often issued for 5, 10, or 20 years.

INVESTMENT BANKERS

An **investment banker** is an individual or company that assists companies with issuing new securities. When raising large amounts of capital, several investment banking companies may work together to sell the new bonds.

Advice to Company One of the significant roles of the investment banker is to guide the company when it issues bonds. Investment bankers will evaluate the company's capital structure (use of debt and equity) to determine if issuing bonds is appropriate and will help to determine the amount of additional debt that might be sold.

Underwriting Process Another task of the investment banker when issuing bonds is underwriting. Underwriting involves setting the price, selling the new bonds, and taking on the risk in this process.

Underwriters make their income from the price difference, or *spread,* between the amount paid to the company issuing the bonds and what investors pay for the bonds. Potential buyers of newly issued bonds include banks, investment companies, pension funds, and individuals. Should the investment bankers not be able to find enough buyers, they hold some bonds themselves. Later, they hope to sell the securities to various investors.

INTEREST RATES

Interest is paid periodically (usually twice a year) to bondholders based on the bond's face value and its stated interest rate. Then, on the bond's maturity date, the face value is repaid to the investor.

Coupon Rate The coupon rate is the stated annual interest rate for a bond. The annual interest is based on the face value of the bond. For example, an 8 percent, $1,000 bond would have annual interest of $80. This amount is paid to the holder of the bond each year until maturity. The total interest for a year is usually made in two semiannual payments, every six months.

The coupon rate is based on current market interest rates for bonds with comparable risk. This rate is determined during the underwriting process. The monetary policy of the Federal Reserve has a major effect on interest rates. When money is *tight,* interest rates tend to move upward. In contrast, an environment of *loose* money results in lower rates.

Current Yield The actual rate of return for investors will often vary from the coupon rate. As interest rates change, the rate of return required by investors may increase or decrease. The current yield of a bond is the relationship between the amount of interest and the cost of the bond. As interest rates increase, bond values decline, so the current yield is higher.

$$\text{Current Yield (\%)} = \frac{\text{Interest Amount}}{\text{Cost of Bond}}$$

$$\text{Current Yield (\%)} = \frac{\$80}{\$940} = 0.085 = 8.5 \text{ percent}$$

In this situation, the cost (market value) of the bond declined from $1,000 to $940 due to higher interest rates. This lower bond value, in relation to the fixed interest payment ($80), results in a higher yield for the investor.

DIGITAL VISION

A successful and competent management team positively affects the bond rating of a company.

Basis Points Bond yield is also reported in terms of *basis points,* which divides 1 percent into hundreds. A basis point is 1/100 of a percentage point. For example, 40 basis points is 0.4 percent. When a bond yield goes from 5.07 percent to 5.32 percent, this change will be reported as an increase of 25 basis points. If a rate changes 50 basis points, it represents a change of one half of 1 percent.

BOND RATINGS

All companies do not pay the same coupon rates. Their coupon rates are affected by the current market level of interest rates and the financial stability of the company. A **bond rating** is a measure of the quality and safety of a company's debt. This evaluation is an indicator of how likely it is that a business will be able to make the interest and maturity value payments on the bonds it issues.

Bond ratings evaluate the possibility of default by a bond issuer. As shown in Figure 7-1, these ratings range from AAA (highly unlikely to default) to D (in default). Two commonly used bond rating companies are Standard & Poor's and Moody's Investors Service.

FIGURE 7-1

Bond Ratings

Quality	Moody's	S&P	Description
High-grade	AAA AA	AAA AA	These ratings are assigned companies judged to be of high quality by all standards; almost no chance of default.
Medium-grade	A BAA	A BBB	Bonds from companies that have many favorable factors with very little chance of default.
Speculative	BA B	BB B	Bonds judged to be somewhat uncertain and a fairly high risk.
Default	CAA CA C	CCC CC C D	Bonds from companies that are of poor standing with extremely poor prospects for making payments to investors; company may have filed for bankruptcy.

Bond ratings are commonly affected by
- The earning power of the company
- Other debts the company currently owes
- The past success and future potential of company management

Bond ratings affect the interest rate a company must offer on its bonds. Lower bond ratings require a high rate to attract investors to the higher risk bond.

checkpoint ✓

What is the purpose of the underwriting process?

7.2 Lesson Assessment

UNDERSTAND CONCEPTS

Determine the best answer for each of the following questions.

1. The federal government debt security with the longest maturity is the
   a. treasury bill
   b. treasury note
   c. treasury bond
   d. municipal bond

2. A bond selling for $1,000 and earning interest of $45 would have a current yield of ____?____ percent.
   a. 10
   b. 45
   c. 4.5
   d. 40.5

3. A ____?____ bond allows investors to exchange the bond for common stock in the same company.
   a. debenture
   b. convertible
   c. mortgage
   d. callable

4. **True or False?** A mortgage bond is considered a secured loan.

5. **True or False?** The bond rating of a corporate bond is based on the earning power of the issuing company.

MAKE ACADEMIC CONNECTIONS

6. **Economics** Research the rates for Treasury bills, Treasury notes, and Treasury bonds for the past five years. What factors affect changes in these rates?

7. **Global Business** Conduct Internet and library research on bonds issued by foreign countries and corporate bonds from around the world. Prepare a short written summary of your findings.

8. **Research** Identify an investment banking company. Conduct research to obtain information about the activities of this organization.

9. **Visual Art** Create a poster or computer presentation to communicate the factors that affect the bond rating of a company.

Goals
- Describe the types of capital stock sold by corporations.
- Explain the process for issuing stock.

Terms
- common stock
- dividend
- preferred stock
- initial public offering (IPO)
- primary market
- secondary market

■Types of Stock

To raise funds for current expansion, future growth, and other company goals, a company may wish to take on additional owners who will provide more equity. A company that sells stock for the first time or sells additional shares is using equity financing.

COMMON STOCK

The most frequently used type of corporate ownership gives participants voting rights and an opportunity to share in profits. **Common stock** is an equity security representing ownership in a corporation with voting rights. Common stock has no stated dividend rate. As part owners of the corporation, common stockholders are invited to the annual meeting of the corporation. They are entitled to one vote per share of common stock owned.

DIGITAL VISION

Common stockholders can attend the annual meeting of the corporation.

teamwork

In your team, prepare a list of advantages and disadvantages of (a) a company regularly paying dividends, and (b) a company not paying dividends.

When sharing in profits, stockholders receive a **dividend**, which is a portion of company profits. Common stockholders receive dividends only after preferred stockholders have been paid their dividends. If the profits of a company are large, the common stockholders may receive additional dividends. For example, suppose that a company has issued $100,000 worth of common stock and $100,000 worth of preferred stock with a stated dividend rate of 6 percent. If the company earns a profit of $20,000 and pays all the profit out as dividends, preferred stockholders would be paid $6,000 in dividends ($100,000 × 0.06). The remainder, or $14,000 ($20,000 − $6,000), would be available to pay dividends to the common stockholders. The common stockholders would earn a return of 14 percent.

Investors who purchase common stock in a corporation

- Have voting rights to elect the company's board of directors at the annual stockholders' meeting

- Are not guaranteed dividends, but may receive higher dividends during the company's prosperous periods

- Are paid after bondholders, other creditors, and preferred stockholders if a company fails or liquidates

PREFERRED STOCK

Preferred stock is the second main class of stock issued by corporations. This security has priority over common stock in the payment of dividends. A preferred stockholder, for example, is paid first if profits are used for any dividends.

The dividends paid to preferred stockholders are usually stated as a dollar amount or as a percentage of the par value. The *par value* of a stock is the minimum price for which a share can be issued. A company sets the par value when the corporation is created. The par value usually has no relationship to the market value of a stock.

Preferred stock has characteristics of both debt and equity. Investors receive a set dividend, similar to bond interest payments, but preferred stock represents ownership.

Stockholders receive dividends, a share in company profits.

For investors, owning preferred stock is less risky than common stock. If liquidation would occur, preferred shareholders are paid before common stockholders. Preferred stockholders generally have no voting rights within the corporation.

Two other characteristics of preferred stock sometimes exist. *Cumulative preferred stock* requires that missed (unpaid) dividends due to low earnings will build up until paid to preferred stockholders. *Convertible preferred stock* allows an exchange into common shares. The conversion process is similar to that of convertible bonds.

checkpoint ✓

What are the main differences between common and preferred stock?

■ Issuing Stock

When a corporation decides to issue stock for the first time or to issue additional shares of stock, various actions are required.

INITIAL PUBLIC OFFERING

When a company offers stock to outside investors for the first time, it is termed an initial public offering (IPO). *Public offering* may refer to the issuing of additional shares of stock by a company.

The IPO for a company is also called "going public." The organization goes from being a *privately held* corporation to one that is *publicly held*. After this process, its shares are sold on a stock exchange. As shown in Figure 7-2, four steps are involved when issuing stock.

1. **Consult with investment banker.** The process starts with contacting an investment banking company. These firms provide advice about issuing stock and will assist with legal approval

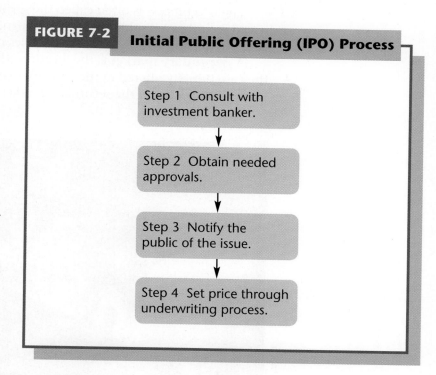

FIGURE 7-2   Initial Public Offering (IPO) Process

Step 1 Consult with investment banker.

Step 2 Obtain needed approvals.

Step 3 Notify the public of the issue.

Step 4 Set price through underwriting process.

from the Securities and Exchange Commission (SEC). Investment bankers will develop a marketing and advertising plan to promote the stock issue. They will also obtain potential customers. Finally,

investment bankers act as agents to distribute very large blocks of stocks and bonds.

2. **Obtain needed approvals.** This step involves two groups. First, a majority of current owners of the company must agree to "go public." Then, the SEC must approve the process. This federal agency assures that the stock offering is legitimate. The public must be protected from any deceptive practices or potential investment fraud.

3. **Notify the public of the issue.** Full disclosure of the upcoming stock issue is another requirement. Through news releases and ads in financial publications, the company communicates with the general public about the shares that will be available. A *prospectus* is prepared and distributed. This document presents the legal and financial information about the company issuing the stock.

4. **Set price through underwriting process.** The underwriters in the investment banking company evaluate various company and market factors to develop a price range for the stock. Then, an *issue price* (also called the *subscription price*) is set. Some questions the investment banking company might consider in setting the price include

- Has the company been profitable over a period of years?
- Have the company's managers made good business decisions?
- Does the company have growth potential in coming years?
- Does the company have an unusually large amount of debt?
- How does the company compare with others in its industry?

The IPO process is often called the **primary market**, where newly issued securities are sold by investment bankers. After the initial selling, all later buying and selling of those securities occurs in the secondary market.

A **secondary market** is the location where securities are traded after they are initially offered in the primary market. The majority of security transactions occur in the secondary market. The New York Stock Exchange,

DIGITAL VISION

Stock brokers trade securities on the secondary market.

other stock exchanges, the NASDAQ, and bond markets are examples of secondary markets.

checkpoint ✓

What factors affect the issue value of a stock?

a question of ethics

Investment Fraud

Each year, investors lose more than $1.2 billion to various scams. Especially vulnerable are elderly consumers, who may not completely understand the opportunities they are offered. And, after being scammed, older consumers may be too embarrassed to report their losses to government authorities.

Some of the most common tactics used to attract people to deceptive investment schemes include

- Developing trust, in which con artists create a friendly connection by telling you about their family and asking about yours.

- Offering an impossibly attractive investment opportunity, for example, land that is cheap compared to other real estate or guaranteed returns of over 50 percent.

- Establishing credibility. The scam artist might imply that the investment is safe because it is advertised in *The Wall Street Journal* or mention that the company is "licensed" with the state.

- Creating social pressure by implying that many other people have made this investment. They may even mention names of people the investor knows.

- Generating fear to close the deal, since "you wouldn't want to miss this opportunity."

- Implying limited availability, such as "these are the last two rare coins available."

To avoid becoming a victim of investment fraud, use these guidelines.

1. Investigate before signing and paying any money. Contact federal and state agencies about any complaints against the company. Also, talk with family members and friends about the investment.

2. Avoid "you must sign up today" opportunities. Take your time to determine if the investment is legitimate and appropriate for your situation.

3. Research the company and type of investment. Understand the costs and potential risks.

4. Most important, remember that deals that seem "too good to be true"…usually are!

Think Critically

1. Why do so many people each year get cheated with phony investments?

2. Conduct an Internet search to obtain additional information about various investment frauds. Prepare a summary of your findings.

UNDERSTAND CONCEPTS

Determine the best answer for each of the following questions.

1. Common stockholders have the right to
   a. vote for members of the board of directors
   b. receive a set amount of dividends
   c. receive payment before preferred stockholders
   d. convert their stock into other types of securities

2. When a company first issues shares of stock, it is referred to as the
   ____?____ market.
   a. stock
   b. bond
   c. primary
   d. secondary

3. An initial public offering refers to ____?____.
   a. issuing foreign bonds
   b. selling stock without using an investment banker
   c. doubling the number of shares of stock
   d. a company going public

4. **True or False?** Most preferred stockholders select preferred stock so
   they will be able to vote for corporate officers.

5. **True or False?** On a daily basis, most investors buy and sell shares
   of stock through the primary market.

MAKE ACADEMIC CONNECTIONS

6. **Research** Obtain additional information about issuing preferred
   stock. Locate the current market value of preferred stock for a
   company.

7. **Visual Art** Research a company that recently had a new stock
   issue. Prepare a visual presentation of the steps of the initial public
   offering (IPO) process using specific information and visuals for the
   situation you researched.

8. **Law** Conduct an Internet search or library research about the role
   of the Securities and Exchange Commission (SEC) in the initial public offering process. Prepare a brief summary of your findings.

9. **Global Business** Identify a multinational company that sells stock
   both in its home country and in the U.S. What are the benefits of
   this action?

Goals
- Identify the activities involved with stock market transactions.
- Explain the purpose of a mutual fund.
- Describe the factors that affect bonds values.

Terms
- stockbroker
- stock exchange
- market value
- stock split
- selling short
- mutual fund
- capital gain
- yield to maturity (YTM)

■ Stock Market Transactions

Each day, hundreds of millions of shares of stock are bought and sold in the secondary market. These shares were previously issued by companies in the primary market, and now they are bought and sold among various investors.

TYPES OF STOCKBROKERS

A **stockbroker** is a licensed specialist in the buying and selling of stocks and bonds. Brokers serve as an intermediary between the issuer of securities (bonds and stock) and potential customers (investors). Through brokers, stockholders state the price at which they are willing to sell their shares. Interested buyers tell brokers what they would be willing to pay for those shares. The brokers then work out a price that is acceptable to both buyers and sellers. For their services, brokers charge a fee called a *commission*.

Two types of brokers are common. A *full-service broker* provides information about securities you may want to buy. Full-service brokers work for brokerage houses with large research staffs. In contrast, a *discount broker* places orders and offers limited research and other services. Discount brokers charge lower commissions than full-service brokers. Investors who do their own research can save money by using a discount broker. Today, both full-service and discount brokers can be reached online handling trades through their web sites.

DIGITAL VISION

Stockbrokers are specialists in the buying and selling of stock.

STOCK EXCHANGES

Brokers work through stock exchanges, which are businesses where securities are bought and sold. The best known stock exchange is the New York Stock Exchange in New York City. The American Stock Exchange is also in New York City. Regional stock exchanges operate in Boston, Chicago, Philadelphia, and San Francisco. More than 150 stock exchanges are in operation around the world.

In the past, stocks of smaller companies were not traded on a stock exchange. The *over-the-counter (OTC)* market is a network where securities transactions occur using telephones and computers rather than on the floor of an exchange. The OTC market in the U.S. is the NASDAQ, which stands for the National Association of Securities Dealers Automated Quotations. Today, the NASDAQ includes many large companies.

CHANGING STOCK VALUES

The market value of a stock is the price at which a share of stock can be bought and sold in the stock market. This current value of a share can change rapidly. If the business is doing well, the market value is likely to go up. If the business has a poor record, the market value usually goes down. The market value may be affected by current economic conditions as well as national and global politics.

The prices at which stocks are being bought and sold are available through stock market listings in newspapers and online. Examine Figure 7-3, which gives an explanation of the stock market listing.

The cost of an online stock trade can range from $5 to $30. The service provided also varies. Investors must decide how much they are willing to pay for assistance and information.

FIGURE 7-3

Stock Market Listing Explanation

STOCK MARKET QUOTATIONS

1	2	3	4	5	6	7	8	9	10	11	12
52-Week					Yld.		Vol.				Net
Hi	Lo	Stock	Sym.	Div.	%	PE	100s	Hi	Lo	Close	Chg.
74.93	56.72	Deere	DE	1.12	1.6	15	21823	70.14	67.38	68.01	−0.42
95.64	64.84	FedExCp	FDX	0.28	0.3	27	14555	94.54	91.78	93.74	+1.22
45	35	Kellogg	K	1.01	2.3	21	6791	44.82	43.67	44.74	−0.24
20.50	15.94	Mattel	MAT	0.40	2.1	16	21682	19.23	17.77	18.80	−0.15
42.95	31.25	Reebok	RBK	0.30	0.8	14	4501	40.47	37.82	39.22	+0.12

1 – Highest price paid for stock during past 52 weeks
2 – Lowest price paid for stock during the past 52 weeks
3 – Abbreviated company name
4 – Symbol used to report company
5 – Current dividend per share (in dollars)
6 – Dividend yield based on current selling price
7 – Price-earning ratio
8 – Number of shares traded, expressed in hundreds, on the trading day
9 – Highest price for a share on the trading day
10 – Lowest price for a share on the trading day
11 – Closing price for the day
12 – Change in closing price compared to previous trading day

Stock Market Indexes Another measurement of investment values is a *stock index*. These indicators of stock values are commonly reported on television, radio, and in newspapers. The Dow Jones Industrial Average (DJIA) includes 30 of the largest U.S. companies. Another commonly reported stock index is the Standard & Poor's (S&P) 500, which is based on stock values of 500 major companies.

Stock Split When the value of a share of stock gets fairly high, many companies decide to lower the price to increase market activity. A **stock split** is the proportional division of a number of stock shares into a larger number. With this action, a lower share value occurs, but there is no change in the proportion of each stockholder's ownership. For example, with a 2-for-1 stock split, the number of shares you own doubles, but the total market value is unchanged. Instead of one share of stock valued at $100, you would have two shares valued at $50 each.

This increase in the number of shares does not change the company's total market value or each shareholder's share of ownership. If you own 20,000 shares, representing 5 percent of the company, you would now have 40,000 shares which would still represent 5 percent ownership. The company hopes that the lower share price resulting from a stock split will create increased interest and market demand for the stock. A stock split can result in strong gains if the price increases to the previous level, since each investor now has more shares.

Selling Short If an investor believes the price of a stock will fall, a method exists to make money. **Selling short** involves selling a stock not actually owned when a lower price is expected. Then, the investor must buy the stock back at the market price to replace the "borrowed" shares.

For example, an investor may decide to "sell short" 1,000 shares of a company's stock on April 20 for $10 a share. Then, on May 1, if the stock is selling at $9 a share, the investor can "replace" the borrowed shares at a lower price. By selling short, this investor made a profit of $1,000, less commission and any other fees.

In this process, investors who sell short hope to buy the needed replacement shares at a lower price. This activity can be quite risky. If the stock increases in value, a loss will occur when the replacement shares must be bought at a higher price.

Consumer spending habits affect stock prices.

teamwork

Discuss various business and economic trends. Prepare a list of stocks which your group believes would be good investments. Explain what factors influenced the selection of these companies.

STOCK SELECTION ACTIONS

As a person decides which stocks to purchase, an investment analysis process can be helpful.

Investment Analysis Process Buying stocks can consist of a process with the following steps.

1. Observe and analyze economic and social trends.
2. Determine industries that will be affected.
3. Identify companies in those industries.
4. Decide whether to buy, sell, or hold the stock of those companies.

By observing various economic and social trends in the U.S. and around the world, you can determine what types of companies could benefit from those trends.

Economic Factors Various economic conditions can affect stock prices, including the following factors.

- **Inflation** Higher prices can result in lower spending by consumers, reducing company profits
- **Interest Rates** As the cost of money changes, company profits can increase or decline
- **Consumer Spending** Profits of companies that sell products and services to households are directly affected by consumer buying habits
- **Employment** As people obtain or lose jobs, the amount of money they have for spending will affect company profits

Industry Trends Societal changes and other factors can have a positive or negative influence on various types of companies. For example, as people live longer, increased health care is required. Companies involved in health care products may be a wise investment. Other industries that investors might analyze and consider for stock purchases include automotive, construction, consumer products, financial services, retailing, technology, and utilities.

Market Trends The overall direction of stock market prices is also a factor to consider. A *bull market* refers to a period of rising stock values. During this time, investors tend to have a positive attitude about the stock market and the economy. In contrast, a *bear market* is a period of declining stock market prices, in which investor attitudes are generally negative.

Dividend Yield Additional information about a company may also be considered. The *yield* of a stock is an important factor if your goal is to earn a good return from your investment.

For example, suppose that a company is paying a quarterly dividend of $0.60 a share. The total dividend for the year would be $2.40, and if the stock is selling for $40 a share, the current yield (return) would be calculated as follows.

$$\text{Dividend Yield} = \frac{\text{Dividend per share}}{\text{Market price per share}}$$

$$\frac{\$2.40}{\$40} = 0.06 \text{ or } 6 \text{ percent}$$

Price-Earnings Ratio The price of a stock should also be considered. Many investors look at the stock's *price-earnings (P/E)* ratio, which is the relationship between a stock's selling price and its earnings per share. The P/E gives you an indication of whether the stock is priced high or low in relation to its earnings per share.

Stock Information Sources When selecting stocks, learn something about the company. Several information sources are available, such as *Moody's Handbook of Common Stocks, Value Line,* and *Standard & Poor's Encyclopedia of Stocks*. These publications provide data about net worth, debt, sales revenue, profits, dividend history, and the future prospects of companies. Many web sites are also available to provide valuable information on companies.

The U.S. Securities and Exchange Commission, which oversees the financial markets, requires all companies that issue publicly traded securities to file detailed reports electronically. Those reports can be accessed online.

checkpoint ✓

What factors are commonly considered when evaluating a company's stock?

¥£€$ finance around the world

Stock Exchanges around the World

Locations of stock exchanges range from Johannesburg to Hong Kong and from Madrid to Lima. More than 150 exist in countries around the world. Each of these organizations serves local companies with trading facilities for buying and selling stocks, bonds, and other securities.

The Prague Stock Exchange started in 1993, the year Czechoslovakia divided into two separate countries—the Czech Republic and Slovakia. As the countries moved from a centrally planned economy under communist rule to a free-market economy, citizens were allowed to invest in stocks.

As the capital of the Czech Republic, Prague is the center of the country's business activities. When it started, the Prague Stock Exchange handled transactions for only seven companies. Today, this exchange has expanded its business to include many more companies. Many of the previously government-controlled businesses are now privately owned. Some of the most popular stocks are companies in the hotel and glass manufacturing industries.

While many local stock exchanges exist, the influence of regional markets is expanding. Euronext was formed in 2000 through a merger of the Paris, Brussels, and Amsterdam stock exchanges. This organization regularly trades stocks of more than 1,250 companies. More recently, Euronext has been acquired by the New York Stock Exchange.

Think Critically

1. How might the activities of stock exchanges in different countries differ from each other?
2. Conduct an Internet search to locate the web site for a stock exchange in another region of the world.

■Mutual Funds

Instead of buying individual bonds and stock, many people buy shares in an *investment company*. A **mutual fund** is an investment fund set up and managed by companies that receive money from many investors. Then, the company buys and sells a wide variety of stocks or bonds. Mutual funds allow investors to spread their risk among many investments.

TYPES OF MUTUAL FUNDS

Over 17,000 different mutual funds are available to investors. These funds have many different objectives. For instance, some emphasize investing in growth stocks, some emphasize stocks that pay high dividends, and some emphasize international stocks. Some of the main types of mutual funds include

- Aggressive growth stock funds, which seek quick growth but also have higher risk
- Income funds that specialize in stocks that pay regular dividends
- International funds that invest in stock of companies from around the world
- Sector funds, which include stocks of companies in the same industry, such as health care, energy, or telecommunications
- Bond funds, which specialize in corporate bonds
- Balanced funds that invest in both stock and bonds

When selecting a mutual fund in which to invest, investors should match their personal investment goals to the type of mutual fund.

The London Stock Exchange is one of many in cities around the world.

MUTUAL FUND VALUES

Mutual fund investors own shares of the mutual fund. The value of each share is based on the total value of all investments made by the mutual fund company. For example, if the investments were worth $400,000 and 80,000 shares existed, each share would be worth $5.

$400,000 \div 80,000 = 5

This amount is called the *net asset value (NAV)* of a mutual fund.

A part of the dividends and interest received from the fund's investments is used to pay operating expenses of the fund. The major portion of earnings is distributed to the mutual fund shareholders or reinvested in the fund.

checkpoint ✓

What are the advantages of investing in mutual funds?

■Changing Bond Values

Bonds are bought and sold in the bond market. The market value of a bond varies based on changing interest rates and the credit rating of the borrowing organization.

REPORTING BOND PRICES

Bond values are reported, like stocks, in daily newspapers and online. Corporate bond prices are stated in 100s, with the bonds sold in $1,000 denominations (ten times the reported amount).

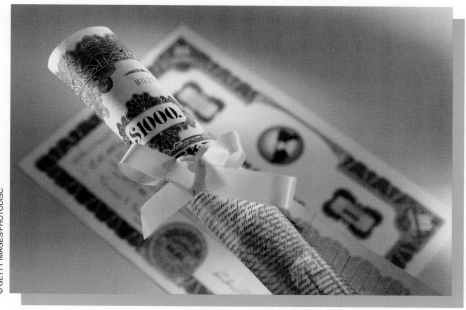

© GETTY IMAGES/PHOTODISC

The price of bonds is affected by changing interest rates.

For example, a bond reported at 100 is selling at its face value of $1000. A bond selling at 105 has a current market value of $1,050. At 100, the bond is being sold at *par*. At 105, it is being sold at a *premium*. Below 100, the bond is being sold at a *discount*.

The price investors are willing to pay for a bond depends upon the *stated interest rate*. If interest rates on similar bonds are higher than the bond's stated rate, investors will want to buy the bond for less than its face value. On the other hand, if the bond's stated interest rate is higher than interest rates on similar bonds, the seller of the bond will want to receive more than its face value.

As shown in Figure 7-4, changing interest rates affect the price of the bond. Since the interest payment is set when the bond is issued, the current yield will be affected by the amount a person pays for the bond.

FIGURE 7-4

Changing Bond Values and the Current Yield

Situation	Bond Sold at	Market Value	Reported at	Interest Payment	Current Yield
Bond issued	par	$1,000	100	$100	10% $100 ÷ $1,000
Higher interest rates	discount	$ 900	90	$100	11.1% $100 ÷ $900
Lower interest rates	premium	$1,100	110	$100	9.1% $100 ÷ $1,100

CAPITAL GAINS

When a person holds a bond until maturity, a **capital gain** may occur. A capital gain is the increase in the value between the purchase price and the maturity value. When a bond is bought at a discount such as $900 and held until maturity, the investor has a $100 capital gain, in addition to the interest payments on the bond.

A *capital loss* can also result. If a bond is bought at a premium, such as $1,100, at maturity the bondholder only receives $1,000. Why would a person do this? The investor has paid for the right to receive the annual interest payments on the bond until the maturity date.

The current yield is the rate of return based on interest earned. Capital gains and losses affect the **yield to maturity (YTM)** of a bond. The yield to maturity is the annual rate of return an investor would receive when a bond is held until maturity. YTM takes into account the price discount below or the premium above the face value of the bond.

As you might expect, the YTM is more than the current yield when the bond is selling at a discount. This rate is less than the current yield when the bond is selling at a premium.

checkpoint ✓

What factors affect bond prices?

7.4 Lesson Assessment

UNDERSTAND CONCEPTS

Determine the best answer for each of the following questions.

1. When a company changes the number of shares of stock to bring the current market price down, this is called
   a. selling short
   b. an initial public offering
   c. a stock split
   d. a mutual fund

2. An investment that allows a person to own a variety of companies is called
   a. a corporate bond
   b. preferred stock
   c. a mutual fund
   d. a municipal bond

3. **True or False?** Only discount brokers allow investors to buy and sell stocks online.

4. **True or False?** As interest rates rise, bond prices tend to rise.

MAKE ACADEMIC CONNECTIONS

5. **Technology** Visit the web site of a stock brokerage company. What services are offered to investors? How might you use this site to select stocks in which to invest?

6. **Data Analysis** Using Figure 7-3, answer the following questions:
   a. What is the amount of the most recent dividend for Federal Express?
   b. What is the yield for Kellogg's stock?
   c. What is the lowest price that Mattel stock sold for over the past year?
   d. What was the closing price of Reebok stock on the previous trading day?

7. **Visual Art** Prepare a poster, computer presentation, or other visual to communicate the main types of mutual funds in which a person can invest.

8. **Research** Using online sources or the financial section of the newspaper, obtain current information about the trend on bond values. What factors have affected bond prices?

Summary

7.1 FINANCING CHOICES

1. The main short-term financing methods used by businesses include buying on account (accounts payable), bank loan, line of credit, promissory note, and commercial paper.
2. Debt (borrowing), equity (selling stock), and leasing (renting) are methods used by organizations to finance business activities.

7.2 DEBT FINANCING: BONDS

3. Bonds are issued by the federal government, state and local governments, foreign governments, and companies.
4. The process for issuing bonds involves the use of an investment banker, who provides advice to the company and helps set the price of the bonds. Rates on new bonds will be affected by current interest rates and the bond rating of the company.

7.3 EQUITY FINANCING: STOCK

5. The two main types of stock issued by corporations are common and preferred.
6. An initial public offering (IPO) is the process of offering stock to outside investors for the first time. When this occurs, a company that was privately owned becomes a public company.

7.4 STOCK AND BOND MARKETS

7. A stockbroker is a licensed specialist in the buying and selling of stocks and bonds. Brokers work through stock exchanges, which are businesses that accommodate the buying and selling of securities. The main factors that affect stock prices are economic conditions, industry trends, and market trends.
8. A mutual fund is an investment fund set up and managed by companies that receive money from many investors. The money from investors is used to buy and sell a wide variety of stocks or bonds. Mutual funds allow investors to spread their risk among many investments. Many different types of mutual funds exist to meet different investment objectives.
9. Bond prices are affected by interest rates. Higher rates will result in a bond being sold at a discount. When rates decline, bonds are sold at a premium. A capital gain is the increase in value between the purchase price and the maturity value on a bond or other investment.

Develop Your Business Language

Match the terms listed with the definitions. Some terms will not be used.

1. Price at which a share of stock can be bought and sold in the stock market
2. Security that has priority over common stock in the payment of dividends
3. Unsecured, short-term debt instruments issued by corporations
4. Stated annual interest rate for a bond
5. Corporate bond without collateral
6. Type of debt secured by a specific asset or property
7. Selling a stock not actually owned when a lower price is expected
8. An equity security representing ownership in a company with voting rights
9. When a company offers stock to outside investors for the first time.
10. Increase in the value between the purchase price and the maturity value
11. Measure of the quality and safety of a company's debt
12. Legal agreement to use property that belongs to another person
13. Business organization where securities are bought and sold
14. A licensed specialist in the buying and selling of stocks and bonds
15. Portion of company profits
16. Proportional division of a number of stock shares into a larger number
17. An individual or company that assists with the issuing of new securities

a. bond rating
b. capital gain
c. commercial paper
d. common stock
e. coupon rate
f. debenture bond
g. dividend
h. initial public offering (IPO)
i. investment banker
j. leasing
k. line of credit
l. market value
m. mortgage bond
n. mutual fund
o. preferred stock
p. primary market
q. promissory note
r. secondary market
s. selling short
t. stock exchange
u. stock split
v. stockbroker
w. yield to maturity (YTM)

Review Concepts

18. A federal government debt security that pays a variable rate that increases with consumer prices is ____?____.
    a. T-bill
    b. T-note
    c. T-bond
    d. I-bond
19. A person interested in current income would select a mutual fund emphasizing
    a. technology stocks
    b. dividends
    c. long-term growth
    d. foreign government bonds
20. The yield to maturity of a bond would be highest when the bond is
    a. sold at a discount
    b. sold at a premium
    c. sold at par
    d. tax deductible

Think Critically

21. What actions might a small company take when needing to borrow funds?

22. What benefits and drawbacks are associated with leasing?

23. What actions can be taken by a company to improve its bond rating?

24. Describe the role of an investment banker when a company is involved in mergers and acquisitions.

25. How can a stock split affect the long-term profits of an investor?

26. What are the economic benefits of capital gains earned by investors?

Business Financial Calculations

27. For each of the following situations, calculate the annual yield.
    a. stock that cost $56 and earned a dividend of $4.20
    b. bond costing $1,000 with annual interest of $106
    c. land purchased for $10,000 and sold a year later for $11,600

28. A bond with a yield of 6.72 percent has dropped 30 basis points. What is the new yield?

29. You call your broker to sell short, asking to sell 100 shares at $42. Within three days, the stock drops to $39 a share and you obtain the required shares. What is the amount of your capital gain in this situation?

30. You own 40,000 shares of stock of a company, representing 6 percent ownership. The company plans a 3-for-2 stock split. After the split,
    a. how many shares would you own?
    b. what percentage of the company would you own?

31. Based on Figure 7-3, answer the following questions.
    a. The number of shares traded on Federal Express stock increased by 10 percent the next trading day. How many shares were traded the next day?
    b. What was the closing price of Deere stock on the previous trading day?
    c. Based on the closing price for Mattel, if the company paid an annual dividend of $1.26, what would be the yield?

32. What would be the market value (in dollars) for a corporate bond selling at 97? What would be the market value of a bond selling at 106?

Analyze Cases

Use the case from the beginning of the chapter, The New York Stock Exchange, to answer the following questions.

33. What activities does the NYSE provide to assist businesses?

34. How do expanded global business activities affect the NYSE?

35. Describe positive and negative aspects of stock exchange mergers for companies and investors.

36. How might technology affect future NYSE activities?

37. What aspect of the NYSE activities poses the greatest challenge for its future? What actions would you suggest to address this concern?

Portfolio Activity

COLLECT an item that reflects the financing alternatives used by various organizations—debt, equity, leasing. This example could be an advertisement, newspaper or magazine article, a web site, photo, or an actual item.

CREATE a visual, such as a table or diagram, to summarize the benefits and drawbacks of the financing methods commonly used by businesses and other organizations. Use photos, ads, actual items, and drawings to illustrate the advantages and disadvantages of debt, equity, and leasing.

CONNECT your visual to other aspects of our economy and society or relate it to an idea you have learned in another class. Make the connection by preparing a brief written summary comparing debt, equity, and leasing.

Stock Market Activity

Issuing stock is a major financing activity of most companies. Organizations may also use debt and leasing. These financing alternatives affect both the company's current business activities and its long-term potential.

Use online and library resources to research the company you have been studying (or select a different company).

1. Compare the use of debt and equity by the company. Use the company's annual report as well as other research sources.

2. Determine if the company has recently issued additional stock or bonds. If so, what was the planned use of these funds?

3. Describe situations in which the company might use leasing.

4. Analyze your findings to determine the effect of these financing decisions on the value of the company's stock. At this point, would you buy, sell, or hold the stock of this company as an investment for your current or future personal financial situation? Explain your reasons.

Planning a Career in Stock Brokerage

When a company needs to raise funds through issuing stocks or bonds, an investment banker will be involved. Investment banking firms help companies and governments issue securities, help investors purchase securities, manage financial assets, trade securities, and provide financial advice.

Expanded public offerings by foreign companies and privatization of firms previously owned by foreign governments will likely increase international investment banking needs.

Stockbrokers work with customers when buying or selling stocks, bonds, mutual funds, and other investment products.

Employment Outlook

- Opportunities for investment and financial services sales agents are expected to grow about 10 percent over the next eight years. Most of these jobs are in securities, commodity contracts, and other financial investment activities.
- Other opportunities exist with banks, credit unions, and other financial institutions. Many people in this field are self-employed.
- Turnover is often high for beginning sales agents who have not yet established a strong base of clients. Opportunities for entry-level positions are very competitive.

Job Titles

- Investment banker
- Stockbroker
- Account executive
- Registered representative
- Brokerage sales manager
- Stock analyst
- Economist
- Security sales agent
- Commodity sales agent

Needed Skills

- A college degree with knowledge of finance, accounting, and economics is a basic requirement
- Sales and interpersonal skills are vital when working with clients
- Research ability and computer competency to keep informed on economic and industry trends
- Knowledge of laws related to securities and financial markets
- Securities and commodities sales agents must pass licensing exams, such as the Series 7 and the Series 63 licenses

What's It Like to Work in Stock Brokerage?

"How might the merger affect the company's stock price?" "Will the company's dividends continue for the next few years?"

These are some of the questions you might address as a stockbroker. Your ability to attract new clients and serve existing ones is a key to success. You will likely work long hours. Your income may be based all or partially on commission.

As you prepare a sales strategy for your clients, you must assess their current financial situation and future needs. Developing a plan to meet clients' investment goals will be the major focus of your work.

What about you? What elements of being a stockbroker might interest you? What additional information would you like to have about this career?

MULTIMEDIA PRESENTATION EVENT

Participants in this event are challenged to use presentation technologies and software to prepare and deliver their message. Most consumers understand the need to invest for their financial future, but do not have a thorough understanding of the investment options. You are to create a multimedia presentation that teaches people about investment options. The presentation should explain stocks, corporate bonds, government bonds, and real estate as investment options. Each type of investment should be carefully defined in the presentation. Definitions should be in terms the average consumer understands. The presentation should also emphasize strengths and weaknesses for each type of investment.

Presentations can be created by 1 to 3 members, and may be submitted using only a CD or DVD. Presentations must be at least two (2) and no more than four (4) minutes in length. They must address the assigned topic, be well organized, and contain substantiated statements.

The oral presentation is an explanation of the multimedia presentation. The oral presentation should explain the development and design process, the use and implementation of innovative technology, the use and development of media elements, and copyright issues with pictures, music, and other features. The individual or team has nine (9) minutes to give the multimedia presentation. Setup time is included in the total presentation time. A timekeeper will stand at eight (8) minutes. Five (5) points will be deducted for any presentation over 9 minutes in length. Following the oral presentation, the judge may conduct a three-minute question-and-answer period during which the presenters should be prepared to defend all aspects of their multimedia presentation.

Performance Indicators Evaluated

- Explain the development of the topic in the presentation.
- Explain the development and design process.
- Demonstrate the use and implementation of innovative technology.
- Compare customer service offerings.
- Explain the use and development of graphics, video, and audio.
- Organize an effective oral presentation.
- Deliver an effective oral presentation that indicates self-confidence.

Go to the FBLA web site for more detailed information.

Think Critically

1. Why is a multimedia presentation a good way to explain different investment options?
2. Why should this presentation compare and contrast investments according to strengths and weaknesses?
3. What is the disadvantage of a presentation that uses too much text?
4. How does the way presenters dress affect the impact of a presentation?

www.fbla.org

Financial Institutions and Banking Services

Point Your [Browser]
www.thomsonedu.com/school/busfinance

Commercial and Global Banking at Wells Fargo

"What are current rates for a commercial line of credit?" "How can we best collect funds from our overseas customers?" These are some of the questions that commercial and international banking experts at Wells Fargo attempt to answer each day.

Started in 1852, today Wells Fargo is the fifth largest bank in the U.S., with about 3,000 branch offices and another 1,000 home mortgage stores. When the company opened for business in San Francisco and Sacramento, California, buying and selling gold was a major focus. Between 1852 and 1918, Wells Fargo used a variety of transportation modes to move gold. These included the Pony Express, stagecoaches, steamships, railroads, and motor vehicles.

Today, the banking services of Wells Fargo are aimed at business customers that have revenues of $10 million or more. The main focus of commercial banking is credit. Wells Fargo provides loans to companies for a variety of purposes. This core product of lending is used to cross-sell other services, such as managing depository needs, coordinating stock transfers, and creating letters of credit for international payments. Working with corporate clients requires developing strong relationships. Wells Fargo employees serve their customers by servicing new loans, assisting with fund transfers, documenting legal requirements, and suggesting risk management strategies. These activities require staff teams to support several large corporate clients in a geographic region.

The company also offers global financial services. The Wells Fargo International Personal Banking (IPB) program for international customers provides online access to many banking services. IPB may be used by a foreign national moving to the U.S. or a U.S. citizen going abroad. Wells Fargo HSBC Trade Bank is a joint venture between Wells Fargo Bank and HSBC, the largest bank in the world, based in London. This agreement allows Wells Fargo customers access to 8,000 HSBC offices in 80 countries. Other international services offered by Wells Fargo include

- Foreign exchange services for buying and selling more than 90 currencies
- Online trade services allowing access to various services for importers and exporters, including letters of credit
- International treasury management providing cash management payments and collections around the world
- Consumer remittance accounts used by customers to electronically send money to Mexico, Hong Kong, Taiwan, and many other international locations

Think Critically

1. How do the commercial and global banking services at Wells Fargo serve its business clients?
2. Conduct an Internet search to obtain current information about the activities of the Wells Fargo Company.

8.1 Banks and Other Financial Institutions

Goals
- Describe the history and development of banking in the United States.
- Explain the organization and activities of commercial banks and other financial institutions.

Terms
- Federal Reserve System
- reserve requirement
- discount rate
- open market operations

■ Banking Systems

People often overlook the fact that a bank is a business and they are its customers. Similar to stores and factories, a bank is a business that sells services such as savings accounts, loans, and investments. Banks are regulated more strictly than most other businesses. If a business fails, some people lose money. If a bank fails, thousands of people are affected.

U.S. BANKING HISTORY

Banking in the United States has evolved from local companies in small towns to multinational corporations. The activities of banks have been affected by historic and economic events.

Federal Currency During Colonial times and just after the American Revolution, several types of currency circulated. In use were the British pound and shilling along with a Spanish coin called the real. In 1792, the Mint Act authorized gold coins in the amounts of $10, $5, and $2.50 along with $1, 50¢, 25¢, 10¢, and 1¢ silver coins, and 1¢ and ½¢ copper coins.

In 1861, paper currency was first issued by the U.S. government. Prior to that, paper money in the form of *banknotes* was issued by individual banks. Between 1793 and 1861, over 1,500 private banks were allowed to print their own paper currency, which was backed by the gold in their vaults. During this time, more than 7,000 different state banknotes were in circulation.

First and Second Banks of the U.S. In 1791, despite varied political opinions, a Bank of the United States was chartered. This bank was privately owned, with the federal government owning about 20 percent of its capital. During its existence, the first Bank of the United States helped stabilize the value of currencies in circulation. Continued political differences resulted in not renewing the bank's charter when it expired in 1811.

As conflicting state bank policies and changing economic conditions continued, a second Bank of the United States was created in 1816. The bank functioned to better regulate credit and the money supply. State banks, however, viewed these actions as a threat. In 1836, this bank also went out of existence when its charter expired.

National Banking Act of 1864 During the U.S. Civil War, many monetary and banking issues surfaced. The National Banking Act of 1864 created the office of the Comptroller of the Currency with the purpose of chartering national banks. As national banknotes were issued, a high tax was imposed on state banknotes. This action resulted in the elimination of state bank currencies and stabilized the value of U.S. banknotes.

Federal Reserve Act After years of economic crises, in 1913, Congress created the Federal Reserve System. This central banking network was designed to be flexible for the changing economic needs of the country.

THE FEDERAL RESERVE SYSTEM

A bank that will not allow you to make deposits is a Federal Reserve Bank, which is a *bank for banks*. The **Federal Reserve System (Fed)** was created to supervise and regulate member banks to help them serve the public efficiently. All national banks are required to join the Federal Reserve System, and state banks may join as well.

Organizational Structure Banks that join the system are known as *member banks*. The United States is divided into 12 Federal Reserve districts, with a central Federal Reserve Bank in each district, as shown in Figure 8-1. These *district reserve banks* serve various functions such as handling banking activities for government agencies and implementing Fed policies. Each regional district bank is governed by a nine-member board of directors.

FIGURE 8-1 The Federal Reserve System

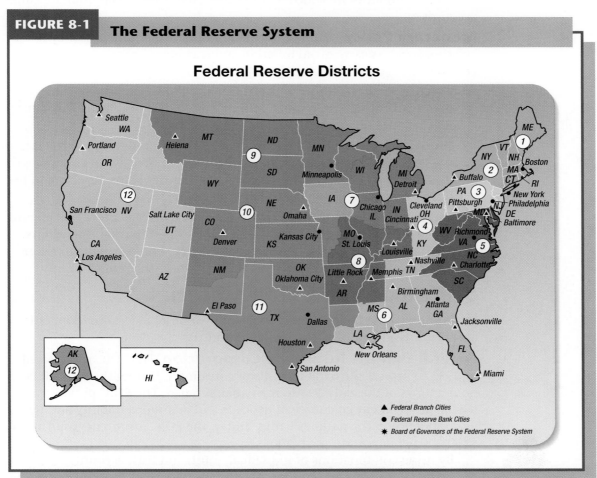

Federal Reserve Districts

▲ Federal Branch Cities
● Federal Reserve Bank Cities
✳ Board of Governors of the Federal Reserve System

The *Board of Governors* of the Federal Reserve System consists of seven members, appointed by the President, who serve a 14-year term. The chair of the Board of Governors, also selected by the President and confirmed by the Senate, serves a four-year term. There is no limit on the number of terms a chair may serve.

Federal Reserve Activities A Federal Reserve Bank serves member banks and the economy in several ways. One service provided by the Fed is the holding of *reserves*. Banks cannot lend all of the money they receive from customers. They are required to keep a part of the money they receive from customers on deposit with the Federal Reserve System. The percentage of funds that a bank is required to hold is the reserve requirement. This amount cannot be used for loans. These funds are held in case additional funds are needed to meet daily customer demand.

As a result of reserve requirements, a bank will lend only a certain percentage of deposits. For example, if a customer deposits $1,000 and the bank is required to hold 15 percent of all deposits in reserve, the bank can lend 85 percent of the new deposit, or $850 (100% − 15% = 85%). This regulation is designed to help the banking system and the economy operate efficiently and to protect depositors.

Another service of the Federal Reserve System is clearing checks in different cities. *Clearing* refers to paying checks among different banks in different cities. The Fed processes millions of checks each day to make sure that the correct amounts are added to and subtracted from the appropriate bank accounts.

Monetary Policy Maintaining an appropriate amount of money in circulation is necessary to avoid inflation and encourage economic growth. The Fed influences the money supply in three ways.

1. **Setting Reserve Requirements** As the Fed adjusts the portion of the deposits that banks must hold, the amount that may be lent out will increase or decrease.

2. **Changing the Discount Rate** The discount rate refers to the rate the Fed charges on loans to member banks. An increase in this rate will usually increase the cost for mortgages and other loans, resulting in reduced borrowing.

3. **Buying and Selling Government Securities** The process of buying and selling government securities is called open market operations. The sale of government bonds to banks, for example, results in fewer funds available for lending. This action reduces the money supply.

OTHER BANK REGULATORY AGENCIES

In addition to the Federal Reserve System, two other federal government agencies actively monitor the banking industry.

Federal Deposit Insurance Corporation The FDIC was created in 1933 to protect the bank deposits of consumers. During the difficult economic times of the early 1930s, many banks failed. The FDIC provides a federal government guarantee of deposits and maintains stability and public confidence in the nation's banks. Today, the FDIC insures deposits up to $100,000 per depositor, per bank.

By using combinations of individual, joint, and trust accounts in different financial institutions, you can obtain federal deposit insurance covering amounts greater than $100,000. Be careful, however, since different branch offices count as the same institution, and mergers in the financial service industry may bring accounts from different banks together.

Comptroller of the Currency Regulation of national banks is the main duty of the Office of the Comptroller of the Currency (OCC). The major activities of OCC are

- Examination of the loans and investments of national banks with regard to liquidity, risk, and banking laws
- Review of the bank's internal controls
- Evaluation of bank management's ability to identify and control risk
- Approval or denial of applications for new bank charters, branches, capital, or other changes in corporate or banking structure
- Rules and regulations governing bank investments, lending, and other banking practices

What are the main activities of the Federal Reserve System?

▮Financial Institutions in Action

The banking system in the United States has become fairly complex as a result of the demand for services by a growing number of consumers and business customers.

BANKING DEPARTMENTS

Banks are usually organized as a corporation. The business elements of the bank are handled by various departments.

Loan Department Reviewing credit applications and approving loans are the primary functions of the loan department. Employees must decide if an applicant is likely to repay the amount borrowed based on past borrowing activity, future income, and any assets pledged as collateral.

Personal Banking Individuals and households usually represent a significant portion of a bank's customer base. Bankers must provide service before and after an account is opened to ensure customer satisfaction. Consumers commonly seek savings, checking, and borrowing services.

Commercial Banking Business clients are a major source of revenue for most banks. Loans, processing cash receipts, making payments, and transferring funds are some of the many commercial banking services.

International Banking More and more banks are working with companies that do business around the world. These customers expect foreign exchange services, international money transfers, letters of credit, and export loans.

teamwork

A wide variety of choices are available as to which financial institution a person or business may use. In your team, prepare a list of questions that you would ask when choosing among various financial institutions.

Trust Department The control and management of money, investments, or other property on behalf of customers commonly occurs. This relationship, called a *trust,* is an important activity for most banks.

FORMS OF FINANCIAL INSTITUTIONS

While a wide variety of financial institutions exist in the United States, these organizations are commonly viewed in two major categories.

Depository Financial Intermediaries Most people say they are "going to the bank" even if they are referring to another type of financial institution. Depository intermediaries have the main functions of storing money and making loans to stimulate economic growth.

1. Commercial banks most often offer the widest range of services to both individuals and business customers.
2. Savings and loan (S&L) associations traditionally specialize in savings accounts and home mortgages.
3. Mutual savings banks, also specializing in savings and mortgages, are owned by depositors rather than by stockholders.
4. Credit unions are nonprofit financial organizations that offer services to meet the needs of their owner-customers.

Non-Depository Financial Intermediaries Customers needing financial services are also served by non-depository financial intermediaries.

1. Life insurance companies provide financial protection for the dependents of people who purchase the policies.
2. Investment companies focus their efforts on pooling funds from many people to select investments with growth opportunities.
3. Consumer finance companies emphasize loans to individuals for motor vehicles, appliances, and other major purchases.
4. Mortgage companies have the primary function of lending money for home buying.
5. Credit card companies mainly offer buying convenience for consumers who want to delay payment for their purchases.

Changing Competitive Environment Non-deposit financial institutions have expanded the services they offer. For example, insurance companies often provide financial planning and investment advice. In addition, services of non-depository intermediaries have been added to many depository companies. Many banks sell various investments to customers in addition to traditional savings plans. Most credit unions provide mortgages along with other types of loans.

For several years, the concept of a *financial supermarket* has existed. These financial institutions offer a complete range of services. Often these financial supermarkets started as a traditional financial business and expanded their services. One advantage of financial supermarkets is one-stop shopping. This convenience must be weighed against possible higher costs and reduced personalized service. Also, some of these financial institutions are not covered by federal deposit insurance.

Another activity to attract customers is offering an *all-in-one account,* also called an *asset management account* or a *cash management account.* For a

Competitive banks provide convenience for their customers.

single fee, investment brokers and others provide a checking account, a debit card, a credit card, online banking, as well as a line of credit for obtaining quick cash loans. These accounts also provide access to stock, bond, mutual fund, and other types of investments.

The competitive environment of financial institutions has been influenced by online banking activities. Electronic banking with virtual branch offices has changed the expectations and behaviors of bank customers. In the past, banks were only open from 9 a.m. to 3 p.m., Monday through Friday. Today, customers have 24-hour access to banking activities anywhere in the world.

Comparing Financial Institutions Always balance your needs with the conditions imposed upon you. When you are not satisfied, shop around! To obtain the best value for your financial services dollar, consider the following guidelines.

1. **Services Offered** In general, select the checking account with the lowest costs. Locate the best interest rate on your savings. Find the lowest interest rate for loans.

2. **Safety** Be sure your financial institution is insured by the FDIC or by the National Credit Union Share Insurance Fund for credit unions. When doing business with an investment broker, look for Securities Investor Protection Corporation (SIPC) coverage. The SIPC exists to protect investors when their brokerage firm is closed due to bankruptcy or other financial difficulties.

3. **Convenience** Decide if you want 24-hour banking or branch offices near your home. A tradeoff usually exists between more convenience and higher costs.

4. **Fees and Charges** Financial services have costs. Compare your needs with the price you pay. A small ATM fee or checking account service charge can add up to hundreds of dollars in a short time.

5. **Restrictions** Costs are not always measured in dollars. If you must keep $500 on deposit for a "free" checking account, you may lose the opportunity to earn interest on those funds at a better rate elsewhere.

checkpoint ✓

How do depository and non-depository financial intermediaries differ?

High-Cost Financial Service Companies

Some people pay $8 to cash a $100 check, or they pay $20 to borrow $100 for two weeks. Many people without access to traditional financial institutions, especially low-income consumers, use financial service businesses that are very expensive.

Pawnshops make loans based on the value of tangible possessions such as jewelry. Many low- and moderate-income families use these companies to obtain cash loans quickly. Pawnshops charge higher fees than other financial institutions. While states regulate the interest rates charged by pawnshops, 3 percent a month or higher is common.

Check-cashing outlets are used to obtain cash by people who do not have a bank account. The more than 6,000 check-cashing outlets (CCOs) in the U.S. charge anywhere from 1 to 20 percent of the face value of a check; the average cost is between 2 and 3 percent. For a low-income family, that can be a significant portion of the total household budget. CCOs also offer other services, including electronic tax filing, money orders, private postal boxes, utility bill payment, and the sale of bus and subway tokens.

Payday loans are also referred to as *cash advances, check advance loans, postdated check loans,* and *delayed deposit loans.* Desperate borrowers pay annual interest rates that sometimes exceed 1,000 percent to obtain needed cash. Payday loans are most commonly used by workers trapped in debt. In a typical payday loan, a consumer writes a personal check for $115 to borrow $100 for 14 days. The payday lender agrees to hold the check until the next payday. This $15 finance charge for the 14 days translates into an annual percentage rate of 391 percent. Some consumers "roll over" their loans, paying another $15 for the $100 loan for the next 14 days. After a few rollovers, the finance charges can exceed the amount borrowed.

Rent-to-own centers allow consumers to obtain televisions, computers, furniture, and appliances with a low initial payment. The leased products may be owned after a certain number of payments. One case in Wisconsin, with more than 10,000 complainants, accused the rental chain of illegally charging interest rates as high as 100 percent to rent televisions and other appliances, often to customers in low-income areas.

Think Critically

1. Why do high-cost financial services exist?
2. What actions might be taken by consumers to avoid these high-cost financial services?

8.1 Lesson Assessment

UNDERSTAND CONCEPTS

Determine the best answer for each of the following questions.

1. To increase the money supply, the Fed would
   a. lower the discount rate
   b. raise the discount rate
   c. raise the reserve requirement
   d. sell government securities

2. **True or False?** The first Bank of the United States later became the Federal Reserve System.

3. When creating a national bank, a charter must be obtained from
   a. the Federal Reserve System
   b. a state banking regulatory agency
   c. the Comptroller of the Currency
   d. the Federal Deposit Insurance Corporation

4. **True or False?** A life insurance company is an example of a non-depository financial intermediary.

MAKE ACADEMIC CONNECTIONS

5. **History** Conduct research on state banknotes used in the United States between 1793 and 1861. Prepare a visual summary of the various types of paper currency issued by state banks.

6. **Law** Obtain information on the legal powers of the Federal Reserve System, the Federal Deposit Insurance Corporation, the Office of the Comptroller of the Currency, or the Securities Investor Protection Corporation. Write a one-page summary of your findings.

7. **Economics** Research recent trends in the level of interest rates, the money supply, and consumer prices. What actions have been taken by the Fed to influence these economic factors?

8. **Communication** Conduct research online or in person about the various departments and services of a specific bank. Create a poster, a computer presentation, or a 3-D model of the various departments of the bank.

9. **Math** A bank is required to maintain a 14 percent reserve requirement and has deposits of $54,000.
   a. What amount must be kept on reserve, and what amount may be lent out?
   b. If the total amount lent out was deposited in other banks, how much of those funds would be required to be kept on reserve?

8.2 Financial Services

Goals
- Describe financial services commonly used by consumers.
- Identify types of commercial banking services.

Terms
- automatic teller machine (ATM)
- debit card
- safe-deposit box
- trust
- lock box
- commercial lending

■ Consumer Services

The financial services available to consumers are continually evolving as a result of technology, changing laws, and new competition. As shown in Figure 8-2, these services may be viewed in five major categories.

FIGURE 8-2

Consumer Financial Services

Electronic Banking	Savings Services	Payment Services	Lending Services	Other Services
ATM	savings accounts	checking accounts	credit cards	safe-deposit boxes
debit cards	certificates of deposit	debit cards	auto loans	investment advice
point-of-sale payments	money market accounts	online payments	mortgages	trust management
direct deposit	retirement accounts	stored-value cards	education loans	
online banking		smart cards	small business loans	

ELECTRONIC BANKING

Electronic funds transfer (EFT) refers to the use of computers and other technology for banking activities. Electronic banking services include the use of automated teller machines, point-of-sale transactions, direct deposit, and automatic bill payment. Online banking with a computer allows a customer to assess many financial services.

Automatic Teller Machines An **automatic teller machine (ATM)**, more commonly called a *cash machine,* allows many banking services. A **debit card**, or *cash card,* is used for ATM transactions.

A debit card is different from a *credit card*. With the debit card you are obtaining or using money that is in your account. With a credit card, you are borrowing to pay later. A lost or stolen debit card can be expensive. If you notify the financial institution within two days of the lost card, your liability for unauthorized use is $50. After that, you can be liable for up to $500 of unauthorized use for up to 60 days.

ATM services have expanded to provide other types of transactions. These machines can be used to buy bus passes, postage stamps, and gift certificates. Be aware that many banks charge fees for ATM usage. To minimize these fees, compare rates at different financial institutions. Use your bank's ATMs to avoid surcharges. Withdraw larger amounts to avoid fees in several small transactions.

Point-of-Sale Payments In a *point-of-sale transaction,* merchants accept debit cards to pay for purchases. Most gas stations, stores, and restaurants accept this type of payment. Vending machines that accept debit cards are becoming more common.

Direct Deposit Many persons use *direct deposit* for paychecks and government payments. Funds are deposited electronically and available automatically.

Automatic Bill Payments Each month, many people pay their rent, mortgage, loans, utilities, and other bills without doing anything. *Automatic bill payment* requires a bank customer to authorize preset amounts for monthly expenses. The payments are deducted from the specified account and transferred to the appropriate companies.

Online Banking Computers and many cell phones have become bank branches. Developments in technology have created a cyber-banking network that allows customers to check balances, transfer funds, and make payments anywhere, anytime. While most traditional financial institutions offer online banking services, Web-only banks also exist. For example, NetBank and E*Trade Bank operate only online while also providing customers access to ATMs.

SAVINGS SERVICES

Safe storage of funds for future use is a common need. One of the main services that financial institutions offer is accepting money from customers for safekeeping. Various types of savings plans are available for this purpose. These range from basic savings accounts and certificates of deposit to money market accounts and various types of retirement accounts.

ATMs are one type of electronic banking service most financial institutions provide.

PAYMENT SERVICES

The ability to transfer money to others is necessary for daily business activities. Money deposited in a checking account can be used by writing a check. Other types of payment services include debit cards and online automatic withdrawals.

Checking Accounts While the number of checks written each year declines, checking accounts are still important for businesses and individuals. A variety of types of checking accounts exist to serve the needs of individuals and businesses. When selecting a checking account, you should consider these factors.

- Minimum balance required to avoid a service charge
- Interest rate earned on the account, if any
- Monthly service charge
- Amount of other fees, such as for printing of checks and stop payment orders
- Availability of other services, such as online banking

Today, stores and other businesses process a check at the time of purchase using an electronic check conversion (ECC) system. The check moves through an ECC reader to obtain the amount, account number, and bank information. After processing, the paper check may be returned to the customer marked "void."

Debit Cards Most retail stores, restaurants, and other businesses accept debit cards issued by Visa and MasterCard. When the debit card transaction is processed, the amount of the purchase is deducted from the checking account. Most debit cards work in two ways.

1. You sign a receipt, similar to when you use a credit card
2. You are asked to provide your personal identification number (PIN), similar to when you use an ATM

Online Payments

Banks and Internet companies serve as third parties to facilitate online bill payments. Some of these include PayPal, CheckFree, and Paytrust. When using these services, be sure to consider the monthly charge as well as online security and customer service availability. Also on the Web are "cyber-cash" or "e-cash" services

© GETTY IMAGES/PHOTODISC

Many people now pay bills online.

designed to serve as financial intermediaries. These organizations create their own *e-money* that serves as a medium of exchange for online transactions.

Other Electronic Payment Methods *Stored-value cards* are prepaid cards for such items as cell phone service, transit fares, highway tolls, laundry service, and school lunches. While some of these stored-value cards are disposable, others can be recharged with an additional amount.

Smart cards, also called "electronic wallets," are similar to ATM cards. An imbedded microchip can store prepaid amounts as well as information about account balances, transaction records, insurance information, and medical history.

LENDING SERVICES

Most people, businesses, and governments borrow money at some time. For example, a business may want to borrow money to build a new warehouse or buy products to resell. Individuals may borrow to buy a car or pay college tuition. Interest earned on loans is a major source of bank income.

Banks offer various types of lending services. These include auto loans, business loans, and mortgages. Credit cards allow users to buy items such as clothing or sports equipment. When a bank issues the credit card, the user is borrowing money from the bank.

Another way that banks lend money is by sending a few checks with a customer's credit card statement. The customer can use one of the checks to obtain cash or to pay a bill. If the customer uses the checks, the amount of each check is charged to the customer's credit card account. In effect, the amount of the check is a loan. Be aware that this type of loan is often more expensive than other kinds of credit.

OTHER FINANCIAL SERVICES

Banks and other financial institutions offer other services to individual consumers and households.

Storage of Valuables Banks offer safe-deposit boxes where customers can store valuables. Because these boxes are in well-guarded vaults, they are safe places to keep valuables such as jewelry, rare coins, investment certificates, birth certificates, wills, and insurance policies.

The box can be opened only by the customer or by someone who has been given the right to open it. Not even a bank has the right to open a safe-deposit box unless it is ordered to do so by a court. Safe-deposit boxes are rented by the year and come in a variety of sizes.

Investment Advice Many financial institutions help customers by offering financial advice and investment services. These advisors can assist customers about whether it is wise to buy a certain house, how to manage money better, or how to exchange U.S. funds for foreign currency. Most banks offer advice on investing savings to earn more money. Types of investments include government bonds, stocks, and mutual funds.

Management of Trusts Many banks manage investments on behalf of customers. A trust is the legal agreement for one party to control property for the benefit of another. When this situation exists, the money or other property that is turned over for the bank to manage is said to be *held*

teamwork

The future of banking is limited only by the imagination of people developing technology. In your group, create a written description of ways in which people may use banking services in the future.

in trust. This service can be offered through a trust company or through trust departments in banks.

Trusts are used by people of all ages, but they are especially useful for young people and for some elderly people. A young person who inherits money may not have the skill and experience to manage it wisely. Elderly people who are ill may ask the trust department of a bank to manage their money. The bank makes investments and keeps the customers informed about what is happening to their money.

checkpoint ✓

What electronic banking services are commonly available for consumers?

technology topics

Body Part Banking

"Look into the camera for your account balance." "Place your finger on scanner to authorize payment." Biometry is the analysis of biological observations, and its use in personal identification is not new. For centuries, scars, complexion, eye color, and height have been used to identify people. Today, technology known as biometrics allows for banking and other security activities based on physical features.

Fingerprint Verification Bank of America created a program to use a person's fingerprint to give individuals access to their online banking services. Law enforcement agencies have long used fingerprint identification techniques. While it is quite accurate, flaws exist. For banking, a chip is used to store a customer's fingerprint. A payment or funds transfer would be authorized when the customer places a finger on a small scanner.

Iris Scanning The pattern of every person's iris is unique. Scanning the characteristics of your eyeball may someday be used as a bank account password or to allow access to your computer. Cameras exist that allow the iris to be scanned from a distance of two or three feet.

Voice Recognition Customers at the American Savings Bank in Hawaii no longer have to enter a number to access their account. Using a voice-activated response system, customers are able to obtain an account balance or make a money transfer.

Hand Geometry This biometric system measures physical characteristics of the hand or fingers. Using a three-dimensional view, this technology allows workers to access a secure area and may be used in the future to permit banking transactions. In a similar way, Mr. Payroll face recognition machines compare two images of the face to authorize check cashing.

Think Critically

1. What concerns might be associated with biometric banking activities?
2. Conduct an Internet search to obtain additional information on recent technology being used in banking transactions.

Commercial Banking

In addition to consumers, banks and other financial institutions serve the needs of business organizations.

CASH MANAGEMENT

The inflow and outflow of funds is a vital element of every business. Banks provide services to assist with cash receipts and payments.

Cash Receipts Collection of cash, checks, and other receipts is a common commercial banking service. A **lock box** is a secured postal box used to receive customer payments. A bank collects receipts from the lock box and deposits the funds into the company's account. The business is then notified of the total amount received. A bank may collect receipts from the lock box several times in a business day.

Cash Payments Most often, a checking account is the basis of a company's cash disbursements. In addition, electronic payment systems are gaining in popularity for payment activities and transfer of funds.

BUSINESS LOANS

Every business organization will likely use credit at some point. **Commercial lending** refers to loans to businesses.

Commercial Loan Purposes Business loans include
- Real estate in the form of buildings or land
- Construction of new or expanded buildings or other facilities
- Equipment needs, such as new machinery or replacement of depreciated vehicles
- Operations, such as financing for repairs, additional inventory, or covering unexpected business costs

NETBookmark

The Small Business Administration maintains a web site with helpful information for small businesses. Access thomsonedu.com/school/busfinance and click on the link for Chapter 8. What information is available on starting a business?

www.thomsonedu.com/school/busfinance

DIGITAL VISION

Banks serve the needs of businesses by offering credit in the form of business loans.

Types of Commercial Loans Common commercial lending activities include

- Term loans, usually from one to five years, used to obtain cash for the purchase of equipment, buildings, land, or to update business facilities
- A line of credit allowing a business to obtain additional funds up to a certain amount without a new loan application
- Company credit cards, which may be used by employees when traveling on business or for other company-related expenses
- Contract financing to finance a project from which income will not be received until it is near completion
- Bridge loans for temporary borrowing between a loan and longer-term financing
- Asset-based lending, a secured business loan in which the borrower pledges a specific company asset to serve as collateral

BUSINESS ASSISTANCE

Banks work with businesses, both large and small, to improve their ratio of success. Continued financial growth of companies also benefits banks. As businesses grow, they will increase their use of banking services. In an effort to help companies succeed, banks offer several services.

Information Services Knowledge of technology, inventory methods, financial planning, economic conditions, and government regulations is a key to success. Banks often offer information to companies through personal contact or group seminars. These programs help small and medium-sized businesses adapt to changing market conditions, expand revenue sources, and reduce costs.

Small Business Administration Programs Banks often work with the Small Business Administration (SBA), a federal government agency that was created to assist and counsel small companies. SBA guidelines for defining a "small business" are based on the number of employees and amount of revenue. These criteria vary for different types of industries.

The SBA coordinates with banks to implement its loan programs. While some direct loans are provided by the SBA, the majority of its efforts involve guaranteeing bank loans to small businesses. SBA programs also include assistance to obtain federal contracts, business management guidance, and specialized efforts for women, minorities, and armed forces veterans.

Since the SBA started in 1953, about 20 million small businesses have received help from one of its programs. Each year, the SBA backs more than $12 billion in loans to assist various types of small businesses.

checkpoint ✓

What are the main commercial services offered by banks?

UNDERSTAND CONCEPTS

Determine the best answer for each of the following questions.

1. The electronic banking service that would be used to transfer funds each month for a mortgage is
   a. direct deposit
   b. automatic bill payment
   c. point-of-sale payment
   d. prepaid debit card

2. **True or False?** Using a debit card is similar to writing a check.

3. An example of a commercial banking service is
   a. a safe deposit box
   b. a bridge loan
   c. an individual checking account
   d. a home equity line of credit

4. **True or False?** Trust management is a type of electronic banking service.

5. A legal agreement created when one party manages property for the benefit of another is a
   a. trust
   b. safe-deposit box
   c. direct deposit
   d. debit card

MAKE ACADEMIC CONNECTIONS

6. **Technology** Conduct a survey of 10 to 15 people about their use of online banking. What services did they use, and how often? Create a table or graph in a spreadsheet program to report your findings.

7. **Research** Locate examples of online payment services and "cyber-cash" companies. What services are provided? What concerns might be associated with these services? Write a summary of your findings.

8. **Culture** Research financial services and payment methods commonly used in various countries around the world. Prepare a written summary of your findings.

9. **Communication** Talk to a local business owner or a small business manager. Obtain information about the types of commercial banking services used. Prepare a brief oral summary.

Goals
- Describe the development of international banking activities.
- Identify organizations that assist with international finance activities.

Terms
- World Bank
- International Monetary Fund
- development bank

▌Global Banking Activities

Many of today's financial services started hundreds and even thousands of years ago. As trade took place among geographic regions, savings accounts, loans, and other banking activities developed.

EARLY INTERNATIONAL BANKING

Evidence exists that banking activities have been in operation for thousands of years. In many societies as early as 2000 BC there were financial activities such as bank deposits, loans, and coining of money.

Ancient Civilizations The valued treasures of ancient Babylonia were the basis of lending money. Religious temples were used as safe-deposit vaults to store valued items. Coins were first used in Greece starting around 500 BC.

The Roman Empire took many of these innovations to the next level. Their banking system included receipt of savings deposits and loans for varied purposes.

European Developments As European explorers expanded trade in the 1400s, banking experienced a renewal. In Italy, moneychangers served the purpose of exchanging currencies from various regions, allowing traders to obtain payment in their home currency.

One of the first enterprises to offer an array of banking services, including checking accounts, was the Bank of Barcelona (Spain). Within a few years, similar banks developed in Amsterdam (The Netherlands), Venice (Italy), and Hamburg (Germany).

In 1800, Napoleon started the Bank of France, which had a strong financial influence in Europe from that point. In Britain, early banking activities were conducted by goldsmiths. They provided safekeeping of valuables and lent money. Gold and silver served as an assurance that the paper money being used was backed by a tangible, valuable asset.

INTERNATIONAL TRADE AND BANKING

Expanded global trade is accompanied by a growth of international banking. Financing of international transactions is generally handled by banks and other financial institutions. Today, nearly 100 U.S. banks have more than

As technology makes the world smaller, global banking activities increase.

1,000 foreign branches. In addition, over 250 foreign banks have offices in the United States.

Because of the expansion of foreign banks in the U.S., Congress passed the International Banking Act in 1978. This legislation requires foreign banks operating in the United States to operate under federal banking regulations. These global companies are required to have deposit insurance in order to do business in the United States.

Increased international banking activity has resulted in more standardized regulations across borders. In recent years, over 100 countries agreed to a global standard for evaluating the financial stability of banks. Banks are required to maintain a certain ratio of capital to reduce the risk of bank failure. However, tradition and economic conditions can create differences among the banking activities in various geographic regions.

Africa Less than half of South Africans have access to a bank and its services, due to distance and lack of documentation of income and address. In addition, the bank fees in the country are some of the highest anywhere. Cell phones in South Africa allow workers to transfer funds hundreds of miles to their families in rural areas. This electronic money can then be used in the local village to buy food and other items. The more than 80 million cell phones users in Africa are able to take advantage of technology to expand business activities and serve family needs.

Asia After the currency crisis in the late 1990s, profits of Japanese banks declined from a gain of $7 billion to a loss of $50 billion. Major banks have realized the need to downsize their scope and focus on specialized services. In contrast to the Asian multinational banks, countries such as Cambodia, Laos, and Vietnam still have areas where more traditional, informal banking takes place. Currency exchange activities and lending can occur with street traders as well as in more formalized bank settings.

Europe Expansion of the European Union (EU) to 25 member nations and attempts to completely integrate financial services created several banking challenges. Conflicting banking regulations in various countries reduce the opportunity for standardization. Many local financial markets are set in their traditions, creating an additional barrier to EU banking integration.

The use of the euro as the official currency is another area of diversity. Long-time EU members Britain, Denmark, and Sweden have opted not to use the euro. Recently admitted members, including the Czech Republic, Hungary, Poland, Slovenia, and Slovakia, hope to meet the economic requirements that will allow them to become part of the euro zone.

Latin America Banking customers in Brazil usually do business with one of the three large banks in the country: Itaú, Bradesco, and Unibanco. These organizations dominated the industry with their thousands of *agências* ("storefront" agencies) and *postos* ("customer-site" agencies) along with *caixas automáticos* (ATMs). These many branches resulted when local areas desired a banking office as a status symbol for their region.

Brazilians do not usually mail checks. Most bills come printed with a bank payment slip. Customers may walk in to a bank branch and pay with a check, cash, or a bank card. Or, the payment may be made at an ATM using the bar code identification on the form. More and more Brazilians are using the Internet to make payments.

Middle East No formal money and banking system existed in the Middle East until 1952 when the Saudi Arabian Monetary Agency (SAMA) was created. Previous to that, foreign coins served the monetary needs of the region. Most of the coins had a value based on their gold or silver content.

The main function of SAMA was to maintain a stable currency value. This central bank used various monetary policy actions, including the setting of interest rates that commercial banks may charge and selling government

The World Bank provides funds to less-developed countries for infrastructure improvements in transportation and utilities.

securities to cover budgetary and balance of payments needs. SAMA also regulated various financial institutions (commercial banks, exchange dealers, and moneychangers) and handled receipts and payments of government funds.

checkpoint ✓

What relationship exists between international trade and global banking activities?

■ Global Financial Organizations

International banking transactions go beyond financial institutions. Several international agencies exist to promote business activities and economic development.

WORLD BANK

The International Bank for Reconstruction and Development, more commonly called the **World Bank**, was created in 1944 to provide loans for rebuilding after World War II. Today, the World Bank has the main function of providing economic assistance to less-developed countries. These funds are used to build communications networks, transportation systems, and utility plants.

The World Bank, with over 180 member countries, has two main divisions. The International Development Association (IDA) makes funds available to help developing economies. These loans can be paid back over many years (up to 50) and have very low interest rates. The International Finance Corporation (IFC) provides capital and technical assistance to businesses in nations with limited resources. The IFC encourages joint ventures between foreign and local companies to stimulate capital investments in the developing nation.

INTERNATIONAL MONETARY FUND

The **International Monetary Fund (IMF)** is an agency that helps promote economic cooperation by maintaining an orderly system of international trade and exchange rates. The IMF was established in 1946, when economic interdependence among nations was escalating at a greater pace than ever before in history.

Before the International Monetary Fund, a country could frequently change the value of its currency to attract more foreign customers. Then as other countries lost business, they would impose trade restrictions or lower the value of their currency. As one nation tried to outdo another, a trade war often resulted. Today, cooperation among IMF nations creates a more orderly trade and monetary exchange.

The IMF, with over 180 member nations, is a cooperative deposit bank that provides assistance to countries experiencing balance of payment difficulties. When a nation's debt increases, its currency declines in value, resulting in even more debt. High debt payments mean less money is available

Several years ago, Ghana had inflation of over 100 percent and quickly declining exports. The IMF suggested various import controls and lower tax rates to stimulate economic gowth for Ghana.

Development banks provide assistance to create sustainable economic growth.

for the country to improve its economic development. To prevent this situation, the International Monetary Fund has three main duties.

1. **Analyze Economic Situations** In an attempt to help countries avoid economic problems, the IMF will monitor a country's trade, borrowing, and government spending.

2. **Suggest Economic Policies** After analyzing the economic focus of a nation, the IMF will suggest actions to improve the situation. If a country imposes restrictions that limit foreign trade, for example, the IMF may recommend changes to encourage global business activities.

3. **Provide Loans** When a country has high foreign debt, the IMF lends money to help avoid major economic difficulties. These low-interest loans can keep a country from experiencing an escalating trade deficit and a declining currency value.

ORGANIZATION FOR ECONOMIC COOPERATION AND DEVELOPMENT

Created in 1961, the Organization for Economic Cooperation and Development (OECD) has 30 member countries. These industrialized nations have a commitment to democratic government and the market economy. In addition to its members, OECD works directly with 70 other countries to expand free trade and encourage economic development among developing economies. OECD also identifies polices to develop appropriate governance by both governments and corporations. Recommendations are offered to promote sustainable development and scientific innovation.

REGIONAL DEVELOPMENT BANKS

Other regional organizations exist to help less-developed countries reduce poverty and expand economic activities. A **development bank** is an organization of several countries created to provide financing for economic development to countries in a region.

Inter-American Development Bank In Latin America and the Caribbean, the Inter-American Development Bank (IDB) was established in 1959. The IDB exists to provide funds and technical assistance programs to enhance economic and social development. The IDB uses a major portion of its resources for the smaller economies in the region. The agency works closely with the IMF and the World Bank, and will often co-finance reforms, projects, and programs. The success of the IDB has resulted in other regions creating their own development banks.

Asian Development Bank With more than 60 member countries (47 in Asia), the Asian Development Bank (ADB) has the goal of improving economic development and quality of life for people in Asia and the Pacific. A strong emphasis is placed on serving the nearly two billion in the region who live on less than $2 a day.

The ADB provides public policy discussions, loans, technical assistance, grants, and guarantees. With headquarters in Manila and 26 other offices around the world, the organization employees more than 2,000 employees from over 50 countries.

African Development Bank Dedicated to reducing poverty and improving the lives of people in Africa, the African Development Bank implements a variety of economic and social programs. Loans, equity investments, and technical assistance are the main tools used to achieve its goals.

Members in the organization include 53 African countries and 24 non-African countries from the Americas, Asia, and Europe. Established in 1964, every action of the African Development Bank is aimed at creating sustainable economic growth and regional economic cooperation.

Other Regional Development Banks The reduction of poverty and expansion of economic activities are concerns throughout the world. Other examples of regional development banks include the Caribbean Development Bank, the Central American Bank for Economic Integration, the European Bank for Reconstruction and Development, and the Islamic

teamwork

Many countries continue to face difficult economic situations. In your team, develop a list of actions that could be taken to encourage improved business development and expanded economic growth in various geographic regions.

Low-interest loans for business needs can support and enhance economic development.

Development Bank. These organizations attempt to stimulate business development and foreign trade and thereby creating jobs and improving quality of life.

checkpoint ✔

What is the purpose of a regional development bank?

Central Banks and Government Financial Activities

Every local and national government uses banking services. Like businesses, government agencies must receive, pay, save, and borrow funds. In nearly every country of the world, a *central bank* exists. These state-owned agencies provide governments with banking services. Every central bank serves one or more of these functions.

1. Maintain a stable money supply using monetary policy tools.
2. Issue adequate amounts of currency to facilitate business activities.
3. Manage the receipts and payments of government agencies.
4. Provide loans for government agencies and other enterprises.
5. License commercial banks operating in the country.

In some countries these financial agencies are called *reserve banks* or a *monetary authority*. Names of central banks around the world include the Reserve Bank of India, the Monetary Authority of Singapore, the Brunei Currency Board, the Central Bank of Cyprus, the Czech National Bank, and the Bank of England.

In some situations, a central bank may have authority over several countries. The European Central Bank, based in Frankfort, Germany, is the central bank for the European Monetary Union (EMU), consisting of EU members that use the euro as their official currency. These "euro zone" countries are all served by one central bank. Each member country also has its own central bank that works with the European Central Bank. The Central Bank of West Africa States issues a monetary unit called the *franc* for the African Financial Community. This currency is used in eight countries (Benin, Burkina Faso, Guinea Bissau, Côte d'Ivoire, Mali, Niger, Senegal, and Togo). These countries are also referred to as the West African Monetary Union (WAMU).

While the primary role of central banks is to provide governments with financial services, they also assist businesses and non-governmental organizations (NGOs). The regulation of banking activities along with a stable currency provides a beneficial economic environment for all participants.

Think Critically

1. How do central banks serve the people of a country?
2. Conduct an Internet search on a central bank in another region of the world. Obtain information about its structure, authority, and activities.

8.3 Lesson Assessment

UNDERSTAND CONCEPTS

Determine the best answer for each of the following questions.

1. Early banking activities in ancient civilizations included
   a. online banking
   b. coins made from precious metals
   c. checking accounts that earned interest
   d. credit cards

2. **True or False?** The World Bank and the International Monetary Fund both provide loans to countries to stimulate economic development.

3. The organization most likely to meet the local needs of a country when improving its economic situation would be the
   a. World Bank
   b. International Monetary Fund
   c. Organization for Economic Cooperation and Development
   d. Regional Development Bank

4. **True or False?** A regional development bank has the main purpose of helping a country stabilize the value of its currency.

MAKE ACADEMIC CONNECTIONS

5. **History** Locate photos or drawings of early banking activities. Prepare a visual presentation and a short written summary of your findings.

6. **Global Business** Research the banking activities in a geographic region. What types of banking institutions and financial services are commonly used in countries in that area?

7. **Research** Conduct research on recent activities of the World Bank and the International Monetary Fund. Prepare a brief oral summary of your findings.

8. **Geography** Select one of the regional development banks discussed in this lesson. Locate a map and indicate the countries that are served by this bank. Obtain additional information on recent activities of the development bank.

Summary

8.1 BANKS AND OTHER FINANCIAL INSTITUTIONS

1. The First and Second Banks of the U.S. were early attempts to create a stable monetary system. Due to political differences, neither bank had its charter renewed when it expired. The Federal Reserve System was created to supervise and regulate member banks to help them serve the public efficiently. The Federal Deposit Insurance Corporation (FDIC) and the Comptroller of the Currency protect banking customers and regulate the activities of national banks.

2. The main departments of most banks are the loan department, personal banking, commercial banking, international banking, and the trust department. The two main types of financial intermediaries are depository and non-depository. In recent years, nearly all financial institutions have begun to offer a wider variety of financial services.

8.2 FINANCIAL SERVICES

3. The main categories of financial services used by consumers are electronic banking, savings, payments, lending, and other services such as safe-deposit boxes, investment advice, and trust management.

4. Commercial banking services include cash management, business loans, and business assistance.

8.3 INTERNATIONAL BANKING

5. As early as 2000 BC, banking activities included accepting deposits, making loans, and coining money. Expanded global trade is accompanied by a growth of international banking. Banking activities in various geographic regions are affected by tradition and economic conditions.

6. The World Bank has the main function of providing economic assistance to less-developed countries. The International Monetary Fund promotes economic cooperation by maintaining an orderly system of international trade and exchange rates. Regional development banks exist to assist less-developed countries reduce poverty and expand economic activities.

Develop Your Business Language

Match the terms listed with the definitions. Some terms will not be used.

1. Electronic banking service machine, more commonly called a *cash machine*
2. Rate the Fed charges on loans to member banks
3. Secured postal box used to receive customer payments
4. International Bank for Reconstruction and Development; created in 1944 to provide loans for rebuilding after World War II
5. Card that allows user to obtain or use money from a checking account
6. Process of buying and selling government securities
7. Percentage of funds that a bank is required to hold
8. Loans to business enterprises for various company needs
9. Boxes in well-guarded bank vaults, rented by customers to store valuable objects and documents
10. Agency that helps promote economic cooperation by maintaining an orderly system of international trade and exchange rates

a. automatic teller machine (ATM)
b. commercial lending
c. debit card
d. development bank
e. discount rate
f. Federal Reserve System
g. International Monetary Fund (IMF)
h. lock box
i. open market operations
j. reserve requirement
k. safe-deposit box
l. trust
m. World Bank

Review Concepts

11. The monetary policy of the Federal Reserve System refers to
    a. lending to assist poor countries
    b. borrowing by the federal government to pay for public services
    c. maintaining an appropriate amount of money in circulation
    d. influencing the exchange rate of currencies in different countries
12. Deposits of consumers are protected from loss by the
    a. Federal Reserve System
    b. Federal Deposit Insurance Corporation
    c. Comptroller of the Currency
    d. World Bank
13. Maintaining an orderly system of currency exchange rates is a primary function of the
    a. International Monetary Fund
    b. Federal Reserve System
    c. World Bank
    d. Organization for Economic Cooperation and Development
14. A ____?____ has the primary purpose of lending money for home buying.
    a. bank
    b. life insurance company
    c. credit union
    d. mortgage company

Think Critically

15. Monetary policy refers to Federal Reserve actions to influence the money supply and economic conditions. Fiscal policy is spending and taxing by the government, which can also affect economic conditions. Describe how changes in spending and taxes can affect economic activities.

16. The Community Reinvestment Act requires that financial institutions provide loans and other funds to assist low-income people with home purchases and for starting businesses. What are the benefits of this federal legislation?

17. As more financial institutions offer a wider variety of services, does competition between them increase or decrease? Explain your answer.

18. Increased use of technology for banking creates convenience for customers. What are some concerns associated with electronic banking activities?

19. Should restrictions be placed on foreign banks doing business in the United States? Explain your answer.

20. Environmentally-friendly sustainable development is a goal of many governments and organizations. How might this goal be achieved?

Business Financial Calculations

21. During a recent six-month period, a customer's balances were April, $148; May, $201.97; June, $101.61; July, $418.53; August, $248.29; and September, $154.36. Monthly service charges for a checking account are based on the bank's rate schedule, as shown below.

Minimum Balance	Charge
0–$199	$5
$200–$399	$3
$400 and over	no charge

   a. How much was the service charge for each month?
   b. What was the total service charge for the six-month period?

22. On June 1, Brad Keller had a checking account balance of $140. He has his paychecks automatically deposited. His earnings for June were $1,080. During the month, he wrote checks for $87, $146, $29, and $292. He had $120 automatically transferred from his checking account to his savings account. In addition, he used his ATM card to withdraw $60 in cash. The bank charges 75 cents for each EFT transfer or withdrawal. Find Brad's bank balance after these transactions.

23. A company needs to borrow $72,000 for 60 days to finance its inventory for the fall selling season. If the annual interest rate of this loan is 5.5 percent, what would be the cost of borrowing these funds? Assume a 360-day financial year.

Analyze Cases

Use the case from the beginning of the chapter, Commercial and Global Banking at Wells Fargo, to answer the following questions.

24. What types of commercial banking services offered by Wells Fargo could be of value to businesses in your community?

25. How might Wells Fargo adapt its commercial banking services to serve the needs of family-run businesses in poor countries?

26. Create some promotional messages that Wells Fargo might use to promote its commercial and international banking services.

27. What are possible benefits and drawbacks of the HSBC joint venture?

28. Wells Fargo hopes to expand its commercial banking among major companies based in other countries.
    a. What services would be appropriate for customers in this new target market?
    b. What actions might be taken by the company to offer commercial banking services in other countries?

Portfolio Activity

COLLECT an item related to banking services and financial institutions in our society. This example could be an advertisement, newspaper or magazine article, photo, or some other actual item.

CREATE a visual to communicate the use of financial institutions. Use photos, other pictures or ads, other actual items, and drawings to illustrate the types of banking services commonly used by consumers and companies.

CONNECT your visual to other aspects of our economy and society or relate it to an important concept you have learned in another class. Make the connection by preparing a brief essay on the use of financial services by consumers, businesses, and governments.

Stock Market Activity

The use of financial institutions is necessary for the success of every business enterprise. Careful selection and use of various banking services can affect the inflow and outflow of funds. Poor cash management and improper borrowing can reduce the financial success of a company.

Use online and library resources related to the use of financial services for the company you have been studying (or select a different company).

1. Identify financial services that are likely used by this company.

2. Explain how effective use of these financial services might create efficient company operations.

3. Describe potential favorable and unfavorable influences on the company's stock price related to the use of various banking services.

Planning a Career in Banking

The banking industry offers a wide variety of career opportunities. Commercial banks employ numerous workers. Other employees work in specialized banks, savings and loan associations, credit unions, and finance companies.

Work activities in this industry range from serving customers and researching economic trends to planning bank marketing activities. Although extensive consolidation has occurred in banking through mergers, more people are employed in commercial banking than in any other part of the financial services industry.

Employment Outlook

- Various careers in banking and financial services expect strong growth.
- Slower growth is expected for certain banking jobs due to industry consolidation and technology.
- Employment of branch managers will grow very little as banks increase the use of electronic banking.
- Electronic banking will create a greater demand for employees with technology skills.

Job Titles

- Branch manager
- Head teller
- Loan officer
- Commercial banking account representative
- Customer service manager
- Personal banking representative
- Financial services sales agent
- Information processing manager

Needed Skills

- Some entry-level jobs require a high-school education with additional college business courses needed for advancement.
- Bank officers and executive positions require a college degree.
- Continuing education classes in cash management, financial analysis, and international banking should be considered.
- Interaction with customers requires strong communication skills and an ability to work effectively under stress.
- Accuracy, professional appearance, and computer competence are vital.

What's It Like to Work in Banking?

Each morning, Kent Latrobe goes online to see how various economic factors are affecting interest rates. He knows that when money is more expensive, borrowing by businesses and consumers declines. But if interest rates are lower, the use of credit will likely increase. This additional borrowing can result in higher earnings for banks.

Changing interest rates are just one area of research for Kent, who works as a research analyst for a bank with offices in 23 states. Today, he must also investigate current trends for employment, consumer spending, and retail sales. These economic indicators provide managers with information to plan strategies for their banking organizations.

What about you? What aspect of banking might be of interest to you as a career? What additional information would you like to have about banking careers?

ADVERTISING CAMPAIGN EVENT

The Advertising Campaign Event provides an opportunity for participants to prepare an advertising campaign for a bank. The participants also will create an appropriate budget and select advertising media. The Advertising Campaign Event can be completed by 1–3 members.

This event consists of outlined fact sheets, a written comprehensive exam, and the oral presentation. The body of the written entry is limited to 10 numbered pages, not including the title page and table of contents. The written portion should consist of the following sections: Executive Summary, Description of the Business, Description of the Client, Objectives of the Campaign, Identification of the Target Market, List of Advertising Media Selection Necessary for the Campaign, Budget, Schedules of all Advertising Planned, Schedules of all Sales Promotion Activities Planned, and Statement of Benefits to the Client.

Participants must only use approved visual aids for their presentations. The oral presentation may be a maximum of 20 minutes long. The first 15 minutes will include an advertising campaign proposal followed by 5 minutes for the judge's questions. Oral presentations will be evaluated for effectiveness of public speaking and presentation skills.

The banking industry has become increasingly competitive. Advertising campaigns for the banking industry have become very creative with funny television commercials and special promotions to capture the attention of the target market. You must develop an advertising campaign for a local bank. The major purpose of the campaign is to increase the number of customers. Your first task is to determine the bank's current advertising. Then you will develop new advertising strategies to improve business.

Performance Indicators Evaluated

- Explain the importance of an advertising campaign.
- Define an effective advertising campaign for an actual business.
- Determine the needs of the target market when creating an advertising campaign.
- Communicate a schedule of events for an advertising campaign.
- Describe special promotions for the advertising campaign.
- Define the benefits the advertising campaign provides the business.
- Deliver an effective oral presentation that indicates self-confidence.

Go to the DECA web site for more detailed information.

Think Critically

1. Why have banks become more dependent on advertising campaigns?
2. Why are banks using humorous commercials as part of their advertising campaigns?
3. What has competition in the banking industry done to promotions offered by banks?
4. Give two examples of promotions that banks can offer potential customers.

www.deca.org

Customer Credit

▶ **Point Your** [Browser]
www.thomsonedu.com/school/busfinance

Visa—Taking Credit Worldwide

Almost from the very beginning of business, there were systems of credit to help sell products when the purchaser did not have ready cash. Neighborhood businesses allowed regular customers to maintain "accounts" where their purchases were recorded. Payments were made later when the buyer had adequate funds. Credit cards expanded the use of credit by allowing businesses to offer credit to customers they did not know. If the customer presented a credit card, the seller knew payment would be guaranteed by the credit card company and that money could be collected from the sale quickly.

The use of credit cards began on a small scale with Diners Club in 1950. Frank McGuire developed an agreement with several restaurants in New York to accept his card in lieu of cash. As he expanded the number of customers who carried the card and the businesses who would accept it, the concept caught on. It was viewed as a convenience for customers and an excellent marketing resource for businesses.

Today there are hundreds of companies that offer credit cards. The uses and acceptance have grown dramatically as have the improvements in the technology supporting the use of the cards. Leading the way in growth is Visa, the world leader in electronic payments. Visa was the brainchild of Dee Hock, a banker in the Bank of America system. He proposed to other bankers that they form an association to develop a common credit processing system. Initially Visa used the same procedures and technology as other credit card companies—a plastic card presented to a merchant by a customer at the time of purchase. Today, customers, businesses, and financial institutions are connected through a worldwide electronic network that instantaneously processes orders, payments, and money transfers.

Today 1.3 billion Visa cards are used worldwide, generating $3.7 trillion in credit sales from over 20 million merchants. Visa International is organized as a private, non-stock for-profit membership corporation owned by 20,000 financial institutions. Visa's transaction processing technology can handle over 10,000 transactions per second with redundant power supplies, communication systems, and data backup capabilities that allow uninterrupted 24/7/365 service to customers and businesses.

Think Critically

1. Why would independent financial institutions want to cooperate in offering one brand of credit card rather than competing and offering their own individual brands?

2. Why are many businesses and consumers willing to accept new technologies for processing credit even though the processes can pose additional risks to personal and financial information security?

Goals
- Recognize basic credit concepts and the reason for the use of credit.
- Describe practices businesses should follow in offering credit.

Terms
- credit
- debtor
- consumer credit
- trade credit
- credit agreement
- self-managed credit plan
- contracted credit plan

■ Credit Basics

Businesses operate through a cycle of production and sales. Products are produced or purchased for inventory that is then made available to customers. Customer purchases result in sales that reduce inventory and provide revenue for the company. A variety of administrative, operating, and marketing costs are generated by company activities in order to achieve customer sales. If revenues from sales are higher than the total of all costs, the company makes a profit.

The goal of all companies in completing the production-sales cycle is to generate a profit. That profit is not possible if products and services remain unsold. Companies look for ways to increase customer purchases of products and services. One of the ways to increase sales is to offer credit to customers. **Credit** is an agreement in which a borrower receives something of value in exchange for a promise to repay the lender at a later date.

IMAGE SOURCE

Most businesses today must offer credit in order to meet customer expectations.

Few businesses today have the choice to offer only cash sales. Almost all business-to-business sales and a large percentage of sales to consumers involve some form of credit. Businesses must make careful choices about the types of credit they will offer, the credit terms, policies, and procedures in order to make credit a profitable tool.

In the same way, businesses will not be able to finance all of their operations and activities with cash. Many of the resources to start a business such as fixed assets are very expensive. The business may not have adequate cash at the time of purchase but will pay for the expensive resource over a period of many years. When manufacturers purchase raw materials and other resources needed for production, they will not make money to pay for those purchases until products are finished and sold to customers. Businesses use credit to finance many of their purchases with the intention of making payment with revenues earned when products are sold. Just as with the decision to offer credit, using credit to finance operations must be considered carefully so that the cost of the credit is not greater than the benefits of its use to the business.

TYPES OF CREDIT AND CREDIT TERMS

Credit extended by a business is a part of a purchase agreement between the company and its customers. Credit is typically offered so customers can buy the company's products and services but delay payment until a later date. The business extending credit is known as the *creditor* or *lender*. The recipient of credit is known as the **debtor** or *borrower*. Credit offered to individual consumers by a business is **consumer credit.** Credit offered to a business customer by another business is **trade credit.** Credit is normally extended through a written document describing the terms under which credit is granted and payment will be made. That written document is called the **credit agreement.** Credit often has a cost attached to it in the form of interest. *Interest* is the price a borrower pays for the use of a lender's money. The agreement between the borrower and lender regarding the interest rate and the time period of the loan is known as the *credit terms*.

If credit is used by a business it must be recorded in the company's financial records. When the business makes a sale on credit, the order is placed, goods are shipped to the customer and subtracted from the company's inventory records, the customer is billed using the agreed-upon credit terms, and a customer record is created in accounts receivable. That account is an asset since it reflects money owed to the business by the customer. When the customer pays for the order, the company receives cash and that amount is subtracted from the customer's account.

The opposite action occurs when a company makes a credit purchase. The order is placed with a supplier and the goods are received. Since it is a credit purchase, no payment is made at the time. Instead the amount owed is recorded in accounts payable, creating a liability for the company. At the time payment is made to the supplier, cash is sent and the amount of the payment is subtracted from accounts payable.

THE CREDIT DECISION

Deciding to extend credit to customers or use credit when making purchases should be viewed primarily as a financial decision. Some businesses feel pressured into offering credit in order to meet customer expectations.

Trade credit is an important way for businesses to obtain financing for their current operations. It makes up the single largest form of short-term debt. For the typical business, trade credit represents about 40 percent of the company's current liabilities.

Businesses reduce their inventory and avoid obsolescence or spoilage by offering credit as a way of increasing sales.

Businesses that are offered credit from suppliers may decide it will be beneficial to obtain and use the purchases and delay payment until they have additional revenues. While almost all businesses offer some type of credit to certain customers and most businesses use credit to finance some of their assets, credit decisions should be made with clear understanding of how the decision will affect the company's financial condition. If the bottom-line result of the decision to offer or accept credit is a negative effect on the company's balance sheet, income statement, or cash flow, it should not be extended or used without a reason that overrides the financial consequence.

There are several costs to the creditor for offering credit. The creditor does not have immediate use of the money, and there is the risk that some customers will not make payments when they are due. There is also the expense of managing the credit system. Those costs need to be balanced against any additional sales that are obtained due to the credit policy and the possibility of collecting a higher sale price or interest payments because of the policy. In addition, the company benefits from a reduction in inventory and the associated costs of storage. If products are sold, there is no risk of obsolescence or damage to the inventory.

When using credit to finance purchases, the primary financial considerations are any interest costs that increase the final price of the purchase, whether a lower price is available for paying cash, and the future effect on cash flow at the time payment must be made. If the purchase allows the company to maintain operations, increase sales, or reduce expenses that would not be possible if the purchase was not made, those results should be considered in making a decision to use credit.

checkpoint ✓

What is the difference between consumer credit and trade credit?

▪Planning to Offer Credit

Most businesses today have little choice about whether to offer credit. Only the smallest businesses and a limited number of personal services businesses can expect every customer to pay cash. Credit is becoming the standard for many business and consumer financial transactions. Even retail transactions for very small amounts such as fast food, postage, transportation toll charges, and online music downloads are now processed using credit as payment.

IMPORTANCE OF CONSUMER AND BUSINESS CREDIT

U.S. consumers used credit cards to finance short-term purchases of over $2 trillion in a recent year. Nearly three quarters of all American households have two or more active credit cards with monthly charges that average over $200 and that carry an outstanding average balance of $1,800. In addition U.S. consumers financed over $1 trillion in purchases using loans from banks, finance companies, and other lenders. That amount does not include home mortgages, which accounted for an additional $8.5 trillion of consumer debt.

The actual amount of credit used by businesses is not as clear. Businesses carry debt in the values of their accounts receivable and accounts payable. Accounts receivable is credit extended to customers. Depending on the business, accounts receivable may include both consumer accounts and business accounts. Accounts payable is credit the company has received from other businesses. The percentage of total assets represented by the value of accounts receivable may range from ten percent to almost 50 percent. Accounts payable as a percentage of total liabilities is typically a smaller percentage but often averages 25 percent of all liabilities or more. Considering the total value of companies' assets and liabilities, extending and receiving credit is an important business activity.

ALTERNATIVES FOR OFFERING CREDIT

Once the decision has been made that offering credit is an important and appropriate strategy for the business, two decisions will follow.

1. What categories of customers will be offered credit?
2. What type(s) of credit plans will be used?

Who Should Receive Credit The choice of which customers will be eligible for credit involves financial and legal questions. Credit should be extended when it improves the financial position of the company. Customers who will pay cash if credit is not offered are not good prospects since the cost of the credit reduces the profit from the sale. Customers who are not good credit risks should not be offered credit since the business will suffer losses when accounts are not paid.

From a legal standpoint, businesses cannot discriminate when deciding who should and should not be eligible for credit. That does not mean that individuals and businesses cannot be evaluated to determine if they are a good credit risk. It does require that credit decisions be based on identified standards and criteria. Anyone who meets the established standards must

teamwork

Develop a list of businesses that you and other team members use regularly that accept credit as a form of payment. Now make another list of businesses that require cash. Which list is longer? What differences do you see in the products and services sold by the businesses in the two lists? Discuss why so many businesses accept credit as a form of payment.

A store may offer credit to increase the number of customers who will purchase larger quantities of products.

be offered credit. Credit terms should be the same for everyone who meets the criteria.

The decision about who should receive credit should be determined by considering the effect of the decision on sales and profits. Will offering credit to business customers rather than final consumers increase sales? Will setting a minimum dollar limit on the use of credit increase the number of customers who purchase more expensive or larger quantities of products?

Types of Credit Plans Businesses have two options when choosing to offer credit. They can use a self-managed credit plan or a contracted credit plan with a financial services firm. With a **self-managed credit plan** the company administers the credit program and assumes all risks and returns. There are several forms of self-managed plans that will be discussed later in the chapter.

With a **contracted credit plan** credit services are provided by a financial services firm for a fee. In general, with contracted plans, the financial services firm assumes the costs and risks of managing the credit plan and receives any profits. In some agreements the financial services company may share the risks and profits with the contracting business.

A common type of contracted credit plan is to accept customer credit cards. Credit card systems are owned and managed by banks (Visa, Master-Card), financial services companies (American Express, Discover), or individual businesses such as retailers, oil companies, and telephone services. In order to accept a credit card, the business needs to establish an agreement with each credit card originator or a third-party company that has established relationships with the credit card companies and serves as an intermediary between the credit provider and the business accepting the card from customers.

To be able to accept credit cards, the business will have upfront costs for transaction processing equipment and usually a small start-up fee from the credit card issuer. In addition there are ongoing costs that can include a monthly statement fee, a per-transaction charge, communication cost, and charge-back fees for sales returns by customers. Finally, the largest expense is a discount from the sale price that the business must pay on each transaction. The discount is a percentage of the sale price normally in the range of 1.5–3.0 percent. The percentage charged by the credit card company is smaller as the volume of credit sales by the business increases. In making the decision to accept credit cards or not, the business will have to balance the convenience and expectations of customers and the reduced credit risk with the upfront and ongoing costs compared with maintaining a self-managed system.

checkpoint ✓

Does a business have to offer credit to every customer? Why or why not?

technology topics

Strengthening Your Online Security

As more and more companies provide their customers with online access to accounts, security becomes a concern. To protect yourself and your family, follow these guidelines.

- Install and update high-quality Internet security software that includes anti-virus and anti-spyware protection and a home network firewall.
- Create and use strong passwords and change them regularly. Use a different password for each account. Don't store passwords on your computer.
- Don't provide personal information online if you didn't initiate the contact. Even then make sure you haven't been transferred to a different web site during your transaction.
- Make sure every web site for online transactions is secure. Do online business only with companies that have strong security records.
- Never click on a link in an e-mail message from someone you don't know or completely trust.
- Always access your accounts from your own computer. Using another computer, especially in a public area such as a school, library, Internet cafe, or hotel, may leave behind your account information.
- Be especially careful when using wireless connections, which are particularly vulnerable.
- Check your accounts regularly and match the account information with your online activities.

Think Critically

1. Why should you take special security precautions rather than relying on companies to maintain your accounts securely?
2. What additional security suggestions can you add to the list?

UNDERSTAND CONCEPTS

Determine the best answer for each of the following questions.

1. ____?____ is an agreement in which a borrower receives something of value in exchange for a promise to repay the lender at a later date.
   a. profit
   b. a payment
   c. credit
   d. a contract

2. The recipient of credit is known as the
   a. creditor
   b. customer
   c. debtor
   d. payee

3. **True or False?** Most businesses today have little choice about whether to offer credit.

4. **True or False?** Accounts receivable can include both consumer accounts and business accounts.

5. Visa and MasterCard are examples of a ____?____ credit plan.
   a. self-managed
   b. contracted
   c. no-cost
   d. none of the above

MAKE ACADEMIC CONNECTIONS

6. **History** Use the Internet or the library to locate information on the earliest uses of credit in early civilizations. Write a brief report on your findings. Make sure to include references for the sources of your information in your paper.

7. **Math** A company decided to implement a credit program for the first time. Before offering credit to customers, sales were $87,000 per month. With the new program, sales increased 25 percent. The monthly cost of managing the program is $13,000. The company is unable to collect 2 percent of total monthly sales due to poor customer credit. Using the figures provided, calculate (1) the dollar increase in monthly sales, (2) total monthly sales, (3) the total cost of the credit program, and (4) the monthly profit or loss resulting from implementing the credit program.

8. **Oral Communication** You represent a credit card company. You are responsible for contacting owners of small businesses who currently only have cash sales. Your goal is to convince them to begin accepting your credit card from their customers. Prepare and deliver a 3-minute presentation for the business owner discussing the benefits of accepting credit cards.

Goals
- Describe the major decisions that are part of a company's credit policy.
- Explain the factors a business should consider when deciding to use credit.

Terms
- credit standards
- creditworthy
- character
- conditions
- factoring

■Developing Effective Credit Policies

When a business decides to offer credit through a self-managed system it can quickly run into trouble if credit is not carefully controlled. Customers are quick to accept credit if it is offered, but sometimes they are not as quick to pay. While most customers will be reliable credit users, a few who end up making late payments or not paying at all will quickly add to the costs of doing business and use up all of the profits that had been anticipated when the decision was made to offer credit.

COSTS OF OFFERING CREDIT

Assume your company just made a $5,000 credit sale to a customer and the payment is due in one month. If you make a 5 percent net profit on your sales you expect to earn $250 profit when the customer pays for the order. However, credit has some immediate costs and potentially some larger long-term costs to your business. The first cost is the loss of $5,000 cash for one month that you would have had if payment was made immediately. If you have to borrow money to finance the sale, $5,000 borrowed at 8 percent for one month equals $33.33. That seems like a very small amount until you begin to add the costs of financing the credit sales of every customer. If you actually have cash on hand so you don't have to borrow money to finance the credit, you lose the interest you could have earned. If you can receive 4.5 percent on a short-term money market account, you give up $18.75 on the $5,000 you could have invested. Again, that is a small amount on one sale but if you had 100 credit customers, the interest you did not earn would be nearly $2,000.

Now consider the possibility that the customer never pays the bill and the products purchased cannot be recovered. First your business loses the $250 of income that will now have to be made up from other sales. But more importantly you have lost the full cost of the product, $4,750, which you will have to recover from additional sales. With a 5 percent profit margin, that will require additional sales of $95,000 just to recover the cost of the loss from offering credit to that customer.

With that example you can see that decisions to offer credit to customers should be made very carefully. If you offer credit to reliable customers who would otherwise not buy or who might increase the amount of their purchases due to the availability of credit, the financial results can be very positive. That same $5,000 sale results in $250 of profit that might not otherwise be obtained. One hundred credit customers averaging $5,000 in sales provides an additional $500,000 of sales and a $25,000 gain in net profit.

CREDIT POLICY DECISIONS

The accounts receivable of a company are the value of products and services that have been sold but for which payment has not been received. The credit policies of the business are an important factor in determining the percentage of sales that will initially be classified as accounts receivable, how long sales will remain in that account, and ultimately how much of the accounts receivable is converted to cash when credit customers pay their accounts. Important decisions in establishing a company's credit policy include when credit will be offered, what standards will be used to offer credit, and what the credit terms will be.

When to Offer Credit Some businesses make credit generally available for all products any time they are offered for sale. That means that if a customer meets the business' credit standards, credit can be used for any purchase. If the business decides to contract its credit services to other businesses or to accept credit cards, that policy is acceptable. The contracted company accepts the risk of offering credit for a fee and maintains the accounts receivable. The business making the sale receives payment quickly rather than having to wait until the customer actually pays the credit company.

With a self-managed credit system, if there is no policy regarding when to offer credit, credit sales can grow rapidly and cash flow may become a problem. With favorable credit terms, customers are likely to use credit and delay payment. The company will not receive cash until the end of that credit period. There are many purchases that customers are likely to make even if credit is not available. Customers are willing to pay for many products immediately. Recognizing when credit is needed to make a sale and when it is not needed provides the business with greater control over both credit sales and cash. Three possible criteria for when to offer credit include

1. Offer credit to specific categories of customers. Examples include offering credit to business customers but not to individual consumers. Credit may be extended only to customers who purchase minimum dollar amounts or quantities of products.

2. Offer credit for specific types of products. High-value, customized, or complex products may warrant credit to encourage sales, while inexpensive products that are regularly purchased do not require credit to stimulate sales.

3. Offer credit during particular sales periods or times of the year. For some companies, there are times of the year when sales do not match production levels. Offering customers credit to purchase during slow sales

Most businesses have a good record of making credit payments. In 2005, 85 percent of all business credit accounts were up to date, with late payments averaging just under 7 days. Less than 1 percent of trade credit accounts were over 90 days past due.

periods may encourage sales. At the end of a sales season as products age, credit may encourage customers to purchase remaining products. Matching credit to cycles of high and low cash flow can help companies maintain healthy cash balances.

Credit Standards Credit standards are the guidelines used by a company to determine if a customer is eligible for credit. A customer who is creditworthy has characteristics making it highly likely that credit payments will be made on time and in full. The characteristics typically considered when determining whether a customer is creditworthy or not are often referred to as the *4 C's of Customer Credit* and are identified in Figure 9-1.

FIGURE 9-1

The 4 C's of Customer Credit	
Character	Collateral (Capital)
Capacity	Conditions

Character is the personal qualities of the credit applicant that demonstrate responsibility and dependability. Character is determined through such things as personal references, good credit in the past, employment history, and circumstances that demonstrate good judgment.

Capacity is often considered the most important of the four factors. *Capacity* is the ability to make the required payments. It is determined by examining the personal and business financial resources of the customer, the current amount of cash available, assets that can quickly be converted to cash, and demands on those assets.

Collateral is the value of assets of the credit applicant that can back the request for credit. Creditors take less risk when the credit applicant has resources that can be claimed if credit is not repaid. For businesses applying for credit, creditors will also look at the value of the business' *capital* or the amount of personal wealth the owners have invested in the business. Persons who have risked a significant amount of their own money in a business provide evidence they are committed to the success of the business.

Conditions refer to factors that are generally outside the control of the borrower or lender but that can affect the risk. Most often conditions refer to the economy and whether it is strong or weak. A strong economy makes it easier for a business to extend credit and for the borrower to have the resources to make payments. As the economy weakens, both the lender and credit applicant may be at greater financial risk. Some specific factors such as changing technology, outdated business practices, or competitive pressures in an industry are conditions that can affect credit decisions.

Before companies offer credit, they need to consider each of the four characteristics and decide what will be acceptable in each category. Some companies develop ratings systems in which customers are classified based on their credit characteristics. "A" customers are strong credit candidates and will be granted the highest amount of credit and best credit terms. "B" customers will have credit limits and restricted credit terms. "C" customers will not be granted credit until their credit characteristics improve.

Credit Terms The final decision when developing a credit policy is to establish credit terms that will be offered to customers. Credit terms define the agreement between the creditor and customer regarding the length of time until credit is due, the interest rate and when it is applied, any early payment discounts, and penalties for late payment.

It is a standard practice when offering business credit to offer a period of time in which the business can pay without interest or penalty. That time period is often 30 days. To encourage early payment, the seller may offer the buyer a price discount if payment is made within a few days, often 10, after the product and invoice have been received. A notation on the invoice identifies the credit terms: "2/10, net 30" means a 2 percent discount is offered if payment is received within 10 days. If that discount is not taken, the full amount (net) is due in 30 days. The terms of "3/10, 1/30, net 60" offers a 3 percent discount for a payment in 10 days, 1 percent discount if paid between 10 and 30 days, or full payment due within 60 days.

Consumer credit terms typically offer a period of time in which payment can be made with no interest charges. Some retailers such as furniture stores offer an extended period, often several months or even a year, when no interest or payments need to be made. At the end of that period, if full payment is not received, the credit customer will be charged a high interest rate that may accumulate from the date of the purchase. Other consumer credit terms are more standard. A specified interest rate is identified that is computed from the date of the sale with a minimum payment that must be made on a monthly basis, or the total amount owed is divided into equal monthly payments for the length of the credit agreement.

MAKING CREDIT DECISIONS

In order to maintain credit standards, a business must have a procedure for gathering information about possible credit customers. Most companies have a simple credit application that asks the applicant for personal and financial information as well as credit references. Then the credit history of the applicant is checked using a credit reporting company. Three companies are the primary sources of consumer credit information in the United States—Equifax, Experian, and TransUnion. The major supplier of business credit information is Dun & Bradstreet. These credit reporting companies collect detailed information on the credit histories of individuals and businesses. They then sell the information including credit rating scores to businesses for use as a tool in making credit decisions.

Businesses submit information to each credit reporting company on the credit transactions of all customers including any credit accounts opened and closed, all purchases made on credit, payments made and missed, dates of late payments, and any other significant customer activities and business actions related to the account. Based on the information accumulated, the credit reporting companies develop a credit score for each individual consumer. An individual credit score is made up of several factors that are shown in Figure 9-2. Each factor is assigned a weighted value based on its importance to make up a percentage of the final score.

In their reports on the creditworthiness of businesses, Dun & Bradstreet provides a number of specific ratings and scores related to the financial strength and credit history of each company. The reports include a financial

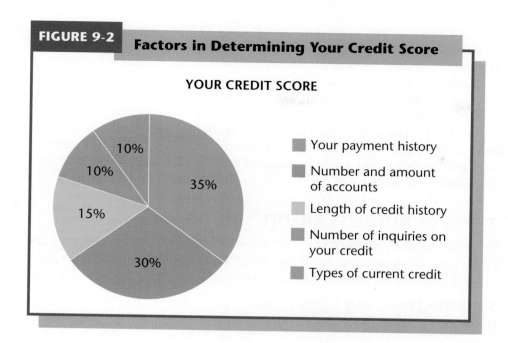

FIGURE 9-2 **Factors in Determining Your Credit Score**

YOUR CREDIT SCORE

- 10%
- 10%
- 15%
- 30%
- 35%

- Your payment history
- Number and amount of accounts
- Length of credit history
- Number of inquiries on your credit
- Types of current credit

stress score, a credit score, a 12-month credit payment rating, an overall credit rating, and a recommendation on the amount of credit that should be extended. A full credit report also provides detailed financial data on the company and other key public information such as bankruptcies, lawsuits, and organizational or ownership changes.

checkpoint ✔

What are the three important decisions to be made when developing a company's credit policy?

▌Deciding to Use Credit

Many businesses must carry high dollar values of inventory as a part of doing business. Manufacturers require raw materials, parts, supplies, and packaging materials in order to produce their products. Retailers must carry a variety of products with adequate assortments of each product to be able to meet customer shopping expectations. The costs of those inventories cannot be recovered until the manufacturer completes production and then sells and distributes the finished goods to its customers or until the retailer's customers make their choices and pay for their purchases.

Inventory costs account for thousands of dollars for those businesses. If the business must pay those costs at the time they are purchased, it will require an expenditure of cash which is likely to put real pressure on the cash balance of the company. Even if products are resold in a few weeks, the cash will not be replaced until money is collected from customers. Often inventories are carried for months and credit is extended to purchasers, delaying even further the time when payment is received.

teamwork

Your team is responsible for preparing a credit policy for a consumer electronics store that sells everything from CDs, MP3 players, and headphones to expensive stereos, televisions, and home theater equipment. Discuss how the company will answer the three important questions that make up a credit policy and then agree on a credit policy the company should follow.

One way to remedy the cash crunch faced by businesses is to use credit to purchase products and services. When credit is accepted, the required payment is delayed until the business will be in a better financial position to pay for the purchases. Of course, the risk associated with the decision to use credit is that there will not be adequate cash at the time payment is due. Also, the credit terms often include a rather high interest rate so the cost of the purchase increases by the amount of interest charges. Businesses must decide whether the risk and increased cost is worth the short-term availability of cash and access to products and services they would otherwise have difficulty purchasing.

TYPES OF BUSINESS CREDIT

There are several sources of credit available to businesses and several types of credit from those sources. Businesses can look to their suppliers, banks, and other financial organizations, or they can issue their own commercial paper.

Supplier Financing Just as a business can offer credit to its customers, it can look to its suppliers for credit on purchases. Suppliers may be willing to offer trade credit to their customers. Trade credit is, in fact, the most important source of short-term credit for most small businesses.

Trade credit from suppliers is offered to businesses with a good credit rating. Usually businesses requesting a large amount or ongoing access to trade credit will have to provide adequate financial information or credit references to the supplier. The supplier may purchase that information from credit reporting businesses such as Dun & Bradstreet.

Most trade credit offers a period of time, often 30–60 days, to pay for an order with no cost to the customer. A discount is often offered to encourage prompt payment, such as 2 percent if payment is made within 10 days. Some trade credit carries an interest charge if payment is delayed for an extended period of time. That interest rate is often quite high. A rate of 1 1/2 percent per month is not unusual, which is equal to an 18 percent annual percentage rate.

Bank Financing Banks that work with businesses recognize the importance of short-term financing and often offer several options for business credit. Those options include promissory notes, lines of credit, and revolving credit.

A *promissory note* is a loan for a specific amount, purpose, interest rate, and time period. It usually is secured by business assets and has a specified payment plan.

A *line of credit* is an informal agreement between the business and its bank identifying a maximum amount of money the business can borrow. The business can obtain a portion of that amount as needed to meet business expenses and will make regular payments to the bank for the interest charges. The business can pay back principal as resources are available to reduce interest charges and to increase the available balance of the credit line.

Revolving credit is similar to a line of credit but is a formal loan agreement for a specified amount of money, time period, and interest rate. The revolving credit agreement commits the bank legally to offer the credit and the borrower usually pays a small annual fee to maintain the agreement.

Credit from Other Financial Organizations There are other financial organizations in addition to banks that provide short-term financing for businesses. They include insurance, commercial finance, and investment companies, and large private companies with financing divisions. Private financial organizations offer the same types of credit products as banks, including secured loans, which are inventory and accounts receivable loans where the borrower's inventory or receivables are pledged as security.

A unique way to obtain cash without the use of credit is through factoring. **Factoring** is the sale of accounts receivable. Private companies, known as factors, will purchase accounts receivable from a company at a discount, often as high as 25 percent. They then become the collection agency and receive payment from the customer. The company selling the account has immediate use of the money and usually no liability if the factor is unable to collect the account. However, factoring is usually expensive and may not be viewed positively by the customer, whose account must now be paid to the company that purchased the account.

Small businesses may use short-term credit to purchase inventory when cash is unavailable.

Commercial Paper Very large companies with strong financial positions can create their own financing through the sale of commercial paper. *Commercial paper* is a short-term unsecured promissory note issued by a business to obtain short-term financing. Commercial paper is issued for a period of 2 to 270 days and is purchased by other banks, investment firms, or other businesses. While the loans are unsecured, they are rated by Moody's and Standard & Poor's, which affects the amount the issuing company receives when the paper is sold.

DETERMINING THE COST OF CREDIT

Using credit usually comes at a cost to the business. As with any financial decision, the company must balance the cost of obtaining credit against the value received from the use of the money. If that value exceeds the cost, it makes sense to obtain the credit. The analysis of costs and benefits should include consideration of any unanticipated risks such as a downturn in the economy or an increase in the business' expenses before payment is due that could affect the ability to pay the cost of the credit.

The Cost of Trade Credit Trade credit may be one of those instances where you can get "something for nothing." Because trade credit is often stated as *net 30,* the business is able to obtain the goods but withhold payment until the end of the 30 days. In that way, the business is using the supplier's money for the full 30 days at no cost. If that is the only variable being considered, there is no reason not to accept the trade credit.

Trade credit often comes with an incentive for early payment in the form of a discount. If the terms of the credit are *2/10, net 30* the purchaser receives a 2 percent discount on the cost of the purchase if payment is made within 10 days. Should the business take the discount and pay early or pay the full amount at the end of 30 days? To make the decision, the business needs to calculate the cost of delaying payment and paying the full cost. Using 2/10, net 30 credit terms, the calculation is

$$\text{Cost of Credit} = \frac{\text{Discount Percent}}{100 - \text{Discount Percent}}$$
$$\times \frac{365}{\text{Payment Period} - \text{Discount Period}}$$

$$\text{Cost of Credit} = \frac{2}{98} \times \frac{365}{30 - 10}$$

$$\text{Cost of Credit} = 0.0204 \times 18.25$$

$$\text{Cost of Credit} = 0.3724 \text{ or } 37.24 \text{ percent}$$

The calculation shows that the cost of delaying payment until the end of the 30 days and forgoing the discount is an annual interest rate of 37.24 percent. That is a very high cost, since it would be possible for most businesses to borrow the money needed to pay the bill at a lower interest rate and earn the discount. If the percentage of discount is lower or if the number of days the business is given to pay the full invoice without interest changes, the cost of credit goes down. The cost of trade credit should be compared to the cost of borrowing funds or the interest rate available for investing unused cash to determine when payment should be made.

The Cost of Loans Before borrowing money from a bank or other financial institution, businesses should determine the real cost of the loan. That cost can then be compared to the costs of other sources of financing and the financial benefits the business will receive from the use of the borrowed funds.

Loans vary in their costs based on a number of factors. The most important factor is the financial condition of the borrower. A financially healthy company can usually obtain a loan at a much lower interest rate than one that has financial problems. A second factor is the general state of the economy and the availability of funds. Somewhat surprisingly, interest rates are usually lower when the economy is weak. Money is usually more readily available at that time and the risk of inflation is low, so interest rates fall. With a strong economy, businesses make strong demands for money, so the money supply is reduced and interest rates begin to increase.

Many business loans are provided with a variable interest rate, meaning the rate can be adjusted up and down by the lender based on changing market rates. Small interest rate adjustments on large loan amounts can dramatically change the cost to the borrower.

The cost of a loan is also affected by the way interest is calculated. Simple interest is calculated on an annual basis. Compound interest is calculated more frequently and adds that amount to the value of the loan. The more frequently interest is compounded, the more expensive the loan. Finally, some lenders add fees to the cost of the loan. Those fees must be added to the loan to determine its actual cost.

checkpoint ✓

How should a business decide if it should accept the discount terms of trade credit rather than waiting to pay at the end of the period?

Building Your Credit Record

Almost everyone uses credit at some point in their lives. Most people use credit regularly and extensively. A good credit record makes it easier to obtain credit, whether for financing a car, purchasing a home, or buying clothing, a computer, or other personal items. While most people can obtain a credit card even if they have a poor credit record, the terms under which the card can be obtained and the interest rate charged will be much higher for those with a poor credit rating. The cost of credit for people with poor credit is always much higher than for people with a good record.

Many people have credit problems and end up with a poor credit rating before they realize the problems it creates for them. Making late payments or ignoring some bills, failing to respond to contacts from collection agencies, and maintaining high balances on a number of credit cards will lead to a low credit score. Once the problem is recognized and a person needs to obtain credit, it may be too late. That credit will be denied and it will take a long time and a great deal of effort to rebuild a strong credit record.

Here are some steps everyone should follow to build a good credit record from the very beginning.

1. Open a savings account in your own name and make regular deposits. This step will establish a relationship with a bank.

2. Once you have adequate savings, open a checking account or obtain a debit card. Maintain a reasonable balance in the account and use it infrequently. DO NOT overdraw the account.

3. Establish credit in your own name. The credit can be with a local retail store, a cellular telephone service, a gasoline company, or a prepaid or secured credit card. Use the credit for small, infrequent purchases and make sure to pay the full balance when it is first due.

4. Maintain a part-time job (full-time in the summer if possible) to develop an employment history. Save a large part of your paycheck to be able to demonstrate a strong financial position when you apply for credit.

5. Protect your personal information and your credit record. Do not share your credit card with friends or let them charge items on your store account with the promise to pay you back. Check your credit record at least once a year to identify and correct any inaccurate information.

6. If you run into credit problems, act to resolve them immediately. Talk with your parents, meet with the company where you have the problem, and make arrangements to pay your debt as quickly as possible. When you ignore a credit problem, it only gets worse.

Think Critically

1. What advice would you give to a friend who appears to be using credit unwisely?

2. Prepare several reasons to discuss with your parents why it is important for you to begin to develop a strong credit record.

9.2 Lesson Assessment

UNDERSTAND CONCEPTS

Determine the best answer for each of the following questions.

1. The value of products and services that have been sold but for which payment has not been received are a company's ____?____.
   a. assets
   b. accounts receivable
   c. liabilities
   d. accounts payable

2. **True or False?** Credit standards are the guidelines used by a company to determine if a customer is eligible for credit.

3. Which of the following is *not* one of the 4 C's of credit?
   a. character
   b. collateral
   c. commitment
   d. conditions

4. Trade credit is an example of
   a. supplier financing
   b. bank financing
   c. factoring
   d. commercial paper

5. **True or False?** A loan with simple interest is more expensive than one with compound interest since simple interest is calculated more frequently.

MAKE ACADEMIC CONNECTIONS

6. **Critical Thinking** Fast food businesses are now starting to accept credit cards. If you were the owner of a local "soda shop," would you accept credit cards? Use a computer to make two lists. The first list should be reasons for accepting credit cards. The second list should be reasons against accepting them. After completing the lists, make a decision and write a one-paragraph rationale to support it.

7. **Communication** You will need to borrow $10,000 next year to help finance your first year of college. Write a letter to a local bank describing your need and the reasons they should grant you a loan. Incorporate information about the 4 C's of credit in your rationale.

8. **Math** Calculate the cost of credit for the following trade credit terms.
   a. 2/15, net 30
   b. 1/20, net 40
   c. 3/30, net 60

9. **Research** Use the Internet to identify three credit cards available to consumers from different companies. Prepare a table that compares the features and costs of the cards. Which card would you recommend (1) to a teenager with no savings and a part-time job, (2) to a young family that has a hard time paying the full balance of a card each month, (3) to a retired couple who live on a fixed income and pay all bills on time each month, (4) for a salesperson who travels extensively and uses the card for business expenses.

Goals
- Describe effective collection procedures for credit accounts.
- Recognize legal requirements for credit and collections.

Terms
- delinquent account
- charge-off
- collection procedures
- aging schedule

Establishing Collection Procedures

One of the greatest costs to a company that operates a self-managed credit system is the loss from unpaid accounts. A credit account that has not been paid by the due date according to the credit terms is a **delinquent account.** Most credit customers pay their accounts. If a company maintains an effective procedure to screen customers, less than five percent of accounts receivable will be behind in payments by more than 30 days. Between one and two percent of accounts will remain uncollected after 90 days, at which point the likelihood of collecting the money owed is very low.

An account that is no longer considered collectible is known as a **charge-off.** To avoid charge-offs, businesses need to develop collection procedures. **Collection procedures** are the steps a business follows to keep customer credit payments up to date. Collection procedures should be planned and put in place before credit is offered to customers. Customer payment of accounts can be improved by offering discounts for early payment and charging interest if accounts are not paid on time. Specific collection procedures should be designed to quickly obtain payment of past due accounts while maintaining positive customer relationships. The steps in effective collection procedures are shown in Figure 9-3.

FIGURE 9-3

A Systematic Collections Procedure

Follow these steps to improve collections of accounts receivable.

1. Carefully screen credit applications
2. Maintain complete and up-to-date account information
3. Ensure speedy and accurate invoicing
4. Monitor accounts receivable
5. Take immediate action following established procedures
6. Use customer-friendly but effective collection strategies
7. Escalate collections before it is too late
8. Establish final collection and charge-off standards

Select Customers Most collection problems can be eliminated before a customer makes a credit purchase. Using a credit application that determines the financial health and credit history of a customer allows the businesses to avoid offering credit to high-risk customers. The business may decide to extend credit to a customer who does not have a strong record but can limit the amount of credit offered and monitor the account carefully.

Maintain Records Complete and up-to-date customer records are critical to effective credit and collections. Accurate contact names, telephone numbers, and e-mail addresses are needed to follow up on billing and payment questions and quickly resolve any problems.

Invoice Purchases Most problems with prompt payments arise from errors or incomplete information on customer invoices or delays in preparing and mailing the invoices. Once an order is shipped, the customer invoice should be mailed immediately. The invoice must accurately bill the customer for the type and quantity of products shipped at the correct price. If the order is incomplete, that information must be clearly communicated to the customer. The credit terms should be printed on the invoice.

Monitor Accounts Each customer account should be monitored to track payment history. Companies prepare an **aging schedule** that categorizes all accounts receivable by the length of time they remain unpaid. Figure 9-4 shows an aging schedule for a company's credit accounts. The schedule can be quickly reviewed to see the age of the accounts and how much of the total accounts receivable is in each age category.

teamwork

Work with a team member to role-play a call from the collections department to a customer who has an account that is overdue by 40 days. The call should be persuasive to convince the customer to pay the account as quickly as possible while keeping their goodwill.

FIGURE 9-4

An Aging Schedule for Accounts Receivable

| Account No. | Age of Account (in Days) | | | | Account Total |
	0–30	31–60	61–90	Over 90	
101		$6,500			$6,500
102	$2,400		$4,900		$7,300
103				$1,025	$1,025
104	$6,950				$6,950
105	$1,950				$1,950
106		$2,100			$2,100
107	$3,250				$3,250
108			$1,990		$1,990
Age Total	$14,550	$8,600	$6,890	$1,025	$31,065
% of Total	46.84%	27.68%	22.18%	3.30%	

Take Action A specific set of collection procedures should be in place that begins immediately when a payment is missed. The procedures should have as their primary goal to retain the customer, but they need to result in prompt payment of the overdue account as well. There are many forms of communication that can be used to contact the customer. Most credit procedures start by sending a copy of the customer's account with a reminder that payment is now due. The reminder should also clearly restate the credit terms including interest charges for late payment.

Use Customer-Friendly Strategies If payment is not received shortly after the first letter is sent, the customer should be contacted by telephone. A well-trained member of the collections staff should remind the customer of the unpaid account, gather information on reasons that the account is unpaid, and discuss procedures for prompt payment. If the customer is not paying because of problems with the order or the product, those issues should be quickly resolved. If payment is delayed due to financial problems, alternatives for payment including a payment schedule should be agreed upon. If it appears that the customer is unwilling or unable to pay the overdue balance, restrictions on future orders should be placed on the customer's account.

Personal contact between customer and creditor can help resolve late account problems.

Escalate Collection Contacts If the late account remains unpaid after the initial contacts, additional formal contacts should be implemented on a regular schedule, usually every two to three weeks. A series of increasingly demanding but positive collection letters should be sent along with a bill of the account that clearly identifies the number of days the account is overdue and the new balance including interest. A telephone call should follow the letter since it is harder to ignore a personal contact than a letter. Neither the letter nor telephone call should be negative or threatening but should express the importance of the customer maintaining a good credit history and the need for prompt payment in order to retain favorable status as a customer. Depending on the location of credit customers, some companies arrange a personal visit as a final step in this stage of the collection process. The visit emphasizes the importance of payment and provides an opportunity for face-to-face discussions about payment plans.

Take Final Steps Only a very small percentage of accounts will be collected that remain unpaid after all of the previous collection steps. A company will have to decide if additional procedures are warranted. The choices are to involve a collection agency, take legal action, or classify the account as a charge-off and terminate the relationship with the customer. A collection agency is skilled at late collections and focuses all of their attention on that effort. Collection agencies charge fees for their services that are in the range of 25–50 percent of the amounts collected. When contracting with a collection agency, it is important to select a company with a good reputation that follows all legal requirements for collections and consumer protection.

A company may decide to take legal action against a debtor. The cost and time involved should be weighed against the likelihood of success and the amount that may be recovered. Many companies decide it is better to classify the account as a charge-off. If credit customers are selected carefully, credit accounts are monitored, and specific collection procedures are implemented quickly, the number and amount of charge-off accounts should be low.

What can be done before credit is offered to a customer to increase the chances that accounts will be paid on time?

■Credit Law

Credit terms can be complex and difficult to understand. The agreement between lender and borrower establishes a legal relationship than may need to be enforced in courts. While most credit transactions are done honestly, some lenders have tried to take advantage of their credit customers. To regulate credit transactions and protect the rights of both lenders and borrowers, a number of federal laws have been enacted. Most states have credit laws that must be followed when business is conducted in that state. Laws have been developed that regulate offering credit, collecting accounts, providing credit information, and protecting the privacy and security of customer information.

THE TRUTH IN LENDING ACT

The Truth in Lending Act is designed to promote the informed use of credit and encourage consumers to compare the cost of cash versus credit as well as to shop for the least expensive credit. The Act requires businesses to disclose specific credit terms in all credit advertising. When granting credit, a business must provide the borrower with a written statement of the cost of credit and the terms of repayment before the agreement is completed. Both the dollar amount and annual percentage rate of a transaction must be specified.

EQUAL CREDIT OPPORTUNITY ACT

The Equal Credit Opportunity Act prohibits discrimination against credit applicants because of age, sex, marital status, religion, race, color, national origin, or receipt of public assistance. All credit decisions must be based on an analysis of financial capability related to the credit for which the person applied. If a consumer is denied credit, the law requires that the person be notified in writing of the reasons for the denial if requested by the consumer.

THE FAIR CREDIT REPORTING ACT

The Fair Credit Reporting Act was developed to increase the accuracy and privacy of information collected by credit reporting companies. Under the Act all consumers have a right to free yearly copies of their credit reports from each of the three national credit reporting organizations. The reports must contain all the information in the file at the time of the request. Each company must disclose who has requested the credit report in the past year. You are also entitled to a free report if a company takes a negative credit action against you. You must be told which credit reporting company provided the information on which the negative action was based.

If you question the accuracy or completeness of information in your report, you have the right to file a dispute with the credit reporting company and the information provider (the person, company, or organization that provided information about you to the credit reporting company). Both the credit reporting company and the information provider are required to investigate your claim and correct inaccurate or incomplete information in your report.

Consumers have the right to dispute mistakes in their credit card bills.

THE FAIR CREDIT BILLING ACT

The Fair Credit Billing Act deals with mistakes in credit bills sent to consumers. If a credit customer believes there is a mistake in a bill, the company must be notified in writing within 60 days. The complaint must then be acknowledged within 30 days unless the mistake has been corrected. The disputed amount does not have to be paid during the time it takes to resolve the complaint. Any finance charges against the disputed amount must be deducted if there was an error. If no error is found, the business must send another bill and can add finance charges on the amount due for the time it has been unpaid.

THE FAIR DEBT COLLECTION PRACTICES ACT

This Act applies to most types of individual and family debts, but it only applies to collection agencies rather than companies who manage their own collection procedures. It prohibits debt collectors from engaging in unfair, deceptive, or abusive practices when dealing with people who have overdue accounts. Specifically they may only make contacts between 8 a.m. and 9 p.m. They cannot make contacts at work and cannot use harassing or abusive language or procedures. They cannot lie or misrepresent what can happen to the borrower if the debt is not paid. Debt collectors must identify themselves when calling on the phone. If specifically requested in writing, they must end all direct contacts.

RIGHT TO FINANCIAL PRIVACY ACT

The Right to Financial Privacy Act recognizes that customers of financial institutions can expect a reasonable amount of privacy for their financial records. The Act establishes requirements and procedures for the release of financial records and imposes requirements on financial institutions for communicating with customers prior to release of personal information.

THE FINANCIAL MODERNIZATION ACT

The Financial Modernization Act includes provisions to protect consumers' personal financial information held by financial institutions. The Financial Privacy Rule requires financial institutions to give customers privacy notices that explain information collection and sharing practices. Customers have the right to limit some sharing of their information. The Act includes the Safeguards Rule, which requires all financial institutions to maintain safeguards to protect customer information. The rule applies not only to financial institutions that collect information from their own customers, but also to companies that receive customer information from the institutions.

checkpoint ✓

Identify the major federal credit laws and the primary purpose of each.

¥£€$ finance **around the world**

Microfinance

How could a loan of $50 result in a life-changing experience? In countries such as Bangladesh, Nepal, Philippines, and Zimbabwe, microfinance has helped to improve the economy and society.

Microfinance, also called *microlending* and *microcredit,* involves programs of small loans to people for self-employment projects. The business activities generate income to provide for life necessities and family needs. Most microcredit efforts involve nonprofit organizations, which helps avoid political influences.

Most microfinance clients are low-income persons with no access to formal financial institutions. They are usually self-employed, often household-based entrepreneurs. In rural areas, clients are small farmers or food processing workers. In urban areas, microfinance activities include shopkeepers, service providers, artisans, and street vendors.

In southeastern Bangladesh, one of the poorest regions in the world, the Bangladesh Rural Advancement Committee (BRAC) loans money to women. Loans are made to help them farm fish, keep cows for milk production, grow vegetables, raise poultry, buy rickshaws, sew clothing, and sell cellular phone time in rural areas where no other phone service is available. The women pay 15 percent interest on loans, which is much less than they would have to pay to loan sharks. BRAC also works to improve the health of women and children. Over 30,000 volunteers have been trained by BRAC to recognize and treat ten common illnesses.

Microcredit has also been successful in Zimbabwe to economically empower the poor. World Vision Zimbabwe provides affordable financing to improve the economy of rural areas. Entrepreneurs operate businesses and live on the income of the projects they started after obtaining inexpensive, small loans from World Vision Zimbabwe.

Over time, some microfinance programs have expanded to include other financial services. In addition to loans, savings accounts and insurance coverage may be provided. These services help borrowers build assets and protect against risks.

Think Critically

1. What are the main benefits of microfinance programs?
2. What are possible concerns of microfinance?
3. Conduct an Internet search to find other examples of microfinance around the world. Prepare a written summary to describe how microfinance has benefited people in various areas.

UNDERSTAND CONCEPTS

Determine the best answer for each of the following questions.

1. A credit account that has not been paid by the designated date according to the credit terms is
   a. an old account
   b. a worthless account
   c. a delinquent account
   d. a current account

2. **True or False?** Collection procedures are not a part of credit procedures, so they should be developed after a customer establishes credit.

3. **True or False?** A primary goal of collection procedures should be to retain the customer.

4. The federal law that is designed to promote the informed use of credit and encourage consumers to understand the cost of credit is the
   a. Truth in Lending Act
   b. Equal Credit Opportunity Act
   c. Fair Credit Reporting Act
   d. Fair Credit Billing Act

5. **True or False?** The Financial Modernization Act was written to require financial institutions to protect the privacy and security of customer information.

MAKE ACADEMIC CONNECTIONS

6. **Writing** Prepare a letter that can be sent to a customer immediately after the credit account payment has become due and payment has not been submitted. The letter should encourage payment while maintaining a positive relationship with the customer.

7. **Math** A company has current accounts receivable of $185,200. If 18 percent of the total is past due, what amount needs to be collected? The company identifies 1.4 percent of accounts receivable as more than 90 days past due and has turned those accounts over to a collection agency. If the agency collects 85 percent of the total owed and keeps 40 percent of the money collected as its fee, how much will the company be paid by the collection agency?

8. **Research** Use magazines or newspapers to locate an advertisement of a company that is selling a product and offering financing to customers. Read the credit information in the ad. After studying the credit information, prepare a two-paragraph written analysis of how the information helped you understand the credit terms and enabled you to make a decision about whether it would be better to obtain the credit from the company, find credit elsewhere, or pay cash for the purchase.

9. **Law** Use the Internet to locate information on laws in your state that regulate credit and collections. Prepare a chart that identifies (1) the name of each law, (2) the purpose of each law, and (3) the requirements businesses and consumers must meet according to the law.

Summary

9.1 CREDIT PRINCIPLES AND PRACTICES

1. Many business-to-business sales as well as sales to final consumers are made using credit. Deciding to extend credit to customers or use credit when making purchases should be viewed primarily as a financial decision.

2. Choosing which customers will be eligible for credit involves financial and legal criteria. When using credit to finance purchases, the primary financial considerations of a company are interest costs that increase the final price of the purchase, whether a lower price is available for paying cash, and the effect on cash flow at the time payment must be made.

9.2 OFFER AND USE CREDIT

3. The credit policies of a business are an important factor in determining the percentage of sales that will initially be classified as accounts receivable, how long sales will remain in that account, and ultimately how much of accounts receivable is converted to cash when credit customers pay their accounts.

4. There are several sources of credit available to businesses and several types of credit from those sources. Businesses can look to their suppliers, banks, and other financial organizations or they can issue their own commercial paper. A company must balance the cost of obtaining credit against the value received from the use of the money.

9.3 COLLECTION PROCEDURES AND LEGAL REQUIREMENTS

5. One of the greatest costs to a company that operates a self-managed credit system is losses from unpaid accounts. Businesses must develop collection procedures that keep customer credit payments up to date and eliminate charge-offs.

6. To regulate credit transactions and protect the rights of both lenders and borrowers, a number of federal laws have been enacted. Laws have been developed that regulate offering credit, collecting accounts, providing credit information, and protecting the privacy and security of customer information.

Develop Your Business Language

Match the terms listed with the definitions. Some terms will not be used.

1. Characteristics making it highly likely that credit payments will be made on time and in full
2. Credit services are provided by a financial services firm for a fee
3. Guidelines used by a company to determine if a customer is eligible for credit
4. Written document describing the terms under which credit is granted and payment will be made
5. Categorizes all accounts receivable by the length of time they remain unpaid
6. Account that is no longer considered collectable
7. Recipient of credit
8. Sale of accounts receivable
9. Factors that are generally outside the control of the borrower or lender but that can affect the risk
10. Credit offered to individual consumers by a business
11. An agreement in which a borrower receives something of value in exchange for a promise to repay the lender at a later date
12. Credit offered to a business customer by another business

a. aging schedule
b. character
c. charge-off
d. collection procedures
e. conditions
f. consumer credit
g. contracted credit plan
h. credit
i. credit agreement
j. credit standards
k. creditworthy
l. debtor
m. delinquent account
n. factoring
o. self-managed credit plan
p. trade credit

Review Concepts

13. When a business makes a sale on credit, the information is recorded in the seller's financial records as
    a. an account payable
    b. a liability
    c. an account receivable
    d. a long-term asset
14. A company can transfer the risks of managing a credit plan by using
    a. a self-managed credit plan
    b. a contracted plan
    c. a collection procedure
    d. all are correct
15. An advantage of using a credit card system for accepting credit is
    a. there is no cost to the business when accepting credit cards
    b. the business receives its money before the customer actually makes payment to the credit card company
    c. no record of the transaction is required
    d. the business can accept any credit card the customer is carrying
16. Which of the following is *not* one of the 4 C's of customer credit?
    a. character
    b. capacity
    c. commission
    d. collateral

Think Critically

17. The average cost per sale to accept credit cards is often higher for a small business than the cost of operating a self-managed credit plan. Based on that, why would businesses choose to use credit cards as their credit system rather than establishing their own credit system?

18. Rank the 4 C's of customer credit in terms of their importance to a business in selecting the best credit customers. Explain your rankings.

19. Most business credit terms allow customers 30 to 60 days to pay invoices without any interest being charged. That means the customer is using the seller's money for free for that time, which adds to the seller's costs. Why do you think businesses offer those credit terms even though they are expensive? Which do you believe is more important to business customers—a discount for paying quickly or no interest charges for 30 to 60 days? Justify your answer.

20. Many people believe that a person's credit score is based only on previous payment history. Instead it includes factors such as the number of credit accounts and their amounts, the length of the credit history, the number of inquiries that have been made by companies, and the types of current credit. Provide reasons why each of those factors are included in calculating a credit score. Which factors do you believe do not fairly represent a person's credit risk? Explain.

Business Financial Calculations

21. If a person pays the minimum amount on a credit card at the end of the month and leaves an unpaid balance of $1,800, how much interest will be owed at the end of the next month if the credit card company charges an annual interest rate of 18 percent?

22. Calculate the total amount each customer must pay based on the following invoice terms and payment dates.

Invoice Date	Invoice Amount	Credit Terms	Payment Date
a. January 1	$74,500	2/10, net 30	January 10
b. March 15	$8,750	1/15, net 30	April 2
c. July 1	$52,000	12 percent APR	December 31

23. Use Figure 9-4 as a model to prepare an Aging Schedule of Accounts Receivable table using the following account information. Assume the current date is July 1. Calculate all totals and percentages.

Account Number	Total Owed	Invoice Date
C-18	$ 565	June 25
C-18	$1,020	May 2
C-22	$1,870	April 15
C-36	$2,100	June 4
C-39	$ 490	January 18
C-39	$ 746	May 28
C-45	$3,205	July 1

Analyze Cases

Use the case from the beginning of the chapter, Visa—Taking Credit World-wide, to answer the following questions.

24. What do you believe accounts for the tremendous worldwide growth of the use of credit cards such as Visa? What recommendations would you make to Visa to increase the numbers of people using their credit cards and the usage of credit cards by those who already own them?

25. Do you believe that credit card companies encourage the misuse of credit? Provide examples to justify your view. What problems are created for consumers, for businesses that accept credit cards, and for Visa if customers charge more than they are able to pay?

26. Provide examples of technology you have seen or heard about that are changing how credit is used by consumers. Use creative thinking and describe new ways that technology might make it easier or safer to use credit to make purchases.

Portfolio Activity

COLLECT several examples of business' credit policies and credit terms that are used to offer consumer credit and trade credit. The information is available in company advertising, product catalogs, and on web sites where they provide ordering information.

CREATE a visual that illustrates important credit concepts and terms.

CONNECT your visual to other items already in your class portfolio or relate it to an important concept you have learned in another class. Make the connection by preparing a one-minute presentation on the importance of carefully developed credit and collection policies to the financial health of a business.

Stock Market Activity

Selling on credit is a fundamental element of doing business. Effective management of consumer credit activities is necessary for company success. Creation and implementation of credit applicant screening activities along with efficient collections can have a strong influence on a company's financial success and stock price.

Use online and library resources along with the annual report of the company you have been studying (or select a different company).

1. Describe the activities of the company with regard to selling on credit.

2. Discuss changes in the amount of the company's receivables over the past few years.

3. Assess to what extent selling on credit might influence the stock price of the company.

Planning a Career in Credit Analysis

Credit analysis is the process of gathering and analyzing information to make credit decisions. Credit analysts evaluate consumer and business financial records and compare them to credit requests. Based on the analysis, decisions about granting credit are made.

Hundreds of thousands of people are employed in the credit industry. Employees are needed to sell credit services, prepare credit reports, maintain and analyze records, manage credit services, and make collections. Varied educational and skill requirements are needed for jobs in credit analysis.

Employment Outlook

- Credit services are increasingly important to the economy so the number of jobs continues to grow.
- People are employed in banks, insurance companies, credit agencies, finance companies, and private businesses that offer their own credit services, such as auto dealerships.
- Many credit analysis activities are now being automated with computer programs, so lower-skilled jobs are disappearing.
- Jobs requiring financial analysis and decision-making skills are growing. The use of credit changes with the strength of the economy.

Job Titles

- Credit analyst
- Credit negotiator
- Credit manager
- Escrow representative
- Factor
- Loan officer
- Underwriter

Needed Skills

- Most credit analysts have a bachelor's degree in accounting, finance, economics, or statistics.
- A master's degree or several years of increasingly responsible experience is needed to advance into top-level jobs.
- A strong background in math and statistics, the ability to interpret financial records, and proficiency with financial software are expected.
- The ability to make objective decisions and to communicate clearly with written reports and charts is also important.

What's It Like to Work as a Credit Analyst?

A credit analyst working for a consumer credit business is responsible for making recommendations on credit applications. A credit analyst will usually be working on many applications at the same time.

The credit analyst reviews each application for completeness and accuracy. Then credit reports on the applicant are obtained, usually via computer. Telephone calls to the retail representative and the applicant may be needed to clarify and add information. For large loan amounts, information may need to be gathered from the applicant's employer, bank, or other sources.

After collecting and studying all information, a credit decision is made and a written report is prepared.

What about you? What do you see as the major changes occurring in the career area of credit and credit analysis? Why do you believe you would or would not like this type of work?

IMPROMPTU SPEAKING EVENT

The ability to express one's thoughts without prior preparation is a valuable asset. Poise, self-confidence, and organization of facts are elements necessary for an effective impromptu speech.

Participants in the Impromptu Speaking Event will be given a current business topic. One (1) 4"-by-6" index card will be given to each participant and may be used during the preparation and performance. Information may be written on both sides of the card. Participants must furnish their own pens and pencils. No reference materials may be brought to or used during the preparation or presentation. Participants will have a lectern to use for their speech but no microphone will be provided.

Participants will be allowed ten (10) minutes to prepare their speeches prior to appearing before the judge. Any notes made during the preparation time may be used when speaking. The note card must be submitted to the teacher/event coordinator at the conclusion of the speech. The speech should be four (4) minutes in length. A timekeeper will stand at three (3) minutes. When the speaker is finished, the time used by the participant will be recorded, noting a deduction of five (5) points for any time under 3:31 or over 4:29 minutes.

Your topic for the impromptu speech will be one of the following concerning credit.

- Consumer Credit: You Are Entering the Danger Zone
- The Responsible Use of Credit
- The Need for Consumer Credit
- Living a Life of Plastic
- Credit—Shop Until You Drop

Performance Indicators Evaluated

- Understand the topic covered by the speech.
- Present an interesting, sincere, clear, and convincing speech.
- Use appropriate gestures and eye contact during the speech.
- Convey professional self-confidence.
- Cover the topic adequately.
- Use facts and convincing rationale to support the speech.

Go to the FBLA web site for more detailed information.

Think Critically

1. Why is credit an important topic in today's society?
2. How can actual credit examples be used for this speech?
3. What is one drawback of credit?
4. What is one advantage of credit?

www.fbla.org

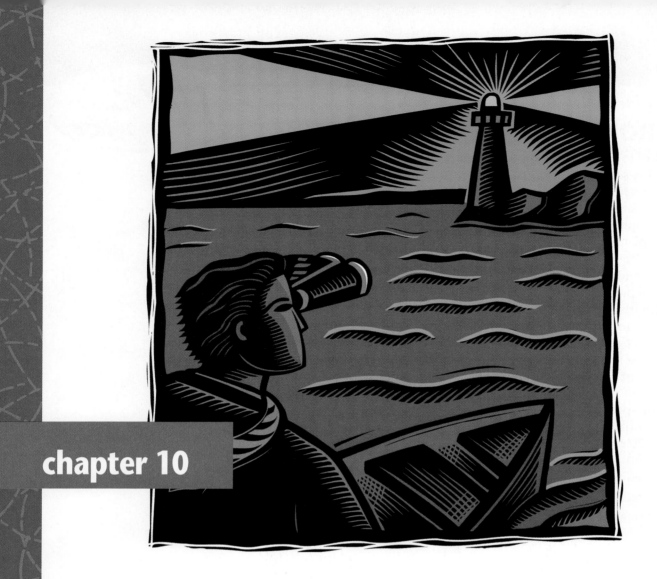

chapter 10

Business Insurance

10.1 MANAGE RISK

10.2 PRINCIPLES OF INSURANCE

10.3 PROPERTY AND VEHICLE INSURANCE

10.4 PERSONNEL AND LIABILITY INSURANCE

Point Your [Browser]

www.thomsonedu.com/school/busfinance

Providing Specialty Insurance

Insurance traditionally spreads the risk of financial loss across a large number of individuals or companies, each of whom faces a similar type of risk. Individuals and businesses may also face financial losses that are unique. A group of investors in a new movie may lose millions of dollars if production problems occur. An athlete's career and earnings will be lost if he or she suffers a major injury. The cargo of a large ship, a major entertainment event that is dependent on good weather, or a fundraiser that offers a large prize for a difficult accomplishment such as a hole-in-one at a golf tournament each presents a possible but reasonably unique risk for the investors or event planners. Those unique risks are difficult to insure and have resulted in the growth of the specialty risk market.

Lloyd's (also known as Lloyd's of London) is the largest source of specialty risk insurance in the world. Surprisingly, Lloyd's is not an insurance company or even an actual company by itself. Instead it is a market where companies and wealthy individuals invest money to insure unique risks. Insurance is provided through *syndicates* or groups of investors who pool their money to insure specific categories of risk. Today Lloyd's has 64 syndicates which specialize in areas such as aviation, catastrophes, and professional risks.

The organization began in 1688 when merchants, ship captains, and ship owners would gather at Edward Lloyd's coffee house in London. Since there was always a risk of loss to ships and cargos, groups formed to pool their money to cover potential losses. Rich investors called *names* were attracted to Lloyd's to speculate on marine insurance. They would put money into a pool that insured a specific ship and its cargo. They would make money if the cargo and ship were safe but would have to pay if loss or damage occurred. Until 1994, most of the capital for Lloyd's came from individual investors. Due to huge losses suffered in the early 1990s, Lloyd's began accepting *members,* or corporations, as investors. Today, members provide about 90 percent of the investment capital while names provide the remaining 10 percent. Among the companies that insure through Lloyd's syndicates are 85 percent of the Fortune 500 companies, the top seven pharmaceutical companies, and the 20 largest global banks. The organization accepted insurance premiums of £13.7 billion in 2005.

Think Critically

1. Why is it difficult and more expensive to get insurance for unique risks? Since premiums are likely to be high for specialty insurance, why would companies and individuals purchase that insurance?

2. Why would names and members want to participate in one of Lloyd's syndicates? What information would you want to have about the syndicate and the risks before you would become an investor?

Goals
- Define risk and the types of risks faced by individuals and businesses.
- Describe the primary methods for managing risks.

Terms
- risk
- economic risk
- pure risk
- speculative risk
- natural risk
- human risk
- controllable risk
- uncontrollable risk
- risk management
- liability

▉ Facing Risk

Each day when you walk out of your door, you face uncertainty and risk. In fact even as you sleep there are risks that can dramatically affect your life. Every business also faces risks that might be so serious that they could result in business failure. **Risk** is the chance or probability of harm or loss.

Individuals face risks that can affect health, income, and property, and can even result in death. Businesses face risks that can have a significant economic affect. Property and inventory can be damaged, lost, or stolen; personnel can become ill, injured, or even die; and the company's products or employees can cause damage to property or harm to people for which the business is liable. Risk carries with it the possibility of financial loss.

THE MEANING OF RISK

Sometimes the word uncertainty is used as a substitute for risk. When you are uncertain, you have doubt about a possible outcome. If you face a risk, there is a chance of a positive outcome and also a chance of a negative outcome. An **economic risk** has a potential financial impact. Some risks are not economic in that they have no direct or immediate financial impact. When you attend a social activity with friends you risk not enjoying yourself. If you forgo studying for an exam, you risk earning a poor grade. But if an employee becomes ill and cannot work for several weeks, the person faces a financial loss of wages that would have been earned. If a business' warehouse is destroyed by fire, the money invested in the building, equipment, and inventory is lost.

Economic risks are either pure or speculative. With a **pure risk** there is no opportunity for financial gain but only loss. If there is a chance that an employee will be injured on a job, there is no additional income that the person will receive because he or she remains healthy. The injury will result in financial loss due to the inability to work. Businesses that face the risk of fire earn no more money if the fire does not occur but suffer financially if property is damaged by fire.

A **speculative risk** has the possibility of either financial loss or gain. Investments carry speculative risks. By investing money where the value of

Uncontrollable risks such as hurricanes cannot be influenced by human action, but the losses they cause can be reduced through planning and preparation.

the investment may rise or fall, the investor can make money or lose money.

Individuals and businesses are willing to take risks because of opportunities. An *opportunity* is the possibility for success. Financial success is one of the possible outcomes of a speculative risk. In addition to financial gain, success can be measured in nonfinancial ways. Recognition and personal satisfaction are viewed by most as successful outcomes that do not carry a financial reward. Both pure and speculative risks provide opportunities for nonfinancial benefits as well as for losses and disappointments.

TYPES OF RISK

Risks to individuals and businesses have many sources or causes. **Natural risks** arise from natural events or are a part of nature. Hurricanes, floods, earthquakes, and ice storms are all natural risks that can result in damage and loss. **Human risks** result from the actions of individuals, groups, or organizations. Injuries suffered by negligent driving, losses from customer or employee theft, or fires that start from unsafe storage of products are results of human risks.

Some risks can be controlled while others cannot. **Controllable risks** can be reduced or avoided by thoughtful actions. Most human risks are controllable. Defensive driving, employee safety programs, and the upkeep and maintenance of buildings can reduce accidents and injuries. **Uncontrollable risks** cannot be influenced by human action. Natural events such as floods and hurricanes cannot be stopped, although careful planning and preparation can reduce the losses that result from many natural risks.

teamwork

With your team brainstorm a list of risks team members and their families face on a regular basis. Classify them as natural, human, controllable, and uncontrollable. Discuss what can be done to reduce the losses that could result from each risk.

checkpoint ✓

What is the difference between a risk and an opportunity?

▪ Managing Risk

Since risk can be expected in almost all activities, efforts should be made to anticipate what risks are most likely to occur and then attempt to reduce the risk and minimize the loss that might be suffered. The process of systematically identifying potential risks and making plans to reduce the impact of the risk on individuals and companies is known as **risk management.** Because most businesses face a large number of risks, many of which can cause significant financial harm or even result in business failure, they employ specialists with the responsibility of planning and coordinating risk management programs. Risk management deals primarily with pure rather than speculative risk. Financial managers are responsible for decision-making about speculative risks or the investment decisions of a business.

RISK MANAGEMENT PROGRAMS

Risk management specialists work at all levels of the business to identify the potential risks the business might face, determine the financial impact each risk may have on the business, develop plans and programs to prevent controllable risks and reduce the financial impact of uncontrollable risks, and provide the necessary resources and training needed to manage the risks. Risk management programs today deal with the security of computer systems, property protection, employee health, and plans to respond to the negative effects of natural and man-made disasters.

The primary sources of risk faced by companies fall into three categories—property risks, personnel risks, and liability risks. Property risks are potential damage or loss to property owned, leased, and used by a business. If a business is responsible for the property of other businesses, that also is a source of property risk. For example, if a company supplies raw materials to a manufacturer, disruption of the supply or quality problems with the raw materials can result in financial loss for the manufacturer as well as the supplier.

Personnel risks include factors that can affect the health, life, or earnings of individuals associated with the business and the role employees play in the work of the organization. If key executives are unable to work due to illness or even die, the business is likely to be disrupted until a new executive is in place. Employee illness, injury, or death can result from poorly maintained equipment, unsafe working conditions, or lack of safety procedures. Large-scale layoffs or retirements can affect production and productivity. The costs of health care, life insurance, disability payments, and retirement are all costs to the business and can affect profitability.

Liability means an individual or business is responsible to others for negligence. Negligence can result from an action taken or from a failure to

Businesses are responsible for controlling their risk by providing safe equipment and working conditions.

act. If people are injured or their property damaged due to the negligence of a business, they can make a financial claim against the business. The injury or damage can result from the use of the business' property or products or the actions of company personnel.

DEALING WITH RISK

People responsible for managing risks go through a careful process of determining the most effective way to deal with each type of risk faced by a business. They choose from four different methods.

Avoid the Risk Some risks can actually be avoided. If there is a chance that one market, group of customers, or type of product presents a particular risk to the business, it may be decided to avoid that choice and select one that doesn't pose the same risk. If a foreign country has an unstable economy, a business can choose to avoid operations in that country. If a particular manufacturer of production equipment has a poor safety record, new equipment can be purchased from another supplier.

Transfer the Risk A common way to avoid a particular risk is to transfer the risk to another company. Rather than assuming the expense and difficulty associated with a credit system, a company may choose to provide credit through a credit specialist or contracted credit card system. Product transportation and storage or information management and security present several types of risks. Using other companies to provide those services transfers much, although not all, of the risk away from the business.

Insure the Risk If the likelihood and amount of a financial loss from a risk can be reasonably predicted, the risk can be insured. By purchasing insurance, the company pays a small percentage of the possible loss to an insurer for protection against the larger loss if the risk occurs. The greater the likelihood of the risk or the larger the possible loss, the more expensive the insurance will be. Taking steps to reduce the possibility or cost of the loss can reduce the insurance costs.

Assume the Risk A company may decide that it will assume the risk rather than choosing one of the other alternatives. If a risk is quite unlikely to occur or if the possible financial loss is relatively small, the company may decide to assume the possible loss because it will do little harm to the business if it occurs. If the cost to the business to insure or transfer the risk is high, it may be more feasible for the company to assume the risk itself. Some companies recognize that a certain amount of equipment will wear out, become damaged, or fail. Rather than insuring equipment for damage, the company may set aside funds each year that can be used to replace equipment. If the company decides to assume a risk, careful risk management planning must be completed to avoid serious financial loss.

In a recent year, 83 percent of the top global financial services firms admitted their computer systems had been compromised. Forty percent of the companies reported that the breaches resulted in significant financial losses to their organization totaling an estimated $456 million.

checkpoint ✓

What are the four methods a business can use to deal with risks that it faces?

UNDERSTAND CONCEPTS

Determine the best answer for each of the following questions.

1. A _____?_____ risk has the possibility of either a financial loss or a gain.
   - a. pure
   - b. speculative
   - c. natural
   - d. human

2. Which of the following is *not* one of the primary sources of risk faced by companies?
   - a. property
   - b. personnel
   - c. liability
   - d. financial

3. Using a financial services company to offer customer credit is an example of _____?_____ the risk.
   - a. avoiding
   - b. transferring
   - c. insuring
   - d. transferring

4. **True or False?** Controllable risks can be reduced or avoided by thoughtful actions.

5. **True or False?** Risk management deals with both pure and speculative risks.

MAKE ACADEMIC CONNECTIONS

6. **Government** Identify one federal department or agency that provides assistance or support to businesses in the areas of risk assessment and risk management. Write a short report that describes the type of risks that are the focus of the department or agency and what assistance is provided to businesses.

7. **Research** Go to the library and review the business section in two weeks of a large newspaper or several monthly issues of a business magazine such as *Business Week* or *Fortune*. From your readings, identify ten risks various businesses faced. Construct a table with four headings—Avoid, Transfer, Insure, Assume. Classify each of the companies and risks you identified in your readings under the appropriate heading to describe how the business dealt with the risk. Present your classifications to other students and justify your decisions.

8. **Law** Businesses are at risk of liability claims filed by customers who use the company's products. Review newspaper articles or search the Internet to locate information on a product liability lawsuit filed against a business. Based on the information you collect, write a report summarizing the case including the type of product, the alleged problem or defect with the product, the damage claimed by the person(s) filing the lawsuit, and the amount of damages requested. Summarize the result of the lawsuit and the reasons for the decision. Based on your study of the case, offer recommendations on what the business might have done to reduce or eliminate the risk that led to the lawsuit.

10.2 Principles of Insurance

Goals
- Identify and define important insurance terms and concepts.
- Understand insurance company organization and operations.
- Describe the key parts of an insurance policy.

Terms
- insurance
- policy
- insured
- insurer
- peril
- policyholder
- insurable interest
- premium
- reinsurance
- deductible
- coinsurance

▎Insurance Basics

The assets of a business are essential. If assets are damaged or destroyed, the business will be unable to continue the work that relies on those assets until they are replaced. Not only will the business need the money to repair or replace whatever has been damaged or destroyed, it will lose potential income from the affected operations until the assets have been restored. Business assets include property, vehicles, equipment, materials and supplies, products, and personnel. The assets vary in cost and importance to business operations. Minimal damage to assets causes little harm and can be repaired quickly at a low cost. Significant damage can totally destroy a key part of business operations and will be expensive and time consuming to replace.

Risk management procedures identify each business asset and determine the importance of each to the business, its cost, and the requirements and time to repair or replace. Risk management also assesses the financial impact of the loss of the asset on business operations. Based on that analysis, decisions will be made on how the business will respond to loss of the asset. For assets where there is a reasonable chance that damage or loss will occur and result in a financial risk the company would not be able to afford, the business should consider purchasing insurance.

INSURANCE TERMS

Insurance is a contract providing financial protection against a specified loss. Insurance is based on three principles.

1. Some risk facing an individual or organization is transferred to others.

2. Risks are pooled or shared among a large group of individuals or companies.

3. Risk for any one individual or business is reduced by controlling the uncertainty of the loss. Purchasing insurance trades a potentially large but uncertain loss for a smaller but certain payment.

Perils that can be insured include fire and vehicle accidents.

Insurance is implemented through a legal contract, or **policy.** The **insured** is the person or business covered by the insurance policy. The **insurer** is the company that assumes the risk and agrees to pay losses covered by the policy. Insurance policies are written to cover losses that result from perils. A **peril** is the cause of a loss. Examples of perils that can be insured are fire, vandalism, vehicle accidents, and personal injury. The **policyholder** is the individual or organization to whom the policy is issued. The policyholder is often but not always the insured. In order to purchase insurance the policyholder must have an insurable interest in the covered loss. An **insurable interest** means that the insured will suffer a financial loss if the insured event occurs. The policyholder is charged a **premium**, which is the amount paid to the insurer to keep the insurance policy in force.

WHAT CAN BE INSURED

The availability of insurance is based on the proposition that the insurer can accurately predict the amount of losses that will be suffered by all of those who are insured for a particular type of loss in a given period of time. It is impossible to predict whether any one business may have a fire that damages a building in a given year. But if thousands of businesses of a certain type and in a particular geographic area are grouped together, accurate estimations can be made of the amount of fire damage that will be suffered during a year.

The accuracy of predictions regarding the amount of losses that will occur among all of the businesses insured for a particular peril is very important. Without the ability to estimate the amount of losses they will need to pay, insurance companies may not accumulate enough money from premiums to pay for all of the losses suffered and make a profit. Companies use principles of statistics to estimate losses. The companies employ *actuaries,* highly trained mathematicians who gather and analyze data and determine risk factors in order to establish premium rates.

Actuaries apply the law of large numbers which means that when very large numbers of an event are considered, they will tend to form a normal distribution. You may be familiar with the view of a normal distribution which is often referred to as a bell curve, as shown in Figure 10-1. Using statistics and data about the amount of losses that have occurred in prior years, actuaries predict the total amount of losses that will result from a particular peril among all policyholders. For example, if an insurance company issues 10,000 fire insurance policies to businesses, their calculations may estimate that 800 businesses will have losses from fires in the next year and the average loss will be valued at $6,800.

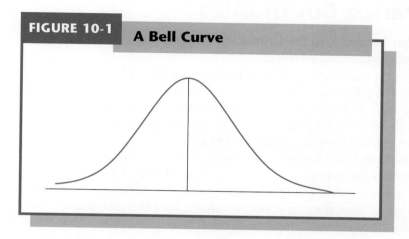

FIGURE 10-1 **A Bell Curve**

In order for a risk to be insurable, the following conditions need to exist.

■ A large number of individuals or businesses must be facing the same type of risk and be willing to purchase insurance. In order to be able to predict the amount of losses and spread the risk across a large number of individuals or groups, insurance companies have to sell a large number of policies.

■ The losses from the perils that are insured must be accidental and uncertain. People cannot take advantage of insurance companies by purchasing insurance and then causing a loss in order to collect money. Insurance fraud is a major problem for insurance companies. It is estimated that fraudulent claims add as much as 25 percent to insurance rates.

■ The actual loss must be identifiable. In order to be paid for a loss by the insurance company, the insured must be able to document that the loss occurred as a result of the peril for which the insurance was purchased. The dollar value of the loss must also be identifiable.

■ The probability of loss cannot be too high and the peril cannot be of a type that may affect a large percentage of insured at the same time. If most businesses suffer losses regularly or at the same time, too much money will be required to pay for the losses. For example, insurance companies become concerned if they sell a large number of the same type of insurance policies in an area that is subject to natural disasters such as hurricanes, earthquakes, or floods. The result could be that almost all policyholders will have claims at the same time if a natural disaster hits that area. To protect themselves against those large losses, insurance companies use a process known as reinsurance. With **reinsurance**, an insurance company sells some of its risk to other insurance companies. The process spreads the risk across more companies and more policyholders.

checkpoint ✓

List the conditions that must exist in order for a risk to be insurable.

■Insurance Companies

In order to offer insurance in the United States, companies must meet requirements and regulations established by each state and by the federal government. Every state has a department of insurance and an insurance commissioner. That department licenses any business that wants to sell insurance in the state and identifies the types of insurance the company is approved to sell. In order to obtain a license, the company must provide information that it has adequate capital for the amount and type of insurance it will sell. Most states also require companies to deposit a minimum amount of securities in order to make sure policyholders' claims can be paid. Finally, states regulate the rates that insurance companies can charge for various types of insurance. In some instances, the rates charged are reviewed to make sure they are adequate to cover potential losses and not exorbitant or discriminatory. In other cases, states actually set the rates that can be charged for types of insurance.

OWNERSHIP STRUCTURES

Insurance companies are generally organized in two types of ownership

In 2004, $1,097,836 million in premiums were paid for insurance in the United States. 45 percent of the premiums were for life insurance while 55 percent were paid for all types of non-life insurance.

© GETTY IMAGES/PHOTODISC

Insurance agents work with customers to determine the amount and type of insurance they need.

structures. *Stock companies* are private corporations that sell insurance as a profit-making venture. The stock is publicly traded, so it is owned by its stockholders and operated by the board of directors and corporate management.

The second form of ownership is a mutual company. A *mutual company* is a nonprofit corporation owned by its policyholders. Since the mutual company is a nonprofit business, any income in excess of expenses is returned to the policyholders in the form of dividends or lower premiums.

Stock companies are the major providers of life and health insurance and of property insurance to businesses. Mutual insurance companies lead in sales of property and vehicle insurance for individual consumers.

INSURANCE OPERATIONS

Insurance companies complete several different activities as a part of their insurance operations. The major activities are rate making, selling, underwriting, investing, and claims processing.

Rate Making The insurance process begins when an insurance company determines the types of insurance it will sell, the types of customers it plans to serve, and the rates it will charge. Rate making establishes the amount per unit of value that will be charged for insurance based on the type of insurance and factors that can affect the frequency and amount of losses. Rates are established by actuaries who carefully review large amounts of data on past loss experiences, specific factors that have increased or diminished losses, and the financial position of the company. Rates must also be set within the guidelines and regulations of the state in which the insurance is sold.

Selling The company must sell an adequate number of insurance policies in order to collect sufficient premiums to pay claims, finance operations, and make a profit. Insurance is typically sold by agents. An *insurance agent* is a person licensed by the state and given authority by the insurer to sell its insurance. An *exclusive agent* is employed by the insurance company and sells only that company's policies. An *independent agent* is self-employed or works for an insurance sales company and represents several insurance companies. Agents work with customers to determine the amount and type of insurance to be purchased. They then write the application and submit it to the insurance company for underwriting. Some simple insurance policies are sold through direct mail or the Internet. In those instances, a customer completes an insurance application and submits it directly to the insurance company for approval often without the need for an agent.

Underwriting Underwriting is the most important part of the insurance process from the viewpoint of the insurer. Each insurance application is carefully reviewed to make sure all information needed to make a decision is available and accurate. In some cases, information is verified through credit agencies, private and public records, or independent investigations. The purpose of underwriting is to determine if the application fits the criteria that make the insurance a reasonable risk. Underwriters will reject applicants if there is evidence that the applicant is likely to have a much higher than average level of loss based on the information reviewed.

Investing Insurance companies receive income from policyholders in the form of premiums paid. Policies are written for a specific period of time, often a year, and the premium is paid in advance. The amount of money collected from premiums alone is normally not enough to ensure payment of all losses. Insurance companies frequently pay more in claims than they receive in premiums for a particular time period. Funds that are received for premiums as well as other types of income are carefully invested in a variety of securities. The regulation of insurance companies restricts how some of the funds can be invested. The companies also need to have adequate liquid assets to pay claims as they occur. Insurance companies have a large amount of assets to invest. Wise decisions by expert investment specialists can contribute to profitability and allow the company to remain competitive in its insurance rates.

Claims Processing When a policyholder suffers a covered loss, the insurance company follows an established process to settle the claim. Claims that involve damage to property usually are handled by an adjuster. An *adjuster* works for the insurance company and determines the extent of a loss and the liability of the insurer. An adjuster can be either an employee of the insurance company or an independent adjuster who works for a fee. Claims for health and life insurance usually are handled by specialists in the claims department who review information and make decisions about payments. Claims processing must be done carefully to make sure that losses are paid according to the conditions of the insurance policy. Some insurance companies develop a reputation of being reluctant to approve settlements. Customers expect insurance companies to be both prompt and fair in processing claims. A negative reputation will spread and will affect the amount of business the company will do in the future. Clear information to customers when an insurance policy is purchased and professional customer service at the time a claim is made will help to increase customer satisfaction.

Customers who have suffered losses expect insurance companies to be prompt and fair in processing claims.

checkpoint ✔

What is the difference between rate making and underwriting?

The Insurance Policy

An insurance policy is a legal contract between the insurer and the insured. As such it must be carefully prepared to make sure it is a legally enforceable agreement and that the coverage provided by the policy is clear. A standard insurance policy contains declarations, the insuring agreement, conditions, and exclusions. There are a number of other provisions of insurance policies that define the coverage offered.

COMMON PARTS OF A POLICY

The *declarations* contain identifying information about the insured and the insured property, the insurance company, agent, type of insurance, the dates and times the insurance is in effect, and the amount of the premium. If others hold an interest in the policy or property, they will be identified as well. A policy number is assigned to each insurance policy.

The *insuring agreement* forms the basis of the insurance contract. It identifies the individuals, activities, or property that are insured, the perils that will be covered, and the actions that must be taken by the insured and the insurer to maintain the insurance and to compensate the insured in the event of a loss.

Conditions identify the stipulations or requirements that must be met in order for the insurance to remain in effect and losses to be paid. Some conditions are standard protections for the insurance company such as a statement that any fraud or misrepresentation by the insured will result in an invalid contract. Other standard conditions are information on how a policy can be cancelled by either party, whether rights in the contract can be assigned to others, and the conditions that must be met to maintain property, report losses, and provide proof of loss.

Exclusions provide specific limitations on the coverage provided. They identify perils that are not covered, limitations on the use of property or activities of the insured, or types of property or losses that will not be covered. For example a life insurance policy may exclude the insured from certain particularly dangerous activities. A property insurance policy may exclude losses caused by flooding from a storm but will cover water damage resulting from a burst water pipe in a building.

Special provisions are added to many insurance policies to control costs. The policy may identify limits on the amount the insurance company will pay to the insured. The limits may be a maximum that will be paid for one loss or a total amount for all losses in a specific time period.

Many property and health insurance policies include a deductible. A **deductible** is an identified amount of a loss that must be paid by the insured before the insurer pays. For example, an automobile policy may have a $500 deductible. If an insured vehicle has $450 of damage, the insured must pay the full amount. If the damage is $1,500, the insured is responsible for the first $500 (the deductible) and the insurance company will pay the remaining $1,000.

With **coinsurance**, the insured and insurer share the risk by paying a defined amount of the costs. Coinsurance is applied in different ways depending on the type of insurance. In health insurance, the insured may pay a specific dollar amount for a covered procedure such as $10 for a visit to a doctor or $15 for a prescription. The insurer than pays the remaining

teamwork

Discuss with team members how you would make the decision whether to accept a higher deductible to an insurance policy in return for a lower annual premium. How does the decision provide an example of risk management?

amount of the covered costs. The coinsurance may be stated as a percentage of the cost. The insured may be required to pay 20 percent and the insurer 80 percent. Depending on the terms of the policy, the coinsurance requirement may apply to each claim or it may have a maximum amount that the insured is required to pay during the term of the insurance. With property insurance, a coinsurance provision requires the insured to pay a percentage of the loss only if the property is underinsured in relation to its actual value. This practice discourages purchasing less insurance than is needed to cover the full value of the property if loss occurs.

checkpoint ✓

Describe the four common parts of an insurance policy.

? ¿ a question of ethics

Insurance Fraud

The Coalition Against Insurance Fraud reports that insurance fraud in the U.S. is an $80 billion-a-year business. They divide fraud into two categories—hard fraud and soft fraud. Hard fraud occurs when crooks set out to deliberately fake an accident, injury, theft, or other loss to collect money illegally from insurance companies. Soft fraud occurs when normally honest people fudge the truth to an insurance company to reduce a premium, cover a deductible, or get a larger settlement. They justify their actions by saying that everyone does it, insurance costs too much, or the insurance companies won't notice a small amount. Examples of soft fraud include

- A car owner includes previous damage to the car after an accident so insurance will cover that repair
- A body shop owner inflates the cost of repair so the customer doesn't have to pay the insurance deductible
- Following a burglary, the homeowner adds items to the list of stolen property that really aren't missing to obtain a larger settlement
- A doctor submits to an insurer a more serious diagnosis of a patient than actually exists in order to receive a larger reimbursement
- A person who slips and falls at a store exaggerates the injury in order to obtain money from the store's insurance company

In a study by Accenture, almost 25 percent of respondents say it is okay to defraud insurance companies. About one in 10 people support submitting claims for items that aren't lost or damaged or for personal injuries that didn't occur. Almost the same number state they would engage in insurance fraud if they could get away with it.

Think Critically

1. From an ethical or moral viewpoint, what if any difference exists between hard fraud and soft fraud? Justify your answer.
2. While the vast majority of Americans do not condone insurance fraud, why do you think many persons believe fraud is acceptable and would be willing to commit insurance fraud?

10.2 Lesson Assessment

UNDERSTAND CONCEPTS

Determine the best answer for each of the following questions.

1. A(n) _____?_____ means that the insured will suffer a financial loss if the insured event occurs.
   a. peril
   b. insurable interest
   c. risk
   d. none of the above

2. The business activity in which each insurance application is carefully reviewed to make sure all information needed to make a decision is available and accurate is known as
   a. rate making
   b. claims processing
   c. investing
   d. underwriting

3. With _____?_____ the insured and insurer share the risk by paying a defined amount of the costs.
   a. dividends
   b. deductibles
   c. coinsurance
   d. premiums

4. **True or False?** Insurance transfers some risk faced by an individual or organization to others.

5. **True or False?** An insurance salesperson can actually represent several insurance companies rather than just one.

MAKE ACADEMIC CONNECTIONS

6. **Government** Use the Internet to locate information on the department of insurance for your state. Describe five services the department provides to consumers and businesses. Identify three ways the department regulates insurance companies in your state.

7. **Math** The table identifies the deductible included in an insurance policy and the loss suffered by the insured. Calculate the amount of the loss that must be paid by the insured and the insurer in each case.

	Amount of Deductible	Amount of Loss
a.	$250	$825
b.	$500	$450
c.	$1,000	$2,420

8. **Critical Thinking** Due to the number of hurricanes that have hit Florida in recent years, many insurance companies have decided not to renew policies for property owners who have filed large claims and to raise rates by as much as 300 percent for renewals of those who didn't file claims. Property owners believe this is unfair since hurricanes are natural disasters. Write a letter to the Insurance Commissioner of Florida to support the decisions of the insurance companies or to argue that the insurance companies should be prevented from taking those actions.

Goals
- Describe common types of business property insurance.
- Identify the main provisions of commercial vehicle insurance.

Terms
- coverages
- self-insurance

■ Insuring Property Risks

Property is a major asset of most businesses. Business operations depend on a variety of types of property that the business owns or rents and even the property of others that is used to support business operations. Because property risks are common to many businesses, the risks can be identified, and damage or loss of property can have a negative financial impact on the business, insurance is available to provide protection against those risks. The common types of property insurance are comprehensive property, business owners, title, transportation, credit, and crime. There are also some more specialized and newer types of property insurance coverage. In addition, within each type a variety of **coverages** (the monetary limits and risks covered by an insurance policy) are available.

Each business will not need and likely cannot afford to purchase each type of property insurance. Planning comprehensive affordable insurance coverage and determining how to minimize risk is an essential part of risk management. Purchasing insurance alone is not adequate to reduce risk and will not be the most cost effective strategy for businesses.

COMPREHENSIVE PROPERTY INSURANCE

Because businesses face so many types of property risks, it would be inefficient to obtain a separate insurance policy for each type of risk. The insurance industry created a comprehensive business property insurance package called the *Commercial Package Policy (CPP)*. Each business can select the appropriate coverage needed but the total set of coverages will be written within one insurance contract with one premium amount.

CPP Coverage Figure 10-2 on the next page lists the full set of perils that can be insured in a Commercial Package Policy. There are of course limitations and exclusions for insurability of each of the perils.

In general, CPP provides protection for all buildings owned by the business and any fixtures and equipment that are considered to be a permanent part of the business. Coverage can be carried on rented buildings to the extent that the building's owner does not provide insurance. The personal property of the business can be insured under the policy as well as the personal property of others that is used in or controlled by the business.

FIGURE 10-2

Commercial Package Policy

Types of Perils Insurable Within a Commercial Package Policy

fire	lightning
explosion	windstorms
hurricanes	tornadoes
hail	smoke
damage by aircraft	damage by vehicle
riot or civil unrest	looting and vandalism
piped water or steam	sprinkler damage
sinkholes	volcanoes
falling objects	snow, ice, and sleet

Coverage can be obtained to restore or replace important business records and papers located within the business' buildings or temporarily located off-premises. It is even possible to insure outdoor equipment used by the business and business landscaping. Many of the coverages have limitations on the maximum amount that can be insured and the perils that are covered, as well as important conditions and exclusions. Some coverages are very expensive and are chosen only because of special circumstances or the type of critical business operations that must be maintained.

Special Coverages Several important coverages are available to businesses that provide assistance if there is damage or failure of important equipment or machinery. *Business income insurance* compensates the business for some of the income that is lost if the business cannot operate for a period of time due to a covered peril. *Extra expenses* that the business incurs to maintain or reestablish operations can also be covered. For example, if a business has to rent or purchase a large generator due to a power failure, that cost may be covered. *Consequential damage coverage* pays for damages to the business that occur after another incident but related to it. In the situation above where the business suffers a power failure, if inventory was damaged as a result of that problem (a supermarket could not maintain the appropriate temperature in coolers and freezers), consequential damage coverage could pay for some losses.

BUSINESS OWNERS POLICY

Small businesses may not see the CPP as appropriate or affordable for insuring their operations. A special property insurance policy has been developed for the unique circumstances of small businesses. It is known as the *business owners policy*. The intent of the business owners policy is the same as the CPP in that it offers comprehensive coverage in one policy. It also allows each business to tailor the policy to the specific characteristics and conditions of the business. Common coverages under the business owners policy are business and personal property, crime (burglary, robbery, employee or customer theft, forgery, employee dishonesty), and lost income. Most policies for small businesses also include business liability coverage.

teamwork

Before studying the information on property risks, brainstorm with team members all of the ways business property can be damaged or destroyed. Then check your list against the perils discussed in the lesson. Discuss how each of the perils could affect business operations.

Business owners policies are usually written with a requirement that insurance must be carried for at least 80 percent of the current value of the property insured in order to receive full payment for losses. If coverage is lower than that requirement, payments for losses will be adjusted accordingly. This provision is similar to coinsurance.

TITLE INSURANCE

Title insurance protects a real estate purchaser against losses due to a defect in the *title,* or the owner's legal interest in the property. Land and buildings have a long life and are often passed from owner to owner. While legal contracts and public records document the transactions, there may be errors in those records that create ownership problems requiring the new owner to pay expenses to correct the problems. A previous owner may not have had full title, there may have been fraud involved in a sale or transfer of property, or a lien may have been placed on the property. A *lien* is a claim against the property as security for a debt owed by the owner. When real estate is purchased, the public records are carefully reviewed and an attorney prepares a report on the validity of the title. If that review fails to uncover an existing problem, the new owner may suffer financial damages.

Title insurance offers protection in two ways. The insurer helps with the defense of the insured in legal proceedings related to the legitimate title to the property. Title insurance also covers losses incurred due to the purchaser relying on the accuracy of the title. Most title insurance policies contain exclusions or possible defects in a real estate title that are not covered. Title insurance is purchased at the time the real estate contract is completed and remains in effect until the property is sold or the title transferred.

TRANSPORTATION INSURANCE

Transportation insurance is one of the oldest forms of business insurance. Whenever goods and materials are moved from one place to another, there is a risk of delay, damage, or theft. Any of those problems can result in financial loss to the businesses that are sending and receiving the goods as well as the company responsible for transportation. Transportation insurance protects against damage, theft, or complete loss of goods while they are being shipped.

Transportation companies are held responsible for losses to shipments while the goods are under their control. As long as they are not negligent in handling, packaging, and transporting the goods, it may be difficult to get a full settlement for losses suffered. Because so many products are now shipped internationally, the transportation laws of several countries may be involved in disputes over losses. To provide protection in those events, it is wise for businesses to purchase transportation insurance. Transportation insurance can be purchased by the transportation company, the buyer, the seller, or others who have a financial interest in the shipment or the assets used as a part of the distribution process.

Transportation insurance is divided into two main categories. *Marine insurance* covers shipment on oceans and inland waterways including rivers and lakes. Insurance is purchased by transportation companies to cover the actual vessel, the cargo, the income earned for shipping, and expenses arising from liability issues. *Inland marine insurance* covers all transportation over land via trains, trucks, and other vehicles as well as storage of products during transit. It also can be used to insure structures that are essential to transportation such as bridges, tunnels, and even communications towers and antennas. Policies can be purchased that cover a specific shipment or all designated types of shipments for a given period of time.

CREDIT INSURANCE

Businesses that make extensive use of credit may consider the use of credit insurance. *Credit insurance* pays off the balance of outstanding loans in the event of death or disability of a debtor. Businesses may require credit applicants to purchase insurance on the amount of a loan, particularly for real estate loans and mortgages when the amount borrowed is close to the actual value of the real estate. This type of insurance is known as private mortgage insurance (PMI). Many retailers that sell merchandise using installment credit offer credit insurance to their customers. If credit insurance is included in the sales contract, for example when a car is purchased, the terms and cost of the insurance to the customer must be fully disclosed. Credit card companies also offer credit insurance policies to cardholders that pay off account balances under certain conditions. *Trade credit insurance* pays for losses suffered when payment is not made by businesses that purchased on credit. In order to encourage international trade, the U.S. government offers export credit insurance to businesses selling goods overseas and making foreign investments.

The federal government insures some types of loans made by private investors through special programs designed for students, small businesses, and veterans, among others. Cities and other government units that issue bonds may purchase insurance against the value of bonds they are issuing that will pay the bondholders in the event of default. The insurance improves the security of the bonds and may result in a higher bond rating and lower cost to the issuer.

CRIME INSURANCE

Crime affects individuals and businesses. All bear the burden of crime, including very high costs. Estimates of the annual cost of crime in the U.S. range from $450–$675 billion dollars. Specific costs to businesses include private security, lost wages and personnel costs, stolen and damaged property including any lost through fraud and embezzlement, and higher taxes resulting from increased costs for the criminal justice system.

Insurance cannot cover all of the costs of crime. Many of the risks related to crime must be controlled and reduced through careful risk management. However, several types of crime insurance are available to businesses. *Burglary, robbery, and theft insurance* covers crimes committed by people that are not owners or employees of the business. Burglary refers to unlawful taking of property from inside the business. Robbery is illegally taking property from another person through force or violence. Theft is a broader term that describes all types of stealing. It can include forgery of checks, negotiable instruments, and other valuable documents.

NETBookmark

The Insurance Information Institute provides information about insurance for businesses and individuals. Access thomsonedu.com/school/busfinance and click on the link for Chapter 10. Find out some of the issues involved in insuring a small business.

www.thomsonedu.com/school/busfinance

Bonds are similar to insurance in that they provide protection against a risk associated with the work provided by one business to another. The company performing the work provides a bond guaranteeing reimbursement of losses suffered by the customer from the failure to perform as agreed. A *fidelity bond* provides protection for losses resulting from dishonest employees. A *surety bond* protects against losses resulting from the failure to complete any part of a contract according to the specified conditions. It is often used in construction to make sure a building is completed on schedule or meets specified construction standards.

checkpoint ✓

Identify six types of property insurance and the purpose of each.

■ Vehicle Insurance

Most businesses own or lease at least one and often many vehicles. Some businesses such as transportation businesses, retailers, manufacturers that ship their own products, and producers such as farmers and timber companies have fleets of trucks and specialized vehicles. Many of those vehicles are expensive, have high maintenance and repair costs, and are crucial to the operation and profitability of the company. There are a number of risks associated with the ownership and operation of vehicles.

Some large companies assume some or all of the cost of risks associated with their vehicles through self-insurance. **Self-insurance** is the advance budgeting of funds to meet the estimated cost of losses. A self-insurance program is risky because losses do not occur on a regular schedule. The amount of losses can be very high in one time period and lower in another.

Businesses often depend on the use of specialized vehicles that must be insured for damage and liability.

With self-insurance, the company must pay all costs whether there are adequate funds reserved or not. One method of balancing that risk is to use self-insurance for more predictable types of losses and purchase insurance for losses that are likely to fluctuate or that may have very high costs.

The components of an automobile insurance policy are similar for individuals and businesses. Policies written to cover business automobiles and other vehicles are called *commercial vehicle insurance* or *business auto coverage*. The common components of a vehicle insurance policy are described in Figure 10-3.

FIGURE 10-3

Vehicle Insurance Policy Coverages

Coverage	Description
collision	Pays for repairs to the insured's vehicle required as a result of a collision with another vehicle no matter who was at fault.
comprehensive	Pays for repairs to the insured's vehicle required as a result of damages resulting from causes other than collision, including fire, hail, vandalism, and theft.
bodily injury liability	Pays the insured's legal defense costs and claims against the business and authorized vehicle operators if the vehicle injures or kills someone.
property damage liability	Pays the insured's legal defense costs and claims if the vehicle damages another's property. Does not cover damages to the business' property or vehicle.
medical payments (personal injury protection)	Pays medical expenses resulting from an accident for the vehicle operator and other occupants. May pay for covered personnel injured while riding in vehicles not owned by the business.
uninsured or underinsured motorist	Pays for costs related to injuries or property damage to authorized drivers and occupants in the business' vehicle caused by an uninsured, underinsured, or hit-and-run driver.

Some aspects of commercial vehicle insurance differ from individual auto insurance policies. Liability costs are a particularly important issue for businesses, especially those that operate large vehicles transporting expensive cargos, vehicles that carry people such as taxis and busses, or vehicles carrying hazardous materials. Such companies will usually have separate liability insurance polices or comprehensive liability coverage as a part of a Commercial Package Policy. The amount of liability coverage may be as high as $5 million or more.

A unique insurance issue is posed by transportation companies that ship goods and materials via semi-trailer. Often the trailer of one company is exchanged with another company's trailer to be transported to a different destination. Normally insurance only extends to the vehicles and cargo identified in the company's insurance policy. A trailer interchange agreement resolves that problem. The trailer interchange agreement is a written arrangement whereby trucking firms exchange the use of their trailers. Under the agreement the company's insurance provides coverage for physical damage to non-owned equipment while in the control of the business.

checkpoint ✓

What is the difference between collision, comprehensive, and property damage liability coverage in a vehicle insurance policy?

technology topics

Protect My Car

Vehicle theft is one of the major crimes affecting both businesses and individuals. It also is a major cost to insurance companies. The financial impact in terms of insurance premiums, out-of-pocket repair costs, and new car costs has now passed $7.5 billion. The National Insurance Crime Bureau recommends a layered approach to reducing vehicle theft that combines basic security procedures with new technology. Here are the layers they recommend.

Layer 1 Common Sense Always remove your keys, close your doors, lock your vehicle, and park in a well-lit public area.

Layer 2 Warning Device Use a visible or audible device that warns thieves the vehicle is protected. It may be an alarm, lockable device on the steering wheel, identification markers, or window etchings.

Layer 3 Immobilizing Device Prevent thieves from hotwiring your car with a smart key, kill switch, or fuel disabler.

Layer 4 Tracking Device A tracking device emits a signal when a vehicle is stolen so it can be located and recovered quickly by police. Most vehicles with the devices are recovered while those without are not.

Experts believe that this combination of theft prevention procedures and technology would put a major dent in the number of vehicles stolen and the cost of vehicle theft.

Think Critically

1. If your auto insurance policy provides protection against vehicle theft, why should you be concerned about reducing the amount of theft that occurs nationwide?
2. Do you believe consumers and businesses should encourage auto manufacturers to install all of the technology recommended by the National Insurance Crime Bureau in every car manufactured so most vehicle theft could be prevented? What if it added $300–$500 to the cost of each vehicle?

10.3 Lesson Assessment

UNDERSTAND CONCEPTS

Determine the best answer for each of the following questions.

1. **True or False?** Businesses can obtain comprehensive insurance coverage on buildings they own but not for those they rent.

2. A special property insurance policy developed for the unique circumstances of small businesses is
   a. title insurance
   b. commercial package policy
   c. business owners policy
   d. business income insurance

3. ____?____ insurance pays off the balance of outstanding loans in the event of death or disability of a debtor.

4. The vehicle insurance coverage that pays for repairs to the insured's vehicle resulting from damages not due to collision is
   a. property damage liability
   b. medical payments
   c. uninsured motorist
   d. comprehensive

5. ____?____ is the advance budgeting of funds to meet the estimated cost of losses.

MAKE ACADEMIC CONNECTIONS

6. **History** Natural disasters result in high losses to property and life around the world. They also contribute to higher costs of insurance when companies provide coverage in the affected areas. Use the Internet to identify up to ten major natural disasters that have occurred throughout the world. On a map of the world, locate and mark each natural disaster. Identify the type of disaster and its estimated cost.

7. **Math** The Bowman Co. is considering self-insuring its vehicles rather than purchasing an insurance policy. It examined three years of losses and listed the costs of vehicle repairs for the three years.
   a. What is the minimum and maximum annual cost of repairs?
   b. What is the average annual cost of repairs for the three years?
   c. If the company wants a one-year balance in the self-insurance account that is 10 percent higher than the highest annual cost of repairs, how much should it save each month?

Year 1	$3,584	$1,215	$794	$5,820
Year 2	$2,505	$13,582	$1,035	
Year 3	$450	$4,267	$6,024	$1,995

8. **Writing** Crime is a major expense to many businesses. The costs result from paying for losses as well as prevention and security. You are working with a small retailer in your community to help them learn more about reducing the impact of crime. Conduct research and prepare a two-page report to the owner making recommendations on new types of security technology that are available and other measures they can take to reduce various types of crime. Make sure to cite the sources of information you use to prepare your report.

10.4 Personnel and Liability Insurance

Goals
- Describe important personnel risks and how they are insured.
- Identify the types of insurance for business liability risks.

Terms
- beneficiary
- criminal liability
- civil liability

■ Providing Personnel Protection

The people who work for a business are certainly a very important asset. They contribute their time and skills to complete the work of the business. Well-trained and motivated employees are an important resource for reducing the risks facing a business by working safely, conserving materials, maintaining equipment, and identifying and reducing hazards and risky procedures. Businesses make a major investment in employees. In addition to salaries and wages, training costs for each employee can be quite high. While the amount spent on training per employee averages just $1,500 per year, the costs can reach $5,000–$10,000 for specialized skills and management personnel. In addition, the average cost of employee benefits is more than 30 percent of the wages and salaries paid. Data from the U.S. Department of Labor's most recent report of employee compensation for private employers in the U.S. is shown in Figure 10-4 on the next page.

REQUIRED INSURANCE BENEFITS

The Old Age, Survivors', and Disability Insurance (OASDI) program was enacted by the federal government in 1935. Better known as *Social Security,* its purpose was to provide a minimum income benefit for retirees when they reached age 65, as well as financial support for workers who became disabled and for the surviving spouse and children in the event of the death of a worker. The program was expanded in 1965 with the addition of Medicare and Medicaid, which provide health insurance, health care, and prescription drug benefits for retired persons, low-income families, and people with certain disabilities. Social Security programs are funded by a combination of employer and employee contributions. In 2006, the contribution rate for employers and employees was 6.20 percent of earnings up to a maximum wage of $94,200. The employer and employee contribution rate for Medicare/Medicaid was 1.45 percent of all earnings. Self-employed persons are responsible for the entire contribution or a total of 15.3 percent of earnings.

FIGURE 10-4

Average Costs of Wages and Benefits for Each Employee

	Goods-Producing Businesses		Service-Providing Businesses	
Total Compensation	$29.36	100.00%	$24.05	100.00%
Wages and Salaries	$19.44	66.20%	$17.31	72.00%
Total Benefits	$9.92	33.80%	$6.74	28.00%
Overtime and Bonuses	$1.16	4.00%	$0.63	2.60%
Life Insurance	$0.06	0.20%	$0.04	0.20%
Health Insurance	$2.47	8.40%	$1.54	6.40%
Disability Insurance	$0.12	0.40%	$0.08	0.40%
Retirement	$1.48	5.00%	$0.77	3.20%
Social Security	$1.34	4.60%	$1.16	4.80%
Medicare	$0.32	1.10%	$0.29	1.20%
Unemployment Insurance	$0.25	0.80%	$0.18	0.70%
Workers' Compensation	$0.87	3.00%	$0.38	1.60%

Unemployment Insurance Two other required benefit programs are unemployment insurance and workers' compensation insurance. *Unemployment insurance* makes payments to workers during periods of unemployment that are beyond the workers' control. Unemployment insurance programs are administered by each state. Benefits are paid out of funds accumulated from payroll contributed by each employer. Each state establishes its own rules for the program under federal guidelines. Generally, unemployment insurance can be received until the person obtains new employment or for up to 26 weeks. Insurance payments are based on the average amount of the employee's earnings during the previous year.

In most states, the rate each employer pays for contributions to the unemployment fund is based on the company's unemployment history. Employers who have had a higher rate of employee layoffs will pay a higher rate than those with very low layoff rates. Employer contribution rates are based on a percentage of each employee's wages. Many states cap the maximum amount of wages on which unemployment fund contributions must be made. Example rates for selected states are shown below.

	Minimum Rate	Maximum Rate
Arkansas	0.8%	6.7%
Maryland	0.6%	9.0%
Missouri	1.3%	4.12%
California	1.6%	6.2%

Workers' Compensation Insurance Medical care, rehabilitation, and lost wages for injured workers as well as death benefits for the dependents of persons killed in work-related accidents are provided by *workers' compensation insurance*. Accidents and illness in business is a serious and expensive problem. A larger volume of insurance is sold for workers' compensation than any other type. The Bureau of Labor Statistics identifies the occupations that have the greatest number of injuries and illnesses. The most recent data is reported in Figure 10-5. Vehicle accidents are the largest cause of occupational deaths.

teamwork

Review and discuss the list of occupations in Figure 10-5. Why do you believe those at the top of the list are most dangerous? Are you surprised by any of the occupations that are in the top ten?

FIGURE 10-5

Top Ten Occupations with the Largest Number of Injuries and Illnesses

Occupation	Number of injuries and illnesses (000)	Percent of total injuries and illnesses
Nonconstruction laborers	89.3	7.1%
Heavy truck drivers	63.6	5.1
Nursing aides, orderlies	51.9	4.1
Construction laborers	37.9	3.0
Light truck drivers	37.2	3.0
Janitors and cleaners	33.6	2.7
Retail salespersons	33.2	2.6
Carpenters	30.5	2.4
Stock clerks, order fillers	24.3	1.9
Maintenance and repair	21.1	1.7
Total, top 10 occupations	422.6	33.6
Total, all occupations	1,259.3	100.0%

Workers' compensation insurance was established as a part of the federal Occupational Safety and Health Act (OSHA) in 1970. Authority to administer the programs was given to each state. In most states, employers are given three choices of how to provide coverage for their employees.

1. Purchase insurance from a private insurance company

2. Purchase insurance from a state or federal insurance fund established under the law

3. Self-insure through contributions to their own fund

EMPLOYEE HEALTH INSURANCE

The percentage of businesses offering health insurance to their workers has declined steadily recently. As the costs of health care increase much faster than the rate of inflation or the cost of business, the percentage of businesses offering the benefit dropped from almost 70 percent to 60 percent in just five years. Large businesses continue to offer health insurance, with nearly 98 percent reporting that they provide coverage. To respond to rising costs, many of those plans have increased the amount that must be paid by employees, reduced coverage, and increased the copayments and deductibles employees pay for medical services.

Health insurance provides payment for expenses related to preventive health care and the treatment of illness and disease. There are two common types of health insurance plans—fee-for-service and managed care. *Fee-for-service insurance* makes payments to doctors and hospitals for each service rendered to the patient. Employees have more freedom in choosing their health care service providers under this plan. *Managed care insurance* is designed to reduce costs by restricting employee choice of doctors and hospitals, negotiating fees for services, and requiring pre-authorization for non-emergency services.

Managed Care Plans Two types of managed care plans are PPO (preferred provider organizations) and HMO (health maintenance organizations). A PPO has arrangements with a network of doctors, hospitals, and other providers who have agreed to accept lower fees from the insurer for their services. An employee can select services within the network and will be charged a small copayment for services. If the employee goes outside the network, there will be higher copayments as well as the requirement to pay any costs higher than those negotiated in the network.

An HMO provides a full range of health services but they must be obtained from the providers that are affiliated with the HMO. Usually employees are assigned or select a primary care physician who makes decisions about the services patients receive and refers them to specialists in the HMO when needed.

Some employers offer other types of insurance as a part of health benefits. Common insurance plans include

- **Catastrophic Coverage** pays for costs of long-term or particularly expensive health care beyond the coverage of typical health plans
- **Medicare Supplement** private insurance that pays for gaps in Medicare coverage
- **Long Term Care** pays costs of nursing care in-home or at special facilities for those unable to care for themselves due to an extended illness or disability
- **Disability Insurance** provides supplementary income for those with short- and long-term disabilities that prevent them from working
- **Dental And Vision Care** contributes to the cost of dental and vision treatment

If these supplementary insurance plans are offered, most employers require employees to pay much of the costs. By negotiating group rates with insurers, the cost of the employer-sponsored plans are usually lower than if the employee obtained an individual plan.

LIFE INSURANCE

Life insurance provides for payment of a sum of money to a beneficiary upon the death of the insured. A **beneficiary** is a person or organization designated to receive the proceeds of the insurance policy. Many companies provide a specified amount of life insurance to full-time or permanent employees. Others offer the opportunity for employees to purchase life insurance but the employee must pay all or most of the cost of the policy. Insuring the lives of key executives of a business is a common practice and

Of the total amount of money paid in liability claims in the U.S., 22 percent was paid for direct economic losses suffered, 25 percent for non-economic losses (pain and suffering), 17 percent for attorney fees of the plaintiff, 16 percent for defendants' legal expenses, and 25 percent for court costs and administrative fees.

the company is named as the beneficiary. The insurance proceeds provide money to help with management transition upon the death of the executive.

Employers offer group life insurance plans that make individual coverage less expensive. Group plans also provide access to insurance for people who might not be able to qualify due to existing health conditions. Generally employees must elect to enroll in group insurance plans soon after beginning employment. If they choose not to participate, they cannot later decide to enroll without meeting higher eligibility requirements.

Most life insurance provided by employers is term insurance. *Term insurance* covers the insured for a specific period of years and does not accumulate any value beyond the death benefit. Because the insurance has a limited life and is not used as an investment tool, it is a lower-cost form of insurance. Often the term insurance provides accidental death and dismemberment (AD&D) coverage. That coverage pays a higher death benefit if death results from an accident. It will also pay specified smaller amounts to the policyholder in the event of dismemberment such as the loss of use of an arm or leg, hearing, or sight.

Alternatives to term insurance are ordinary and universal life insurance. *Ordinary* or *whole life insurance* provides permanent coverage for the life of the policyholder as long as premiums are paid. The policy accumulates a small cash value over time. With *universal life insurance,* part of the premium buys term insurance coverage that will be paid if the insured dies. The rest of the premium is invested in high-yield securities as a savings tool for the policyholder.

RETIREMENT PLANS AND PENSIONS

As people expect to live into their 80s and even their 90s, they are increasingly concerned about the income they will need after retirement. Most believe that Social Security and personal savings will not be adequate to provide the standard of living they want and to pay for increasing health care and medical costs in old age. Employers can offer retirement and pension plans to employees to aid them with their long-term financial planning. In the past large companies developed private pension funds and paid a large percentage of employee contributions into those plans. With rising business costs and pension costs much higher than predicted, many private plans have been dramatically modified or even dropped.

A traditional pension plan is designed to pay benefits to the employee for a prescribed number of years after retirement. Regular contributions are made to the plan by the employer and employee based on a percentage of wages and salaries. Pension plan managers invest the funds to increase their value in order to meet the amount needed to pay retirement benefits. A *defined contribution pension plan* does not guarantee an employee a fixed level of benefits upon retirement. Instead, the employer contributes a fixed amount to an account set up for the employee and benefits are determined by the amount of contributions and the performance of the investments. A *defined benefit plan* promises the employee a fixed or determinable monthly payment upon retirement. This more traditional form of pension requires the employer to contribute adequate funds to provide the promised benefit, resulting in higher than anticipated costs for many companies.

Newer forms of employer-sponsored retirement plans try to reduce the direct costs to the employer but provide employees with incentives for savings. Many of the plans are no longer managed by the business but use financial planners and investment firms to develop and manage the retirement funds. The federal government has provided a number of tax incentives in qualified investment plans designed to encourage employer and employee contributions. Examples of those plans are

- Deferred profit-sharing, stock bonus, or stock-ownership plans in which employers share profits in the form of cash or stock or allow employees to purchase stock on a tax-deferred basis.

- 401(k) savings plans in which employees can invest money in qualified savings and investment plans on a pre-tax basis. The amount of savings is deducted from the employee's salary before income tax is withheld.

- Individual retirement accounts (IRAs) allow employees to supplement their retirement savings by additional contributions to private plans selected by the employee. The savings can be made through payroll deduction.

Each of the retirement plans that are approved for special tax treatment has restrictions and requirements that must be met in terms of who can invest, the maximum amounts that can be contributed, and how and when funds can be withdrawn.

checkpoint ✓

Why are employers willing to contribute 30 percent or more of the cost of employee salaries and wages to pay for benefits?

■ The Need for Liability Insurance

One of the greatest risks to a business is liability. In its broadest sense, liability means being legally responsible. More specifically, when a business has a legal liability it is responsible for paying others because of negligent actions. That liability extends to harm and damage resulting from the use of a business' products and services, from actions of business personnel or those acting under the direction of the business, and that occur in and around the property of the business. The results of business liability appear in the settlement of court cases for millions of dollars. Even if those large settlements are not enough to drive the business into bankruptcy, they will have a major effect on the long-term financial performance of the company as well as the image and reputation of the business in the eyes of customers and the public.

Two types of penalties can be applied in liability cases. Criminal liability results from breaking a law. People guilty of crimes may serve prison sentences and pay fines. Recent public examples of business criminal liability are the convictions of Enron, Tyco, and WorldCom executives. Civil liability results from negligent acts against individuals or organizations. Individuals or organizations bring a lawsuit against others

Professionals can purchase special liability coverage for the unique activities of their business.

for damages suffered from negligent actions. When a civil judgment is made against a person or a business, the penalty is payment of damages to those who were harmed. It will also usually require that the negligent actions be stopped.

MANAGING LIABILITY RISKS

Because business liability can result in financial costs in the millions of dollars, companies must be proactive in managing those risks. The process of managing liability means identifying all possible areas of potential liability for the business, the particular products, people, activities, and actions (or lack of action) that can contribute to liability, and taking direct action to reduce and remove any liability problems. These actions will include product design, development of specific service procedures, careful employee training, developing and enforcing safe operating procedures, providing clear product information, and quick and effective responses when harm or injuries occur.

Companies often purchase liability insurance that provides coverage for the areas and activities where the business has liability exposure. Liability insurance can be very expensive for areas where damages can affect hundreds of people or the costs can be in the millions of dollars. Companies must not avoid purchasing adequate liability insurance because of the cost. Taking actions to reduce the probability of negligence or limit the effects of damage can help reduce the costs of liability insurance. But if liability is reasonably possible, insurance will be needed to avoid a liability judgment that can financially ruin the business.

TYPES OF LIABILITY INSURANCE

Several liability coverages have already been identified in the discussions of property and vehicle insurance. Workers' compensation is also a type of liability insurance, as are elements of health and life insurance. Almost every type of business insurance offers liability coverage as a part of the basic policy or as an optional coverage. In developing a liability insurance plan, risk managers should carefully review existing insurance policies to determine existing coverages and their costs. Then any new coverage should avoid duplication or provide the same coverage at a lower cost so that the liability coverage in the specialized policy can be removed or reduced.

Commercial General Liability Commercial general liability (CGL) insurance provides very broad coverage to people and property and the types of actions and activities of a business that typically provide liability exposure. The actions of owners, executives, and employees acting on behalf of the business are covered. Even stockholders of corporations acting in their official roles and vendors performing required work of the organization can be included.

Other liability coverages in a CGL include damages resulting from

- The use of the company's products and services
- Any contracts entered into on behalf of the business
- Harm or injury to property or people caused by personnel, products, or assets of the business
- The business' advertising or other communications

Commercial Liability Umbrella Insurance Companies with liability exposures in the millions of dollars can also purchase an umbrella liability policy. An *umbrella policy* is a separate policy providing a higher limit of coverage over and above any other basic liability policies an insured may have. If each liability policy owned by a business carried coverage for millions of dollars, the cost would be prohibitive. The likelihood of having a large claim against each of those types of risks is not great, but it is possible that one area may suffer a very large loss. An umbrella policy picks up coverage above the limits of the underlying or specialized policies at a lower cost that having the coverage in each policy. Usually the specialized policies are required to have coverage of $500,000–$1 million. The umbrella policy then extends the liability coverage as high as $100 million or more.

Other Liability Insurance Several other types of liability insurance policies are available to provide coverage for special circumstances or unique activities and operations of a business. Examples are shown in Figure 10-6.

FIGURE 10-6

Special Business Liability Coverages

Directors and officers	Protects the directors and officers of corporations for wrongful acts in connection with management.
Employment practices	Cover claims for harassment, discrimination, or wrongful termination of employees.
Cyberspace liability	Protects businesses that use online technology for actions resulting from libel, slander, copyright or trademark infringement, and errors.
Professional liability	Protects professionals such as accountants, attorneys, and architects from negligent acts, errors, or omissions in performing their professional services.
Medical malpractice	Covers physicians, dentists, and other medical practitioners for their actions or the actions of others under their supervision for their professional actions and the results. Coverage is also extended to the insured's business since many doctors are a part of a professional practice association.

checkpoint ✓

How does an umbrella liability policy benefit a business?

Responding to Instant Messaging

Instant messaging (IM) is the communication method of choice for many computer users, but it causes headaches for businesses. Businesses are not only concerned about lost productivity from non-business use of IM, but more seriously about the business risks posed by its use. Publicly available IM services open unsecured electronic access into the organization that is quickly being attacked by hackers, virus-writers, and spammers. Research by FaceTime Security Labs shows that security incidents involving the use of chat, IM, and P2P networks were up 2,200 percent between 2004 and 2005.

Some businesses respond by banning the use of IM by employees. But that presents two problems. First, it is almost impossible to enforce the ban since IM programs can be easily downloaded onto any computer and the software is able to bypass most firewalls and security systems. Second, IM is a proven productivity enhancement tool for business. 70 percent of large businesses using IM and 84 percent of mid- and small-sized businesses report significant improvement in communications and cost reductions due to decreased phone usage. Banning IM reduces the security risks faced by the businesses but puts them at a competitive disadvantage with businesses that embrace the new technology.

Businesses face risk management issues when dealing with IM. If companies attempt to ban the use of the technology they risk upsetting employees, customers, and business partners and creating an environment where policies will be violated and increased monitoring of employees will be needed. On the other hand, if companies embrace the use of IM but don't recognize and deal with the major security threats opened up by the technology, they will face the likelihood of data theft and attacks on information technology systems.

Risk management personnel are installing new comprehensive instant communication tools on their computer systems and on each employee's computer. The new tools offer vast improvements over publicly available IM, integrating video and desktop tools for conferencing and collaboration. Most importantly they offer significant security protection that can be controlled by the business. While the initial cost may be high, it allows employees access to the use of IM while greatly reducing potential security threats and costs.

Think Critically

1. Why would banning the use of IM reduce employee productivity if it reduced the amount of time employees spend on non-business communication?
2. Do you believe the communications of individual employees through IM and e-mail present security risks to a business? Why or why not? Recommend policies a business could implement to make sure the use of IM and e-mail by employees does not harm the business.

10.4 Lesson Assessment

UNDERSTAND CONCEPTS

Determine the best answer for each of the following questions.

1. ____?____ provides medical care, rehabilitation, and lost wages for injured workers as well as death benefits for the dependents of persons killed in work-related accidents.
   - a. unemployment insurance
   - b. Social Security
   - c. workers' compensation
   - d. Medicare

2. Which of the following is *not* one of the penalties that can be applied in the case of liability?
   - a. a fine
   - b. a jail sentence
   - c. payments to those who suffer damage
   - d. All of the above are penalties for liability

3. A separate policy providing a higher limit of coverage over and above any other basic liability policies an insured may have is a(n)
   - a. umbrella policy
   - b. all causes policy
   - c. malpractice policy
   - d. general conditions policy

4. **True or False?** Businesses can choose not to offer Social Security benefits to their employees.

5. **True or False?** Businesses are unable to reduce the liability risks they face so they should carry liability insurance for every risk they face.

MAKE ACADEMIC CONNECTIONS

6. **Math** A business located in Missouri has a total payroll of $8,563,928. If they are required to pay worker's compensation on the first 8 percent of their payroll costs, what would be the minimum and maximum amount they would have to contribute based on the information in the lesson?

7. **Critical Thinking** Spend some time thinking about your daily activities at home, school, on your job if you are employed, and in your community. List 10 risks you regularly face that can result in personal harm, damage to your property, or personal liability for your actions. Prepare a table in which you list each of the risks, the possible perils related to each risk, actions you can take to reduce each risk, and the type of insurance that you could purchase (if any) to provide financial protection.

8. **Law** Based on the potential major negative consequences a terrorist attack could have on the U.S. economy, the federal government passed the Terrorism Risk Insurance Program. Use the Internet to research the law and develop a short computer presentation summarizing the purpose of the program and the help it provides to businesses and insurance companies.

Summary

10.1 MANAGE RISK

1. Risk is the chance or probability of harm or loss. Individuals face risks that can affect health, income, property, and can even result in death. Businesses face risks that can have a significant economic effect.

2. Natural risks arise from natural events or are a part of nature. Human risks result from the actions of individuals, groups, or organizations. Risks can be avoided, transferred, insured, or assumed.

10.2 PRINCIPLES OF INSURANCE

3. Insurance is based on three principles. (1) Some risk facing an individual or organization is transferred to others. (2) Risks are pooled or shared among a large group of individuals or companies. (3) Risk for any one individual or business is reduced by controlling the uncertainty of the loss.

4. Insurance companies can be stock companies or mutual companies. Their major activities are rate making, selling, underwriting, investing, and claims processing. An insurance policy is a legal contract between the insurer and the insured. A standard insurance policy contains declarations, the insuring agreement, conditions, and exclusions.

10.3 PROPERTY AND VEHICLE INSURANCE

5. Property risks to businesses can be identified and insurance is available to provide protection against those risks. The common types of property insurance are comprehensive property, business owners, title, transportation, credit, and crime.

6. Automobile insurance policies are similar for insurance purchased by individuals and businesses. Policies covering business vehicles are called commercial vehicle insurance or business auto coverage.

10.4 PERSONNEL AND LIABILITY INSURANCE

7. The federal government requires business to provide Social Security, unemployment, and workers' compensation insurance. Two common types of health insurance plans are fee-for-service and managed care. Life insurance pays a beneficiary upon the death of the insured. Employers offer retirement and pension plans to employees to aid long-term financial planning.

8. Companies must be proactive in managing liability risks. They can purchase liability insurance that provides coverage for the areas and activities where the business has liability exposure. Commercial general liability insurance provides broad coverage to people and property. An umbrella policy provides coverage beyond other policies.

Develop Your Business Language

Match the terms listed with the definitions. Some terms will not be used.

1. An individual or business is responsible to others for negligence
2. Can be reduced or avoided by thoughtful actions
3. A chance of financial gain or loss
4. A person or organization designated to receive the proceeds of the insurance policy
5. The individual or organization to which the policy is issued
6. A contract providing for financial protection against a specified loss
7. Results from breaking a law
8. The insured and insurer share the risk by paying a defined amount of the costs
9. Cannot be influenced by human action
10. No opportunity for financial gain but only loss
11. The chance or probability of harm or loss
12. The cause of a loss

a. beneficiary
b. coinsurance
c. controllable risk
d. coverages
e. criminal liability
f. deductible
g. economic risk
h. insurance
i. insured
j. insurer
k. liability
l. natural risk
m. peril
n. policy
o. policyholder
p. premium
q. pure risk
r. risk
s. self-insurance
t. speculative risk
u. uncontrollable risk

Review Concepts

13. A word that is used as a substitute for risk is ____?____.
    a. peril
    b. insurance
    c. uncertainty
    d. opportunity

14. Purchasing insurance trades a potentially large but uncertain loss for a smaller but certain ____?____.
    a. gain
    b. risk
    c. result
    d. payment

15. Which of the following must exist for a risk to be insurable?
    a. only a small number of individuals or businesses can face the risk
    b. losses from the risk must be both accidental and uncertain
    c. the cost of the losses cannot be estimated
    d. all of the above must exist

16. The part of the insurance policy that forms the basis of the contract between the insured and the insurer is the
    a. exclusions
    b. conditions
    c. insuring agreement
    d. declarations

17. ____?____ life insurance covers the insured for a specific period of years and does not accumulate any value beyond the death benefit.
    a. term
    b. AD&D
    c. ordinary
    d. universal

Think Critically

18. Do you believe a pure risk poses greater problems for a business than a speculative risk? Why or why not?

19. If you were the risk manager for a company, how would you go about attempting to identify all of the risks facing a business? How would you decide which risks should be insured and which should not?

20. What is meant by the insurance concept that risks are pooled or shared? How does each business benefit from pooling risks? Are there any disadvantages to a business from pooling its risks with others?

21. Use Figure 10-1 to describe how a bell curve represents the number and amount of damages that are likely to result from the number of fires that occur in a large number of businesses over several years.

22. Why do insurance companies need to identify both conditions and exclusions in an insurance policy? Why should businesspeople purchasing insurance make sure they clearly understand the conditions and exclusions?

23. Discuss the advantages and disadvantages to a young employee of the following options for retirement planning: (1) relying on Social Security only, (2) relying on a personal investment plan, (3) combining Social Security with a personal investment plan.

24. Choose a business and describe examples of situations where the business might need business income insurance and consequential damage coverage.

Business Financial Calculations

25. Using the information from the FYI in Lesson 10.2, calculate the total value of life insurance premiums and non-life insurance premiums sold in the U.S. in 2004.

26. A health insurance policy has a coinsurance clause that requires the insured to pay the first $250 of charges and 20 percent of additional charges up to a maximum total payment of $1,250. The bills for health care are

January 5	$120	March 30	$45
April 18	$375	June 20	$63
August 25	$560	October 2	$190
November 1	$35	December 20	$95

Calculate the amount the insured must pay for each of the bills. Then determine the total amount of the health care costs and the percentage paid by the insured and by the insurer.

27. John Eros is a carpenter and his wife Janell works as a bank teller. John earns a rate of $23.22 before overtime and benefits and Janell earns a rate of $18.50. Using the percentages shown in Figure 10-4, calculate the amount of compensation John and Janell would earn for each of the benefits listed in the figure. What is the total compensation for each person?

Analyze Cases

Use the case from the beginning of the chapter, Providing Specialty Insurance, to answer the following questions.

28. Why are the types of significant and unique losses described in the case such as a one-time entertainment event or the production of a movie difficult to insure?

29. What makes Lloyd's different in both organization and operations from traditional insurance companies? Why would a wealthy individual or corporation want to participate in a syndicate?

30. Insurance is offered to provide protection for pure risk, meaning there is no opportunity for financial gain. Do you believe the investments of the Lloyd's syndicates are pure risks or speculative risks? Justify your answer.

31. Why do you believe most of the investment capital in Lloyd's syndicates today comes from corporations rather than names?

32. What type of risks would you expect the Fortune 500 companies, global banks, and pharmaceutical firms to insure through Lloyd's that they would not be able to insure through traditional insurance policies?

Portfolio Activity

COLLECT examples that illustrate the variety of types of insurance policies and plans used by businesses.

CREATE a visual to illustrate a business dealing with a variety of risks through a comprehensive risk management program including insurance.

CONNECT your visual to other items already in your class portfolio or relate it to an important concept you have learned in another class. Make the connection by preparing a one-minute presentation on the importance of insurance to businesses, employees, and others.

Stock Market Activity

Financial and other business risks are common in every organization. These uncertainties regularly affect the financial performance and stock value of a company. Attempts to reduce or eliminate risks through insurance will influence an investor's decision to buy, sell, or hold a stock.

Use Internet and library resources to research the company you have been studying (or select a different company).

1. Identify common risks the company may encounter. Point out both internal (company) risks and external (economic, social, political) risks of the business.

2. Explain actions that might be taken to reduce or eliminate these risks.

3. Describe how various risks may have affected the market value of the company's stock over the past 12 to 18 months.

Planning a Career in Insurance

Insurance is a broad industry with many types of jobs and career opportunities. The industry is changing dramatically as new types of insurance products are developed, insurance is offered as part of a broad set of finance and investment products and services, and the Internet and other technology is used more extensively to deliver and support insurance sales and service activities.

Insurance jobs are found in two basic types of businesses. Insurance carriers are the large companies that offer policies and carry the risk of insurance that is sold. Insurance agents and brokers sell insurance, process applications, and are often the main contacts with customers.

Employment Outlook

■ Technology that allows direct sales and information processing using the Internet and other technologies is reducing the demand for sales and customer service personnel.

■ The growing demand for new insurance products and the blurring of insurance and investment services is increasing the demand for people with technology skills and careers in medical and health insurance and financial services related to investments and insurance.

Job Titles

■ Customer service representatives
■ Appraisers
■ Adjusters
■ Investigators
■ Loss control specialists
■ Underwriters
■ Actuaries

Needed Skills

■ Clerical and administrative personnel may need only a high school diploma with technical and math skills

■ Insurance specialists require a college degree

■ An aptitude for mathematics is required

■ Strong customer service and communication skills are important

■ Most advanced jobs require specialized coursework, degrees, or licenses in insurance products, procedures, and legal requirements

What's It Like to Work as an Actuary?

Actuaries are one of the smallest career areas in insurance but the most important. Actuaries work in all parts of the economy although mostly in financial services, including insurance companies, banks, and retirement funds.

Actuaries spend their time identifying and studying risk and its impact on financial resources. They gather and analyze data on the occurrence of risks, the costs of damage from those risks, and ways to minimize risk. Actuaries are responsible for deciding if specific risks are insurable, the conditions and exemptions of coverage, and the cost of insuring the risk. They monitor the profitability of insurance companies and recommend corrective action. They ensure that insurance companies have set aside enough funds to pay claims. They provide advice on how to invest the insurance companies' assets.

What about you? What type of insurance career is most appealing to you? What will you have to do to prepare for a career in the insurance industry?

BUSINESS PRESENTATION MANAGEMENT EVENT

The Business Presentation Management Event challenges individuals to use current desktop technologies and software to prepare and deliver an effective multimedia presentation.

You will design a computer-generated multimedia presentation for Worldwide Insurance about managing business risks through property, vehicle, liability, and other types of insurance. The presentation must be on the contestant's computer hard drive or on CD-ROM. No VCR or laserdisc may be used for this presentation. Charts and other graphics must be used in this presentation. All text and graphic materials must follow the organization's graphic standards and make proper use of the organization's logo and/or name. All contestants are responsible for securing a release form from any individual whose name, photograph, or other information is included in the presentation. No photographs, text, registered trademarks, or names may be used without permission. Although a work may be freely accessible on the Internet and contain no statement of copyright, the law protects these works.

Fifteen minutes will be allowed for preparation and setup of the presentation. The presentation shall last a minimum of seven (7) minutes and a maximum of ten (10) minutes. Up to five (5) minutes will be allowed each contestant for questions from the judges. The contestant must make effective use of current multimedia technology in the presentation. Presentations will be evaluated for effective use of space, color, and text as design factors.

Performance Indicators Evaluated

- Demonstrate knowledge of multimedia software and components.
- Demonstrate effective oral communication skills.
- Apply technical skills to create a multimedia presentation which enhances the oral presentation.
- Use the best typography, functional graphics, charts, graphs, and color for an effective presentation.
- Develop the stated theme for the presentation.
- Understand the topic presented.

Go to the BPA web site for more detailed information.

Think Critically

1. How can a multimedia presentation heighten the need for the product or service being advertised?
2. What information about insurance should be included?
3. Who is the target market for this presentation?
4. What is the advantage of a multimedia presentation over an informative brochure?

www.bpa.org

chapter 11

Technology and Financial Management

11.1 FINANCIAL INFORMATION MANAGEMENT

11.2 TECHNOLOGY IN FINANCE

11.3 INFORMATION PRIVACY AND SECURITY

Point Your [Browser]
www.thomsonedu.com/school/busfinance

Personal E-Finance

Marcella was up early Saturday morning and seated at her computer. She was meeting friends for brunch before they headed to the auto show and then to a concert. She had several tasks to do to get her financial resources organized but was going to make a big effort to get it all done.

Her first stop was her virtual bank web site. She wanted to see if her commission check had been transferred to her bank account via direct deposit. Seeing that it had not and worried that her checking balance was a bit low for some of her weekend spending, she transferred money from a money market account. She had an e-mail message that one of her CDs was up for renewal in 10 days. She checked the renewal interest rate and quickly went to a web site that showed CD rates being paid by banks across the country. She was happy to see that her bank was near the top so she sent a reply to her banker to renew the CD.

Marcella's next stop was her online brokerage account. She checked the performance of her stock portfolio. It wasn't performing as well as she had expected so she sent a question to her online broker and was surprised when she got an immediate response. He was waiting for a plane and had responded to her message using his BlackBerry. She also saw that her automatic trading program had activated a purchase of 100 shares of the tech stock she had been watching. Marcella was glad the order was placed without her having to constantly monitor the market or rely on a broker. The automatic calendar pop-up on her computer screen showed that she needed to make a quarterly contribution to her Roth IRA. She set up an electronic funds transfer from her bank to the mutual fund account to be sent the following Wednesday.

Marcella saw an e-filing reminder from the Internal Revenue Service in her e-mail. She filed her state and federal income taxes last year using e-filing. Since it was so simple and she had received her tax refund quickly she knew she would do it again. She was now doing her own income taxes using a tax preparation software program that linked to financial records she maintained using a personal finance software program.

Her final task was to gather information on new auto models. Marcella was planning to trade her car in the next few months and thought the auto show would be a good chance to look at choices. But before she went, she wanted information on safety, fuel efficiency, and reliability. Later she could get pricing information as well as compare insurance costs before she made a final choice. In fact, Marcella thought she might try an online buying service this time. Why waste time going to a dealer when she could probably get a better deal online?

Think Critically

1. How is Marcella's lifestyle different as a result of using online services and computer technology? Discuss how each of the tasks would be performed differently without the technology.
2. How do the businesses Marcella uses for her financial services benefit from using the Internet to deliver their products and services? What are some problems the businesses might face?

Goals
- Discuss how computers and the Internet are changing the finance industry.
- Describe the parts of a financial information system.

Terms
- electronic document
- electronic record
- electronic information exchange procedures
- financial information system
- electronic spreadsheet
- what-if planning

Changes in Financial Information Management

Finance is an information industry. For the most part, consumers are buying information when they make purchases from businesses in the finance industry. They expect a great deal of information to help them make decisions and manage their financial resources. Savings and investment products marketed by banks, investment businesses, and other financial services companies are selected by consumers based on an understanding of costs, returns, and risks. Insurance products are sold on the basis of protections provided, rates, conditions, and policy terms. To be successful in an information industry, businesses must be able to create, store, access, analyze, update, and transmit information. Customers need to be able to access, understand, analyze, and compare information and, most importantly, use it to make decisions and solve problems.

In the past, most of the information in the finance industry was paper-based. Companies handled large quantities of paper that moved slowly within the company, between businesses, and to and from customers. Businesses and customers relied on large filing systems to hold all of the paperwork and secure storage to protect important papers. Many clerical workers were needed to prepare, process, file, and retrieve the paperwork. Documents were mailed, sent through express delivery, and required security personnel for secure distribution. Days and even weeks were needed to prepare and process complex financial documents.

ELECTRONIC INFORMATION

Today many businesses in the finance industry are shifting to electronic documents and records and electronic information exchange procedures. An **electronic document** (paperless document) is information contained in a computer file prepared for a specific purpose. It can be text, images, graphics, or any combination of those formats. An **electronic record** is a document containing information that is intended to be preserved for a period of time to document an event, activity, or transaction. Electronic documents and records can be created originally in electronic form, meaning there is no paper document. They can also be developed as electronic "duplicate" versions of documents and records that are first created on paper. **Electronic information exchange procedures** provide a way to share information in electronic forms, including text, graphics, audio, and video. The exchange procedures must maintain the authenticity and accuracy of the information and provide privacy and security.

For many years, businesses and consumers believed they could not replace paper documents and records with paperless alternatives. There was concern that the electronic form could be lost or damaged. Many people were uncomfortable working with electronic documents due to lack of experience. There also were legal restrictions on the use of electronic documents and signatures that prevented the complete replacement of paper records. Today advances in computer technology have created vastly improved quality and speed for developing electronic documents and for copying and scanning paper documents and records into electronic form. Electronic data storage and security procedures are enhanced. People are becoming more experienced and comfortable with using many forms of electronic documents. Laws are now in place to validate the use of electronic documents, records, and signatures for contracts and other legal agreements.

A recent study found that 90 percent of all new business records are either created in electronic form or are scanned and stored electronically. Businesses are moving to electronic records to gain productivity and reduce costs. A study of banking services discovered that the average cost to complete a typical customer transaction face to face with a teller was over one dollar. The cost of ATM and call center transactions was about 25 cents. If the customer completed the transaction using the Internet, the cost was close to a penny.

The cost of maintaining paper records can be expensive. Ten hours of the average employee's time each week is spent managing documents, representing about 10 percent of payroll costs. The cost of preparing, copying, storing, and retrieving the documents in just one four-drawer file is between $4,000 and $6,000 a year.

THE USE OF TECHNOLOGY

More important than cost savings for many businesses are changes in consumer expectations. Computers, the Internet, and a variety of emerging electronic tools are now commonplace in businesses and increasingly being used by individuals and families. In the United States, 207 million people use the Internet regularly at home, work, or school. That is 69 percent of the total population of the country and the most users of any country in the world. It also reflects 117 percent growth in the use of the Internet in just six years. The second largest user population is China with 123 million Internet users, which represents only 9 percent of the country's population. Worldwide, there are 1.43 billion Internet users, or about 16 percent of the world population.

© GETTY IMAGES/PHOTODISC

Consumers are increasingly comfortable using computers to transact business.

A slightly higher number of U.S. consumers, 219 million, have mobile phones. Currently, about 50 percent of mobile phone users have web-accessible cell phones with multimedia capability. Worldwide, mobile phone usage is exploding. The number of mobile phone users passed 2.5 billion and is expected to reach 3 billion within three years.

Having access to high-speed Internet connections increases the likelihood that businesses and consumers will use their computers for business services. Currently 50 million high-speed (broadband) connections serve U.S. businesses and consumers. The number of connections is increasing by about 33 percent each year. Most of those connections are residential, with 43 million high-speed Internet connections in American homes. The types of high-speed service are nearly evenly divided between cable (cable television) modem service and DSL (telephone line) connections.

With Internet access, both home-based and mobile, consumers are increasing their use of financial services provided via the Internet. Figure 11-1 illustrates some of that use.

FIGURE 11-1

Internet Access to Financial Services in the U.S.

Online Financial Service	Percent of Consumers with Internet Access
Use a banking web site	43%
Pay bills	38%
Obtain financial information; e.g., stock quotes, interest rates	44%
Buy and sell stocks	12%
Obtain auto insurance quotes	7%
Invest in a mutual fund	11%
Shop for a home mortgage	10%

Most financial services businesses are adapting to the online environment. Online trading accounted for over 40 percent of all stock trades on both the New York Stock Exchange and NASDAQ by the early 2000s. The average assets of Internet-only banks are over three times greater than that of traditional banks—$3.5 billion to $1 billion. Two-thirds of U.S. banks currently accept online payments or are implementing the technology to do so. Businesses are spending about $5 billion a year on equipment and procedures to support mobile commerce from cell phones and other wireless devices. Overall, businesses report that currently about 15 percent of all interactions with consumers and 20 percent of all interactions with suppliers occur online. The most productive companies report online interaction rates with consumers as high as 80 percent.

checkpoint ✓

What advantages do electronic documents offer to businesses compared to paper documents?

Financial Information Systems

Effective information systems are essential for companies, especially those that provide financial services. The need for information is steadily increasing, the forms in which information is developed, stored, and transmitted are expanding, the speed required to access information constantly accelerates, and the concern for privacy and security is growing. An *information system* is a structured set of processes, people, and equipment for converting data into information. It integrates hardware, software, information, data, applications, communications, and the people who generate, record, and use the information.

Financial information is a key part of information systems in every company. Within financial services companies a specialized information system is required. A **financial information system** supports managers in the financing of a business and the allocation and control of financial resources. The main financial decisions supported by the specialized information system are shown in Figure 11-2.

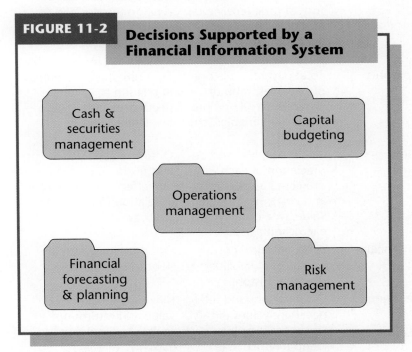

FIGURE 11-2 Decisions Supported by a Financial Information System

- Cash & securities management
- Capital budgeting
- Operations management
- Financial forecasting & planning
- Risk management

MANAGING FINANCIAL INFORMATION

A financial information system is used to (1) gather, (2) organize, (3) store, (4) analyze, and (5) report financial data. The activities are managed through a system of data collection procedures, computer technology, software, and electronic information exchange procedures. The system allows an organization to obtain financial information and use that information in decision-making.

Several factors provide the basis for financial planning and management. Figure 11-3 describes the information that should be included in a financial information system and the basic financial goals managers attempt to achieve by the analysis of that information. Notice that the categories of financial factors match information included in a company's financial statements. Other key financial planning and performance data included in financial information systems are sales, inventory, operating expenses, personnel and payroll costs, insurance expenses, tax liabilities, and profitability. In addition to the company's financial performance data, the financial information system should also collect, analyze and report external information including economic and competitive data, information about investment alternatives, and data on risks that the company faces.

FIGURE 11-3

Information Needs and Goals in Financial Management

Financial Factor	Information Needed	Management Goal
Cash flow	Cash inflows and outflows; cash needs; cash balances; cash investment options and results	Efficiency in use of cash; minimum cash balance; maximum return on cash investments
Accounts receivable	Total receivables; history of total receivables and of each account; account aging	Minimize receivables in relation to sales and inventory; minimize overdue and uncollectible accounts
Accounts payable	Total payables; history of payables; ratio of payables to related performance variables; cost of credit	Optimize cost of credit in relation to purchase needs and cash investments
Capital assets	Value, age, life, and depreciation of each asset; projected asset needs and costs; net present value; rate of return on each capital asset	Optimize asset value and resource use; maintain effective asset mix in relation to company strategy
Long-term liabilities	Type, amount, cost, and term of liabilities; payment histories	Optimize long-term debt to total capital
Stockholder's equity	Classifications and total/per share values of stock; profit or loss; dividend payments; retained earnings; stock actions (splits, purchases, new issues)	Maximize stockholder value and return; optimum use of retained earnings

MAKING DECISIONS

Financial management involves analyzing a company's financial performance, identifying ways to use financial resources as efficiently as possible, and developing strategies to use current resources to improve the financial position of the company. Specifically, financial management activities include

- Matching available resources to the activities planned by the organization
- Identifying additional sources of financing to meet deficiencies or to finance new initiatives

- Monitoring the effectiveness of current resource use
- Identifying ways to reduce and recover expenses
- Studying past resource usage to determine future budget requirements, project cash needs, and forecast financial growth
- Managing and investing company assets to make them profitable
- Developing long-term financial plans to meet future resource requirements and maximize financial returns
- Forecasting, controlling, and attempting to prevent major risks

Before the availability of computerized information systems and decision tools, analyzing financial data was a time-consuming and complex task. Today, the primary tool for financial analysis is the electronic spreadsheet. An **electronic spreadsheet** is a software program that organizes and presents data in columns and rows and allows analysis using integrated mathematical formulas. The spreadsheet makes it possible for managers to complete what-if planning. With **what-if planning**, alternatives for financial decisions are considered by applying assumptions to the financial data in an electronic spreadsheet. The spreadsheet automatically computes the effects of the assumptions on financial performance.

SHARING INFORMATION

An important function of a financial information system is to provide access to appropriate information for stockholders, managers, employees, business partners, and customers. Information must be accessible at the time and in the form required by each type of user. The system needs to provide access to the information each group needs but restrict access to confidential and private information.

teamwork

Identify a type of business with which all team members are familiar. As a team, brainstorm a list of the types of information that business uses in its day-to-day operations. Divide the list into information that would be a part of a financial information system and information that would be a part of the larger company information system.

DIGITAL VISION

Information must be accessible at the right time and in the right format for each type of user.

The ability to collaborate in the analysis of financial information and decision-making is another important requirement of information systems. Today, companies need to be connected around the world. Computer networks must provide that access in business offices and allow for mobile access as well. Computerized information systems provide worldwide access in multiple languages and various currencies and recognize the legal requirements and tax laws of each of the countries in which a business operates.

checkpoint ✓

List several types of decisions managers make with information available in a financial information system.

technology topics

Overcoming Virtual Communication Limitations

One of the objections many people have to participating in online virtual meetings is the lack of the types of feedback they are used to receiving in face-to-face communications. Body language, facial expressions, and visual evidence of interest or boredom provide useful information to both leaders and participants.

People responsible for planning and managing virtual communications need to respond to those concerns to make team members and meeting participants comfortable. The use of web cams is a simple and inexpensive way for people to see and hear other participants rather than just viewing text and graphics. Older camera technology restricted participant views to only one person at a time or just the speaker's face on the computer screen. Newer group meeting software and better placement of cameras make it possible for all team participants, local meeting groups, and full images of people to be seen on a computer screen. Participants can click around among people and locations on their own computers to get the visual image they want.

There are other useful virtual communication tools that increase involvement and feedback. One helpful tool is *emoticons* (small symbols used to convey feelings and emotions in a text message). Some emoticons useful for giving group feedback are "Applause," "Let's take a break," or "I don't understand." Voting tools allow leaders to poll participants to determine areas of agreement or disagreement. A hand-raising icon allows a participant to seek recognition in order to ask a question or provide input.

Think Critically

1. Do you believe that with experience virtual teams and meetings can be as effective as or more effective than traditional face-to-face experiences? Why or why not?
2. In your view, what effect if any does a person's age, gender, or culture have on comfort with virtual teams and meetings? What other factors might affect a person's motivation and effectiveness in virtual groups?

11.1 Lesson Assessment

UNDERSTAND CONCEPTS

Determine the best answer for each of the following questions.

1. Which of the following statements about electronic documents and records is correct?
   a. businesses are required to make paper backups of both
   b. electronic documents are intended to be preserved for a period of time while electronic records are not
   c. few businesses are currently using electronic documents or records
   d. none of the statements are correct

2. The reasons businesses and consumers believed they could not replace paper documents and records with paperless alternatives include all of the following except
   a. concern that the electronic form may be lost or damaged
   b. lack of comfort in working with electronic documents
   c. legal restrictions on the use of electronic documents and signatures
   d. all of the statements are correct

3. **True or False?** Access to high-speed Internet connections increases the likelihood that consumers will use computers for business services.

4. A ____?____ supports financial managers in the financing of a business and the allocation and control of financial resources.

5. ____?____ planning applies assumptions to the financial data in an electronic spreadsheet.
   a. what-if   c. if-then
   b. what-was   d. profit-loss

MAKE ACADEMIC CONNECTIONS

6. **Math** If a bank processes 180,225 transactions in a month, what will it cost if all transactions are (a) paper-based at a cost of $1.09 per transaction, (b) completed through ATMs and call centers at a cost of $0.27, and (c) completed by consumers using the Internet at $0.02? How much can the bank save if it changes the way transactions are completed from 100 percent paper based to 50 percent paper-based, 35 percent through ATMs and call centers, and 15 percent Internet?

7. **Technology** Use an electronic spreadsheet to show the 5-year return on a $150,000 investment with interest compounded annually at the following interest rates: 4 percent, 5.5 percent, 6 percent.

8. **Communication** You have been hired as a customer service manager for a small local bank. It has been a part of the community for over 70 years and the customers are mostly middle-aged and older. The bank does not yet have a web site or use Internet technology. You want to attract younger customers and believe technology will appeal to them. Write a one-page memo to the bank president giving your rationale for introducing the technology and your recommendations for the first steps the bank could take.

Goals
- Describe factors businesses consider when making technology decisions
- Discuss how technology is changing the financial industry

Terms
- adoption curve
- cost-benefit analysis

A Focus on Technology

The environment is changing dramatically for almost all businesses in the finance industry. A new focus on technology is required. Financial services are delivered globally, providing new opportunities but at the same time creating new competitors. The speed of financial transactions is becoming instantaneous. Customers expect more choices and higher levels of customer service. At the same time they are able to access more information on which to base their decisions and can compare the prices and features of products and services.

Most businesses do not feel they have a choice about whether to increase the use of technology. They see evidence of the success many businesses have had in attracting customers through technology and the potential cost savings they might realize. At the same time they are challenged by the many types of technology, the effects that changes may have on current and new customers as well as on the company's employees, and the high initial costs of the changeover.

MAKING TECHNOLOGY DECISIONS

When businesses plan to adopt new technology, they make three decisions.

1. What types of technology will benefit the business?
2. How will technology be used in the business? Will it replace a current process, duplicate and provide an alternative to a current process, or will it offer a new process, product, or service?
3. What will be the timeline for implementing the technology?

Type The type of technology can be directed at consumers or at business processes. A consumer technology improves the customer experience. It may offer more convenient, timelier, or faster access. Technology can make it easier for customers to gather and analyze information and make comparisons of the business' products and services with its competitor's. It can provide improvements to existing products and services or even brand new choices the business could not offer without the technology.

Technology can also be used to improve the way business processes are completed. That can mean improvements in quality and efficiency and often savings in the cost of completing business activities. Another benefit of technology is that the business process may be performed in different locations by more people to allow easier business expansion or more effective use of business resources.

NETBookmark

Career clusters are a tool to use when you are considering career possibilities. Access thomsonedu.com/school/busfinance and click on the link for Chapter 11. Find information on a career in information security or technology.

www.thomsonedu.com/school/busfinance

Use One of the greatest challenges to businesses when considering new technology is the effect it will have on existing products, services, and processes. For example, when banks began using ATMs it didn't mean that bank tellers could be replaced. While the increased use of ATMs frequently resulted in the need for fewer tellers, many customers still want personalized service at times but the convenience of ATMs at other times. Other customers will never use ATMs if they can avoid it. So ATM technology in effect duplicates existing services. Insurance companies that provide web sites where customers can obtain information and complete applications or file claims almost always still need agents and customer service personnel to work directly with customers. Some of the personnel may now devote a portion of their time to Internet business, but the company cannot eliminate traditional service methods. As new technology is considered, the business must evaluate how it will affect existing operations immediately and in the long run.

Some technologies actually introduce new products, services, and processes that create new business opportunities. In those instances, the company must decide if the new business will replace older or more traditional products, if it will compete with existing products and services and likely reduce the revenues they generate, or if it adds to the business and will require additional resources since the existing products and services must still be maintained.

Timing When will new technology be introduced and how long will it take to be fully implemented? The introduction of new technology and its acceptance by consumers follows a common set of stages that can be shown in an adoption curve. An **adoption curve** represents the stages in which an innovation is accepted by individuals and businesses. Figure 11-4 on the next page shows an adoption curve with five typical responses to an innovation.

Innovators are the small percentage of consumers or businesspeople who are risk takers and want to be the first to try something new. They are willing to pay more and put up with early problems in order to be the first to obtain the innovation.

Early adopters are viewed as opinion leaders and are quick to adopt an innovation after they have seen its use and value. They will take a bit more time to gather information and consider risks and benefits than innovators, but will make a decision quickly when they determine that the innovation offers benefits.

The *early majority* is one of the two largest groups of adopters. They are more cautious than the first two groups, but they want to be seen by others as accepting and using innovation. They respect and follow the lead of early adopters but are more value conscious and not as willing to take a risk.

The *late majority* is the other large group of innovation users. By the time they made a decision, the product is no longer considered an innovation and is widely used. This group is cautious and conservative. They want clear evidence of the effectiveness of an innovation. They will wait until it is thoroughly tested and proven and the cost has dropped.

Laggards are very resistant to change and very conservative in their purchase behavior. They do not trust innovation and will avoid spending money on products and services they have not used in the past until they have little other choice. They do not view themselves as a part of the group and may even take pride in being different.

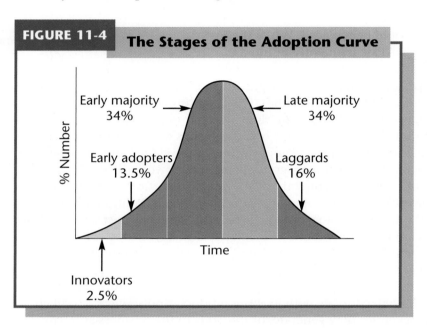

FIGURE 11-4 **The Stages of the Adoption Curve**

After decisions about the type, use, and timing of technology adoption have been analyzed, the final step is to complete a standard cost-benefit analysis. A **cost-benefit analysis** compares the total expected costs with the total expected benefits of one or more choices in order to choose the most profitable option. When completing a cost-benefit analysis of a technology choice, the actual monetary value of both the cost of purchasing and implementing the technology and the financial benefits from its implementation must be calculated. The costs to purchase and implement new technology are relatively easy to determine, although the continuing cost of its use over a period of years may be more difficult. The people responsible for the cost-benefit analysis will have to estimate how successful the new technology will be and how quickly and widely it will be used.

It is often much more difficult to determine the monetary value of the benefit of the technology. Increases in sales and revenues can be estimated but must be matched to any possible decreases from existing products, services, and technologies. Will the technology increase the number of new customers? The new technology might actually result in the loss of some customers who don't like it. Will it increase the average amount current customers spend? It might simply spread the current amount customers spend across the old and new technologies.

An important part of cost-benefit analysis is determining opportunity costs. An *opportunity cost* for a technology decision is the cost of adopting

teamwork

Discuss with your team how the adoption curve is demonstrated by people in your school, family, and neighborhood by the purchase and use of new technology products. Discuss whether you can see examples of the adoption curve in how businesses in your community begin to use new technology.

the technology compared to what the same amount of money could have earned if it was used for the next best alternative. For example, a brokerage firm could compare the cost of investing in web-based software so customers can make stock purchases online versus the cost of hiring and training more stockbrokers and customer service personnel to provide personalized customer service.

checkpoint ✔

What are the differences among the five groups identified in the adoption curve?

■ Technology Applications in the Finance Industry

All parts of the financial services industry are affected by technology. Every category of financial services is expanding the types of products and services offered. Financial services businesses such as banks, stockbrokers, investment companies, and insurance companies compete with each other offering similar savings, investment, and insurance products. There is a smaller number of larger businesses as competitors merge and small businesses are driven from the market by competition. Customers demand higher levels of service and personalized attention no matter how they contact the business. They want convenient access to financial services at any time and any place through traditional as well as mobile and electronic services. Companies must use technology to provide employees and customers with quick access to information and fast service, but with attention to both accuracy and security.

TECHNOLOGY AND BANKING

New banking technology provides consistent service no matter what method of contact customers choose. The concept of branch banking is expanding to provide banking and financial services through traditional branch offices, but also through staffed banking centers in supermarkets, discount stores, and other businesses. The number of ATMs is expanding as are the types of financial transactions that can be completed through the automated technology. Banking services and financial resources are accessed with smart cards that can be used at many types of retail businesses as well as standalone financial services kiosks. The kiosks offer easy-to-use touch screen technology with audio, text, graphics, and video and often the capability to talk directly to a customer service representative when help is needed.

Early bank web sites primarily provided information. Now customers can complete most banking transactions online, such as account management, bill paying, loan applications, and accessing customer service and financial advice through direct personal contact with bank personnel. Mobile banking using cell phones is the newest form of customer service technology. It is expected that interactive television may provide personalized banking services at home in the future.

Banks are implementing sophisticated technology and improving internal processes that collect, store, and provide instantaneous access to customer and product information for use by employees and customers in any location using any type of technology. The technology used to support those processes must be accurate, efficient, and secure, and it must greatly reduce the per-transaction cost to keep the business competitive and profitable. Converting most paper-based transactions to electronic transactions will be an important part of reducing costs and increasing accuracy. Electronic data will increase security issues facing both the banks and their customers.

TECHNOLOGY AND INVESTING

Investing in stocks and mutual funds has traditionally been done by direct contact with a stockbroker who then placed orders via telephone or computer to the trading floor. Beginning in 1971, the NASDAQ exchange removed the floor trading component and made trading on its exchange entirely computer-based. The growth of personal computers and the Internet opened electronic trading to individual investors who could place orders through an account with an online stockbroker. It also provided the individual investor with a growing and easily accessible amount of information that was previously available primarily through direct contact with a stockbroker.

The early growth of online investing was initially accomplished through specialized electronic brokerage firms such as Ameritrade and E*Trade. They offered limited investor information and support, but placed investor orders at greatly discounted prices compared to full-service brokers. Over time, traditional full-service brokers recognized the importance of offering online trading for their customers, while specialized electronic brokers recognized that their customers wanted more information and investment advice. Many of the electronic brokerage companies have now merged with full-service brokers. The products and services they offer have expanded into a variety of savings, investment, money management, retirement, and insurance products.

Most investors with Internet access now use the Internet for a number of investment services. They expect to be able to access investment information that is understandable and current. They want immediate access to stock quotes. Most importantly, they want their buy and sell orders to be placed instantaneously so the price doesn't change between the time the order is placed and the transaction is completed. As with other financial services businesses, each customer has unique needs and expectations for information, services, and access to technology. Most investment firms continue to offer the services of investment advisors and brokers who can be contacted personally via telephone or computer, or even in person. They also offer technology services that allow investors to complete most investment activities without the help of a company employee.

Many companies have entered the investment services market to provide information to consumers and businesses. Some of the information services are available free and supported by advertising, while others charge a fee to customers. Most of the companies provide information in multiple formats including e-mail updates, cell phone alerts, special reports, charts, graphs, and the streaming of current stock price and market information. The technology allows customers to customize the type of information they

Gen Yers spend about 12 hours online every week. That compares to 9 hours for Gen Xers and 6 for Boomers. They are also active social users of the Internet. For example, they are 50 percent more likely than Gen Xers to send instant messages, twice as likely to read blogs, and three times as likely to use social networking sites.

want and the form in which they receive it. The volume of information, the customization capabilities, and the need to provide immediate information requires sophisticated technology.

Other investment services are also becoming increasingly computer-based. Information on available bond offerings and the purchase of new bond issues as well as bond trading can be completed via computer. The federal government now sells treasury securities through computer-based auctions and the securities themselves are now paperless.

TECHNOLOGY AND INSURANCE

The insurance industry has been one of the last categories of financial services to accept and implement consumer-oriented technology. Companies have internal systems and procedures to maintain their own records. That technology only recently has begun to extend to accepting, processing, and updating applications and adjusting claims. Recent surveys indicate that only 31 percent of insurance companies allow customers to access quotes on their web sites and only 7 percent enable their customers to make simple applications or basic changes to existing policies online. Even insurance agents and adjusters often don't have online access to much of the information they need or are unable to enter policy and claims information online. Insurance companies claim that policies must be personalized and underwriting is too complex to allow it to be managed by people without specialized knowledge and training.

Several small insurance companies led by auto insurers have been implementing a number of web-based consumer services, including comparing insurance rates and applying for basic coverage. That has spurred larger companies to increase their web presence to compete. Another focus of online customer service is providing current customers with access to policy information and the ability to make basic changes such as address or beneficiary. Some companies have added online billing and payment processes. One of the innovations being implemented by companies that offer multiple types of insurance is to consolidate policy information and billing of several types of insurance so customers can access, review, and pay for all policies in one place and at one time if they choose.

Financial customers expect to receive current, correct, and understandable information online.

Technology services are being developed to allow agents, adjusters, and other personnel to easily access company records and input new data from any location. The technology can be used on wireless computers, PDAs, cell phones, and other mobile computing devices. Insurance agents can gather and submit information from the customer's home or business. An adjuster can access a specialized form to be used on site to assess and document damage, determine the amount the insurance company will pay, and even process a partial or full payment for the customer immediately.

THE EFFECT OF TECHNOLOGY ON CONSUMERS

As consumers gain more access to and experience with technology, their preferences for interacting with businesses often change. Figure 11-5 illustrates consumer views of some common types of technology.

FIGURE 11-5

Consumer Use of Technology

Type of Technology	Currently Use or Would Use if Available
Gas pump payments	79%
ATMs	75%
Debit/credit keypads at checkout	66%
Self-service grocery checkouts	55%
Automated financial/banking services	49%
Automated ticket purchases	48%

In addition, research shows that

- Consumers currently make 33 percent of their in-store payments with cash, 14 percent with a paper check, 19 percent with a credit card, and 23 percent with a debit card. Debit cards are the fastest growing as well as the most widely used form of electronic payment, while the use of cash and checks are declining.

- For online payments, consumers choose credit cards for 55 percent of purchases, debit cards for 25 percent, and checks and money orders for 6 percent.

- When paying monthly bills, checks are still the preferred choice of 49 percent of consumers. Automatic bill pay where payments are transferred from a bank account is used by 21 percent, and 24 percent use a credit or debit card for an online payment.

- Four web sites that combine money-management content with financial services ranked among the 20 most popular consumer sites for business information: AOL Money & Finance, MSN Money, Yahoo! Finance, and CNN Money.

- Internet users who have used an e-commerce or financial management site are more trusting of online banking sites, automatic bill pay sites, credit history sites, and others.

- Internet users who have bought items online are more likely to say they have a lot of trust in online security.

Provide an example of the use of technology in banking, investment, and insurance businesses.

¥£€$ finance around the world

Informal Currency Traders

As you are walking the streets of Addis, Ethiopia, you need to exchange some U.S. dollars for birr. You can go to a bank and get 8.5 birr per dollar or you can do business with a street trader and get 10 per dollar. What should you do?

When traveling, most of your currency exchanges will be done through banks, currency exchange bureaus, and travel agencies. Exchange services often are also available at hotels, airports, railway stations, and small shops. In many countries, another alternative exists—the black market currency exchange, also referred to as informal currency traders.

In some major towns in Ethiopia, there are black market money exchange kiosks. Often, they use a legitimate business enterprise, such as selling food items, as a cover for their currency exchange activities. In general, it is illegal for a person to participate in foreign exchange transactions except in banks, major hotels, and travel agencies.

In Zambia, black market foreign exchange dealers offer better rates for several currencies, including the U.S. dollar, the British pound, the South African rand, and the Botswana pula. It is not uncommon to see individuals offering bundles of Zimbabwean banknotes for sale on the roadside near the Zambia border with Zimbabwe. You might also find freelance currency traders in the marketplaces of larger towns and cities.

Many opportunities exist in Peru to exchange currencies in settings other than banks and other formal financial institutions. Individuals on street corners in large cities change money, mostly involving transactions between U.S. dollars and Peruvian sol.

Informal currency trading is not always possible, especially in countries where strong government controls exist. In Tunisia, you are not allowed to import or export dinars. Transactions outside the formal financial system are forbidden. Violation can result in heavy penalties. A similar situation exists in Morocco, where no currency trading of the dirham outside of banks is allowed. In Thailand, a person must have a license issued by the Bank of Thailand to be authorized to do currency exchange.

Think Critically

1. What are benefits and concerns associated with informal currency traders?
2. Conduct a web search to obtain additional information about currency exchange activities for travelers.

UNDERSTAND CONCEPTS

Determine the best answer for each of the following questions.

1. Which of the following is not one of the decisions businesses make about the adoption of technology?
   a. type
   b. competition
   c. use
   d. timing

2. An ____?____ curve represents the stages for an innovation to be accepted by individuals and businesses.

3. ____?____ are very resistant to change and very conservative in their purchase behavior.
   a. innovators
   b. early adopters
   c. late adopters
   d. laggards

4. **True or False?** Mobile banking through the use of cell phones is the newest form of customer service technology.

5. When making online payments, the most common form of payment used by consumers is
   a. cash
   b. paper check
   c. credit card
   d. debit card

MAKE ACADEMIC CONNECTIONS

6. **Technology** Prepare a computer presentation of at least three slides describing how technology is changing the way consumers purchase and use financial services.

7. **Debate** Form two teams and prepare for a debate on the topic "The major factor businesses should consider when adopting technology is cost-benefit analysis rather than consumer preferences."

8. **Communication** Write a one-page persuasive paper convincing an insurance company it should allow its agents and customers to complete most of their transactions using the Internet.

9. **Math** In 2006 there were 219.4 million wireless subscribers in the U.S., each of whom paid an average monthly bill of $51. Use that information to calculate the total revenues collected in one month and for the full year by the wireless service providers.

10. **Sociology** The amount of Internet use and type of online activities varies based on people's age, gender, income level, and race/ethnicity. Use the Internet to collect information on those differences. Prepare three tables or charts that present your findings. For each chart or table, develop a conclusion about the meaning of the information to financial services businesses.

11.3 Information Privacy and Security

Goals

- Describe important responsibilities of companies in protecting business and customer information
- Identify specific risks to customer information privacy and security

Terms

- data integrity
- information privacy
- information security
- identity theft
- account hijacking
- phishing
- pharming
- pretexting

▌Business Responsibility for Private Information

Data security has become an important issue for both businesses and consumers. As more and more personal information is collected, stored electronically, and shared among employees and between businesses, the risks of lost or stolen data increases. According to the Privacy Rights Clearinghouse, in a recent two-year period companies and institutions of every type and size have collectively mishandled nearly 94 million private records. Examples of the data security problems include the following.

- ■ Personal data on more than 26 million U.S. veterans was missing after the burglary of a computer disk from the home of a computer analyst working for the Department of Veterans Affairs.

- ■ Two laptop computers with personal information on about 31,000 Navy recruiters and their prospective recruits were stolen from a local recruitment office in New Jersey.

- ■ Chase Card Services notified 2.6 million current and former Circuit City credit card holders that computer tapes containing their personal information had been inadvertently tossed in the trash.

- ■ The names, addresses, and credit and debit card numbers of some 243,000 customers of Hotels.com were on a laptop that was stolen from an employee of Ernst & Young who was auditing the company's records.

- ■ ChoicePoint, which provides consumer data services to insurance companies and other businesses, was duped by thieves who set up fraudulent accounts with the company by posing as collection agencies that were looking to run background checks on potential customers. Over 100,000 records were stolen.

- ■ CardSystems' computers were breached when a script was installed on its servers by company insiders or hackers that periodically looked for specific file types. Three files containing information for 263,000

teamwork

You have just received a notice from your credit card company that your account information has been stolen. Discuss with team members how you would feel about the business upon receiving the news and what you believe individual consumers can do to protect their personal information.

accounts were removed from the computers. CardSystems processed credit card data for both MasterCard and Visa.

- Blue Cross and Blue Shield inadvertently printed customer Social Security numbers on mailing labels. Also, a contractor e-mailed a data file containing personal information on employees and vendors to his home computer in violation of company policy.

Each of the companies when informing the public of the lost information claimed that they had specific security procedures in place that were designed to protect the data. In each case either the procedures were violated or security systems were breached. The lost data created problems for the individuals whose personal information was compromised and for the companies responsible for the resulting damages and financial losses.

MAINTAINING DATA INTEGRITY

Businesses require customers to provide personal information in order to establish accounts, approve credit, and offer customer services. Customers submit the information to businesses with the belief that it will be protected and not misused. Very large databases of customer information are regularly used by many employees to complete a variety of business activities. Data may be shared with business partners and vendors that have been contracted to provide specific services. As a part of providing effective and efficient customer service, customers may be given access to the data in order to manage their own accounts and update information. Each part of the information management process involves security risks where data may be lost, stolen, damaged, or altered.

Developing effective information management systems is a significant challenge for today's businesses. An information management system must have the capability to handle large amounts of information while complying

IMAGE SOURCE

Businesses must provide assurance to online consumers that their personal information will be protected and not misused.

with company policies and legal requirements. The system needs to provide access to data in multiple ways from hundreds of locations while maintaining data integrity. **Data integrity** means that information has not been altered or destroyed in an unauthorized manner. The protection includes making sure data can be recovered and restored if the original information is damaged or destroyed as a result of error, equipment failure, or disaster. Both hardware and software must be up to date and reliable. Information management policies and procedures need to address data confidentiality and privacy safeguards. Transactions cannot be completed without proper authorization and procedures to check the accuracy of data when it is entered, analyzed, and used.

LEGAL RESPONSIBILITIES OF FINANCIAL BUSINESSES

Financial businesses are legally required to protect the privacy of consumer information they collect. **Information privacy** is the right of an individual to be secure from unauthorized disclosure of information. The Financial Services Modernization Act of 1999 requires companies to give consumers privacy notices that explain the institutions' information-sharing practices. In turn, consumers have the right to limit some sharing of their information. The law applies to companies that offer financial products or services to individuals such as loans, financial or investment advice, and insurance.

Consumers that are not regular customers of a business are entitled to receive a privacy notice only if the company shares the consumers' information with other companies. Customers must receive a notice every year for as long as the customer relationship lasts. The privacy notice must be a clear statement of the company's privacy practices including what information the company collects, with whom it shares the information, and how it protects or safeguards the information. Consumers have the right to say no to having their information shared with certain third parties. Companies must make it easy for the customer to refuse information sharing. Companies are able to share data with other companies that provide data management services or when legally required to release the information.

Information security is another important issue facing companies as they increase their use of technology. **Information security** is the protection of information from unauthorized accidental or intentional access, modification, destruction, or disclosure while being transmitted or stored. In 2002, The Federal Trade Commission (FTC) issued the Safeguards Rule, which requires financial institutions to have measures in place to keep customer information secure. The Safeguards Rule requires companies to develop a written information security plan that must

- Designate one or more employees to coordinate its information security program
- Realistically identify and assess the risks to customer information in each area of company operation, design and implement a safeguards program, and regularly monitor and test it
- Require service providers to maintain security safeguards and oversee their handling of customer information

Not all privacy rules and procedures result from laws. The Direct Marketing Association (DMA) developed and adopted online privacy guidelines

Fingerprint readers used with personal computers offer an alternative to entering a password. First, you record your fingerprint on the fingerprint reader that is integrated into the computer or keyboard. The first time you are required to enter a password. You touch the reader, type your user id and password, and touch the reader again to confirm your identity. After that, whenever you want access you just touch the fingerprint reader and you're in.

for businesses and organizations to follow. The five guidelines for protecting consumer information privacy are

1. The right of consumers to receive notice of policies
2. The right of consumers to choose not to allow information sharing
3. The right to access and correct personal information
4. The right to expect information to be secured and protected
5. The right to redress if policies are violated

The DMA guidelines have been accepted by many businesses even though the businesses are not legally required to follow them. A recent survey found that most business web sites post a privacy policy, although many of the policies do not include all five of the consumer rights stated in the DMA guidelines.

INFORMATION SECURITY PROCEDURES

The Federal Trade Commission has issued a list of procedures businesses should follow to increase the security of their information systems and to protect business and consumer information. The most important steps they identify are

- Make sure all employees understand the importance of information security
- Review information security policies and procedures with all personnel
- Check backgrounds of employees who handle sensitive information
- Verify employee qualifications for the use of information technology
- Classify sensitive information and restrict access to such information
- Remove access and information when an employee leaves or a customer account is closed
- Employ firewalls to protect personally identifiable information

Conducting employee background checks on new hires is one aspect of information security procedures.

- Use current virus protection and security programs and update them regularly
- Respond to security alerts released by software vendors
- Require users to regularly change passwords and use complex passwords
- Use authentication measures to verify personnel and consumer use of personally identifiable information and monitor access
- Routinely test vulnerabilities to hardware, software, and data entry and storage
- Develop procedures to identify and stop potential security breaches
- Recognize and study all attempted intrusions and unusual data requests
- Have a recovery/backup plan and a secondary site to maintain data in case of a security breach or natural disaster
- Destroy or shred data when it is no longer needed and eradicate data from equipment prior to disposal
- Be careful about sharing networks with business partners and vendors
- Develop decoys and monitor company and vendor data management procedures

checkpoint ✓

What law requires financial businesses to protect the privacy of consumer information they collect?

Consumer Privacy and Security

Today business procedures and technology provide greater and easier access to information than ever before. You can conduct business over the Internet with companies from your local community or around the world at any time of the day. But that access comes at a price. The number of U.S. adult victims of identity fraud was 8.9 million in 2006. The total amount lost by consumers to fraud was $56.6 billion or an average of $6,383 per victim. In addition to the losses suffered, victims reported it took them about 40 hours of personal time to resolve the problems.

Consumers are concerned about the security risks of using computers. The most active users report the greatest concern, even though their concern doesn't reduce their use. According to information reported in the Online Fraud Report, two-thirds of consumers who conduct online financial transactions are extremely or very concerned about giving their personal or financial information to a fake web site and having hackers steal financial information from their computer. In another study, while 87 percent of consumers polled said they were confident they could recognize fraudulent e-mails, when tested, 61 percent were unable to identify which e-mails were legitimate and which were not. The study also presented images of sample web sites and asked consumers whether they could identify whether a site was secure or not. Sixty-seven percent could not identify a secure web site. Seventy-four percent of Americans don't believe using only an ID and password to log in is very safe.

TYPES OF ONLINE SECURITY RISKS

Online fraud steals consumer identities and personal information and hijacks customer financial accounts. **Identity theft** occurs when someone uses your personal information without your permission to commit fraud or other crimes. A great deal of personal data is available online, although most of it is not accessible in one location. By obtaining one or two pieces of personal information such as a Social Security, account, or driver's license number, identity thieves are able to obtain additional information from other sites. **Account hijacking** is obtaining access to another person's financial accounts through fraud and then stealing the funds. Account hijacking is the fastest growing form of consumer financial crime in the U.S., with $2.4 billion stolen from 2 million people in one year. Account hijackers are now attacking investment accounts maintained by online brokerage firms as well as more traditional financial accounts in banks.

Online fraud occurs in several ways. **Phishing** involves creating e-mails with legitimate-looking addresses and web sites designed to look like familiar businesses, financial institutions, and government agencies to deceive Internet users into disclosing their personal information. Pharming is more sophisticated than phishing. **Pharming** attacks a legitimate business' server to redirect traffic from that site to another web site. Consumers who believe they are submitting information to the legitimate business are actually sending it to the illegitimate site. **Pretexting** is the practice of obtaining personal information through illegal contacts with organizations that maintain consumer databases. The criminal poses as a legitimate business or official to secure access to the organization's computer files or to purchase available information from the database. The information is then used for identify theft or other types of fraud.

STEPS TO REDUCE SECURITY RISKS

Consumers express concern about online security risks and many take steps to protect their personal information and reduce the chance they will be a victim of Internet crime. Figure 11-6 shows some methods consumers use to prevent identify theft.

FIGURE 11-6

Consumer Actions to Protect Their Identity

Method	Percentage
Review bank/credit card statements for fraud	88%
Shred/destroy credit card receipts/other financial papers	77%
Check credit reports	64%
Never give out Social Security number	51%

The National Cyber Security Alliance recommends the following actions to protect yourself from Internet crime.

- If you receive a request for personal information through an e-mail, online form, or application, make sure you know who it is from and how the information will be used.

- If you get an unknown e-mail or pop-up message, do not open the message, reply, or click on a link in the message. Delete the e-mail message. Use pop-up blocking software whenever possible.

One method of protecting against identity theft is to shred receipts and statements.

- If you believe there is a legitimate need to supply personal information to a company with whom you have an account or have placed an order, contact that company directly in a way you know to be genuine. You may want to supply the information the first time through the mail or via a telephone call you place to the company.

- Never send personal information via e-mail even if you originate the message. E-mail is not a secure transmission method.

- When making an online purchase, never provide personal information or a credit or debit account number through a company's web site unless you are certain about the company's integrity and you have checked for indicators that the site is secure. Unfortunately, no indicator is foolproof since scammers are able to forge security icons.

- Even though it takes time and is not always easy to do, read company privacy policies posted on their web site. Determine what personal information the company collects, how the information is used, and whether it is shared or sold to other businesses. Find out whether you have the right to review your personal information as well as what security measures the company uses to protect your information. If you don't see a privacy policy or it is difficult to understand, think about finding another business to use.

checkpoint ✓

What is the difference between identity theft and account hijacking?

finance in your life

Using Online Financial Tools

As a consumer you will make many financial decisions in your lifetime. Some financial calculations are quite complex. There are many Internet web sites and online resources that provide financial tools and software to help you with financial planning and decision-making. Here are a few of the most popular and helpful.

Financial Calculators

http://money.aol.com/calculators
A large number of calculators for specific financial tasks including autos, budgeting, college planning, savings, stocks, and retirement.

Financial Planning Tools

http://www.finance.cch.com/tools/tools.asp
Forms and tools to help you organize and manage your personal finances including an insurance policy inventory, self-employment tax planning, life expectancy tables, and a mortgage planning worksheet.

Interest Rate Finder

http://bankrate.com
Searches for and presents the best current rates for various types of loans, investments, credit cards, and insurance policies.

Virtual Spreadsheet

http://spreadsheets.google.com
An online spreadsheet template for budget preparation, financial analysis, and what-if comparisons. Spreadsheets can be created and saved online as well as shared with others for collaborative work. (This site requires that you create a Google account with a password.)

Social Security Benefits Calculator

http://www.ssa.gov/retire2/AnypiaApplet.html
Allows you to calculate your estimated lifetime Social Security benefits based on current wages and benefit rates.

Financial Planning WebQuest

http://www.sbzinak.com/webquest
A comprehensive WebQuest activity where you to set up a budget for the lifestyle you choose. It includes decisions on a house, automobile, other personal expenses, and a job that will provide adequate income to meet your income requirements.

Think Critically

1. Why is it important to keep financial records and make careful financial calculations as a part of financial planning?
2. In addition to the tools listed above, what other types of financial planning do you believe consumers should complete? Use the Internet to see if you can locate online tools and software to help with each type of planning.

11.3 Lesson Assessment

UNDERSTAND CONCEPTS

Determine the best answer for each of the following questions.

1. The total number of private records that have been mishandled by businesses in one year is nearly
   a. 10 million
   b. 50 million
   c. 100 million
   d. 1 billion

2. **True or False?** Businesses cannot require consumers to provide personal information in order to do business with them.

3. Data _____?_____ means that information has not been altered or destroyed in an unauthorized manner.

4. _____?_____ is the protection of information from unauthorized accidental or intentional access, modification, destruction, or disclosure while being transmitted or stored.
   a. information security
   b. information management
   c. hijacking
   d. a privacy policy

5. _____?_____ theft occurs when someone uses your personal information without your permission to commit fraud or other crimes.

MAKE ACADEMIC CONNECTIONS

6. **Technology** Use the Internet to identify a new technology product that is being developed to provide greater security for protecting personal information. Based upon your research about the product, prepare a one-page magazine advertisement promoting the new product to prospective customers.

7. **Critical Thinking** Use the Internet or locate an article in a magazine that describes a situation where a business lost a large amount of personal consumer data. Analyze the reasons it occurred. Make several recommendations to the company of security procedures they should follow to prevent the problem from occurring again.

8. **Communication** Schedule an interview with an information technology specialist from your school or a local large business. You can conduct the interview by telephone or via e-mail if the person agrees. Ask the person about the procedures the organization follows to protect the information it collects and maintains electronically. Based on information in the chapter, write a two-page report analyzing the effectiveness of the organization's security procedures.

9. **Visual Art** Prepare a chart that can be posted in your home or in another location where family or friends use a computer to access the Internet. The chart should provide tips and reminders of how to use the Internet safely.

Summary

11.1 FINANCIAL INFORMATION MANAGEMENT

1. Finance is an information industry. Consumers buy information when they purchase financial products. They expect a great deal of timely and accurate information to help them make purchasing decisions and manage their financial resources.

2. Within financial services companies a specialized financial information system is required. The system allows an organization to obtain needed financial information and use that information in decision-making.

11.2 TECHNOLOGY IN FINANCE

3. When businesses plan for the adoption of technology, they make decisions about the types of technology to adopt, how the technology will be used, and the timeline for implementing the technology. Final decisions are made using a cost/benefit analysis.

4. All parts of the financial services industry are affected by technology. Large customer databases and more product information demand that companies use technology to provide quick access to information and faster services with accuracy and security.

11.3 INFORMATION PRIVACY AND SECURITY

5. As more personal information is collected, stored on computers, and shared, the risks of lost or stolen data increase. Financial businesses are legally required to protect the privacy of the consumer information they collect.

6. Online fraud is used to steal consumer identities and personal information and to hijack customer financial accounts. Online fraud occurs through phishing, pharming, and pretexting.

Develop Your Business Language

Match the terms listed with the definitions. Some terms will not be used.

1. The practice of obtaining personal information under false pretenses
2. The right of an individual to be secure from unauthorized disclosure of information
3. Attacks a legitimate business' server to redirect traffic from that site to another web site
4. Represents the stages for an innovation to be accepted by individuals and businesses
5. Information contained in a computer file prepared for a specific purpose
6. Obtaining access to another person's accounts through fraud and then stealing the funds
7. Alternatives for financial decisions are considered by applying assumptions to the financial data in an electronic spreadsheet
8. The protection of information from unauthorized accidental or intentional access, modification, destruction, or disclosure while being transmitted or stored
9. Compares the total expected costs with the total expected benefits of one or more choices in order to choose the most profitable option

a. account hijacking
b. adoption curve
c. cost-benefit analysis
d. data integrity
e. electronic document
f. electronic information exchange procedure
g. electronic record
h. electronic spreadsheet
i. financial information system
j. identity theft
k. information privacy
l. information security
m. pharming
n. phishing
o. pretexting
p. what-if planning

Review Concepts

10. Which of the following statements is *not* true about electronic documents in business?
    a. most new business records today are either created in electronic form or are duplicated and stored electronically
    b. the cost of electronic transactions is actually just about the same as the cost of paper-based transactions
    c. laws now allow the use of electronic signatures for contracts
    d. all of the statements are true
11. Which category of financial service businesses has been one of the last to accept and implement consumer-oriented technology?
    a. banking
    b. investments
    c. consumer finance
    d. insurance
12. Which of the following is not a legal requirement of financial businesses regarding the use of consumer information they collect?
    a. they must give consumers privacy notices
    b. they cannot share customer data they have collected with business partners
    c. they must develop, monitor, and test information safeguards
    d. all of the above are legal requirements of business

Think Critically

13. What is meant by the statement, "Finance is an information industry"? Why does that make technology an important part of offering products and services to customers? Why does that put pressure on businesses to maintain effective, secure, and up-to-date technology?

14. A car insurance company is considering a new process where customers can notify the company of an accident and track the claims process by cell phone. Explain how they can use the stages of the adoption curve to decide how to implement the new technology.

15. The number of data security problems in the U.S. has actually declined in the past few years, but the total cost to businesses and consumers has increased. Why do you believe both of those changes have happened at the same time?

16. Identify and justify the three most important things consumers can do to protect personal information when they use the Internet.

Business Financial Calculations

17. A company is developing a new smart card technology that allows customers to maintain all financial and investment account information on one card that they can use at ATMs. The company estimates the total number of possible users of the technology to be 58 million. If 3 percent of the consumers are innovators, 10 percent early adopters, 36 percent early majority, 32 percent late majority, and the remainder laggards, how many users are in each of the adoption categories?

18. Consumers currently make 33 percent of in-store payments with cash, 14 percent by check, 19 percent with a credit card, and 23 percent with a debit card. If a store has $589,200 of sales, what was the amount paid using each method? Prepare a pie chart to illustrate the percentage breakdown of payment methods.

19. Research by Celent Communications compared the total amount of fraud in the U.S. with the amount of online fraud. Their findings were:

Year	Total Fraud (in millions)	Online Fraud Rates
2003	$2,373.2	2.5%
2004	$2,664.9	2.4%
2005	$2,745.4	2.2%
2006	$3,028.8	2.0%
2007	$3,212.7	2.0%

Calculate the dollar amount of online fraud for each year and the total cost of fraud and online fraud over the five-year period. Using those totals, what was the average online fraud rate for the entire time?

Analyze Cases

Use the case from the beginning of the chapter, Personal E-Finance, to answer the following questions.

20. Identify the different financial institutions, services, and technologies Marcella used while completing her work on Saturday morning.

21. Marcella's father questioned her when she told him she was using an online bank. He said he would want to be able to walk into a bank and talk to a real person. He also liked the security his bank provided for his deposits. How should Marcella respond to her father's concerns?

22. Describe some other financial activities Marcella probably completes and how technology could help her complete those activities.

23. Discuss the security risks Marcella faced during her work session. What do you believe the businesses Marcella used should do to make sure her identity and finances are protected? What security precautions would you recommend to Marcella for her activities?

Portfolio Activity

COLLECT an example of hardware, software, and methods businesses and consumers can use to protect privacy and increase security. The example could be an ad, written article, product, or other type of example.

CREATE a visual to illustrate a business environment or an individual's computer work area demonstrating the use of security procedures. Use photos, other pictures, or drawings to show the security applications.

CONNECT your visual to other items already in your class portfolio or relate it to an important concept you have learned in another class. Make the connection by preparing a one-minute presentation on how poor security procedures can harm both individuals and businesses.

Stock Market Activity

Technology continually affects business operations. The use of computerized information, production, and distribution systems can increase an organization's efficiency. Effective technology management is vital to compete successfully in most industries.

Use Internet and library resources to research the company you have been studying (or select a different company).

1. List examples of the use of technology by this company. Describe situations in which the organization's operations and information systems have been enhanced with the use of computers.

2. Obtain information on potential technology that may affect this type of company in the future.

3. Identify potential influences of technology on the recent financial performance and stock value of the company.

Planning a Career in Information Security

As people increase their computer use and connect to the Internet with a number of technologies, they increase their awareness of the risks they face in those activities. Businesses also are focused on security as they expand their use of information technology and work to deliver more services to more customers using the Internet. Information security specialists plan, coordinate, and implement the organization's plans to protect business and customer hardware, software, and data. They develop security plans, educate employees and customers about computer security, develop and maintain security software, monitor computer networks for security breaches, and respond to cyber attacks, security breaches, and a wide variety of information integrity issues.

Employment Outlook

- The number of jobs and types of jobs in information security are growing rapidly as technology applications are improved and expanded to more and more employees and customers.
- Security professionals work as a part of information technology staffs in all types of businesses including finance, engineering, healthcare, education, government, and law enforcement.

Job Titles

- Security risk analyst
- Manager of information security
- Data recovery specialist
- Software security developer
- Technology access manager
- Security architect

Needed Skills

- Minimum of a bachelor's degree in computer science, mathematics, or business information systems
- Specialized preparation in computer programming, software development, and network management
- Excellent analytical and problem-solving skills, ability to work as a team member and leader, effective written and oral communications skills with technical and non-technical audiences

What's It Like to Work as an Information Security Specialist?

Jessica is an entry-level security specialist working in Internet security for her company. She spends well over half of her time most days monitoring the company's web site and evaluating use by employees, customers, and others. She looks for problems that might slow or bring down the web site and unusual activity that might present a security risk. She also is responsible for reviewing and responding to technical questions, complaints, and problems that are submitted via e-mail. The problems range from the amount and type of spam received by customers to forms and procedures that don't work and problems with account access and passwords. Once a week she participates in a team meeting to review the latest security threats, hardware and software issues, and plans for new technology.

What about you? What appeals to you about the career area of information security? What types of jobs in this career area do you currently find most interesting?

GRAPHIC DESIGN PROMOTION EVENT

The Graphic Design Promotion Event requires participants to demonstrate the ability to create a computer-aided graphic design for promotional purposes.

You must produce a three-fold professional brochure. The theme of your Graphic Design Promotion (brochure) is Identity Theft—Protecting Yourself from Being the Next Statistic. Your Graphic Design Promotion must provide the consumer with strategies to protect financial security and privacy.

Dimensions of your original work must be 8 ½" by 11" or less. The product may be black and white or color and printed on white or colored paper. The graphic design should not be professionally or commercially produced. All graphics must be computer generated. Public domain and contestant-prepared graphics may be used for this project. No copyrighted items may be used. No photographs, text, registered trademarks, or names may be used without permission. All state and federal copyright laws must be respected. Although a work may be freely accessible on the Internet and contain no statement of copyright, copyright law provides that such works are protected.

Each participant will have no more than ten (10) minutes for the judges' question and answer session. The participant will be asked questions about how the graphic was developed and produced.

Performance Indicators Evaluated

- Use principles of design, layout, and typography in graphic design.
- Demonstrate knowledge of graphic design and rules for layout.
- Demonstrate effective use of color, lines, text, graphics, shapes, etc.
- Generate a promotional flyer for marketing purposes.
- Use appropriate artwork and design techniques for a given theme.
- Apply technical skills to manipulate graphics, artwork, and images.

Go to the BPA web site for more detailed information.

Think Critically

1. Why is a brochure about protecting against identity theft a good idea?
2. What is a good source for this topic?
3. Why is it important to use current identity theft statistics in the brochure?
4. Where is a good place to distribute identity theft brochures for consumers?

www.bpa.org

chapter 12

International Finance

12.1 INTERNATIONAL BUSINESS AND TRADE

12.2 ECONOMIC DEVELOPMENT AND MONETARY SYSTEMS

12.3 INTERNATIONAL FINANCIAL MARKETS

12.4 GLOBAL PAYMENTS AND FINANCIAL RISK

Point Your [Browser]
www.thomsonedu.com/school/busfinance

Case STUDY

Global Banking Activities of HSBC

With almost 10,000 offices in nearly 80 countries, HSBC Holdings is the largest bank in the world. HSBC is named after its founding bank— Hong Kong and Shanghai Banking Corporation, created in 1865 to finance the growing trade between China and Europe. Today, with headquarters in London, HSBC has a strong financial presence in Europe, Asia, the Americas, the Middle East, and Africa.

HSBC is listed on the London, Hong Kong, New York, Paris, and Bermuda stock exchanges. Shares of the company are owned by about 200,000 stockholders in 100 countries. In the United States, shares traded on the New York Stock Exchange are in the form of American Depository Receipts (ADRs). The U.S. operations of HSBC are a subsidiary of HSBC Holdings, which operates more than 400 branch offices. This network allows HSBC Bank USA to provide customers with the full array of personal and commercial banking services.

Recently, HSBC obtained Household International, a U.S. company. This consumer lending division serves customers in the United States, the United Kingdom, Canada, Ireland, the Czech Republic, and Hungary. The selling focus of HSBC Finance involves home mortgages, automobile loans, credit cards, and other types of personal loans.

HSBC Canada, previously called the Hong Kong Bank of Canada, is the Canadian subsidiary for HSBC. In recent years, HSBC Canada was the seventh largest bank in Canada. It was also the largest foreign-owned bank in the country.

Through the use of its computer technology network, HBSC is able to provide a wide variety of online services. This financial service e-commerce capacity allows the company to provide personal, commercial, and investment banking services throughout the world. In addition to its core banking services, HBSC also offers credit cards, investment portfolio management, insurance, and leasing.

Think Critically

1. How might HSBC be different from U.S. banks?
2. Locate the web site of HSBC to obtain current information on the company. Prepare a brief summary of recent activities.

Goals
- Describe common international business activities.
- Identify methods for encouraging and measuring foreign trade.

Terms
- absolute advantage
- comparative advantage
- imports
- exports
- quota
- tariff
- embargo
- foreign debt
- balance of trade
- balance of payments

■Foreign Trade Activities

Most business activities and financial transactions occur within a country's own borders. The making, buying, selling, and financing of goods and services within a country is called *domestic business*. In contrast, *international business* refers to business and financial activities necessary for creating, shipping, and selling goods and services across national borders. International business is often referred to as *foreign* or *international trade*.

The countries of the world are interdependent and so are their economies. The United States conducts trade with over 180 countries. Consumers have come to expect goods and services from around the world.

© GETTY IMAGES/PHOTODISC

The natural resources of a country may give it an absolute advantage in foreign trade.

ABSOLUTE ADVANTAGE

Buying and selling among companies in different countries is based on two economic principles. An absolute advantage exists when a country can produce a good or service at a lower cost than other countries. This situation may result from the natural resources or raw materials of a country. For example, some South American countries have an absolute advantage in coffee production; Canada, in lumber sales; and Saudi Arabia, in oil production.

COMPARATIVE ADVANTAGE

A country may have an absolute advantage in more than one area. If so, it must decide how to maximize economic wealth. A country, for example, may be able to produce both computers and clothing better than other countries. The world market for computers, however, might be stronger. The country would better serve its own interests by producing computers and buying clothing from other countries. This situation, in which a country specializes in the production of a good or service at which it is relatively more efficient, is called comparative advantage.

IMPORTING

Goods and services bought from other countries are called imports. In the United States, imports account for the total supply of bananas, coffee, cocoa, spices, tea, silk, and crude rubber. In order to manufacture certain goods, U.S. companies must import tin, chrome, manganese, nickel, copper, zinc, and several other metals. Without foreign trade, many things you buy would cost more or would not be available at all.

EXPORTING

The goods and services sold to other countries are called exports. Just as imports benefit you, exports benefit consumers in other countries. Workers throughout the world use factory and farm machinery made in the United States. They eat food made from U.S. agricultural products and use chemicals, fertilizers, medicines, and plastics. Exports by U.S. companies create about one of every six jobs in this country.

TRADE BARRIERS

Government actions can create *trade barriers,* which are restrictions to reduce free trade. These political actions are known as *formal* trade barriers. In contrast, the culture, traditions, and religion of a country can create *informal* trade barriers. Informal barriers are not based on formal government actions but they do restrict trade. Three common formal trade barriers are quotas, tariffs, and embargoes.

Quotas One action by governments to regulate international trade sets a limit on the quantity of a product that may be imported or exported in a given period of time. This limit is referred to as a quota. Quotas may be set for many reasons. Countries that export oil may put quotas on crude oil so that the supply will remain low and prices will stay at a certain level. Quotas may also be imposed by one country on imports from another to express disapproval of the policies or social behavior of that country. A quota can be set to protect an industry from too much foreign competition.

Tariffs Another device that governments use to regulate international trade is the tariff. A **tariff**, also referred to as an *import duty,* is a tax that a government places on certain imported products. Suppose you want to buy an English bicycle. The producer charges $140, but our government collects a 20 percent tariff ($28) on the bicycle when it is imported. You will have to pay $168 plus shipping charges for the bike. The increased price may cause you to decide to buy a U.S.-made bike at a lower price.

Embargoes If a government wishes to do so, it can stop the export or import of a product completely. This action is called an **embargo.** Governments may impose embargoes for many reasons. They may wish to protect their own industries from international competition to a greater degree than either the quota or the tariff will accomplish. The government may wish to protect sensitive products, particularly those important to national security. Like a quota, an embargo also may be imposed to express disapproval of the actions or policies of another country.

checkpoint ✓

What are common actions by government to discourage global trade?

■ Encouraging and Measuring Trade

Expansion of foreign trade is an ongoing goal of most countries. Governments attempt to create jobs and enhance economic development through exporting.

ACTIONS TO ENCOURAGE TRADE

Specific government actions can promote international business activities. Common efforts to encourage international trade include free-trade zones, free-trade agreements, common markets, and regional trade organizations.

Free-Trade Zones To promote international business, governments often create free-trade zones in their countries. A *free-trade zone* is a designated area, usually around a seaport or airport, where products can be imported duty-free and then stored, assembled, and/or used in manufacturing. Only when the product leaves the zone does the importer pay any taxes.

Free-Trade Agreements A growing trend is for countries to establish *free-trade agreements* with other nations. With this arrangement, member countries agree to eliminate duties and trade barriers on products traded among them. Trade is then increased between members. For example, the United States, Canada, and Mexico created the North American Free Trade Agreement (NAFTA) in 1993. This pact eliminates taxes on goods traded among the three countries and eases the movement of goods. NAFTA is designed to enlarge the markets and economic bases of the countries involved. The Central American Free Trade Agreement (CAFTA), which includes the Dominican Republic, has a similar purpose.

To encourage trade, countries may engage in free-trade agreements.

A free-trade agreement may be between two or more countries. The United States has agreements with many individual nations, including Australia, Bahrain, Chile, Israel, Jordan, Malaysia, Panama, and Peru.

Common Markets Countries may join together in a common market to promote more trade among them. In a *common market,* also called an *economic community,* members eliminate tariffs and other trade barriers, allow companies to invest freely in each member's country, and allow workers to move freely across borders. Common market members also have a common external duty on products being imported from non-member countries. Examples of common markets include the European Union (EU), the Latin American Integration Association (LAIA), and Mercosur, the Southern Common Market, whose original members were Argentina, Brazil, Paraguay, and Uruguay. In recent years, other countries have joined as full or associate members. The goals are to expand trade among member nations and promote regional economic integration.

Regional Trade Organizations In most regions of the world, countries unite to promote economic development and trade. Examples of these efforts include the following:

- The Association of Southeast Asian Nations (ASEAN) promotes political and economic cooperation among its 11 member countries. The goals of ASEAN include acceleration of economic growth, social progress, and cultural development in the region.

- The Caribbean Community and Common Market (CARICOM) was established to provide for free movement of goods, labor, and capital among the member countries. CARICOM attempts to improve living and work standards and coordinate economic development and trade.

- Economic Community of West African States (ECOWAS) was organized to promote development among the 15 member countries. Economic issues (agriculture, trade, and infrastructure) along with social concerns (children, education, and public health) are the foundation of ECOWAS activities.

teamwork

In your team, describe three specific actions a country might take to encourage international trade with nations in other regions of the world.

Money moves between countries through tourism.

TRADE MEASUREMENTS

Like households, nations are concerned about balancing income with expenditures. When people buy more than their income allows, they go into debt. In the same way, when the businesses in a country import more than they export, they owe money to others. **Foreign debt** is the amount a country owes to other countries.

Balance of Trade The difference between a country's total exports and total imports is called the **balance of trade.** Countries like to have a favorable balance of trade. That happens when they export more than they import.

When a country exports (sells) more than it imports (buys), it has a *trade surplus,* and its trade position is said to be *favorable.* But, if it imports more than it exports, it has a *trade deficit* and its trade position is *unfavorable.* A country can have a trade surplus with one country and a trade deficit with another. Overall, a country tries to keep its international trade in balance. After a long history of a favorable balance of trade, the United States has had a trade deficit in recent years. Figure 12-1 shows the U.S. trade balance with various nations.

FIGURE 12-1

United States Trade Balances

Goods Exported (in billions)	Country	Goods Imported (in billions)	U.S. Trade Balance
904.3	All countries	1,671.4	−767.1
211.9	Canada	290.4	−78.5
120.4	Mexico	170.1	−49.7
55.5	Japan	138.0	−82.5
26.5	Netherlands	14.9	+11.6
15.8	Australia	7.3	+8.5
15.4	Brazil	24.4	−9.0
22.1	Taiwan	34.8	−21.7
41.9	China	243.5	−201.6
186.4	European Union	308.8	−122.4

Balance of Payments In addition to exporting and importing goods and services, other financial exchanges occur among nations. Money goes from one country to another through investments and tourism. For example, a citizen of one country might invest in a corporation in another country. A business may invest in a factory in another country. Or, a government might give financial or military aid to another nation. When tourists travel, they contribute to the flow of money from one country to another.

The difference between the amount of money that comes into a country and the amount that goes out is called the **balance of payments**. A country's balance of payments can either be positive or negative. A *positive* or *favorable* balance of payments occurs when a nation receives more money in a year than it pays out. A *negative* balance of payments is *unfavorable*, which is the result of a country sending out more money than it brings in.

checkpoint ✓

How does balance of trade differ from balance of payments?

technology topics

Online Foreign Trade Resources

The U.S. Department of Commerce and other federal government agencies provide extensive assistance to companies involved in international trade and global financial transactions. Some of the most valuable include

- The U.S. Government's Export Portal, also referred to as export.gov
- The USA Trade Center
- The International Trade Administration, also known as trade.gov
- The Small Business Administration Office of International Trade
- The Foreign Agricultural Service (FAS) of the U.S. Department of Agriculture (USDA)

Web sites that have a specific emphasis on financing global business activities include

- The Export-Import Bank of the United States
- The Overseas Private Investment Corporation
- The Foreign Credit Insurance Association

Think Critically

1. Why does the U.S. government provide assistance to companies involved in international trade?
2. Locate a web site that provides information for companies involved with exporting or other international business activities. Prepare a summary of the content of this web site.

12.1 Lesson Assessment

UNDERSTAND CONCEPTS

Determine the best answer for each of the following questions.

1. A limit on the quantity of a product that may be imported or exported is
   a. an absolute advantage
   b. a comparative advantage
   c. a quota
   d. a tariff

2. **True or False?** A country may have an absolute advantage because of its natural resources.

3. An action to encourage trade is
   a. a quota
   b. an economic community
   c. a tariff
   d. an embargo

4. **True or False?** A favorable balance of trade results from a country importing more than it exports.

5. A commonly used trade barrier is
   a. an economic community
   b. a tariff
   c. a free-trade zone
   d. a free-trade agreement

MAKE ACADEMIC CONNECTIONS

6. **International Studies** Check the labels of various clothing items you own to determine the countries of origin. Make a list of the nations. Prepare a short essay on why certain products may be manufactured in certain countries.

7. **Visual Art** Use photos and other visuals to create a poster or computer presentation to communicate various trade barriers and various actions countries take to encourage international trade.

8. **Technology** Explain the benefits of the Internet and other technology for expanded and improved international trade and global financial transactions.

9. **Geography** Select a common market or a regional trade organization discussed in this lesson. Conduct research to determine the countries involved in this organization. Prepare a map showing the member nations. Create a brief oral summary of the organization's activities.

Goals
- Describe factors that affect economic development.
- Explain how countries influence foreign exchange values.

Terms
- infrastructure
- industrialized country
- less-developed country (LDC)
- developing country
- exchange controls

◼Economic Development

Every country and every individual continually makes decisions about the use of time, money, and energy. A nation's economic situation is a significant element in its international business and global financial activities.

ECONOMIC DEVELOPMENT FACTORS

In some countries, people travel to work on a high-speed bullet train to manage a computer network in a high-rise building. In other countries, people go by oxcart to a grass hut to operate a hand loom to make cloth for family members and people in their village. These differences in living and work environments reflect the *level of economic development*. The main influences on a country's level of economic development are

- ◼ **Literacy Level** Countries with better education systems usually have more productive facilities.

- ◼ **Technology** Automated production, distribution, and communications systems allow for the efficient creation and delivery of goods, services, and ideas.

- ◼ **Agricultural Dependency** An economy with an emphasis on agriculture will not likely have manufacturing to provide a high quantity and quality of products.

  Another element that supports economic development is infrastructure, which is the transportation, communication, and utility systems of a nation. Countries with efficient transportation systems and modern telecommunications are better prepared for global business activities than nations with a weak infrastructure.

TYPES OF INFRASTRUCTURE

The infrastructure of a country provides the foundation for economic development and efficient business activities. Going beyond the basic facilities needed for financial transactions, infrastructure may be viewed from several perspectives.

1. **Physical Infrastructure** Refers to the transportation, communication, and utility systems that facilitate business activities, including computer systems and telecommunications facilities that are necessary for global business success.

2. **Natural Infrastructure** Involves climate, waterways, farmland, and other natural resources that contribute to a nation's economic development. These natural resources can provide an advantage for countries when creating and distributing goods and services.

3. **Social Infrastructure** Family relationships, labor unions, religious influences, schools, and other social organizations often must be considered when interacting with customers, suppliers, investors, and employees.

4. **Financial Infrastructure** This element involves the availability and efficiency of a country's banks, financial markets, and other financial institutions.

5. **Managerial or Entrepreneurial Infrastructure** The ability of a nation's people to organize and implement business activities. For example, when McDonald's first opened a restaurant in Russia, company representatives worked with local businesspeople to teach managerial skills. They taught how to obtain, coordinate, and use the food products, workers, buildings, and equipment necessary to operate a fast-food restaurant.

LEVELS OF ECONOMIC DEVELOPMENT

The degree to which a country provides food, housing, health care, and other consumer needs is commonly viewed in three categories.

Industrialized Countries Nations with the greatest economic power have the ability to provide extensive goods and services. An industrialized country is a country with strong business activity that is usually the result of advanced technology and a highly educated population. Such countries have attained a high level of industrialization and an extensive network of financial institutions. Population is centered in large cities and suburbs rather than in rural areas. Industrialized countries are actively involved in foreign trade. Nations commonly described as industrialized include Canada, England, France, Germany, Italy, Japan, and the United States.

Less-Developed Countries Many countries of the world have a very low standard of living. A less-developed country (LDC) is a country with little economic wealth and an emphasis on agriculture or mining. About four billion people living in LDCs have an income of $2 or less per day. As a result, citizens often cannot afford adequate housing, food, and health care. This situation results in a high death rate among newborns, a shorter life expectancy than in other countries, and potential for political instability. Examples of LDCs include Afghanistan, Bangladesh, Bolivia, Chad, Ethiopia, Kenya, Liberia, Nepal, Nigeria, Pakistan, and Somalia. Future economic development for less-developed countries presents a challenge for all nations.

teamwork

The economies in less-developed countries often lack infrastructure and strong educational systems. In your team, create a list of actions that could improve economic conditions in these countries.

Developing Countries Between the extremes of economic development are the **developing countries**, attempting to evolve from less developed to industrialized. These nations are characterized by improving educational systems, increasing technology, and expanding industries. These factors result in an increasing national income. Examples of developing countries include Brazil, Bulgaria, Czech Republic, India, Mexico, and Thailand.

checkpoint ✓

What factors affect a country's level of economic development?

International Currency

A major challenge faced by businesses involved in international trade is the varied currency systems in use around the world. Nations have their own banking systems and their own kinds of money. For instance, Russia uses the ruble; the European Union uses the euro; Brazil, the real; India, the rupee; and Saudi Arabia, the riyal.

The value of a country's currency is important for international business success. If trading partners do not accept certain currency, the country may have to make payment in another currency. A currency that is not easy to exchange for other currencies is called *soft currency*. While the monetary unit serves as a medium of exchange in the home country, the currency has limited value in the world marketplace.

In contrast, monetary units such the Japanese yen, the euro, the Swiss franc, and the U.S. dollar are accepted for most global financial transactions. These monetary units are examples of *hard currency*, which refers to monetary units that are freely converted into other currencies.

Industrialized countries have the physical infrastructure to support business activities.

© GETTY IMAGES/PHOTODISC

FOREIGN EXCHANGE RATES

The process of exchanging one currency for another occurs each day. The value of a currency in one country compared with the value of a currency in another is called the *exchange rate*. The value of currency, like most things, is affected by supply and demand. The approximate values of various currencies on a recent date in relation to the U.S. dollar (USD) are shown in Figure 12-2.

FIGURE 12-2

Recent Exchange Rates for Selected Countries

Country	Currency	Symbol	Code	Value in USD	Units per USD
United Kingdom	pound	£	GBP	$1.89	0.53 pounds
Canada	dollar	$	CAD	0.90	1.11 Canadian dollars
European Union	euro	€	RUR	1.27	0.78 euro
India	rupee	Rs	INR	0.0215	46.5 rupees
Japan	yen	¥	JPY	0.0086	116.34 yen
Mexico	peso	Mex$	MXN	0.09	10.9 pesos
Saudi Arabia	riyal	SRIs	SAR	0.267	3.75 riyals
South Africa	rand	R	ZAR	0.14	7.15 rand
Brazil	real	R$	BRL	0.466	2.14 reals
Venezuela	bolivar	Bs	VEB	0.00047	2,146 bolivares
China	yuan	Y	CNY	0.13	7.98 yuan

When a U.S. company sells products to a Canadian firm, for example, the U.S. firm must convert the Canadian dollars received in payment into U.S. dollars. If each Canadian dollar is worth 90 cents in the United States, what would the U.S. firm charge if goods worth approximately $10,000 in the United States were sold to a Canadian firm? The U.S. firm would have to charge about $11,111 in Canadian dollars (10,000 ÷ 0.90 = 11,111). That makes a U.S. dollar worth about $1.11 in Canadian currency.

FACTORS AFFECTING CURRENCY VALUES

Currency exchange rates among countries are affected by three main factors: the country's balance of payments, economic conditions, and political stability.

Balance of Payments When a country has a favorable balance of payments, the value of its currency is usually constant or rising. Increased demand for both the nation's products and its currency are the basis of this situation. In contrast, when a nation has an unfavorable balance of payments, its currency usually declines in value due to lower demand for the monetary unit.

Economic Conditions When consumer prices increase and the buying power of the country's money declines, its currency will not be as attractive. Inflation reduces the buying power of a currency. High inflation in Brazil, for example, would reduce the demand for the real.

Foreign exchange controls help maintain the value of a country's currency.

Interest rates, the cost of using someone else's money, also affect the value of a country's currency. Higher interest rates mean more expensive products and lower demand among consumers. This, in turn, reduces the demand for a nation's currency, causing a decline in its value.

Political Stability Companies and individuals want to avoid risk when doing business in different nations. If a government changes unexpectedly to create an unfriendly business environment, a company may lose control of a factory or money on deposit in local banks.

Political instability may also occur when new laws and regulations are enacted. These rules may not allow foreign businesses to operate as freely. Uncertainty in a country reduces the confidence businesspeople have in its currency.

FOREIGN EXCHANGE CONTROLS

In an effort to maintain the value of its currency, a nation may place limits on the flow of money out of the country. **Exchange controls** are government restrictions to regulate the amount and value of a nation's currency. These controls can be in the form of either fixed exchange rates or limits on the amount and cost of currency. One common exchange control limits the amount of local currency a person can take out of a country. For example, in past years, Australia, Bangladesh, France, Italy, Japan, Portugal, South Africa, Spain, and Sweden have all placed some restrictions on exporting local currency.

checkpoint ✔

What factors affect the value of a country's currency?

UNDERSTAND CONCEPTS

Determine the best answer for each of the following questions.

1. A less-developed country is characterized by
   a. a strong infrastructure
   b. a low literacy level
   c. modern technology
   d. a well-educated population

2. The value of a country's currency would likely decline as a result of
   a. inflation
   b. a favorable balance of trade
   c. expanded exports
   d. decreased foreign debt

3. **True or False?** Infrastructure commonly refers to a nation's trade activities with other countries.

4. **True or False?** Most currencies of the world have a value that stays fairly constant from day to day.

MAKE ACADEMIC CONNECTIONS

5. **Science** Describe how new scientific discoveries might improve the economic development of a country.

6. **Economics** Research the economies of a less-developed or developing country. Prepare a short report that communicates possible actions that might be taken to improve economic conditions in these countries. Also, point out how all nations benefit when economic conditions improve in less-developed countries.

7. **Communication** Talk to a person who has lived in or visited another country. Obtain information about experiences with obtaining and using local currency.

8. **Visual Art** Conduct an Internet search for pictures of currency from various countries. What types of images appear on these banknotes? What is the significance of the images?

12.3 International Financial Markets

Global Security Markets

International companies use stocks and bonds to finance global business activities. Stock and bond exchanges around the world create a network for issuing, buying, and selling equity and debt securities.

INTERNATIONAL STOCK EXCHANGES

While the New York Stock Exchange is the largest in the world, other major stock exchanges exist, including Euronext (Paris, Amsterdam, and Brussels), Bombay, Copenhagen, Dusseldorf, Istanbul, Milan, Rio de Janeiro, Seoul, Stockholm, Taiwan, Tel Aviv, Toronto, and Zurich.

Every hour of the day, investors buy and sell stocks. On the trading floor of the stock exchange and through computer systems, representatives of buyers and sellers interact to determine the prices of shares of stock.

Completely computerized stock exchanges, without trading floor representatives, are becoming common. These high-speed, low-cost automated systems are used by most major stock exchanges. Some of the world's largest screen-based systems for buying and selling global stocks are based in Europe. Computerized stock trading allows a broker in London to buy and sell stocks of multinational companies listed on stock exchanges in Istanbul, Rio de Janeiro, or Taiwan. The system allows investors to complete buy and sell orders anytime, day or night.

World Federation of Exchanges This private organization exists to coordinate the activities of the hundreds of financial markets and stock exchanges around the world. The World Federation of Exchanges attempts to communicate among the exchanges to enhance the efficiency of these financial markets. This group also attempts to meet the needs of capital markets in emerging economies.

Global Stock Indexes Investors use a stock index as an indication of market changes and trends. A global stock index is based on a group of stocks selected to reflect the overall progress of all stocks being represented. More than 50 stock indexes exist to communicate market trends, including the Toronto S&P, London FTSE, Tokyo Nikkei, DJ Pacific Pan-Asia, Milan S&P, Oslo All-Share, Kuala Lumpur Composite, and the Sao Paulo BOVESPA.

teamwork

In your team, create a list of factors that might affect the value of bonds in different countries of the world.

American Depository Receipt Citizens of the United States are restricted from buying stocks in foreign companies. To allow U.S. investors to buy shares in corporations based in other countries, an **American depository receipt (ADR)** may be issued. The value of this document, which originates with a U.S. bank, is based on the value of the shares of the foreign stock. ADRs are traded on U.S. exchanges and are valued in U.S. dollars. With this procedure, the foreign stock shares are held in trust by the bank. While ADRs reduce transaction costs for investors, currency rate and economic risks still exist. The dividends and capital gains earned on the shares are converted to U.S. dollars, which are then distributed to investors.

International Mutual Funds International mutual funds exist to attract investors who wish to buy stock in hundreds of companies around the world. These investments are managed by a company that combines invested money from many people to purchase a portfolio of stocks.

A major benefit of these mutual funds is *diversification*. By pooling money from many investors, a mutual fund manager is able to invest in many types of stocks and bonds, spreading out the risk for the investors.

Global mutual funds eliminate the high brokerage commissions and high currency conversion fees that an individual investor might encounter. International funds reduce the risk that exchange rate changes may wipe out profits even when stocks increase in value.

Other types of international mutual funds include regional funds. For example, a Latin America fund invests in companies with long-term growth in Central and South America. A Pacific fund would invest in companies in that region.

THE OVER-THE-COUNTER MARKET

Large companies that meet financial requirements of a stock exchange and are traded regularly are called *listed stocks*. In contrast, the *over-the-counter (OTC) market* is a network of stockbrokers who buy and sell stocks not listed on a stock exchange.

The National Association of Securities Dealers Automated Quotations (NASDAQ) is the major computerized trading system for OTC stocks in the U.S. The Unlisted Securities Market is the over-the-counter market for companies in England. In Germany, the Neuer Markt trades stocks of emerging companies in the European Union.

GLOBAL BOND MARKETS

Debt instruments such as bonds and notes are used by most companies, governments, and other organizations. These securities are bought and sold through financial markets in most major cities of the world.

International Bonds Issuing bonds provides debt financing for companies and governments. The issue value of a corporate bond will vary based on the nation. Examples of this issue value, also called the *face value* or *maturity value,* include the following:

People often confuse the euro and Euro-dollar. The euro is the official currency of the European Union. A Eurodollar is a U.S. dollar on deposit in a bank outside the United States. It was originally called the Eurodollar since most of the deposits were in Europe. Today, the U.S. dollar is used throughout the world.

Country	Bond Issue Amount
United States	$1,000 (dollar)
United Kingdom	£100 (pound sterling)
Brazil	R$1,000 (real)
South Africa	100 R (rand)

The global bond market faces various problems, especially in emerging economies where economic and political uncertainty can affect interest rates and default potential. International financial analysts mention the following concerns regarding bonds issued in developing economies in an attempt to drive economic development.

■ Projected returns from bonds can face strong uncertainty when issued by companies with no past record of financial success.

■ Risk levels can quickly increase due to economic difficulties, political instability, and cultural differences.

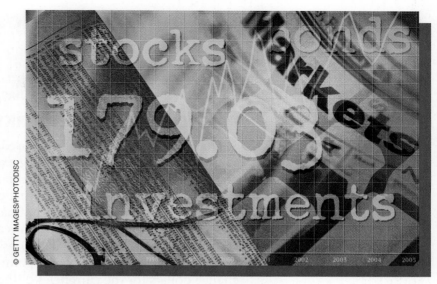

Bonds are sold by companies and governments around the world to finance debt.

■ Local rating agencies may not have analysis techniques and reporting standards comparable to industrialized countries.

■ The buy or sell decisions of institutional investors, such as mutual funds and insurance companies, can affect the bond market values for small, vulnerable companies.

Inflation-Linked Bonds A debt security that can provide protection against economic uncertainty is the *inflation-linked bond*. This bond increases in value based on the rate of inflation. Examples of inflation-linked bonds are the Canadian real return bond (RRB) and the British inflation-linked gilt (ILG). With these securities, the loan principal of the bond increases with the inflation rate. Investors receive interest payments based on the inflated principal. At maturity, the repaid amount is the inflated principal.

International Asset-Backed Securities Market The *asset-backed security* is a specialized type of global debt instrument. These bonds and notes are secured by various company assets. Common items used as collateral include loan receivables, accounts receivable, and other types of receivables. These asset-backed securities have short maturities and involve steady, definite cash flows, such as payments from loans or leases.

The international asset-backed securities market has grown extensively in recent years, with continued growth expected. Most regions of the world will expand use of this financial security. In Asia, for example, some asset-backed securities are supported by the Asian Development Bank and others are funded by the Japanese government.

checkpoint ✓

What are the benefits of international mutual funds for investors?

■ Other International Financial Markets

In addition to stock and bond markets, other global financial markets are in operation, including foreign exchange, futures, and options markets.

FOREIGN EXCHANGE MARKET

The value of a country's currency used to be set by its government. More recently, most countries use **floating exchange rates**, in which currency values change based on supply and demand. These values and the process of exchanging one currency for another occur in the *foreign exchange market,* which consists of banks and other financial institutions that buy and sell different currencies. Most large banks are part of the foreign exchange market and may provide currency services for businesses and consumers.

Travelers and businesspeople going outside of the United States can exchange dollars for the currencies of the countries they will visit. This exchange can be done at large banks, online, or at travel agencies that specialize in foreign currency services. When in another country, travelers can go to a currency exchange window at the airport, train station, or local bank and buy local currency. How much of the local currency they will get depends on the value of the two currencies at that time. Rates are posted at exchange windows, and there is a charge for exchanging currency.

FUTURES MARKET

If a company knows it will need a certain currency in the future, it can enter into an agreement to buy that monetary unit later at a price agreed upon today. **Currency futures** are contracts to purchase for a fee a foreign currency at today's rate with payment and delivery at a later date. For example, an Australian company needs 20 million yen in two months to pay for imports from a Japanese company. By buying a currency future contract, the importer will get the yen in two months at today's rate. This protects the Australian importer from having to buy the currency later at a higher price.

Farmers want to get a fair price for their grain. Food companies want to avoid paying high prices for grain that will be used to make breakfast cereals. By agreeing to a price now for delivery in the future (usually three or six months from now), a farmer is protected against receiving a lower price, while the cereal company is protected against higher costs.

The *futures market* allows investors to buy or sell contracts on the future prices of commodities, metals, and financial instruments. Futures markets involve contracts on corn, oats, soybeans, wheat, cocoa, sugar, oil, gold, silver, treasury bonds, and currencies—yen, euro, and Eurodollars.

OPTIONS MARKET

An *option* is the right to buy or sell a security or commodity at a specific price within a limited time period, usually three, six, or nine months. This contact can take one of two forms. A *call option* is the right to buy the item. In contrast, a *put option* is the right to sell some type of investment.

When buying an option, you are *not* buying the investment (stock or commodity). You are only purchasing the *right* to buy or sell the investment in the future at a certain price. For example, a call option to buy a certain stock might allow the purchase of that stock at $40. This gives the investor the opportunity to buy those shares, before a certain date, for $40.

This option would be used if the current market value of that stock is more than $40. However, if the stock sells for less than the option price, the investor will not exercise the option. The investor is not required to exercise an option. In general, the buyer of a call option hopes the price of the stock will rise. In contrast, an investor who buys a put option is expecting the market price to decline so the stock can be sold later at a higher price.

Options markets exist around the world. In New York, Chicago, London, Tokyo, and elsewhere, investors are buying call and puts on everything from stocks and gold to soybeans and euros.

checkpoint ✓

What is the purpose of a futures contract?

business in action

Carrefour's Cross-Border Cash Flows

The name of the Carrefour company, which is French for "crossroads," describes the company's global business activities. This French company, which is the largest retailer in Europe (and second largest in the world), has consumers crossing roads to get to their stores in 29 countries in Europe, Latin America, and Asia. Carrefour has more than 12,000 retail outlets operating under more than 20 different store names. Shoppers may encounter hypermarkets, supermarkets, convenience stores, and discount stores. The company offers everything from vegetables and frozen dinners to socks and banking. The diverse product line allows Carrefour to adapt to the needs of various cultures and geographic regions.

At the crossroads of southern Europe, Carrefour Italia has a significant presence with about 1,500 hypermarkets, supermarkets, and convenience stores. The company obtains over 90 percent of its fresh foods from local producers. This strategy keeps costs low and freshness and quality high. Carrefour brands in Italy include Terre D'Italia and ScelgoBio.

Centros Comerciales Carrefour operates in Spain. Also called Carrefour España, this subsidiary owns or franchises about 3,000 hypermarkets, supermarkets, and discount stores under the Dia and MaxiDia banners.

In Latin America, Carrefour faced many cultural, economic, and political barriers. Despite setbacks, the company has been able to establish itself as the largest retailer in this region. Countries where Carrefour has strong market presence include Argentina, Brazil, Chile, Colombia, and Mexico.

In Asia, the company's success has been a result of careful planning and interaction with knowledgeable citizens. Facing regulatory risks along with currency crises, Carrefour effectively used local partners in the region.

Think Critically

1. What strategies of Carrefour enhance the company's profits?
2. What costs and risks are associated with the company's operations?
3. Conduct an Internet search for current information about the activities of Carrefour. Prepare a short written summary of your findings.

12.3 Lesson Assessment

UNDERSTAND CONCEPTS

Determine the best answer for each of the following questions.

1. An investor in the United States may buy shares in foreign companies through
   a. the World Federation of Exchanges
   b. a global market index
   c. an ADR
   d. NASDAQ

2. A company may contract a price today for a product that will be delivered months from now though the ____?____ market.
   a. foreign exchange
   b. futures
   c. international bond
   d. over-the-counter

3. The global ____?____ market involves the use and trading of equity securities.
   a. stock
   b. bond
   c. foreign exchange
   d. futures

4. **True or False?** International corporate bonds represent ownership in a foreign company.

5. **True or False?** Most countries of the world use a fixed exchange rate rather than a floating exchange rate.

MAKE ACADEMIC CONNECTIONS

6. **Economics** Conduct library and online research for a global stock market index. In a written summary, describe the index and the recent trend of its movement.

7. **Culture** Talk to a person who has lived or worked in another country. Obtain information about the financial markets and investment activities in that country.

8. **Research** Conduct online or library research on an international mutual fund. Locate information about the name of the fund, the investment goal, and recent performance results. In what types of companies does the fund invest? In what countries are these companies located? How has the fund performed in recent years?

9. **Visual Art** Select a currency from another country. Research the value of that monetary unit in relation to the U.S. dollar over the past three months. Prepare a graph to communicate the exchange rate. Describe possible factors that may have affected the changing value.

Goals
- Describe global payment methods and financial documents.
- Identify agencies that help companies reduce global financial risks.

Terms
- letter of credit
- bill of exchange
- commercial invoice
- proof of insurance
- credit risk insurance

International Payments and Financial Documents

Sometimes when buying an item, you pay cash or write a check. Other times, you may buy the item on credit. In a similar way, global companies must decide how to pay for imported goods. Three types of payment methods are commonly used for international transactions: cash in advance, letter of credit, and sale on account.

CASH IN ADVANCE

Making payment before the shipment of goods can be risky for the buyer. When paying in advance, you may not receive the items or you may have difficulty obtaining a refund for damaged or returned goods. Cash in advance is not often used. This method may be required for first-time customers, small orders, or customers in high-risk countries.

Global companies may use commercial invoices to provide a description of the merchandise and calculate import duties.

LETTER OF CREDIT

A **letter of credit** is a financial document issued by a bank for an importer in which the bank guarantees payment. This payment method involves the importer paying for goods before they are received, but after the goods are shipped. This agreement, issued by the importer's bank, promises to pay the exporter a set amount when certain documents are presented. A *bill of lading* might be required as proof that the goods have been shipped.

SALE ON ACCOUNT

Almost every business buys or sells on account, allowing its regular customers to make payments in a certain time period, such as 30 or 60 days. Credit terms describe the time required for payment and other conditions of a sale on account.

OTHER GLOBAL FINANCIAL DOCUMENTS

Varied business environments may result in the use of other types of documents for foreign trade transactions.

Promissory Note A promise to pay a set amount by a certain date is a *promissory note*. These notes are signed by buyers to confirm their intention to make payment. A promissory note communicates to both the buyer and the seller the amount of a purchase, the date by which it must be paid, and any interest charges.

Bill of Exchange A written order by an exporter to an importer to make payment, usually through a third party, is a **bill of exchange.** The instructions to the importer include the amount, the due date, and the payment location, such as a bank or other financial institution.

Electronic Funds Transfer Each day, more and more payments are being made online. Electronic funds transfer (EFT) moves payments through banking computer systems. After an importer receives the ordered goods, a bank can be instructed to transfer the payment for the merchandise to the bank of the exporter.

Commercial Invoice Prepared by the exporter, a **commercial invoice** provides a description of the merchandise and the terms of the sale. This document includes details about the buyer, seller, merchandise, amounts, prices, shipping method, date of shipment, and terms of payment. Commercial invoices are also used at the port of entry to calculate any import duties that may be due.

Proof of Insurance Often required in import-export transactions is **proof of insurance.** An insurance certificate explains the amount of insurance coverage for fire, theft, water, or other damage that may occur to goods in shipment. This document also lists the names of the insurance company and the exporter.

teamwork

Various business transactions may require different payment methods. In your team, describe situations in which each of these payment methods might be appropriate: cash in advance, letter of credit, and sale on account.

checkpoint ✓

What three payment methods are commonly used in foreign trade transactions?

■International Financial Agencies

Companies involved in global transactions must protect their merchandise and other assets. The services of several agencies are available to reduce foreign trade risk.

EXPORT-IMPORT BANK

The Export-Import Bank of the United States (EXIM) is a U.S. government agency that helps finance the export sales of U.S. products. EXIM provides loans to exporters, along with loan guarantees and export credit insurance. An exporting company can purchase an export credit insurance policy from EXIM that will provide 100 percent political risk protection for international sales, including protection from foreign governments that refuse to convert local currency to dollars. EXIM also covers damage or destruction of a shipment caused by wars, revolutions, and civil disorders.

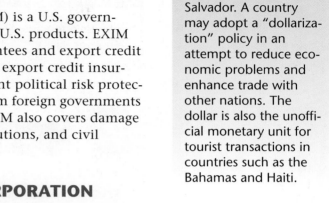

OVERSEAS PRIVATE INVESTMENT CORPORATION

The Overseas Private Investment Corporation (OPIC) provides investment insurance to U.S. companies that establish operations in developing countries. A company can protect its overseas investment by purchasing OPIC insurance to shield the company from several types of political risk, including expropriation and damage or destruction caused by war, revolution, terrorism, and sabotage. If any of these political actions occur, the business can file a claim with OPIC to recover its losses.

FOREIGN CREDIT INSURANCE ASSOCIATION

One financial hazard of conducting business in other countries is not receiving payment. **Credit risk insurance** provides coverage for loss from non-payment for delivered goods. Credit risk insurance is available through the Foreign Credit Insurance Association (FCIA), a private association that insures U.S. exporters. FCIA enables exporters to extend credit to overseas buyers.

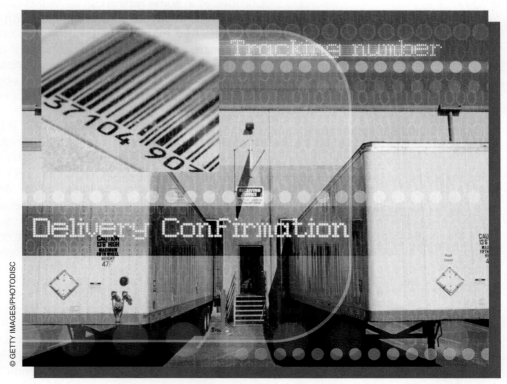

© GETTY IMAGES/PHOTODISC

Companies that engage in international trade protect their delivered goods with insurance against non-payment, damage, or political disruptions.

Credit insurance covers 100 percent of losses for political reasons, such as war, asset seizure, and currency inconvertibility. This insurance covers up to 95 percent of commercial losses, such as non-payment due to insolvency or default. About 200 banks in the United States have purchased policies from FCIA and can insure loans made to U.S. exporters.

checkpoint ✓

Name agencies that exist to help companies reduce global finance risk.

a question of ethics

Bribery and Gift Giving

In the United States, it is considered unethical for a businessperson to pay bribes to government officials or to other businesspersons in exchange for favorable treatment such as the awarding of contracts. In fact, it is against the law, whether the recipient is an American or someone in another country. The Foreign Corrupt Business Practices Act of 1977 outlawed the payment of bribes by Americans to foreign officials, companies, or individuals. At times, not paying bribes may put U.S. businesses at a competitive disadvantage.

Companies in some regions of the world commonly use payoffs to gain access to new markets. Some countries consider bribes to be tax-deductible business expenses. U.S. companies can face heavy fines and prison sentences when U.S. laws are violated. But sometimes companies cave in to local customs. A U.S. computer company offered Chinese journalists the equivalent of $12 to attend its news conference. The company said the money was for taxi fares; but the amount was equal to a week's pay for some journalists.

While it is relatively easy to outlaw bribes, it is much harder to define the difference between a bribe and a gift given as a token of appreciation. Gift giving among businesspeople is relatively limited and infrequent in the United States and Canada. In other cultures it is very common and regarded as entirely appropriate. Many organizations have policies that limit the monetary value and type of gifts that are acceptable. A social dinner invitation is usually meant to influence the recipient's behavior, even if in a subtle way. As more countries recognize how harmful bribes are to economic progress, the practice is ending.

Think Critically

1. How can U.S. businesspeople handle situations in foreign countries where officials expect bribes to be paid as a condition for doing business there?
2. Suppose you work for a manufacturing company. A plastics supplier who is trying to get more business sends you a case of golf balls made with one of its high-tech composite materials. What would you do?

12.4 Lesson Assessment

UNDERSTAND CONCEPTS

Determine the best answer for each of the following questions.

1. The payment method with the lowest risk is
   a. a sale on account
   b. a letter of credit
   c. a bill of exchange
   d. cash in advance

2. The ____?____ provides investment insurance when U.S. companies establish operations in developing countries.
   a. Export-Import Bank
   b. Foreign Credit Insurance Association
   c. World Federation of Exchanges
   d. Overseas Private Investment Corporation

3. **True or False?** Letters of credit are commonly issued by a federal government agency.

4. **True or False?** A commercial invoice documents that an exporting company has insurance coverage.

MAKE ACADEMIC CONNECTIONS

5. **Visual Art** Obtain photos and other visuals that reflect the various payment methods and financial documents discussed in this lesson. Create a poster, computer presentation, or other visual summary to communicate your knowledge of these items.

6. **Law** Conduct research to obtain information about the payment methods and other legal documents required when exporting to another country. Prepare a short oral summary of your findings.

7. **Research** Select one of these agencies: the Export-Import Bank, the Foreign Credit Insurance Association, or the Overseas Private Investment Corporation. Conduct online and library research about this organization. Prepare a brief written summary of its current activities.

8. **Careers** Investigate what types of legal agreements a person might encounter when applying for a job to work for a multinational company in another country.

Summary

12.1 INTERNATIONAL BUSINESS AND TRADE

1. A country that can produce a good or service at a lower cost has an absolute advantage. A comparative advantage exists when a country produces a good or service at which it is more efficient. Items bought from other countries are imports. Items sold to other countries are exports. Some formal trade barriers are quotas, tariffs, and embargoes.

2. Free-trade zones, free-trade agreements, common markets, and regional trade organizations encourage international trade. The difference between a country's total exports and total imports is its balance of trade. Balance of payments is the difference between the amount of money that comes into a country and the amount that goes out.

12.2 ECONOMIC DEVELOPMENT AND MONETARY SYSTEMS

3. An industrialized country has strong business activity resulting from advanced technology and a highly educated population. A less-developed country (LDC) has little economic wealth and an emphasis on agriculture or mining. Developing countries are attempting to evolve from less developed to industrialized.

4. The value of a country's currency is affected by the nation's balance of payments, economic conditions, and political stability.

12.3 INTERNATIONAL FINANCIAL MARKETS

5. The World Federation of Exchanges coordinates financial markets and stock exchanges around the world. International mutual funds allow investors to buy stock in companies around the world. The global bond market is used to issue and trade debt securities.

6. Floating exchange rates are set in the foreign exchange market. The futures market allows investors and others to buy or sell contracts on the future prices of commodities, metals, and financial instruments.

12.4 GLOBAL PAYMENTS AND FINANCIAL RISK

7. Three types of payment methods are used for international transactions: cash in advance, letter of credit, and sale on account. Other global financial documents include promissory notes, bills of exchange, electronic funds transfer, commercial invoices, and proof of insurance.

8. The Export-Import Bank of the United States (EXIM) helps finance the export of U.S. products. The Overseas Private Investment Corporation (OPIC) provides investment insurance to U.S. companies that establish operations in developing countries. Credit risk insurance is available through the Foreign Credit Insurance Association (FCIA).

Develop Your Business Language

Match the terms listed with the definitions. Some terms will not be used.

1. Exists when a country can produce a good or service at a lower cost than other countries
2. Tax that a government places on certain imported products
3. A country specializes in the production of a good or service at which it is relatively more efficient
4. Exists when a government stops the export or import of a product
5. Items bought from other countries
6. Difference between a country's total exports and total imports
7. Difference between the amount of money that comes into a country and the amount that goes out
8. The transportation, communication, and utility systems of a nation
9. A country with little economic wealth and an emphasis on agriculture or mining
10. Nations characterized by improving educational systems, increasing technology, and expanding industries

a. absolute advantage
b. balance of payments
c. balance of trade
d. bill of exchange
e. commercial invoice
f. comparative advantage
g. credit risk insurance
h. currency futures
i. developing country
j. embargo
k. exchange controls
l. exports
m. floating exchange rates
n. foreign debt
o. global stock index
p. imports
q. infrastructure
r. less-developed country (LDC)
s. letter of credit
t. quota
u. tariff

Review Concepts

11. If more money flows out of a country than flows in, the result is
    a. a lower foreign debt
    b. an unfavorable balance of payments
    c. a favorable balance of payments
    d. a favorable balance of trade

12. ____?____ countries are often characterized by low economic wealth and a dependence on agriculture or mining.
    a. industrialized   c. developing
    b. less-developed   d. infrastructure

13. ____?____ would likely increase the value of a country's currency.
    a. inflation   c. expanded exports
    b. extensive foreign debt d. expanded imports

14. Credit risk insurance providing coverage for loss from non-payment for delivered goods may be obtained from
    a. Export-Import Bank of the U.S   c. FCIA
    b. International Monetary Fund   d. OPIC

Think Critically

15. High tariffs are sometimes used by a country to protect its new and developing industries. What are two examples of new and developing industries either in the United States or in other countries? Do you think that such industries should be protected by high tariffs? If so, how long should they be protected? Give reasons for your answer.

16. What are some concerns associated with an unfavorable trade balance? What actions might be taken by a country to reduce an unfavorable trade balance?

17. Describe situations in which the financial markets of a country might affect the economies and companies of other countries.

18. To what extent should the government of a country help companies expand their exports?

Business Financial Calculations

19. In a certain year, a country has exports of $6.7 billion and imports of $7.1 billion. Do these numbers represent a favorable or unfavorable balance of trade? For what amount?

20. To make their exports suitable for use in other countries, U.S. manufacturers must produce goods that are measured in the metric system. Using this metric conversion table, determine the following amounts.

When you know:	Multiply by:	To find:
ounces (oz)	28.35	grams (g)
pounds (lb)	0.45	kilograms (kg)
pints (pt)	0.47	liters (l)
quarts (qt)	0.95	liters (l)
gallons (gal)	3.79	liters (l)

   a. A 14-ounce package of pasta would weigh about ____?____ grams.
   b. Six pounds of beef would about ____?____ kilograms.
   c. Eight pints of fruit juice is about ____?____ liters.
   d. Three quart bottles of soft drinks equals about ____?____ liters.
   e. Estimate how many gallons are equal to 12 liters. Then check your answer with a calculator. How accurate was your estimate?

21. Using Figure 12-2, determine how many U.S. dollars could be bought for these amounts from other countries:
   a. In Japan, 1,200 yen
   b. In Canada, 5 Canadian dollars
   c. In Saudi Arabia, 150 riyals

22. A corporate bond in the Philippines selling for 1,000 pesos and earning annual interest of 80 pesos has a current yield of 8 percent (80 ÷ 1,000). If the risk of this bond increased, investors would require a higher rate of return. If the bond value declines to 840 pesos (with the interest payment staying the same), what would be the new yield?

Analyze Cases

Use the case from the beginning of the chapter, Global Banking Activities of HSBC, to answer the following questions.

23. Explain actions that might be taken by HBSC to better understand its customers in different regions of the world.

24. Describe possible differences in financial activities in other countries that might require HSBC to adapt its product offerings.

25. What are benefits and drawbacks of technology that HSBC might encounter when doing business around the world?

26. Select a country in which HSBC currently does business or might start doing business. Conduct research to (a) describe the current financial market of the country, (b) identify the financial products of HSBC that would be appropriate for that country, and (c) suggest actions HSBC might take regarding doing business in that country.

Portfolio Activity

COLLECT an item that illustrates global business activities. This example could be an ad, written article, photo, product package, or some other item.

CREATE a visual to show various international financial activities related to the item. Use photos, other pictures or ads, other actual items, and drawings to illustrate how geography, culture, economic conditions, and government activities influence a company's international financial activities and the use of global financial markets.

CONNECT your visual to other aspects of our economy and society or relate it to an important concept you have learned in another class. Make the connection by preparing a brief explaining how various factors affect international financial decisions.

Stock Market Activity

The value of a company's stock is often affected by its international operations as well as competition from foreign companies. Every business exports, imports, or competes against companies that import or export.

Use online and library resources along with the annual report of the company you have been studying (or select a different company).

1. Describe the international activities of the company. In how many countries does the company do business?

2. Determine the portion of revenue and profit that the company obtains from outside its home country.

3. Discuss actions the company takes to adapt its products, advertising, and financial activities to varied cultures and foreign business environments.

4. Determine to what extent international operations may have influenced the stock price of the company.

Planning a Career in Global Finance and International Business

International finance and global business offer many employment opportunities. These positions include people who work with financial transactions and selling across borders as well as international banking and global shipping. While the skills necessary to perform these tasks are increasingly important, job titles may not reflect global activities.

Workers will also have duties unrelated to importing and exporting. Transportation managers will usually oversee both foreign and domestic shipping. A loan officer will approve loans for both exporting and local business activities.

Employment Outlook

- Faster than average growth in employment for interpreters and translators is expected.

- Employment of inspectors will likely increase with the need for security compliance.

- Continued growth of many global finance and international trade positions is expected as companies expand global operations.

Job Titles

- Foreign exchange trader
- International loan officer
- Customs inspector
- Interpreter, translator
- Global purchasing manager
- Cargo and freight agent
- Cross-cultural trainer
- International sales agent

Needed Skills

- International finance and business positions require a college degree along with experience in a field, such as accounting, banking, investments, marketing, or sales.

- Advanced study in international banking, global financial markets, and economics is required for some positions.

- Computer skills and technology competencies are increasing in importance.

- Fluency in another language is required for many jobs.

- A foreign exchange or overseas study program will contribute to cultural awareness and language proficiency.

What's It Like to Work in International Finance?

"What is the yen doing compared to the euro?" This type of question can be the focus of a foreign exchange trader. You will need to assess various factors affecting local economies. The political environment may create risk and uncertainty.

Your clients will expect you to get them the best exchange rates for their foreign sales and purchases. The buying and selling of currencies requires information in the quickly changing foreign exchange marketplace.

You work long hours since it's always the middle of the business day somewhere in the world.

What about you? What aspects of international finance are of interest to you? Why? What are some actions a person might take to achieve success in this career field?

EMERGING ISSUES EVENT

The Emerging Issues Event gives FBLA members an opportunity to demonstrate skills in researching and presenting an emerging business issue. This team event helps members learn research skills. Team participants develop speaking ability and poise through oral presentation.

The global economy has presented opportunities and challenges for increased trade. Businesses in the United States have a code of ethics or rules for honest and fair business practices. American companies outsource jobs to countries like India and China with large populations and lower wages than the United States. These countries also have large markets for products and services made in America. The home-building and agriculture industries count on illegal workers from Mexico.

Participants will be expected to research the topic prior to the presentation. They must be prepared to present an affirmative or negative argument for the business practice.

Each team must be composed of two to three (2–3) members. Each team's presentation must be the result of independent work. Facts and working data may be secured from any credible source. All members of the team must participate in research on the topic and in the actual presentation. Teams are allowed to use note cards for their presentations. No other materials or props are allowed for this presentation.

Ten (10) minutes before their presentation time, team members will draw to determine whether they will present an affirmative or negative argument. Teams will then have five (5) minutes to finalize their preparations. Each presentation may last no longer than five (5) minutes. Following each oral presentation, the judges may conduct a five (5) minute question-and-answer period during which the presenters should be prepared to defend their affirmative or negative argument.

Performance Indicators Evaluated

- Define clearly the ethical issue(s) involved in the business situation.
- State clearly the team's position about the ethical issue(s).
- Present an affirmative or negative argument for the business practice.
- Organize thoughts and solutions in a clearly understandable format.
- Demonstrate self-confidence, poise, and good voice projection. Involve all team members in the presentation.

Go to the FBLA web site for more detailed information.

Think Critically

1. Why are outsourcing and illegal employees hot issues in the U.S.?
2. How does this competitive event require you to keep an open mind about a topic on which you may have formulated a definite opinion?
3. What is the best argument for an affirmative response to this issue?
4. What is the best argument for a negative response to this issue?

www.fbla.org

Appendix A

PRESENT VALUE OF $1 (SINGLE AMOUNT)

Period	1%	2%	3%	4%	5%	6%	7%	8%	9%	10%	11%	12%
1	0.990	0.980	0.971	0.962	0.952	0.943	0.935	0.926	0.917	0.909	0.901	0.893
2	0.980	0.961	0.943	0.925	0.907	0.890	0.873	0.857	0.842	0.826	0.812	0.797
3	0.971	0.942	0.915	0.889	0.864	0.840	0.816	0.794	0.772	0.751	0.731	0.712
4	0.961	0.924	0.888	0.855	0.823	0.792	0.763	0.735	0.708	0.683	0.659	0.636
5	0.951	0.906	0.863	0.822	0.784	0.747	0.713	0.681	0.650	0.621	0.593	0.567
6	0.942	0.888	0.837	0.790	0.746	0.705	0.666	0.630	0.596	0.564	0.535	0.507
7	0.933	0.871	0.813	0.760	0.711	0.665	0.623	0.583	0.547	0.513	0.482	0.452
8	0.923	0.853	0.789	0.731	0.677	0.627	0.582	0.540	0.502	0.467	0.434	0.404
9	0.914	0.837	0.766	0.703	0.645	0.592	0.544	0.500	0.460	0.424	0.391	0.361
10	0.905	0.820	0.744	0.676	0.614	0.558	0.508	0.463	0.422	0.386	0.352	0.322
11	0.896	0.804	0.722	0.650	0.585	0.527	0.475	0.429	0.388	0.350	0.317	0.287
12	0.887	0.788	0.701	0.625	0.557	0.497	0.444	0.397	0.356	0.319	0.286	0.257
13	0.879	0.773	0.681	0.601	0.530	0.469	0.415	0.368	0.326	0.290	0.258	0.229
14	0.870	0.758	0.661	0.577	0.505	0.442	0.388	0.340	0.299	0.263	0.232	0.205
15	0.861	0.743	0.642	0.555	0.481	0.417	0.362	0.315	0.275	0.239	0.209	0.183
16	0.853	0.728	0.623	0.534	0.458	0.394	0.339	0.292	0.252	0.218	0.188	0.163
17	0.844	0.714	0.605	0.513	0.436	0.371	0.317	0.270	0.231	0.198	0.170	0.146
18	0.836	0.700	0.587	0.494	0.416	0.350	0.296	0.250	0.212	0.180	0.153	0.130
19	0.828	0.686	0.570	0.475	0.396	0.331	0.277	0.232	0.194	0.164	0.138	0.116
20	0.820	0.673	0.554	0.456	0.377	0.312	0.258	0.215	0.178	0.149	0.124	0.104
25	0.780	0.610	0.478	0.375	0.295	0.233	0.184	0.146	0.116	0.092	0.074	0.059
30	0.742	0.552	0.412	0.308	0.231	0.174	0.131	0.099	0.075	0.057	0.044	0.033
35	0.706	0.500	0.355	0.253	0.181	0.130	0.094	0.068	0.049	0.036	0.026	0.019
40	0.672	0.453	0.307	0.208	0.142	0.097	0.067	0.046	0.032	0.022	0.015	0.011

Appendix B

FUTURE VALUE OF $1 (SINGLE AMOUNT)

Period	1%	2%	3%	4%	5%	6%	7%	8%	9%	10%	11%	12%
1	1.010	1.020	1.030	1.040	1.050	1.060	1.070	1.080	1.090	1.100	1.110	1.120
2	1.020	1.040	1.061	1.082	1.103	1.124	1.145	1.166	1.188	1.210	1.232	1.254
3	1.030	1.061	1.093	1.125	1.158	1.191	1.225	1.260	1.295	1.331	1.368	1.405
4	1.041	1.082	1.126	1.170	1.216	1.262	1.311	1.360	1.412	1.464	1.518	1.574
5	1.051	1.104	1.159	1.217	1.276	1.338	1.403	1.469	1.539	1.611	1.685	1.762
6	1.062	1.126	1.194	1.265	1.340	1.419	1.501	1.587	1.677	1.772	1.870	1.974
7	1.072	1.149	1.230	1.316	1.407	1.504	1.606	1.714	1.828	1.949	2.076	2.211
8	1.083	1.172	1.267	1.369	1.477	1.594	1.718	1.851	1.993	2.144	2.305	2.476
9	1.094	1.195	1.305	1.423	1.551	1.689	1.838	1.999	2.172	2.358	2.558	2.773
10	1.105	1.219	1.344	1.480	1.629	1.791	1.967	2.159	2.367	2.594	2.839	3.106
11	1.116	1.243	1.384	1.539	1.710	1.898	2.105	2.332	2.580	2.853	3.152	3.479
12	1.127	1.268	1.426	1.601	1.796	2.012	2.252	2.518	2.813	3.138	3.498	3.896
13	1.138	1.294	1.469	1.665	1.886	2.133	2.410	2.720	3.066	3.452	3.883	4.363
14	1.149	1.319	1.513	1.732	1.980	2.261	2.579	2.937	3.342	3.797	4.310	4.887
15	1.161	1.346	1.558	1.801	2.079	2.397	2.759	3.172	3.642	4.177	4.785	5.474
16	1.173	1.373	1.605	1.873	2.183	2.540	2.952	3.426	3.970	4.595	5.311	6.130
17	1.184	1.400	1.653	1.948	2.292	2.693	3.159	3.700	4.328	5.054	5.895	6.866
18	1.196	1.428	1.702	2.026	2.407	2.854	3.380	3.996	4.717	5.560	6.544	7.690
19	1.208	1.457	1.754	2.107	2.527	3.026	3.617	4.316	5.142	6.116	7.263	8.613
20	1.220	1.486	1.806	2.191	2.653	3.207	3.870	4.661	5.604	6.727	8.062	9.646
25	1.282	1.641	2.094	2.666	3.386	4.292	5.427	6.848	8.623	10.835	13.585	17.000
30	1.348	1.811	2.427	3.243	4.322	5.743	7.612	10.063	13.268	17.449	22.892	29.960
35	1.417	2.000	2.814	3.946	5.516	7.686	10.677	14.785	20.414	28.102	38.575	52.800
40	1.489	2.208	3.262	4.801	7.040	10.286	14.974	21.725	31.409	45.259	65.001	93.051

Appendix C

PRESENT VALUE OF A SERIES (ANNUITY)

To use the table, find the vertical column under your interest rate (or cost of capital). Then find the horizontal row corresponding to the number of years it will take to receive the payment. The point at which the column and the row intersect is the present value of $1. You can multiply this value by the number of dollars you expect to receive in order to find the present value of the amount you expect.

Period	1%	2%	3%	4%	5%	6%	7%	8%	9%	10%	11%	12%
1	0.990	0.980	0.971	0.962	0.952	0.943	0.935	0.926	0.917	0.909	0.901	0.893
2	1.970	1.942	1.913	1.886	1.859	1.833	1.808	1.783	1.759	1.736	1.713	1.690
3	2.941	2.884	2.829	2.775	2.723	2.673	2.624	2.577	2.531	2.487	2.444	2.402
4	3.902	3.808	3.717	3.630	3.546	3.465	3.387	3.312	3.240	3.170	3.102	3.037
5	4.853	4.713	4.580	4.452	4.329	4.212	4.100	3.993	3.890	3.791	3.696	3.605
6	5.795	5.601	5.417	5.242	5.076	4.917	4.767	4.623	4.486	4.355	4.231	4.111
7	6.728	6.472	6.230	6.002	5.786	5.582	5.389	5.206	5.033	4.868	4.712	4.564
8	7.652	7.325	7.020	6.733	6.463	6.210	5.971	5.747	5.535	5.335	5.146	4.968
9	8.566	8.162	7.786	7.435	7.108	6.802	6.515	6.247	5.995	5.759	5.537	5.328
10	9.471	8.983	8.530	8.111	7.722	7.360	7.024	6.710	6.418	6.145	5.889	5.650
11	10.368	9.787	9.253	8.760	8.306	7.887	7.499	7.139	6.805	6.495	6.207	5.938
12	11.255	10.575	9.954	9.385	8.863	8.384	7.943	7.536	7.161	6.814	6.492	6.194
13	12.134	11.348	10.635	9.986	9.394	8.853	8.358	7.904	7.487	7.103	6.750	6.424
14	13.004	12.106	11.296	10.563	9.899	9.295	8.745	8.244	7.786	7.367	6.982	6.628
15	13.865	12.849	11.938	11.118	10.380	9.712	9.108	8.559	8.061	7.606	7.191	6.811
16	14.718	13.578	12.561	11.652	10.838	10.106	9.447	8.851	8.313	7.824	7.379	6.974
17	15.562	14.292	13.166	12.166	11.274	10.477	9.763	9.122	8.544	8.022	7.549	7.120
18	16.398	14.992	13.754	12.659	11.690	10.828	10.059	9.372	8.756	8.201	7.702	7.250
19	17.226	15.678	14.324	13.134	12.085	11.158	10.336	9.604	8.950	8.365	7.839	7.366
20	18.046	16.351	14.877	13.590	12.462	11.470	10.594	9.818	9.129	8.514	7.963	7.469
25	22.023	19.523	17.413	15.622	14.094	12.783	11.654	10.675	9.823	9.077	8.422	7.843
30	25.808	22.396	19.600	17.292	15.372	13.765	12.409	11.258	10.274	9.427	8.694	8.055
35	29.409	24.999	21.487	18.665	16.374	14.498	12.948	11.655	10.567	9.644	8.855	8.176
40	32.835	27.355	23.115	19.793	17.159	15.046	13.332	11.925	10.757	9.779	8.951	8.244

FUTURE VALUE OF A SERIES (ANNUITY)

To use the table, find the vertical column under the interest rate being earned. Then find the horizontal row corresponding to the number of years of the investment. The point at which the column and the row intersect is the factor for the future value of $1. You can multiply this value by the number of dollars of the investment to calculate the future value of the investment.

Period	1%	2%	3%	4%	5%	6%	7%	8%	9%	10%	11%	12%
1	1.000	1.000	1.000	1.000	1.000	1.000	1.000	1.000	1.000	1.000	1.000	1.000
2	2.010	2.020	2.030	2.040	2.050	2.060	2.070	2.080	2.090	2.100	2.110	2.120
3	3.030	3.060	3.091	3.122	3.153	3.184	3.215	3.246	3.278	3.310	3.342	3.374
4	4.060	4.122	4.184	4.246	4.310	4.375	4.440	4.506	4.573	4.641	4.710	4.779
5	5.101	5.204	5.309	5.416	5.526	5.637	5.751	5.867	5.985	6.105	6.228	6.353
6	6.152	6.308	6.468	6.633	6.802	6.975	7.153	7.336	7.523	7.716	7.913	8.115
7	7.214	7.434	7.662	7.898	8.142	8.394	8.654	8.923	9.200	9.487	9.783	10.089
8	8.286	8.583	8.892	9.214	9.549	9.897	10.260	10.637	11.028	11.436	11.859	12.300
9	9.369	9.755	10.159	10.583	11.027	11.491	11.978	12.488	13.021	13.579	14.164	14.776
10	10.462	10.950	11.464	12.006	12.578	13.181	13.816	14.487	15.193	15.937	16.722	17.549
11	11.567	12.169	12.808	13.486	14.207	14.972	15.784	16.645	17.560	18.531	19.561	20.655
12	12.683	13.412	14.192	15.026	15.917	16.870	17.888	18.977	20.141	21.384	22.713	24.133
13	13.809	14.680	15.618	16.627	17.713	18.882	20.141	21.495	22.953	24.523	26.212	28.029
14	14.947	15.974	17.086	18.292	19.599	21.015	22.550	24.215	26.019	27.975	30.095	32.393
15	16.097	17.293	18.599	20.024	21.579	23.276	25.129	27.152	29.361	31.772	34.405	37.280
16	17.258	18.639	20.157	21.825	23.657	25.673	27.888	30.324	33.003	35.950	39.190	42.753
17	18.430	20.012	21.762	23.698	25.840	28.213	30.840	33.750	36.974	40.545	44.501	48.884
18	19.615	21.412	23.414	25.645	28.132	30.906	33.999	37.450	41.301	45.599	50.396	55.750
19	20.811	22.841	25.117	27.671	30.539	33.760	37.379	41.446	46.018	51.159	56.939	63.440
20	22.019	24.297	26.870	29.778	33.066	36.786	40.995	45.762	51.160	57.275	64.203	72.052
25	28.243	32.030	36.459	41.646	47.727	54.865	63.249	73.106	84.701	98.347	114.41	133.33
30	34.785	40.568	47.575	56.085	66.439	79.058	94.461	113.28	136.31	164.49	199.02	241.33
35	41.660	49.994	60.462	73.652	90.320	111.43	138.24	172.32	215.71	271.02	341.59	431.66
40	48.886	60.402	75.401	95.026	120.80	154.76	199.64	259.06	337.88	442.59	581.83	767.09

Glossary

A

Absolute advantage exists when a country can produce a good or service at a lower cost than other countries

Account hijacking obtaining access to another person's financial accounts through fraud and stealing the funds

Account payable amounts owed to creditors for goods and services

Account payable one of the most common current liabilities

Account receivable the money owed for the purchases customers buy on credit

Accounting organizing a system of financial records, recording financial data, and preparing, analyzing, and interpreting financial statements

Accounting cycle a series of steps performed to ensure the completeness and accuracy of accounting records and to prepare summary financial statements

Accounting transaction the act of recording an activity that results in a change in value of an organization's resource

Accounts the financial records for each of the specific assets, liabilities, and categories of owner's equity

Accrual accounting the accounting procedure that recognizes revenues and expenses when they are incurred rather than when cash is received or spent

Actuaries highly trained mathematicians who gather and analyze data and determine risk factors in order to establish premium rates

Adjuster person who works for an insurance company and determines the extent of a loss and the liability of the insurer

Adoption curve represents the stages for an innovation to be accepted by individuals and businesses

Aging of accounts receivable the categorizing of credit accounts owed based on how long they have been due

Aging schedule schedule generated when performing the aging of accounts receivable; categorizes all accounts receivable by the length of time they remain unpaid

American depository receipt (ADR) issued to allow U.S. investors to buy shares in foreign companies

Annual report a statement of a company's operating and financial performance issued at the end of its fiscal year

Asset-backed security a specialized type of global debt instrument; bonds and notes that are secured by various company assets

Assets all of the things a business owns and uses as a part of business operations

Automatic bill payment convenience offered by a bank to its customers in which the customer can authorize preset amounts paid regularly

Automatic teller machine (ATM) electronic banking service machine, more commonly called a cash machine

B

Balance of payments the difference between the amount of money that comes into a country and the amount that goes out

Balance of trade the difference between a country's total exports and total imports

Balance sheet identifies the assets, liabilities, and equity of a business as of a specific date

Bear market a period of declining stock market prices

Benchmark company a competitor that has historically demonstrated outstanding financial performance used to establish financial performance goals

Beneficiary a person or organization designated to receive the proceeds of the insurance policy

Bill of exchange a written order by an exporter to an importer to make payment, usually through a third party

Bond a financial instrument that obligates the issuer to pay the bondholder the principal plus agreed-upon interest at the end of a designated period

Bond money that is borrowed by a company or government

Bond markets offer newly issued bonds of companies and government agencies for sale as well as buying and selling existing bonds

Bond rating a measure of the quality and safety of a company's debt

Bonds provide protection against a risk associated with the work provided by one business to another

Breakeven point a calculation that determines the approximate sales volume required to just cover costs, below which production would be unprofitable and above which it would be profitable

Budget a wise spending plan

Budget discrepancies differences between budgeted amounts and actual financial performance

Bull market a period of rising stock values

Burglary, robbery, and theft insurance covers crimes committed by people that are not owners or employees of the business

Business financial goals goals that establish direction for the financial plans of a business

Business income insurance compensates the business for some of the income that is lost if the business cannot operate for a period of time due to a covered peril

Business owners policy special property insurance policy for the unique circumstances of small businesses

C

Call option the right to buy some type of investment

Callable bond allows the company to pay off the debt before the maturity date at a specified price

Capacity the ability of the borrower to repay money owed

Capital the amount of personal wealth the owners have invested in the business

Capital budget a plan to acquire and finance long-term assets of a business

Capital expenditures long-term spending for items that will be used over a longer period of time (more than a year)

Capital gain the increase in the value between the purchase price and the maturity value

Capital markets markets in which debt and equity securities that are issued for more than a year are sold

Capital project construction or purchase of a long-term asset, such as buildings and equipment

Capital resources the human-made goods used in the production of other products and services

Cash budget an estimate of future cash receipts and cash payments for a specified period of time

Cash flow statement shows how cash is used by a business during a specified time period

Cash flows the yearly amounts of increased sales or decreased costs

Centralized organization organization in which business decisions are made at company headquarters

Certificates of deposit (CDs) a common form of money market financing

Character the personal qualities of the credit applicant that demonstrate responsibility and dependability

Charge-off an account that is no longer considered collectible

Chief executive officer charged with carrying out the strategy and policy of the board of directors

Chief financial officer responsible for planning and managing a company's financial resources

Chief operating officer directs the actual operations of the business

Choice deciding which wants and needs will be satisfied and which will go unsatisfied

Civil liability results from negligent acts against individuals or organizations

Clearing paying checks among different banks in different cities

Coinsurance the insured and insurer share the risk by paying a defined amount of the costs

Collateral an asset promised by a business to a creditor if repayment of a loan isn't completed

Collection procedures the steps a business follows to keep customer credit payments up to date and eliminate charge-offs

Command economy form of economy in which the government has the primary influence on economic decisions

Commercial invoice provides a description of merchandise and the terms of the sale

Commercial lending loans to business enterprises for various company needs

Commercial Package Policy (CPP) comprehensive business property insurance package

Commercial paper unsecured, short-term debt instruments issued by corporations

Commercial vehicle insurance policies written to cover business automobiles and other vehicles

Commission a fee charged by brokers for their services; also, compensation earned by salespeople or others as a percentage of sales

Commodity markets markets where raw materials and other basic production resources are traded

Common market market in which members eliminate tariffs and other trade barriers, allow companies to invest freely in each member's country, and allow workers to move freely across borders; also called an economic community

Common stock an equity security representing ownership in a corporation with voting rights

Comparative advantage a country specializes in the production of a good or service at which it is relatively more efficient

Compensation the wages or salary along with other financial benefits paid to employees

Complementary projects two or more projects that are dependent on one another

Compound interest interest is paid not only on the total amount borrowed but also on the interest that has been earned

Conditions factors that are generally outside the control of the borrower or lender but that can affect the risk; also, the part of an insurance contract that identifies the stipulations or requirements that must be met in order for insurance to remain in effect and losses to be paid

Consequential damage coverage pays for damages to a business that occur after another incident but related to it

Consumer credit credit offered to individual consumers by a business

Consumer price index (CPI) index used to measure the average change in prices

Contracted credit plan credit services provided by a financial services firm for a fee

Controllable risks risks that can be reduced or avoided by thoughtful actions

Controller in charge of accounting and the financial records of the organization and provides support for executives and other managers in understanding and using financial data and reports

Convertible bond can be exchanged for common stock in the same company

Convertible preferred stock stock that can be changed into common shares

Corporate bonds bonds issued by corporations

Corporation a distinct legal entity formed by completing required legal documents in a specific state

Cost of capital the interest rate used to evaluate a capital project

Cost of debt the rate of return required by creditors

Cost of equity the required return of the owners in a company

Cost-benefit analysis compares the total expected costs with the total expected benefits of one or more choices in order to choose the most profitable option

Coupon rate the stated annual interest rate for a bond

Coverages the monetary limits and risks covered by an insurance policy

Credit an agreement in which a borrower receives something of value in exchange for a promise to repay the lender at a later date

Credit agreement a written document describing the terms under which credit is granted and payment will be made

Credit insurance insurance that pays off the balance of outstanding loans in the event of death or disability of a debtor

Credit policy the guidelines used for approval of credit customers

Credit risk insurance provides coverage for loss from nonpayment for delivered goods

Credit standards the guidelines used by a company to determine if a customer is eligible for credit

Credit terms the conditions under which credit is extended by a lender to a borrower

Credit union user-owned, not-for-profit, cooperative financial institution

Creditor an individual or an organization that provides funds to a business, with repayment of the funds and agreed-upon interest due at a future date; also, a business that extends credit to a customer

Creditworthy characteristics making it highly likely that credit payments will be made on time and in full

Criminal liability liability that results from breaking a law

Cumulative preferred stock requires that missed (unpaid) dividends due to low earnings will build up until paid to preferred stockholders

Currency futures contracts to purchase for a fee a foreign currency at today's rate with payment and delivery at a later date

Current assets items of value in an organization that will likely be converted into cash within a year

Current expenses include rent, materials, wages and salaries, utilities, repairs, advertising, supplies, and other necessary business costs

Current liabilities amounts owed that need to be paid within the next year

Current ratio a number calculated by dividing current assets by current liabilities

D

Data integrity information has not been altered or destroyed in an unauthorized manner

Debenture bond a corporate bond without collateral

Debit card bank card that allows user to obtain or use money from a checking account

Debt financing the use of borrowed money to obtain needed capital

Debt securities represent borrowing by companies or governments

Debtor the recipient of credit

Decentralized organization organization in which business decisions are made at lower levels rather than at company headquarters

Declarations contain identifying information about the insured and the insured property, the insurance company, agent, type of insurance, the dates and times the insurance is in effect, and the amount of the premium

Deductible an identified amount of a loss that must be paid by the insured before the insurer is liable

Defined benefit plan promises an employee a fixed or determinable monthly payment upon retirement

Defined contribution pension plan type of pension plan that does not guarantee an employee a fixed level of benefits upon retirement. Instead, the employer contributes a fixed amount to an account set up for the employee and benefits are determined by the amount of contributions and the performance of the investments

Delinquent account a credit account that has not been paid by the designated date according to the credit terms

Demand the amount of a product or service that individuals want to buy to satisfy their wants and needs

Deposit institution accept deposits for people and businesses to use in the future

Depreciation a decline in the value of an asset as it ages

Developing country a nation characterized by improving educational systems, increasing technology, and expanding industries

Development bank an organization of several countries created to provide financing for economic development to countries in a region

Direct compensation money received for work

Direct deposit a system that electronically transfers net pay into an employee's bank account

Direct materials unfinished goods used by a manufacturer to create a finished product

Discount the amount of money subtracted from a loan at the time of lending equal to the interest charged by the lender

Discount broker lower-cost broker who places orders and offers limited research and other services

Discount rate the rate the Fed charges on loans to member banks

District reserve bank a Federal Reserve Bank; one of which is located in each Federal Reserve district

Diversification the offering of a variety of products or services; also, investing in a variety of assets

Dividends a portion of corporate earnings allocated to each share of stock

Domestic business making, buying, selling, and financing of goods and services within a country

Due care a commitment to completing all tasks thoroughly and with the highest level of quality

E

Early adopters opinion leaders who are quick to adopt an innovation after they have seen its use and value

Early majority one of the two largest groups of innovation adopters; they are cautious, but they want to be seen by others as accepting and using innovation

Economic risk a chance of financial gain or loss

Economics the science of decision making about the allocation of scarce resources

Electronic document information contained in a computer file prepared for a specific purpose

Electronic funds transfer (EFT) the use of computers and other technology for banking activities

Electronic information exchange procedures developed to share information in electronic forms including text, graphics, audio, and video

Electronic record a document containing information that is intended to be preserved for a period of time to document an event, activity, or transaction

Electronic spreadsheet a computer software program that organizes and presents data in a series of columns and rows allowing analysis using integrated mathematical formulas

Embargo exists when a government stops the export or import of a product completely

Equities the financial claims on a company's resources

Equity financing offers an ownership interest in the company to investors

Equity securities securities that represent ownership. The most common type of equity security is stock

Exchange controls government restrictions to regulate the amount and value of a nation's currency

Exchange rate the value of one currency in terms of another

Exclusions provide specific limitations on insurance coverage

Exclusive agent insurance agent employed by an insurance company who sells only that company's policies

Expected return the amount of future cash inflows

Exports the goods and services sold to other countries

Extra expenses expenses that a business incurs to maintain or reestablish operations that can also be covered by insurance

F

Face value indicates the amount being borrowed; also called the maturity value or par value

Factoring the sale of accounts receivable

Federal Reserve System a bank for banks; created to supervise and regulate member banks to help them serve the public efficiently

Fee-for-service insurance makes payments to doctors and hospitals for each service rendered to the patient

Fidelity bond provides protection for losses resulting from dishonest employees

Finance activities involved with saving, investing, and using money by individuals, businesses, and governments

Financial budget a projected financial statement for a specific future time period

Financial information system supports managers in the financing of a business and the allocation and control of financial resources

Financial institutions handle money receipts, payments, and lending. These organizations, also called financial intermediaries, provide a wide range of financial services

Financial leverage using debt financing to increase the rate of return on assets

Financial market an organized process for the exchange of capital and credit

Financial plan a formal report with a summary of the current financial situation along with plans for future financial activities

Financial ratios comparisons of important financial data used to evaluate business performance

Financial return a profit earned from an investment

Financial risk the possibility that an expected profit will not be achieved

Financial statements specific reports prepared according to accepted accounting standards that provide financial information about an enterprise

Financial supermarket a type of financial institution offering a complete range of services

Financial system financial relationships between people, businesses, and governments in a country

Finished goods products that have completed the manufacturing process and are ready to sell

Fixed costs business expenses that do not change as the level of production changes

Floating exchange rates currency values change based on supply and demand

Foreign currency the currency of another country

Foreign debt the amount a country owes to other countries

Foreign exchange market a market where one currency is exchanged for another

Foreign exchange rate the value of a country's currency in relation to the value of the money of another country

Free enterprise economy a form of economy based on principles designed to protect and promote the economic freedoms of individual consumers and businesses

Free-trade agreements member countries agree to eliminate duties and trade barriers on products traded among them

Free-trade zone a designated area, usually around a seaport or airport, where products can be imported duty-free and then stored, assembled, and/or used in manufacturing

Full-service broker broker who provides information about securities you may want to buy

Fundamental accounting equation Assets = Liabilities + Owners' Equity

Future value the amount to which an amount of money will grow in a defined period of time at a specified investment rate

Futures market allows investors to buy or sell contracts on the future prices of commodities, metals, and financial instruments

G

General obligation bond a bond backed by the full faith, credit, and taxing power of the government issuing the bond

Global business a company that transcends national boundaries and is not committed to a single home country

Global stock index a group of stocks selected to reflect the overall progress of all stocks being represented

Gross pay a person's total earnings

Gross profit the difference between variable costs and selling price

H

Hard currency monetary units that are freely converted into other currencies

Health insurance provides payment for expenses related to preventive health care and the treatment of illness and disease

Horizontal integration a merger between two or more companies in the same type of business

Human resources people and their skills, including both physical and mental abilities; sometimes referred to as labor

Human risks risks that result from the actions of individuals, groups, or organizations

I

Identity theft occurs when someone uses another person's personal information without permission to commit fraud or other crimes

Imports items bought from other countries

Income statement provides a view of the financial changes in a business that have occurred during a specific period of time

Income tax a tax levied on the income of individuals

Independent agent an insurance agent who is self-employed or who works for an insurance sales company and represents several insurance companies

Independent projects projects that are not affected by each other

Indirect compensation payments made by an employer on behalf of an employee

Industrialized country a country with strong business activity that is usually the result of advanced technology and a highly educated population

Inflation a rise in the general level of prices

Inflation-linked bond a bond that increases in value based on the rate of inflation

Information integrity information remains unchanged from its source and has not been accidentally or maliciously modified, altered, or destroyed

Information privacy the right of an individual to be secure from unauthorized disclosure of information

Information security the protection of information from unauthorized accidental or intentional access, modification, destruction, or disclosure while being transmitted or stored

Information system a structured set of processes, people and equipment for converting data into information

Infrastructure the transportation, communication, and utility systems of a nation

Initial investment the cost of a project, such as new equipment or a building; also called the start-up cost or the initial outlay

Initial public offering (IPO) when a company offers stock to outside investors for the first time

Inland marine insurance covers all transportation over land via trains, trucks, and other vehicles as well as storage of products during transit

Innovators the small percentage of consumers or businesspeople who are risk takers and want to be the first to try something new

Insurable interest the insured will suffer a financial loss if the insured event occurs

Insurance a contract providing for financial protection against a specified loss

Insurance agent a person licensed by the state and given authority by the insurer to sell its insurance

Insured the person or business covered by the insurance policy

Insurer the company that assumes the risk and agrees to pay losses covered by the policy

Insuring agreement identifies the individuals, activities, or property that are insured, the perils that will be covered, and the actions that must be taken by the insured and the insurer to maintain the insurance and to compensate the insured in the event of a loss

Intellectual property intangible assets used by companies

Interest the amount paid for the privilege of borrowing money

Interest rate the cost of borrowing money, expressed as a percentage of the amount borrowed, usually over a period of one year

Internal rate of return (IRR) the discount rate at which the net present value is zero

International business business and financial activities necessary for creating, shipping, and selling goods and services across national borders; often referred to as foreign or international trade

International Monetary Fund an agency that helps promote economic cooperation by maintaining an orderly system of international trade and exchange rates

Intrastate commerce business transactions involving companies that do business only in one state

Inventory the merchandise an organization plans to sell to customers

Inventory turnover a measure commonly used to determine how many times inventory is sold and replaced

Investment banker an individual or company that assists companies with issuing new securities

J

Joint venture an agreement between two or more companies to share a business project

Journal entry identifies the key information for an accounting transaction, including date, amount, purpose, and the accounts affected

Journals business records in which transactions are recorded

L

Laggards consumers who are very resistant to change and very conservative in their purchase behavior; they do not trust innovation and will avoid spending money on products and services they have not used in the past until they have little other choice

Late majority one of the two largest groups of innovation users. By the time they make a decision, the product is no longer considered an innovation and is widely used. This group is cautious and conservative; they want clear evidence of the effectiveness of an innovation

Leasing a legal agreement to use property that belongs to another person

Less-developed country (LDC) a country with little economic wealth and an emphasis on agriculture or mining

Lessee the user who rents an item

Lessor the owner of property that is leased

Letter of credit a financial document issued by a bank for an importer in which the bank guarantees payment

Liabilities claims against business resources by those to whom the business has financial obligations; also, an individual or business responsible to others for negligence

Lien a claim against the property as security for a debt owed by the owner

Life insurance provides for payment of a sum of money to a beneficiary upon the death of the insured

Limited liability company (LLC) form of organization that combines features of the partnership and corporation, offering some of the advantages of each

Limited partnership form of organization that includes one or more general partners and other limited partners

Line of credit an agreement that allows a company to obtain additional loans without a new loan application

Liquidity the ease and speed with which an investment can be converted into cash

Lock box a secured postal box used to receive customer payments

Long-term assets assets that have a life of a year or more and often define the nature of the business

Long-term liabilities any liabilities for which payment will not be made in full for more than a year

M

Macroeconomics economic decisions made at a national level

Managed care insurance health insurance designed to reduce costs by restricting employee choice of doctors and hospitals, negotiating fees for services, and requiring pre-authorization for non-emergency services

Marine insurance covers shipment on oceans and inland waterways including rivers and lakes

Market where and to whom a business sells

Market economy an economy based on the combination of the decisions made by individual consumers and businesses

Market price the price at which an equal number of products will be produced and purchased

Market value the price at which a share of stock can be bought and sold in the stock market

Maturity date the date when the bond, which is a loan, must be repaid

Member banks banks that belong to the Federal Reserve System

Microeconomics the level of economic decisions related to the choices of individuals and businesses

Money any item that serves as a method of payment

Money markets markets that specialize in buying and selling financial instruments for short time periods of a year or less

Mortgage bond a type of debt secured by a specific asset or property

Municipal bond a debt security issued by a state or local government

Mutual company a nonprofit insurance corporation owned by its policyholders

Mutual fund an investment fund set up and managed by companies that receive money from many investors

Mutual savings bank a bank that provides a variety of services, but it is organized mainly for savings and home loans; this type of financial institution is owned by the depositors

Mutually exclusive projects the acceptance of one project does not allow acceptance of others

N

Natural resources the materials in the world around us

Natural risk risk that arises from natural events or as a part of nature

Net pay the amount, after various deductions, which is paid to each employee

Net present value (NPV) the present value of cash flows for a project minus the initial investment

Non-deposit institution life insurance companies, investment companies, consumer finance companies, mortgage companies, check-cashing outlets, and pawnshops

O

Open market operations the process of buying and selling government securities

Operating budget budget that projects all income and expenses for the operations of a business for a specific future time period

Operating income the company's earnings before interest and taxes

Opportunity the possibility for success

Opportunity cost the value of the alternative that is given up when a decision is made

Optimal capital structure the financing combination of a low cost of capital and maximum market value

Option the right to buy or sell a security or commodity at a specific price within a limited time period, usually three, six, or nine months

Over-the-counter (OTC) market a network where securities transactions occur using telephones and computers rather than on the floor of an exchange

Owner's equity the total value that all owners and investors have in the firm

P

Par value the minimum price for which a share of stock can be issued

Partnership a business owned and managed by two or more people under the conditions of a legal written agreement

Payback method used to determine how long it will take for the cash flows of a capital project to equal the original cost

Payroll record the form that documents each employee's pay history

Payroll stub provides employees with a summary of their total pay and deductions for the current pay period as well as for the year to date

Peril the cause of a loss

Personal financial goal a desired outcome for financial planning

Personal financial planning the process of managing your money to achieve personal economic satisfaction

Pharming attacks a legitimate business' server to redirect traffic from that site to another web site

Phishing creating and using e-mails with legitimate-looking addresses and web sites designed to look like familiar businesses, financial institutions, and government agencies to deceive. Internet users into disclosing their personal information

Piece rate earnings determined on the basis of each unit of output

Point-of-sale transaction type of sale in which merchants accept debit cards to pay for purchases

Policy a legal contract through which insurance is implemented

Policyholder the individual or organization to whom the policy is issued

Preferred stock a security that has priority over common stock in the payment of dividends

Premium the amount paid to the insurer to keep the insurance policy in force

Prepaid bank card a bank card that holds the amount of a worker's pay; also called stored value cards, these electronic devices may be used to obtain cash and make purchases at stores

Present value the current value of an amount of money to be received at a future date based on a specified investment rate

Pretexting the practice of obtaining personal information under false pretenses

Price-earnings (P/E) ratio the relationship between a stock's selling price and its earnings per share

Primary market market where newly-issued securities are sold by investment bankers

Primary offering when an organization makes stock available for the first time or issues new bonds

Principal the amount of money borrowed

Private corporation a business that can limit the number of owners and who is allowed to purchase stock

Promissory note a loan for a specific amount, purpose, interest rate, and time period; it usually is secured by business assets and has a specified payment plan

Promissory note a signed, written promise to borrow money between a borrower and a lender

Proof of insurance a certificate that explains the amount of insurance coverage for fire, theft, water, or other damage that may occur to goods in shipment

Property tax tax based on the value of land and buildings

Prospectus document that presents legal and financial information about a company issuing stock

Public corporation a business that issues stock that is sold on the open market

Pure risk no opportunity for financial gain but only loss

Put option the right to sell some type of investment

Q

Quota a limit on the quantity of a product that may be imported or exported within a given period of time

R

Rate of return (or yield) the relationship between the amount received and the cost of an investment

Ratio analysis analysis done to study relationships in a company's financial resources in order to understand and improve financial performance

Reinsurance occurs when an insurance company sells some of its risk to other insurance companies

Reserve requirement the percentage of funds that a bank is required to hold

Resources the means available to develop solutions for unsatisfied wants and needs

Retained earnings profits earned by a company that are not paid to shareholders as dividends

Revenue bond a bond that is repaid with the income from the project that the bond was issued to finance, such as a toll bridge or stadium

Revolving credit a formal loan agreement for a specified amount of money, time period, and interest rate

Risk the chance or probability of harm or loss

Risk management the process of systematically identifying potential risks and making plans to reduce the impact of the risk on individuals and companies

S

Safe-deposit box boxes in well-guarded bank vaults, used by customers to store valuable objects and documents

Salary earnings calculated on the basis of a time period, usually weekly, bi-weekly, or monthly

Sales tax a state or local tax on goods and services that is collected by the seller

Savings and loan association (S&L) specializes in savings accounts and making loans for home mortgages

Scarcity people have wants and needs that are greater than can be satisfied with the available products and services

Secondary market market where securities are traded after they are initially offered in the primary market

Secondary offering when an investor offers stocks and bonds for resale

Security an investment instrument issued by a corporation, government, or other organization representing ownership or a debt

Self-insurance the advance budgeting of funds to meet the estimated cost of losses

Self-managed credit plan a company administers its own credit program and assumes all credit risks and returns

Selling short selling a stock not actually owned when a lower price is expected

Shift differential type of compensation in which a person may be paid a higher rate for working nights or weekends

Simple interest the amount of interest calculated at the end of each year based on the total amount loaned

Soft currency currency that is not easy to exchange for other currencies

Sole proprietorship a business owned and managed by one person

Solvency the capability of an organization to meet its financial obligations as they become due

Source document the original record of a transaction

Source of funds the inflow of cash that can be used for paying various expenses

Speculative risk the possibility of either financial loss or gain

Spot markets markets where products are bought and sold for immediate (on-the-spot) delivery

Stock a security representing ownership in a corporation

Stock companies private corporations that sell insurance as a profit-making venture

Stock exchange business organization where securities are bought and sold

Stock index indicators of stock values that are commonly reported on television, radio, and in newspapers

Stock market the organized exchange of the ownership shares of public corporations

Stock split the proportional division of a number of stock shares into a larger number

Stockbroker a licensed specialist in the buying and selling of stocks and bonds

Subchapter S corporations small corporations that have special tax rules from the Internal Revenue Service and many states

Sunk cost expenses that have been incurred and cannot be recovered

Supply the quantity of a product or service that has been produced by businesses with the hope of making a profit from sales to customers

Surety bond protects against losses resulting from failure to complete any part of a contract according to the specified conditions

Syndicates groups of investors who pool their money to insure specific categories of risk

T

Tariff a tax that a government places on certain imported products

Tax revenue government income

Term the length of time invested money is controlled by others

Term insurance insurance that covers the insured for a specific period of years and does not accumulate any value beyond the death benefit

Time value of money the difference in purchasing power of an amount of money at a future date

Title insurance protects a real estate purchaser against losses due to a defect in the title, or the owner's legal interest in the property

Trade barriers restrictions to reduce free trade

Trade credit credit offered to a business customer by another business

Trade credit insurance pays for losses suffered when payment is not made by businesses that purchased on credit

Trade deficit situation that exists when a country has more imports than exports

Trade surplus situation that exists when a country exports more than it imports

Trade-offs resources you give up (money or time) that have a value that is lost

Traditional economy economy in which economic decisions are made in much the same way they always have been

Treasurer responsible for the management of a company's cash, investments, and other financial resources as well as relationships with investors and creditors

Treasury bills short-term securities offered by the federal government

Trend analysis examining financial performance over several periods of time to determine patterns

Trust the legal agreement for one party to control property for the benefit of another

U

Umbrella policy a policy providing a higher limit of coverage over and above any other basic liability policies an insured may have

Uncollectible an account that is overdue and unlikely to be paid

Uncontrollable risks risks that cannot be influenced by human action

Unemployment insurance makes payments to workers during periods of unemployment that are beyond the workers' control

Universal life insurance insurance in which part of the premium buys term insurance coverage that will be paid if the insured dies, while the rest of the premium is invested in high-yield securities as a savings tool for the policyholder

Unsecured loans loans that have no specific collateral

Use of funds outflow of money by a company

V

Variable costs business costs that change from month to month, such as labor costs, production materials, and utilities

Vertical integration expansion through increased involvement in different stages of production and distribution

W

Wages the earnings of workers calculated on an hourly basis

Weighted average cost of capital (WACC) calculated by multiplying the proportions of debt and equity by the capital cost for each

What-if planning alternatives for financial decisions that are considered by applying different assumptions to the financial data in an electronic spreadsheet

Whole life insurance provides permanent coverage for the life of the policyholder as long as premiums are paid

Work in process manufactured items in various stages of completion

Workers' compensation insurance provides medical care, rehabilitation, and lost wages for injured workers as well as death benefits for the dependents of persons killed in work-related accidents

Working capital the difference between current assets and current liabilities

World Bank International Bank for Reconstruction and Development; created in 1944 to provide loans for rebuilding after World War II

Y

Yield to maturity the annual rate of return an investor would receive when a bond is held until maturity

Index